Introduction to Statistics for Psychology and Education

McGRAW-HILL SERIES IN PSYCHOLOGY
CONSULTING EDITORS
Norman Garmezy   Lyle V. Jones

Adams Human Memory
Berkowitz Aggression: A Social Psychological Analysis
Berlyne Conflict, Arousal, and Curiosity
Blum Psychoanalytic Theories of Personality
Bock Multivariate Statistical Methods in Behavioral Research
Brown The Motivation of Behavior
Brown and Ghiselli Scientific Method in Psychology
Butcher MMPI: Research Developments and Clinical Applications
Campbell, Dunnette, Lawler, and Weick Managerial Behavior, Performance, and
   Effectiveness
Cofer Verbal Learning and Verbal Behavior
Crafts, Schneirla, Robinson, and Gilbert Recent Experiments in Psychology
Crites Vocational Psychology
D'Amato Experimental Psychology: Methodology, Psychophysics, and Learning
Deese and Hulse The Psychology of Learning
Dollard and Miller Personality and Psychotherapy
Edgington Statistical Inference: The Distribution-free Approach
Ellis Handbook of Mental Deficiency
Ferguson Statistical Analysis in Psychology and Education
Fodor, Bever, and Garrett The Psychology of Language: An Introduction to
   Psycholinguistics and Generative Grammar
Forgus Perception: The Basic Process in Cognitive Development
Franks Behavior Therapy: Appraisal and Status
Ghiselli Theory of Psychological Measurement
Ghiselli and Brown Personnel and Industrial Psychology
Gilmer Industrial and Organizational Psychology
Gray Psychology Applied to Human Affairs
Guilford Psychometric Methods
Guilford The Nature of Human Intelligence
Guilford and Fruchter Fundamental Statistics in Psychology and Education
Guilford and Hoepfner The Analysis of Intelligence
Guion Personnel Testing
Haire Psychology in Management
Hirsch Behavior-Genetic Analysis
Hirsh The Measurement of Hearing
Horowitz Elements of Statistics for Psychology and Education
Hurlock Adolescent Development
Hurlock Child Development
Hurlock Developmental Psychology
Jackson and Messick Problems in Human Assessment
Krech, Crutchfield, and Ballachey Individual in Society
Lakin Interpersonal Encounter: Theory and Practice in Sensitivity Training
Lawler Pay and Organizational Effectiveness: A Psychological View
Lazarus, A. Behavior Therapy and Beyond
Lazarus, R. Adjustment and Personality

Lewin   A Dynamic Theory of Personality
Lewin   Principles of Topological Psychology
Maher   Principles of Psychopathology
Marascuilo   Statistical Methods for Behavioral Science Research
Marx and Hillix   Systems and Theories in Psychology
Miller   Language and Communication
Morgan   Physiological Psychology
Mulaik   The Foundations of Factor Analysis
Novick and Jackson   Statistical Methods for Educational and Psychological Research
Nunnally   Introduction to Statistics for Psychology and Education
Nunnally   Psychometric Theory
Overall and Klett   Applied Multivariate Analysis
Porter, Lawler, and Hackman   Behavior in Organizations
Restle   Learning: Animal Behavior and Human Cognition
Robinson and Robinson   The Mentally Retarded Child
Rosenthal   Genetic Theory and Abnormal Behavior
Ross   Psychological Disorders of Children: A Behavioral Approach to Theory, Research, and Therapy
Schwitzgebel and Kolb   Changing Human Behavior: Principles of Planned Intervention
Shaw   Group Dynamics: The Psychology of Small Group Behavior
Shaw and Constanzo   Theories of Social Psychology
Shaw and Wright   Scales for the Measurement of Attitudes
Sidowski   Experimental Methods and Instrumentation in Psychology
Siegel   Nonparametric Statistics for the Behavioral Sciences
Spencer and Kass   Perspective in Child Psychology
Stagner   Psychology of Personality
Townsend   Introduction to Experimental Methods for Psychology and the Social Sciences
Vinacke   The Psychology of Thinking
Wallen   Clinical Psychology: The Study of Persons
Warren and Akert   The Frontal Granular Cortex and Behavior
Winer   Statistical Principles in Experimental Design
Zubek and Solberg   Human Development

Introduction to Statistics for Psychology and Education

Jum C. Nunnally
Professor of Psychology
Vanderbilt University

With the Collaboration of
Robert L. Durham
L. Charles Lemond
William H. Wilson

McGraw-Hill Book Company

New York St. Louis San Francisco Düsseldorf Johannesburg
Kuala Lumpur London Mexico Montreal New Delhi Panama
Paris São Paulo Singapore Sydney Tokyo Toronto

To Kay

Library of Congress Cataloging in Publication Data

Nunnally, Jum C
  Introduction to statistics for psychology and
education.
  1. Psychometrics. 2. Educational statistics.
I. Title.
BF 39.N79   519.5'02'415   74-8052
ISBN 0-07-047583-0

**INTRODUCTION TO STATISTICS FOR
PSYCHOLOGY AND EDUCATION**

1 2 3 4 5 6 7 8 9 0 KPKP 7 9 8 7 6 5 4

This book was set in Press Roman by Publications Development Corporation.
The editor was Richard R. Wright; the designer was Publications Development
Corporation; the production supervisor was Milton J. Heiberg.
Kingsport Press, Inc., was printer and binder.

Contents

Preface

The purpose of this book is to provide a comprehensive text for one-term undergraduate courses in statistics for psychology and education. It might also prove useful in courses relating to other aspects of behavioral science. The following five principles were held in mind while writing the book.

First, whereas an understanding of statistics is essential for learning about the behavioral sciences, most undergraduate students do not like the topic; consequently, efforts were made to simplify the subject and make it as interesting as possible. Second, while the book is sufficiently broad in scope to provide a stepping stone to graduate level courses in statistics, it is assumed that most readers of this book will mainly be consumers of statistical reports rather than producers of statistics themselves. For this reason, the text emphasizes an understanding of statistics rather than attempting to develop a high level of skill in the actual use of statistics.

The third principle upon which the book is based is that only those statistical methods which are actually used widely in psychology and education should be discussed. Many books on the topic are filled with "museum pieces," which even the authors would find little occasion to use. The selection of statistical methods was based on a pragmatic recourse to what researchers in psychology and education frequently employ.

The fourth principle upon which the book is based is that, while inferential statistics have their place in the scientific enterprise, they have been grossly overrated. Parts Three and Four of the book provide the student with an ample introduction to the probabilistic nature of statistical inference; however, the reader is warned at many points that such inferential statistics provide only meager information and should not be ends unto themselves. Therefore, the reader is advised of the necessity to go on and employ various types of descriptive statistics regarding research results after applying inferential statistics. These descriptive statistics are described throughout the text, most notably in Part Three of the book.

The fifth principle underlying the book is that there is really no need to overwhelm the reader with mathematics and computational procedures; rather, the more important thing is to provide an understanding of what statistical procedures mean. Consequently, the book emphasizes the major principles underlying the importance of statistical procedures and their use. At the same time, many statistical methods are discussed in the text, and ample references to more complex methods are given.

At this point in the preface, it is customary for the author to say that he is indebted to many people for their advice and help, and indeed I am. I am indebted to the Literary Executor of the late Sir Ronald A. Fisher, F.R.S., to Dr. Frank Yates, F.R.S., and to Longman Group, Ltd., London, for permission to reprint four tables from their book *Statistical Tables for Biological, Agricultural and Medical Research.* In addition, my vigorous, young collaborators forced me to take account of recent developments and emphases in the use of statistics in psychology and education. It was a real pleasure working with them on the book. Dr. Keith Clayton gave me line-by-line advice on the technical accuracy and lucidness of the presentation. Above all, I want to express my deep gratitude to three talented ladies who worked on the manuscript: Mrs. Martha Gregory, Mrs. Connie Lee, and Mrs. Nancy deZevallos. If the book is not successful, it will be because I mismanaged some very talented people.

Jum C. Nunnally

Part One

Fundamental Concepts

1

The Nature and Importance of Statistics

In everyday life, we swim in a sea of statistics. The king sends the royal census takers out to determine the incomes, landholdings, possessions, numbers of children, and other characteristics of the people in his realm. In the morning newspaper, the Gallup Poll announces that 48 percent of all registered voters prefer Henshaw for president, 42 percent prefer Bradley, and 10 percent have never heard of either. A high school teacher is poring over the scores of his students on a final examination in algebra. He is busy ranking students from highest to lowest, computing averages, and performing other analyses of the results.

A research specialist in a large commercial testing firm is completing an investigation concerning the effectiveness of a new test of college aptitude. He has the test scores of students from many schools around the country before they enter college and their grade-point averages at the end of the freshman year. He performs statistical analyses to determine the extent to which aptitude test scores actually predict college performance.

A psychological experiment is being conducted on three groups of college students in which lists of words are given in different manners to test the students' memorizing ability. One group of students hears the words spoken on a tape recorder; the second group of students sees the words presented on a screen; and a third group of students sees the words and hears them spoken simultaneously. The results suggest that the group which received both oral and visual presentation performed better than the other two groups. However, there were numerous inconsistencies in the results. For example, several members of the group that performed best on the average did not perform as well as members of the visual group, and one member of the oral group obtained the best score of all three groups. In spite of the inconsistencies in results, inferential statistics led the experimenter to the conclusion that the results were "real" and not due to chance.

MAJOR CONCEPTS IN STATISTICS

Whereas the term *statistics* is used in the singular in referring to an overall discipline, it really is plural in the sense that a number of important concepts are involved. Each of these will be discussed in this section.

The Meaning of Statistics

All of the previous examples concern statistics, which is the topic of this book. *Webster's* has been kind enough to supply us with a definition which covers most of what we mean by the term statistics: "Facts or data of a numerical kind, assembled, classified, and tabulated so as to present significant information about a given subject" (*Webster's New World Dictionary,* 1970, p. 1391). The concepts implied by the definition will be discussed throughout this section.

Collection and Analysis of Data

Statistics always concern data or facts. An item of data is that a particular household has three children, and another item of data is a score of 97 by a student on a scholastic aptitude test. However, statistics consist of more than the collection of data alone. Thus, until something is *done* with the data, sheets compiling numbers of cows, test scores of students, opinions about political candidates and others are not yet statistics.

The most crucial aspect of applying statistics consists of *analyzing* the data in such a way as to obtain a comprehensive summary of the overall results. Such methods of analysis will be considered throughout this book. A very simple method of analysis is to compute the percentages of people who say they will vote for different candidates. A slightly more complex form of analysis is to compute the average score on the final examination for students in freshman algebra. By computing an average, the teacher can determine how well his students are performing in comparison to those in other classes in the same school. A still more complex form of analysis consists of computing measures of correspondence (or degree of agreement) between aptitude test scores and grade-point averages of students in college. This involves correlational analysis, which will be discussed in detail in Part Two of this book. One can continue up the scale in terms of complexity, finally moving into highly complex methods of analysis that are used by experts in research.

Descriptive Statistics

Research results are usually obtained only from a sample of individuals rather than from all of the persons in question. Analyses like those discussed in the previous section result in *measurements* which help to summarize or describe the data as a whole. Consequently, analyses performed to obtain such measurements are said to constitute *descriptive statistics*. A percentage which measures the relative preference of people for one political candidate over another describes one aspect of the overall results of the study and thus constitutes a descriptive statistic. The average performance of a group may be used to measure and thus describe its achievement in comparison to other groups. A measure of the relationship between aptitude test scores and college grades can be used to predict college performance. All methods of analysis that lead to measurements of overall results constitute descriptive statistics.

Inferential Statistics

Whereas descriptive statistics can be computed on any set of data from any group of persons, they are usually computed only on a *sample* of the persons in question. A sample is a subset of all of the persons from some larger group. The purpose of studying the sample is to estimate some characteristics of the population as a whole. The *population* is the larger group from which the sample is drawn. It is desirable to select the sample in a random or at least partially random manner from the population as a whole. Descriptive statistics can be computed on data obtained from the sample; and if it were feasible, the same descriptive statistics could be computed on the population as a whole. In order to do this, it is necessary to estimate the likelihood (or probability) that the measurements made on the sample would be the same if they could be made on the whole population of subjects. Thus, although an opinion poll may ask questions of several thousand persons, these are only a very few of the millions of voters to which the descriptive statistics (percentages in this case) are generalized. If all of the voters in the country were questioned in the Gallup Poll, it might be found that 45 percent intended to vote for Henshaw rather than the 48 percent found in the sample. In this example, all the voters in the country constitute the population. The voters who were polled constitute a sample of that population. The concepts of population and sample will be discussed in detail in Chapter 3. For now, it is necessary for the reader to understand only that population refers to *all* people in a particular category, and sample refers to those people which are selected by an experimenter for use in a particular research project. By employing *inferential statistics* on results from the sample, it might be concluded that the odds are only one in ten thousand that more persons would say they intended to vote for Bradley than for Henshaw if all of the voters in the country were polled.

In the study of the predictiveness of a college aptitude test, the experimenter might study many hundreds of students; but he would not study the millions that enter college every year. Consequently, there is some danger of erroneously generalizing from the descriptive statistics obtained from his sample of subjects to the larger population. Again, inferential statistics would be useful in providing confidence about some results and cautions about others. Inferential statistics might indicate that the odds are less than one in a thousand that there would be no correlation at all if the whole population were studied; however, inferential statistics may also indicate that it is risky to conclude that the test being investigated predicts grade-point averages better than do tests that have routinely been employed for years. There are many different types of inferential statistics, depending on the descriptive statistics to which they are applied and the kinds of questions posed about the descriptive statistics.

Quantification and Measurement

Our definition of statistics relates to some other important matters. The analyses of data that produce descriptive statistics are always quantitative in nature. Thus, as simple a descriptive statistic as a percentage is obtained by adding up the number of events that are in one category and dividing by the total number of events, for example, the percentage of people who intend to vote for Henshaw. More complex forms of quantitative analysis are required to produce other descriptive statistics. In order to perform quantitative analyses of data, however, the data themselves must be rather precisely measured in numerical form. In other words, unless one can make precise measurements of the original data in numerical form, it is not possible to perform any descriptive or inferential statistics on the results. For this reason, some important aspects of psychological measurement will be considered in Chapter 2.

Although quantification and measurement are intimately related, it is important to realize that they are not exactly the same. Some examples will serve to illustrate why this is the case. It would be conceivable to make very fine measurements of the intelligence of students but simply let the results sit in file cabinets and not make any quantitative analyses of them, for example, as with respect to progress in school. Intelligence might be measured with respect to an illogical procedure, such as how rapidly students could run a mile. This method would produce precise numerical results and could be subjected to numerous forms of quantitative analysis, but the quantitative analyses would be foolish. Intelligence might be measured only impressionistically in terms of above or below average, and thus be so crudely measured that possible quantitative analyses would be quite limited. Therefore, some measurements simply do not lend themselves to complex quantitative analyses; on the other hand, it is possible to perform complex analyses on highly precise but illogical measurements. Thus, precise, valid measurement and quantitative analysis may go hand in hand, but they certainly are not identical.

Experimental Design

The dictionary definition of statistics spoke of presenting "significant information about a given subject." In order to obtain meaningful information from both descriptive statistics and inferential statistics, it is necessary for the data to be collected on the basis of an explicit, appropriate *experimental design*. Essentially, an experimental design is a blueprint of how an experiment will be conducted.

A simple example of an experimental design is a study concerning three methods of instruction in reading skills. The experiment is conducted on three sections of the fourth grade in a particular school. The experimenter decides to randomly assign one-third of the students in each section to each of the three methods of instruction. Students are given measures of reading skills before the instruction takes place and two months later, after the instruction is completed. The same test is administered after the instruction as before. This set of decisions on the conduct of the experiment constitutes an experimental design; however, there are many other ways that the experiment could have been conducted, each of which would constitute a different design. For example, it might be impractical to randomly assign students from each class to each of the three treatment conditions. Instead, a whole class could have been assigned to each of the three methods of instruction. Rather than continue instruction for only two months, it might have been extended to a period of four months. Rather than employ the same test afterwards, a different test might have been given. As illustrated above, the final set of decisions regarding how research will be conducted and measurement of results made constitutes an experimental design. As will be discussed in the pages ahead, some types of designs are generally better than others or more appropriate in particular circumstances than others.

INFORMATION OBTAINED FROM STATISTICS

A skeptic could question whether or not any real information is obtained from all of the data collection and analyses that statistics entail. In rebuttal, one can muster up examples of where statistics have provided very valuable information indeed. As one example, it had been thought that as much as 10 percent of the returning veterans from the Vietnamese War were addicted to heroin. A systematic screening of these veterans was undertaken by the Armed Forces. Analyses of urine specimens were made which could detect lingering effects of heroin on the body. The percentage of soldiers who had used heroin was found to be much smaller than the estimate of about 10 percent. This finding had a marked impact on the planning of a treatment program for drug addiction.

A second example of the usefulness of statistics is in obtaining norms (statistical standards) for commercially distributed tests of achievement for the elementary grades. Such norms are obtained by testing thousands of children throughout the country and computing the percentages of students who make scores at each level. This permits one to make a direct, quantitative comparison of the scores of one student with students across the country. In this way, it might be found that Fred Jones in the fourth grade performs as well as or better than 60 percent of the fourth-grade students across the country in reading comprehension. In addition, it might be found that the average score of 25 students in Fred's class is below that of 70 percent of students across the country, which would indicate that the class, as a whole, is doing rather poorly in reading. Obviously, such information as this is valuable in counseling students, understanding the ability levels of students in a school system, and planning instruction.

A third example of the importance of statistics is in research on psychological tests. Statistical methods are required to select the best items for tests to ensure that the items as a group tend to measure the same thing in a reliable or consistent manner. A more obvious use of statistics with psychological tests is in the selection of people for a particular activity, such as entrance into college, a program of training in the Armed Forces, and job placement in industry. Unless statistical methods were used to determine how well tests actually predicted the performance of people, invalid tests might be used for these purposes. It is frequently the case that tests which appear valid (or effective) actually are not valid at all when data are gathered and analyzed. In contrast, some test materials that might appear to be trivial simply from looking at them are predictive of success in training programs or job performance. Purely on an impressionistic basis such tests would be relegated to the wastebasket, but statistical analyses of test scores in comparison to actual performance show the worth of the test.

Interpretation of Statistics

If our skeptical friend is overwhelmed with the examples of important information supplied by statistics, he might retreat into condemning statistics on another basis. He might say, "You can prove anything with statistics." (A facetious rebuttal is that statistics do not lie, but some statisticians do.) There are many instances in which statistics would be misleading without proper interpretation. An example comes from statistical analyses of the income in a very small town, the hub of which is the home of a multimillionaire. The remaining households in the community consist of people who perform menial service jobs for the millionaire. Statistics are computed on the yearly incomes of residents of the small town. By one method of analysis, the conclusion is reached that the average yearly income in the community is over $89,000, but of course this would be highly misleading. As in all other cases where statistics are misleading, the fault is in the interpretation and not in the statistics. It would have been a very poor research worker indeed, who did not analyze the data in a number of ways to provide different perspectives on the situation. Rather than speak of various statistics as being misleading, it is more proper to speak of misleading interpretations of statistics.

Another example of a misleading interpretation of statistics frequently occurs when the police force in a city is markedly upgraded. The customary finding is that the number of recorded crimes jumps up noticeably the first and second year after the police force is improved. An irresponsible or unknowing newspaper reporter might headline his column, "Crime Increases 80 Percent in City Over Last Year." The interpretation could be entirely false, since the apparent increase in crime might just be the result of better gathering of information about crimes and better bookkeeping of reported crimes. A more correct interpretation would have followed from examining only those types of crimes for which bookkeeping procedures had remained constant.

A third example of misinterpreting statistics comes from a study of the correlation between school grades of children and numbers of books in their homes. Two variables are found to correlate positively: children who make high grades tend to have many books in their home and vice versa for children who exhibit low grades. If the person reporting the results was either naive or dishonest, he could interpret this to mean that quantity of books was *causing* good grades in school, but such an interpretation would be most unwise. It is probably more likely that quantity of books in homes was a by-product of general economic affluence. Thus, the children who had more books in their homes also had more radios, more bathtubs, more of everything. Consequently, an equally plausible interpretation would be that the availability of bathtubs causes children to make good grades. Alternative statistical approaches would shed a more accurate light on the correlation between numbers of books and school grades of children. Essentially, these statistics would supply much the same information if one correlated numbers of books and school grades for those children of the same economic backgrounds rather than different economic backgrounds.

From the foregoing examples, we can see that statistics per se are not inherently evil or misleading; instead, what is frequently at fault is the misinterpretation of statistics by unwitting or unscrupulous people. Throughout this book, numerous principles and procedures will be discussed for properly applying statistics and properly interpreting the results.

Forecasting the Future

When people criticize statistics, they frequently assume that (1) statistics are used almost exclusively for predicting future events, and (2) statisticians assume that present trends will continue indefinitely. Under these two assumptions, it is very easy to poke fun at statistics. One example relates to the fact that the number of psychologists is increasing percentage-wise with respect to the population of the United States every year. Obviously, if this percentage increase continues, 100 percent of the population of the United States would be psychologists in the far future. As another example, if one simply projected the current rate of population growth in the world, one would come to the conclusion that in another 100 or more years, the world's population will be so dense that people will have to stand upon one another's shoulders. Obviously, there are other factors which come into play in preventing such trends from continuing indefinitely; for example, there would be no one to hire psychologists even if they represented as much as 10 percent of the population, and people would be starving to death long before such physical crowding of overpopulation occurred.

The first criticism of statistics is unjustified because statistics is by no means limited to forecasting future events. Statistics are often used for analyses of present and past events, rather than forecasting future events. One cited example is in studying numbers and kinds of crimes that occur each year.

A number of things need to be clarified about the second conception of statistics. Very seldom do scientists assume that present trends in any phenomenon will continue indefinitely. Rather it is almost always the case that predictions of future trends are based on assumptions regarding how the trend will *change* as different matters come to pass. For example, to estimate the yearly coal usage in 1990, assumptions about population size, amount of energy consumed per capita, efficiency of transforming coal to energy resources, and other things that are likely to be different would be introduced.

As another example, to estimate the number of textbooks in geography that will be used in 1980, would require making assumptions about school population size, competition from other types of educational material (for example, educational TV), changes in emphasis in the study of geography, and other such matters. Similarly, with phenomena in the behavioral sciences such as crime rates, rates of incidence of various mental illness, costs for medical treatment, numbers of people in different professions, and many other phenomena, it is necessary to make a set of assumptions in order to attempt accurate predictions of future states of affairs.

HOW STATISTICS CAN BE USEFUL TO THE READER

Students taking courses in statistics frequently complain that they see little relevance of statistics for their other courses, for daily life, and for careers in the years ahead. This is certainly not a fault of statistics but rather of the ways in which statistics sometimes are presented in lectures and in books. The chapters ahead will be filled with many examples of how statistical methods are used in school, in daily life, and in various careers; however, it might be wise at this point to summarize some of the major ways in which they can be useful.

Undergraduate Study

Students who major in education, psychology, and other behavioral sciences must have an adequate grasp of statistics in order to understand their own subject matter. Without a knowledge of statistics, students in education courses could not understand such important matters as (1) how achievement tests are developed and interpreted, (2) how research on educational practices is designed and analyzed, and (3) how students are selected for college on the basis of grades and aptitude tests. Without a knowledge of statistics, students in psychology would be unable to comprehend (1) the analysis of results from a study of human memory, (2) the computation of the correlation between the trait of anxiety and the trait of intelligence, and (3) the extent to which perception of size is distorted by visual illusions. Because a prior knowledge of statistics is necessary to understand much of the subject matter in education and psychology, a course on the topic should be required in most curricula.

Graduate Work in Psychology and Education

If students go on from undergraduate study into graduate study, they will find many uses for statistics. The needs for a knowledge of statistics at the level of graduate training are much the same as those at the undergraduate level (for example, to understand research reports); however, the graduate student must understand statistics at a higher level than is required of his undergraduate counterpart. Also, graduate students are usually involved in research, and a knowledge of statistics is required for the adequate design and analysis of investigations. For these reasons, nearly all graduate students in psychology and education are required to take advanced courses in statistics.

Professional Goals

After students complete their formal education, they will find many uses for statistics in their careers. Persons who receive higher degrees are frequently involved in research, and, as mentioned previously, such research could not be adequately planned, undertaken, or the data analyzed without the employment of statistical principles. Persons with advanced degrees who function primarily as administrators (for example, a psychologist directing a counseling center, or a person with a doctorate in education directing a school system) find many uses for statistics in understanding research reports and performing research on institutional functions.

Persons who seek jobs at the end of undergraduate training will also find many uses for statistics in their work. A prime example is the classroom teacher who must perform statistical operations on test scores, understand statistics presented in test manuals, and grasp the meaning of statistics presented in research reports. Similarly, a person with an undergraduate degree in psychology will find an understanding of statistics useful for such vocations as welfare work, career guidance, assistant on psychological research projects, and computer technician for a commercial testing agency.

In Daily Life

Even if a person has no intention of entering any career in psychology and education, he will find statistics very helpful in daily life. It is helpful, for instance, to understand such things as (1) projections of birth rate trends for the future, (2) the amount of error to be expected in decisions based on public opinion polls, (3) the meaning of research findings reported on television regarding the effectiveness of different commercial products, (4) the reasons for employing some types of tests for selecting college freshmen and reasons for not employing other indices, (5) the odds against winning various dice tosses, (6) the meaning of safety factors built into bridges, and (7) many concepts concerning individual differences among people. We live in a world in which many things can be best analyzed and described in statistical terms, and consequently, a knowledge of statistics is an important aid to becoming a well-informed person.

FOUNDATIONS FOR THE PROPER USE OF STATISTICS

The purpose of this text, essentially, is to create an understanding of statistics and how they are most fruitfully employed. To set the stage for detailed discussions in subsequent chapters, we will briefly outline some of the prerequisites for employing statistics correctly:

1 *Purposes.*   It should go without saying that a sound background in statistics includes a thorough understanding of what statistics are, why they are used, how they are interpreted, and what they can and cannot do; however, it is frequently the case that students develop a moderate understanding of the technical details of elementary statistics but do not really understand the general principles regarding the nature of statistics. Efforts will be made in the pages ahead to help develop this understanding.

2 *Research design.*   Statistical concepts should be brought to bear on the design of research rather than introduced after mountains of data have been obtained. Designs are frameworks for planning research rather than statistical tools that are employed after research is completed. Although it is obvious that statistical consideration should be brought in when planning the research rather than later, it is appalling to consider in how many instances statistics

are given scant attention until nearly all of the data are collected. For example, it is frequently found that a number of psychological tests are administered to patients in mental hospitals. In many instances, such data is collected without regard for any future use. Afterwards, it might be desirable to compare two types of mentally ill patients on a personality trait; however, it may then be found that the test was administered to only one of the two groups of patients in question, or that the number of patients in one group was too small for meaningful comparisons to be made. Such examples are legion; they result in much misspent time and much uninterpretable data.

3 *Measurement.* It is a waste of time to plan research or employ statistics unless the variables under consideration can be measured. Thus, research in psychology and education requires adequate measures of (1) intelligence, (2) reading achievement, (3) anxiety, (4) memory, (5) perceptual ability, and other attributes. Furthermore, measures must be reliable in the sense that people obtain essentially the same IQ or other trait score when tested on two different occasions. Measurement methods must demonstrate other characteristics before they can be accepted as actually indexing what they are purported to measure.

4 *Sampling of subjects.* Frequently, one of the most difficult things in performing research is to obtain the proper human subjects. Questions regarding the proper selection of subjects would be encountered in (1) undertaking an opinion poll about the value of college education, (2) determining the usefulness of a college entrance examination, (3) comparing the perceptual abilities of mental hospital patients and normal persons, (4) comparing the effectiveness of two approaches to learning mathematics, and (5) comparing men and women in terms of different types of learning tasks. Principles regarding the adequate sampling of subjects will be given special attention in Chapter 3.

5 *Selection of statistics.* As mentioned earlier, the statistical techniques for analyzing results of research should logically follow from the statistical design. The design should be selected in such a way that proper data can be collected and proper statistical analyses of the results can be made. It is important to set the stage for subsequent discussions of this by saying that (1) researchers, either by mistake or lack of sophistication, sometime formulate and carry out designs for which proper methods of statistical analysis are not yet available or are logically unobtainable, and (2) there are usually choices among methods of statistical analysis, even when an excellent research design has been selected and implemented. Regarding the latter, considerable attention will be given throughout the book to provide principles for selecting the most appropriate and most informative methods of analysis. The important point to grasp is that the experimenter has a choice in selecting methods of analysis.

6 *Computation.* After research is completed, the data in hand, and proper

methods of statistical analysis selected, the statistical results must be computed. Although this comment seems obvious, it is depressing to find so many instances in which statistics are incorrectly computed (for example, as is frequently uncovered when recomputing some statistics on data borrowed from a colleague). Such inaccurate computation occurs mainly because of (1) lack of understanding of what the equations entail, and (2) confusion about various steps in the computational routines. Both of these matters should be kept in mind throughout this book.

7 *Interpretation.* In addition to understanding the nature of statistics themselves, it is necessary to understand the results obtained from applying them. For this end, numerous principles for the proper interpretation of statistics will be discussed in the text. Additional wisdom in this regard can be obtained only by working with and keeping in mind the meaning of various types of statistical results.

SUMMARY

The term *statistics* refers, in general, to the gathering and analyzing of data for the purpose of obtaining comprehensive results. Statistical results are mentioned very frequently in everyday life. Some examples are the report of an opinion poll concerning voter preferences for different political candidates or claims on television regarding the effectiveness of a headache remedy. More important for the reader, statistical concepts and techniques are absolutely essential for research in psychology and education. Without a knowledge of introductory statistics, the reader would be incapable of either understanding the currently available research reports in his field or of performing any meaningful research on his own.

There are many aspects related to the topic of statistics. First, statistics concern the gathering of actual data rather than dealing with subjective impressions. Thus, an opinion poll concerns the number of persons who say that they will vote for one candidate rather than another, and a study of intelligence concerns the actual test scores.

Second, before any data is collected, there must be a research design, or blueprint, for gathering of data so that it will address itself to research issues. The mere gathering of data for its own sake does not meet this requirement. No sensible geologist, for instance, would wander around picking up rocks indiscriminately; rather he would select rocks that helped answer some question regarding the geological features of a particular region. Similarly in psychology and education, the mere gathering of vital statistics, test scores, and other items of data do not necessarily lead to important conclusions. An experimental design leads to the collection of data that will help provide information about important research issues.

Third, statistics are compiled on a sampling of persons from a population. It is almost always the case that research is performed on only a subset of the persons to which the results will be generalized. It is necessary for the sample to be as representative as possible of the total population.

Fourth, various descriptive statistics which summarize the overall results can be employed. Examples are the percentage of persons who say that they will vote for one political candidate over another, the degree of correlation between a college aptitude test and actual performance in college, and the difference in average performance of two groups of students who are provided different types of instruction in mathematics.

Fifth, inferential statistics can be employed to estimate the extent to which descriptive statistics obtained from a sample are likely to apply to the population as a whole. Depending upon the experimental design and type of data, a wide variety of methods of inferential statistics can be applied.

All of these aspects of statistics are omnipresent in psychology and education, and the reader must understand them if he is to work effectively in his field of study.

EXERCISES

Study Questions

1 Describe the essential differences between descriptive and inferential statistics.

2 What is a sample? What is a population? Can they ever be the same group of people?

3 Why is measurement an essential consideration in any use of statistics?

4 Discuss the assumption that one statistic is just as good as another (in other words, it does not make any difference which statistic is used in analyzing the results of a research project).

5 Discuss the importance of an adequate experimental design before research is undertaken.

6· Why is it useful for students in psychology and education to have an understanding of statistics?

7 List and discuss the major requirements for the proper use of statistics.

SUGGESTED ADDITIONAL READINGS

Campbell, D. T., and J. C. Stanley. *Experimental and quasiexperimental designs for research.* Chicago: Rand McNally, 1966, Chap. 1.

Guilford, J. P., and B. Fruchter. *Fundamental statistics in psychology and education*, 5th ed. New York: McGraw-Hill, 1973, Chap. 1.

Nunnally, J. C. *Introduction to psychological measurement*. New York: McGraw-Hill, 1970, Chap. 1.

Scott, W. A., and M Wertheimer. *Introduction to psychological research*. New York: John Wiley, 1967, Chaps. 1, 2, and 3.

2

Quantification, Measurement, and Probability

It is frequently assumed that statistics are essentially concerned with arithmetic computations and that nothing else is very important. This is definitely a misunderstanding. The proper use of statistics is based on a number of underlying concepts which will be discussed in this chapter. Several examples will indicate why it is necessary to understand some general principles before statistical methods can be meaningfully applied.

One cup of cornflakes, one cup of milk, three strawberries, and three spoons of sugar might add up to a good breakfast, but they would not add up to eight units of anything in the same sense that we would talk about eight feet of lumber or eight hours in the working day. While playing poker, one person has not won a hand for hours; still, he assumes that the probability is high that luck will turn his way in subsequent hands. In Omaha, Nebraska, the radio "man-in-the-street" interviews 25 individuals at a shopping center regarding a possible curfew for persons under eighteen. The persons questioned consist of 16 middle-aged housewives with shopping bags in hand, 3 disgruntled husbands who had been cajoled by their wives into coming along, 2 teen-aged boys who were rather vague about their reasons for not being in high school that day, the policeman directing traffic, and 3 construction workers during their lunch hour. Fifteen members of this motley crew say that they are in favor of the curfew; consequently, the announcer states that 60 percent of "the people" are in favor of such a curfew.

The above examples concern misunderstandings regarding the nature of quan-

·tification, probability, and statistical inference. The author would like to flatter the reader by saying that such misunderstandings are ludicrous to the point where they would not occur in the minds of sophisticated adults, but even people who otherwise are sophisticated frequently accept such fallacies. The remainder of this chapter will be devoted to a discussion of some fundamental concepts underlying the development and proper use of statistics.

HISTORY OF QUANTIFICATION

Statistical results are always reported in some quantitative form such as (1) the percentage of people who intend to vote for one candidate rather than another, (2) the billions of dollars spent on foreign aid during the last ten years, or (3) the average intelligence test score of students who enter the University of Pennsylvania. As a result, we take mathematics for granted as something that has always been available to us. Actually, it took thousands of years for these simple systems of quantification to become established. For example, it was only in the middle ages that the use of zero became widespread in arithmetic computations. Some primitive people are still limited to a counting system that consists only of one, two, and many. [A very interesting book concerning the history of the development of arithmetic is by Eves (1964).]

Numbering systems were used before people had any symbols for the numbers themselves. The ancient Phoenicians traded by lining up a collection of shells to indicate the extent to which they would barter one form of goods for another; but they had no symbols to stand for these numbers.

Even as late as the middle ages, anyone who could perform long division was considered a mathematical expert. Only during the last several hundred years have higher forms of mathematics of a kind required for the development of complex statistical methods been invented. The purpose of this book is not to present the complex mathematical methods that were used in deriving important statistics; rather, it is to present statistical methods in an understandable manner for the reader who is only lightly trained in mathematics. However, it is of value to realize that many of the statistical methods which will be discussed were not developed until the turn of the century, and that those developed since 1950 surely far outnumber all that were developed up to that point in time.

MEASUREMENT

Having numbers and mathematical procedures for working with them is not enough for the meaningful application of statistics. Statistics make sense only when they are applied to important *measures.* For example, it would be meaningless to average the numbers on the uniforms of football players at Notre Dame, since the numbers themselves would not measure anything. Examples of important measures in the behavioral sciences are (1) the time it takes to recognize words that are presented briefly, (2) scores on intelligence tests, (3) achievement test scores in mathematics, and (4) number of words correctly recalled after three minutes of rehearsing a list of 40 words. Although tomes have been written on the nature of measurement, in the end it boils down to something rather simple: *Measurement consists of rules for assigning numbers to objects in such a way as to represent quantities of attributes.* In this definition, the term *rules* indicates that the procedures for assigning numbers must be explicitly formulated. In some instances, the rules are so obvious that detailed formulations are not required. This is the case when a yardstick is employed to measure lengths of lumber. What should be done is intuitively obvious; consequently, it is not necessary to study a thick manual of rules before undertaking the measurement. Such examples are, however, the exception rather than the rule in science. For instance, measuring the amounts of various components in chemical compounds often requires complex procedures that are not intuitively obvious. Similarly, the rules for measuring most psychological attributes are not intuitively obvious, for example, the intelligence of schoolchildren, the amount of retention in a study of paired-associate learning, drive level in a study of rats, and attitudes toward political parties.

Frequently in this book, reference will be made to the *standardization* of measures of psychological attributes. Essentially, a measure is said to be *well standardized* if different people employ the measure and obtain very similar results with the same, or at least comparable, techniques of measurement. Thus, a method of measurement for the surface temperature of planets in the solar system is well standardized if different astronomers who employ the method obtain very similar numerical results for particular planets on specific occasions. Similarly, an intelligence test is well standardized if different examiners give approximately the same scores to the same children, or if the same examiner gives approximately the same scores to the same children when employing two versions of a test. If a measure is well standardized in this way, it is said to be *reliable.* If a measure is not highly reliable, statistical analyses of data obtained from applying the measure (for example, a measure of personality) will produce rather jumbled results that cannot be clearly interpreted.

In our definition of measurement the term attribute indicates that measurement always concerns some particular feature of objects. Strictly speaking, objects are not measured, but rather their attributes are measured. For example, while it makes no sense to speak of "measuring" a child, it makes sense to speak of measuring the intelligence of a child. Although the distinction may sound like mere hairsplitting, it is important. First, it demonstrates that measurement requires a process of abstraction. An attribute concerns comparisons among objects on a particular dimension, for example, weight or intelligence. A red rock and a white rock may weigh the same, and two white rocks may have different weights.

Thus, the attribute of weight is an abstraction which must not be confused with all the particular features of objects. This point should be obvious, but unfortunately, it isn't always. Children, for example, have difficulty distinguishing between a particular attribute of objects and all recognizable attributes of objects, as do adults in many primitive societies. The failure to abstract a particular attribute makes concepts of measurement difficult to grasp. To some extent, adults in modern society experience this same difficulty. For example, it is difficult for some people to understand that a criminal and a well-behaved member of society can have the same level of intelligence (as measured by intelligence tests).

A second reason for emphasizing that measurement always concerns a particular attribute is that it forces us to carefully consider the nature of the attribute before attempting to measure it. We may reach the conclusion, for instance, that the attribute does not exist. As an example, the lack of any consistent results in the efforts to measure an attribute of "rigidity" in people makes it doubtful that there is such an attribute. It is not necessarily the case that all the terms used to describe people are matched by measurable attributes, for example, ego strength, strength, extrasensory perception, and dogmatism.

Still looking at the definition of measurement, the term *numbers* is used to represent quantities. Quantification concerns *how much* of an attribute is present in an object; numbers are used to communicate the amount. Quantification is so intimately interwoven with the concept of measurement that the two terms are often used interchangeably; however, it is important to make a fine distinction between them. Any set of numbers represent quantification, for instance, adding together people's heights, IQs, or miscellaneous other numbers; but such quantification would not relate to any important psychological attributes. Quantification is important when it concerns relations among carefully measured psychological traits concerning abilities, personality, and other human characteristics. Thus, quantification is a necessary aspect of research in psychology and education, but only if the quantification concerns measurements of important human characteristics.

Measurement is closely related to counting. Essentially what one does in any measurement method is to count similar units. Length is measured by counting equal units of extension such as inches or centimeters. Weight is measured by counting equal units of ounces, pounds, or grams. The amount of gasoline placed in an automobile is determined by counting the number of gallons. The physical characteristics of measuring instruments are valuable in that they do the counting for the observer. Thus, one can simply read off the number on a ruler, the number on a scale for weight, and the number of gallons shown on the gasoline pump.

Psychological measures are also intimately related to counting. A clock counts the fractions of a second used to measure reaction time. By counting the number of word pairs correctly remembered in a study of paired-associate learning, one arrives at a measure of the amount learned; by counting the number of items correctly answered on a test of ability, one arrives at a measure of ability; and by counting the number of answers indicative of personal adjustment, one arrives at a measure of adjustment.

Measurement is legitimately derived from counting operations only if it is reasonable to assume that the units counted are qualitatively and quantitatively the same. For example, a count of 12 does not constitute a legitimate qualitative measure if 6 units are inches and 6 units are pounds or if 6 items relate to intelligence and 6 items relate to adjustment. Similarly, a count of 14 is not a legitimate quantitative measure of length unless all 14 units are inches, feet, centimeters, meters, or other equivalent units of length. Perhaps less obvious than these examples, if one interprets the interval between an IQ of 100 and an IQ of 110 as equal to that between an IQ of 110 and an IQ of 120, strictly speaking, he is assuming that each of the 20 units of IQ between 100 and 120 are quantitatively equal to one another. On pages 23-27 a more extensive discussion about the nature of units on psychological measures will be presented. In part, it will illustrate that it is reasonable to liberalize these strict standards while employing statistical methods.

Our definition of measurement also states that numbers are assigned to *objects*. The objects in psychology and education are usually people or lower animals. In some instances, however, they are material objects. For example, when people rate the pleasantness of each word in a list, the words are measured, and the people act as part of the measurement process.

Although any set of rules for quantifying psychological traits constitutes a measure, this does not mean that all measures are useful for any purpose. The proof of usefulness is determined by the extent to which it enhances scientific explanation. A measure of intelligence is valid or useful to the extent that it is predictive of grades in college, relates to teachers' ratings of intelligence, and is predictive of results in research. Since we think of intelligence as relating to these matters, a measure of intelligence is useful to the extent that it manifests these expected relationships. After such expected relationships are found, then one can trust the results obtained in subsequent investigations where the nature of relationships are difficult to anticipate. In addition, a measure is useful to the extent that it fits into a rich network of relations in science. Thus, in physics, such measures as weight, velocity, and electrical resistance fit into networks of relationships with other measures of physical quantities. In the same way, measures of intelligence, adjustment, and others in the behavioral sciences are connected with other scientific variables through such networks. Essentially, a measure is *valid* to the extent that it fulfills expectations regarding hypothesized relationships with other variables; and a measure is scientifically useful to the extent that it fits into a network of relationships with other scientific variables.

ADVANTAGES OF STANDARDIZED MEASURES

Although the reader probably has a healthy respect for the importance of measurement in science, it might be useful to look at some of the particular advantages which measurement provides. To examine the advantages of standardized measures, it is necessary to consider what would be left if they were not available; for example, if there were no measures of temperature or intelligence. What would be left would be subjective appraisals, personal judgments, or whatever one would call the intuitive processes involved. While intuitive processes can sometimes be accurate, they do not provide the essential elements needed to form a solid basis for standardized measures.

Objectivity

The major advantage of measurement is that it takes the guesswork out of scientific observation. A key principle of science is that any statement of fact made by one researcher should be independently verifiable by other researchers. The principle is violated if there is room for disagreement among researchers about the observation of empirical events. For example, since we have no standardized measure of ego strength, two psychologists could disagree widely about the ego strength of a particular person. Obviously, then, it is not possible to make scientific tests of theories about ego strength. On the other hand, theories concerning atomic particles, temperature of stars, intelligence of children, drive level in rats, and so on, are testable in that they involve unambiguous procedures for documenting empirical events. Standardized measures provide such procedures.

Quantification

The quantitative results provided by standardized measures have two advantages. First, numerical indices make it possible to report results in finer detail than would be possible with personal judgments. Thus, the availability of thermometers makes it possible to report the exact increase in temperature when two chemicals are mixed, rather than only the fact that the temperature increases. Similarly, whereas teachers may be able to reliably assign children to broad categories of intelligence such as "bright," "average," and "below normal," intelligence tests provide finer differentiations.

A second advantage of quantification is that it permits the use of powerful methods of mathematical analysis. This is essential in the elaboration of theories and in the analysis of experiments. Although it may be a long time off for psychology and education, it is reasonable to believe that all theories will eventually be expressed in mathematical form. Only when theories are in mathematical form is it possible to make precise predictions for experimental investigation. Without powerful methods of analysis, it would be all but impossible to assess the results of research.

Communication

Science is a highly public enterprise in which efficient communication between researchers is essential. Each researcher builds on what has been learned in the past, and day by day he must compare his findings with those of other research-ers working on the same types of problems. Communication is greatly facilitated when standardized measures are available. Suppose, for example, that in an ex-periment concerning the effects of stress on anxiety reaction, it is reported that a particular treatment made the subjects appear anxious. This would leave many questions as to what the experimenter meant by "appear anxious"; consequently, it would be very difficult for other experimenters to investigate the same effects. Much better communication would be achieved if standardized measures of anxi-ety were available. Even if subjective evaluations of experimental results are very carefully done, they are much more difficult to communicate than statistical analyses of standardized measures. The rate of scientific progress in a particular area is limited by the efficiency and fidelity with which researchers can commu-nicate their results to one another.

Economy

Although it frequently requires a great deal of work to develop standardized measures, once developed they are usually much more economical of time and money than subjective evaluations. For example, even if a teacher was a good judge of intelligence, he would probably need to observe a child for some months to make a sound judgment. A better appraisal could usually be obtained from one of the group measures of intelligence, which would take no more than an hour to administer and might cost less than 25 cents per child. Rather than have clinical psychologists individually interview each recruit for the Armed Forces, a large group of recruits can be administered a printed test. In a study of the effects of a particular drug on amount of activity of white rats, it would be far more eco-nomical to employ standardized measures such as the activity wheel, than to have trained observers sit for hours noting the amount of activity.

MEASUREMENT SCALES

A term that frequently is used interchangeably with measure is that of *scale*. Ex-amples of scales are the yardstick for measuring length, a scale that the butcher uses to measure amounts of meat, and a scale for measuring the intelligence of students. Although there are many types of measures or scales used for a variety of scientific purposes, they can be categorized according to a small number of characteristics which are important for the use of statistics. It is necessary to un-derstand classifications of measurement scales because even the simplest statisti-cal operation must take account of the type of scale being employed. Essentially, we are concerned with what sorts of "interpretations" can be made of the num-bers obtained from psychological measures. More precisely, we are concerned with the legitimacy of employing various types of statistical procedures in measuring human attributes. Can the same statistics be legitimately applied to scores on an intelligence test as they can to the results of using a yardstick to measure heights of children? Can the same statistics be applied to rate of learning to read as can be applied to changes in measurements of humidity from day to day?

Different types of measurement scales use numbers in different ways. The type of measurement scale being employed determines the types of statistical methods that are appropriate. This is much like determining the grade of gasoline that should be used in an automobile or the type of battery to employ in a portable radio. Measurement scales can be rank ordered from those that supply rather meager information about the trait in question to those that supply the most information possible. A discussion of this ordering of scales follows.

Labels

Numbers are frequently used to keep track of things, without being subjected to mathematical analyses. For example, a geologist working in the field might choose to number his specimens of rocks 1, 2, 3, etc., in which case the numbers would be used purely as *labels* without being applied to mathematical analyses. It would make no sense to add the numbers representing the first and second rocks and equate that sum in any way with the 3 relating to the third rock. Examples of numbers used as labels are the numbers on the shirts of football players, social security numbers, and bank account numbers on checks.

It must be emphasized that any measurement scale concerns an *intended use* of numbers. One intended use of numbers is for labeling. In this instance, there is no intention of performing mathematical analyses of the numbers, and the numbers are not considered to represent quantities of attributes. It may be the case, however, that numbers as labels happen to correlate with quantities of attributes. Thus, in the example of the geologist and his rocks, it may be that as his sack of rocks grows heavier he discerningly picks smaller and smaller specimens; consequently the numbers used as labels would incidentally relate to the weights of the rocks. Similarly, high-numbered highways may in some way be quantitatively different from low-numbered highways, and atomic elements further along in the numbering scheme may be quantitatively different from earlier-positioned elements. The crucial point is that in discussing the nature of measurement scales, one must justify the use of the numbers. Whether or not there are incidental quantitative correlates of a particular set of numbers is not relevant to a discussion of the legitimacy of the intended use of the numbers. Since labels are not intended to imply quantities of attributes, no justification is required for the employment of numbers as labels; however, it should be clear that the numbers are only being used in this capacity.

Categories

Closely related to the use of numbers as labels is their use to represent groups of objects, or *categories.* For example, the geologist might classify each of his rocks into one of the categories of sedimentary, igneous, or metamorphic and refer to these categories-as 1, 2, and 3. Other classification schemes include different professions, the two sexes, and brain-damaged and normal people. For different professions, it might be simpler to give numbers to the professions for keeping track of them in a computer rather than coding them in any other way. The only difference between employing numbers as labels and employing them to represent categories is that in the latter case (1) more than one object goes with each number, and (2) all the objects assigned to the same number are alike with respect to some attribute. As is true of numbers used as labels, numbers used to represent categories in a classification scheme have no quantitative implications; similarly, they may have many incidental correlates with quantities of attributes. Thus, on the average, males and females differ in height, athletic ability, and a host of other attributes, but that is entirely unrelated to justifying the use of the numbers 1 and 2 to stand for males and females respectively. Since numbers used to represent categories are not intended to have quantitative implications, no justification is required for the use of numbers for that purpose.

In discussing categorization, a distinction should be made between using numbers to represent categories and using them to signify the frequency with which objects appear in different categories. The geologist might categorize 22 of his specimens as igneous rocks, and a psychologist might classify 86 of the mental patients in a study as being depressive. In such instances, it is sometimes said that one "measures" the number of cases in different categories. It would be more proper to say that one *enumerates*, or *counts* the objects in categories.

Ordinal Scales

An *ordinal scale* is one in which (1) a set of objects or people is rank ordered from "most" to "least" with respect to an attribute, (2) there is no indication of "how much" in an absolute sense any of the people possess the attribute, and (3) there is no indication of how much the people differ with respect to the attribute. Rank ordering is the most primitive form of measurement (excluding labels and categories). It is primitive in that it is basic to all higher forms of measurement, and it conveys only meager information.

An example of an ordinal scale is one which rank orders a group of boys from tallest to shortest. This scale would give no indication of the average height: as a group the boys might be relatively tall or relatively short. An example of rank order in education would be the gradual elimination of students in a spelling bee. The final group of contestants contains six students. First, one is eliminated leaving five, another is eliminated leaving four, and so on to the student remaining. The six students are thus rank ordered in terms of how well they performed in the contest.

What is frequently not understood is that the numbers employed with ordinal scales in the behavioral sciences provide only a convenient shorthand for designating relative positions of people. A rank-order scale is obtained when, for any N

persons, it is known that one person is higher than all the rest, the second person is higher than those below him, and so on to the person who is last with respect to the particular attribute.

Some have claimed that most measures in psychology and education (for example, intelligence tests) should be interpreted as a rank ordering of people rather than classified as another form of measurement; however, the general contention is that it is sensible to treat measurements in both psychology and education as constituting interval scales and to apply appropriate methods of statistics.

Interval Scales

An *interval scale* is one in which (1) the rank ordering of objects is known with respect to an attribute, (2) it is known how far apart the objects are from one another with respect to the attribute, but (3) no information is available about the *absolute* magnitude of the attribute for any object. Examples of interval scales are (1) scores on intelligence tests, (2) scores on an inventory of personal adjustment, and (3) ratings of attitudes toward the United Nations. Most measures in psychology and education can be considered as interval scales, and data obtained from them can be analyzed by statistical methods that assume interval scales. [The basis for this assumption is discussed in detail in Nunnally (1967), Chap. 1.]

There are some measures in psychology and education that cannot be considered as "high" in the hierarchy of scales as the interval scale. Examples of these were given with respect to categories and rank-order scales. When this is the case, many powerful statistical methods cannot be employed; special methods required in this circumstance are discussed in Chapter 13.

A potentially important item of information not supplied by interval scales is the absolute magnitude of the attribute for any particular person or object. An interval scale concerns differences among people regarding the trait in question but provides no information about the overall level of people in general. Thus, tests might provide useful information about how much people vary in intelligence and personal adjustment, but such measurements would not be capable of revealing how intelligent or how well-adjusted people are in an absolute sense. Therefore, it makes no sense to say, as some nonexperts have said, that the average person is low in intelligence.

Ratio Scales

A *ratio scale* is obtained when (1) the rank order of persons with respect to an attribute is known, (2) the intervals between persons are known, and (3) the distance from a *rational zero* is known for each person. In other words, a ratio scale is a particular type of interval scale in which distances are stated with respect to a rational zero. A rational zero is an obvious starting point for measurement, such as the empty space at the end of a yardstick and nothing on a scale for weight measurement. Such scales are referred to as ratio scales because it makes sense to divide measurement results by one another. A good example of a ratio scale is weight. It makes sense to say that the weight of a boy in the sixth grade is 1½ times that of a boy in the second grade. In contrast, on an interval scale measuring reading skills, it does not make sense to say that the reading ability of a boy in the sixth grade is 1½ times that of a boy in the second grade.

Assumptions about Scale Properties in the Choice of Statistics

Investigations in psychology and education are concerned with all the types of scales just discussed. Some investigations are concerned with categorical data, such as the numbers of mental patients of different kinds, comparisons of brain-damaged people with normal people, and the comparison of smokers and non-smokers.

In some cases, data in psychology and education are expressed in rank form. To repeat some examples: the rank ordering of mental patients in terms of improvement and the rank ordering of students in a spelling bee. Other examples would be the ordering of men in a branch of the Armed Forces according to eligibility for promotion and the ordering of the top three winners in a beauty contest.

There are some forms of psychological data that are considered ratio scales, for example, the length of time required for a rat to traverse a maze or reaction time in human subjects. In such cases, zero amount of time is a meaningful concept, and it is also meaningful, for example, to speak of one subject taking twice as much time as another subject.

Another instance in which experimental results are correctly considered to be ratio scales is that in which a number of "things" are responded to in one way rather than another. This would be the case in giving three groups of students three different amounts of time to solve 100 simple arithmetic problems. If a group that was given 25 minutes solved, on the average, twice as many problems as the group that was given only 10 minutes, there is nothing wrong with quoting that ratio and taking it seriously in any necessary statistical analyses.

The examples of ratio scales are the exception rather than the rule; most psychological data are legitimately interpreted only as interval scales rather than ratio scales. It makes no sense, for example, to speak of zero intelligence or zero self-esteem, just as it makes no sense to say that one person is twice as anxious as another or that one person has 1½ times as much reasoning ability as another. Having only interval scales rather than ratio scales for most attributes does not present a serious problem. Most methods of mathematical and statistical analysis needed in psychology and education require only interval scales. These are the statistics that will be discussed throughout the book except for the special statistics concerning categories and ranks that will be discussed in Chapter 13.

The concept of *probability* is omnipresent in daily life. The TV weatherman says there is an 80 percent chance of rain tomorrow. A high school counselor advises a student that the odds are less than 50-50 that he will perform successfully in a local university. The batting average of a baseball star is 390. The physician gives the patient a 99 percent estimate for the success of an operation. The odds are 1 out of 54,145 of drawing four aces in five cards dealt in a poker game. Despite its widespread use, however, the concept of probability is poorly understood by most people. Because it is a concept so fundamental to statistics, it is necessary to understand some of the basic elements of probability.

Probability as an Estimate of the Unknown

Probability is always concerned with the relative frequency with which something will occur before the results are actually known. Usually these unknown results concern future events—future outcomes of weather conditions, horse races, performance of students in college, outcomes of psychological experiments, results of elections, and other unknown outcomes.

In a strict sense, it is more correct to speak of unknown outcomes rather than future outcomes, because probabilities can be applied to past events in time where the results are not known. For example, it would be perfectly proper to apply concepts concerning probability to the use of a particular word in different paragraphs of Shakespeare's plays. Thus, if a scholar guessed that a particular word had been employed in 5 percent of all of the paragraphs written by Shakespeare (a probability of 0.05), he could actually analyze the works of Shakespeare to see to what extent this probability estimate was accurate. In the same sense, it is logically feasible to make probability estimates of crimes committed long ago as well as other events of the past.

The major point is that probabilities always concern unknown events; after the events are known, probability is not an issue. In short, it makes no sense to talk about probabilities after the facts are already known about raining on Tuesday, the outcome of a horse race, or the actual performance of a student in college.

Probability and Relative Frequencies

Inevitably, probability concerns estimates of frequencies, frequency being a technical term for number of events of one kind or another. Considered in an absolute sense, a frequency seldom is directly interpretable. Usually more important is the *relative frequency,* which quite simply is the ratio of the frequency of events of one kind as compared to the frequency of events of another kind. For example, one might quote the frequency with which a baseball player made a hit during the season. However, much more information would be obtained by dividing the frequency of hits by the total number of times that the player was at bat. We would know more about a batter who made 90 hits after coming to bat 300 times during a season than one who we just were told made 100 hits. Knowing that in a large study of children it is found that 365 begin to walk before the age of one year has no meaning until a relative frequency is computed by dividing the number of children who did walk by the total number of children investigated. Relative frequencies are used as indices of probability; however, it is important to remember that probabilities concern estimates of relative frequencies obtained before the fact.

A statement of probability (relative frequency) is meaningful only in the context of a strictly specified state of alternative possibilities. Most of the examples already cited concern only two possibilities, for example, making a hit or not making a hit in baseball, or completing college training or not completing college training. Using the example of college training, any probability statement regarding completion would imply the following simple relationship

$$\text{Probability} = \frac{\text{Estimated number of students who will complete training}}{\text{Estimated number who will complete training plus estimated number who will fail to complete training}} \quad (2\text{-}1)$$

Because it is obviously awkward to spell out all of the terms in equations such as Equation (2-1) it is very useful to have some standard symbols for abbreviating the terms. The convention is to symbolize probability with p. The terms on the right-hand side of the equation above stand for *variables*; that is, each of them can take on many different values in terms of the frequencies involved. Examples of variables that would relate to probability statements are numbers of persons who complete college training, pass a scholarship examination, enter one occupation rather than another, correctly identify a word projected upon a screen, or belong in one category of mental illness rather than others. Each of these categories represents a variable in the sense that the numbers of people falling in each can vary from zero up to the total number of persons in an investigation. An example would be in sampling 1,000 mental patients around the country with respect to the numbers (or frequencies) in each of three categories. The possible range of frequencies in each category varies from zero up to the total number of subjects in the study. It is common to symbolize variables with letters late in the alphabet, X and Y when there are only two variables, and W, Z, and others when there are three or more variables.

The above probability statement can be rephrased as follows

$$p = \frac{X}{X + Y} \quad (2\text{-}2)$$

where p = the probability of completing college, X = the estimated number of students in a particular study who will complete college, and Y = the estimated number who will fail to complete college.

It is often the case that more than two possible events are involved in a probability estimate. As an example, a college offers four programs of study leading to four different degrees. All students are enrolled in one and only one of the four programs. If, from previous experience, good estimates are available regarding the frequency with which students enroll in the four programs, then the probability of any student selected at random enrolling in a particular program (X) would be as follows

$$p = \frac{X}{X + W + Y + Z} \qquad (2\text{-}3)$$

where p = the probability of enrolling in program X, X = estimated number of students who will enroll in one of the four programs, and W, Y, Z = estimated numbers who will enroll in other types of programs.

In establishing such probabilities, it is usually much simpler to insert in the denominator the total numbers of frequencies, t, involved in all possibilities rather than to list them individually. Thus, in Equation (2-3) or in any other probability statement, the probability can be very simply stated as follows

$$p = \frac{X}{t} \qquad (2\text{-}4)$$

where p = the probability of any particular event occurring, X = the estimated frequency of such events, and t = the estimated total numbers of events.

Some Characteristics of Probabilities

Probabilities are expressed in terms of ratios ranging from zero to 1.00. Obviously, a probability cannot be negative, because that would imply less than a zero possibility of an event occurring. Similarly, a probability could not be greater than 1.00, because that would imply a level of certainty above 100 percent of an event occurring. It is convenient to think of probabilities in terms of percentages, estimated percentages of times that something will occur out of a specified number of other possibilities. Probabilities are frequently stated in other ways, such as in stating a batting average of 300 rather than 0.300, or the odds of winning a poker hand as 1 out of 10 rather than 0.10.

In discussing probabilities, one must make a distinction between complete and incomplete sets of possibilities. Complete sets of possibilities are the odds that a person will or will not complete college successfully in a specified period of time, whether or not the next person to walk in the door will be a male or a female, and whether or not the results of an experiment indicate that one method of instruction in mathematics is superior to another. Such sets of possibilities are complete in the sense that there are no alternatives other than the ones stated. In these examples, there is an "either-or" set of possibilities, but the same would be true if there were three or more possible outcomes. In contrast, a set of possibilities under investigation may be incomplete, or not include all the possible outcomes that could occur. An example of an incomplete set of possibilities would be one concerning students entering college for training in engineering, liberal arts, or law. Since the students could also go into medicine, divinity, and other areas, the probabilities of their being trained in the former courses would not add up to 1.00.

Many issues in statistics concern the probability with which one event will occur rather than another. The best known example is that of flipping a coin a number of times and having it come up "heads," for example, five times in a row. This simple experiment illustrates a number of points about probability. Probability statements are formulated in four ways. First, probabilities are formulated on the basis of the *principle of indifference.* Since there is no reason to believe that the coin will come up "heads" rather than "tails," one must make a sheer guess or, in other words, be indifferent about the two possibilities. An example of how the principle of indifference applies to experiments in psychology and education is as follows. An experimenter is contemplating an investigation of the effectiveness of three different types of driver training. Ninety students are randomly divided into three groups with respect to the three types of training. After the experiment is over, all students are given a comprehensive test on driver safety, and comparisons are made of the average results in the three groups. Numerically, the average scores are different, but the experimenter wonders whether these could be due to the happenstance of how students were randomly sorted into groups. Purely by chance, some of the students in one group might have had more of the necessary motor skills, intelligence, and other attributes that would make for rapid success in that type of program of instruction. If students with higher aptitude were accidentally placed in one group rather than another, average differences on the test might have been unrelated to the program of instruction. Instead of actually submitting students to the courses of instruction, he might have performed a "random experiment" as follows. Initially, the names of all 90 students would be placed in a box. These would be drawn out one at a time and placed in three piles. Then, rather than submit the students to three different courses of training, all would be submitted to the same type of training. Average scores would then be compared for the randomly selected groups. In this way, it might have been found that differences among randomly selected groups actually were as large as those found in the experiment, or differences in the actual experiment may have been much larger. Because in the random experiment there would be no reason for students to differ on the average any more than could be expected by chance, the principle of indifference would hold. To the extent to which groups in the actual experiment differed considerably more than in the random experiment, the principle of pure chance would be rejected in favor of the conclusion that the three types of training had different effects on subsequent performance.

When the principle of indifference must be applied in order to establish probabilities, it is frequently said that prediction concerns *sheer chance.* Later it will be shown that statistics employed in research often are concerned with demonstrating that the results of an experiment probably are *not* due to sheer chance. Suppose that a coin is tossed 30 times and comes up "heads" every time. Statistical methods would indicate that the probability for this set of events to occur by chance alone is so minute that there is sufficient cause to suspect that a two-headed coin is being flipped. In the same way, the odds are extremely low that all 30 of the students in one experimental group will perform better than the highest scoring student in another experimental group by chance alone. Such findings would give the experimenter great reason to believe that the results could not come from a random sorting of students as was initially established.

The second method of asserting probabilities is by the *empirical* approach, or through the gathering of evidence. Polling agencies estimate the percentages of people who are watching different programs each time period. Thus, it might be found that 42 percent of the TV sets which are on at seven o'clock are tuned to "The Sheriff's Daughter," 26 percent to "Fred and Mary," and the remaining 32 percent to "What Happened This Week." The principle of indifference would not be applied here because there is more than chance guessing involved. With prior information available, the wisest course is to establish probabilities for subsequent events on the basis of the relative frequencies found in the past. Thus, one could phone the homes of friends and ask them whether or not they were watching television, and if so, which of the three programs they were watching. Considering those people who actually were watching television, the best bet in advance would be that 42 percent ($p = 0.42$) would be watching "The Sheriff's Daughter." Of course, the principle of indifference will lead to the statement of $p = 0.33$.

There are many cases where information is gathered specifically for the purpose of obtaining probabilities that accurately forecast future events. For example, research is undertaken to determine the numbers of students at different IQ levels who successfully complete different college programs. In this way, it might be found that 80 percent of the people who have IQs of 120 or higher are successful—actually graduate or quit on their own initiative without having failing grades. Then in future cases, one could say that $p = 0.80$ that any candidate for entrance into that college would be successful if he has an IQ of 120 or higher. The means by which probabilities are determined empirically concern descriptive statistics, which will constitute a major part of the chapters that lie ahead. A percentage is a descriptive statistic; for example, the percentage of people watching one television program or another. There are many other descriptive statistics which are useful in establishing probabilities for predicting the outcomes of future events.

A third method of establishing probabilities is to derive them from a theory about the behavior of people or lower animals. A recent trend in psychology and education has been to express theories in probabilistic terms, these theories being referred to as *mathematical models.* An oversimplified example will illustrate mathematical models and how probabilities are derived from them. The model concerns a learning experiment with kindergarten children. The child is shown a series of cards, one at a time. He is told that when some of the cards appear he should say "right" and when the other cards appear he should say "wrong." Half of the cards have a black triangle in the middle, and the other half have a circle. For half of the children, the triangle is "right," and for the other half, the circle is "right." A second deck of cards with each triangle colored red and each circle colored green is composed. A random half of the children in the study learn the task with the circle and triangle in solid black and the other half learn it with the circle and triangle in different colors. In the former group, the triangle would always be "right" for a particular child, and since both the triangle and the circle are black, the child would have only one cue, shape, for correct responding. For a child in the second group, the triangle would always be "right," but since the triangle is red and the circle green, the child has two valid cues; judging the correct card in each case can be determined by shape, color, or both.

A mathematical model in this case might assert that children who have two valid cues would completely learn the task twice as fast as children with only one valid cue. This ratio then could lead to the statement of numerous probabilities regarding performance of children in comparison to one another and at different points in the learning experience. (This is a very oversimplified example. A true mathematical model in this case would consider other factors in the situation.)

A fourth way of obtaining probabilities (predictions of unknown events) is through the *intuitive* approach. In this approach, someone simply uses his own judgment about the probability with which an event will occur in the future. This is, of course, what gamblers do in setting the odds for betting in those situations where probabilities cannot be established in terms of the three previously described methods. In some cases, probability is established partly in terms of intuition and partly in terms of prior experience. If two of the horses in competition had participated in a number of previous races, this would provide some evidence regarding the probability of one horse coming in ahead of the other; however, it would be extremely unlikely that enough information of this kind would be available on all horses to permit the establishment of probabilities entirely on an empirical basis. Even if such information were available, the gambler would still have to use his intuition in judging the probability of winning, because there are many other factors such as condition of the track which enter into horse races.

There are many other areas besides gambling where probabilities are established mainly on an intuitive basis. For example, when a physician tells a patient that the odds are 99 out of 100 that a particular operation will be successful, he is doing this at least partly on an intuitive basis. He may have some relative frequencies from facts gathered previously about the type of operation, but the probability estimate must necessarily contain a large component of judgment on the part of the physician. Although people do not usually verbalize probabilities with respect to their actions or even realize that probability is involved, they use judgments regarding probabilities for many things that they do every day. For example, when a person decides to go on an automobile trip even though one of the tires is quite worn, he is basing his decision partly on a subjective estimate that the probability of the tire lasting until arrival at the destination is high. When a housewife rushes to the store and decides not to stop long enough to lock the front door, she is (or at least should be) entertaining a very low probability that a thief will steal the family possessions.

The major lesson to be learned here is that a probability is *any* estimate of the relative frequency with which one event rather than other specified events will occur in unknown circumstances—usually in the future. By definition, such relative frequencies necessarily range between 0.00 and 1.00. Probabilities can be based on the principle of indifference, research on relative frequencies obtained in the past, mathematical models, or sheer intuition. With regard to intuition, the probability can be a wild guess or even based on the most absurd assumptions, but it is a probability nevertheless.

The proof of the pudding is in how well the stated probability actually forecasts events in the future, and that can be learned only by patiently gathering the relative frequencies as they accumulate. In some cases this is entirely feasible, as in research on the effectiveness of tests, different methods of instruction, effects of drugs, and most other research issues in psychology and education. In many other cases, it is simply not feasible to actually determine relative frequencies to the point that they can be truly realized. This would be the case in formulating a subjective probability regarding which of two prize fighters will win. They are not going to fight on enough future occasions to obtain any stable indication of the actual relative frequency of one winning rather than the other.

When probability statements are made about a unique event (a prize fight) or only a small number of events, then the probabilities can never be tested for accuracy. Such probabilities serve only to provide some comfort in making decisions. The essence of research in psychology and education is that problems are posed in such a way that verification of probability statements can be tested by future events. The remainder of this book will *not* be concerned with probabilities based on mathematical models or intuition; rather, it will concern probability based on the principle of indifference and on empirical research.

Mathematical Aspects of Probability

The subject of probability constitutes a whole subarea in mathematics. It would be far beyond the scope of this book to provide even a cursory introduction to such mathematics, but several important principles are necessary for understanding certain concepts. [An excellent source for an introduction to the mathematics is Hays (1973).]

One important issue is whether or not various events entering into relative frequencies are independent of each other. Put quite simply, events are independent if the occurrence of one has no influence on the occurrence of others. Usually, it is assumed that coin flips are independent, that is, whether or not "heads" or "tails" comes up on one toss has no influence on whether "heads" or "tails" comes up on any successive toss. As another example, if students are randomly placed in two groups for an experiment on perception, it is assumed that the placements of the students in the two groups are independent. If Mary is placed in group A, proper procedures of randomization would ensure that this did not influence whether John was placed in group A or group B. In drawing a sample of people for an opinion poll, independence is achieved by ensuring that the choice of one respondent does not influence the choice of any other respondents.

There are many ways in which nonindependence occurs. One might invent a machine that is so delicately tuned in flipping coins that if it landed "heads" one time the probability would be much higher than 0.50 that it would land "tails" the next time. If in selecting people for an opinion poll, the pollster asked the first respondent to recommend several friends to be questioned, this would constitute a possible lack of independence. The friends most likely would have similar opinions. If psychological tests are used to measure the results of an experiment and some of the students copy answers from one another, this would also be a lack of independence. Students who are tested in an experiment on perception regarding recognition of words rapidly presented on a screen, would exhibit a lack of independence if they are tested in groups and verbalize their answers rather than write them.

The concept of independence will come up numerous times in the study of statistics because it relates to the all-important matter of determining relative frequencies. In essence, a lack of independence causes the experimenter to interpret more data than he actually has. Because they would be independent, 30 tosses of a coin would constitute 30 separate items of information about the extent to which the coin was biased to turn up "heads" or "tails." In the situation where a pollster let persons recommend friends for polling, the sampling would not be independent; consequently, the number of persons in the so-called sample would be misleadingly large with respect to the actual amount of data that was obtained. Similarly, in all experiments concerning the study of people, a lack of independence results in an illusory sample size with respect to the actual amount of interpretable data. One of the major purposes of carefully designing an experiment is to ensure the necessary forms of independence required for the employment of statistics. This will be discussed in more detail in Chapter 3.

When probabilities are independent, a few simple principles underlie calculations of outcomes even in the most complex situations. It is frequently the case that rather powerful methods of mathematical analysis such as those involved in calculus, are required to derive the exact probabilities for complex outcomes in research, although these methods all rest on a number of rather simple ideas. One must start by defining the set of outcomes that are of interest in the particular problem, for example, being male versus female, making different scores on psychological tests, or effects of different drugs on motor coordination. If the set of outcomes is complete, then the probabilities of all possible outcomes necessarily add up to 1.00. This is frequently called a *closed set.* A set can be closed by adding a "wastebasket" category, for example, some occupation other than doctor, lawyer, or professor.

One important and obvious principle is that the probability of an event being in at least one of two or more categories consists of the sum of probabilities of being in either category. To take an extremely simple case, the probability of the next person walking in the door being *either* male or female equals the sum of the two separate probabilities, namely 1.00. A somewhat less obvious example would be that concerning the effects of different degrees of novelty on visual attention. Students are shown four pictures, each on one corner of a screen. The pictures represent four levels of novelty, for instance, outline drawings of a cow in which the features are purposely distorted to make the animal appear novel. The four levels are (1) an ordinary cow, (2) a cow with symmetrical polka dots, (3) a cow with polka dots and long legs, and (4) a cow with polka dots, long legs, and the trunk of an elephant. A hidden camera is used to record which picture students are looking at during any point in time. From previous research it has been found that the percents are 10, 20, 30, and 40 respectively. Thus, in future cases it would be reasonable to assume that, for any student picked at random at any given time, the probabilities of the student being caught looking at any one of the pictures would be 0.10, 0.20, 0.30, and 0.40 respectively. By the *principle of additivity*, one could also state that the probability would be 0.70 of the student being photographed while looking at *either* of the two most novel stimuli rather than the other two. The probability would be 0.40 that the student was looking at either the ordinary cow or the third picture in the series. In this way, one could obtain as many probabilities of compound events as there are possible combinations of pictures.

The additivity principle is only one rule for combining probabilities of separate outcomes into overall probabilities. One example would be that of the probability of obtaining three "heads" in a row from tossing a coin. In that case the odds would be $1/2 \times 1/2 \times 1/2$, thus $p = 1/8$ or 0.12. In general, the probability of obtaining a predicted string of successive outcomes equals p^c where p is the probability of the outcome and c is the number of outcomes. Thus the probability of obtaining five heads in a row equals 1/2 to the fifth power (1/32), so that $p = 0.03$.

Rules for combining probabilities and equations for deriving the actual results are available for all possible combinations of simple outcomes into probabilities for complex outcomes. [See discussion in Hays (1973), Chap. 2.] These rules for combining and computing probabilities are essential for the derivation of all inferential statistics. It is not necessary for the reader to understand the mathematics of probability in detail for grasping the essentials of introductory statistics, but it is important to know that all statistics rest upon some fundamental principles regarding probability.

SUMMARY

The foundations of statistics comprise quantification, measurement, and probability. In the eyes of many persons who have not studied the topic, statistics is associated with the sheer arithmetic involved in analyzing data. Quantification is very impõrtant in statistics, but there is much more to it than that. The experimenter has a choice as to the types of mathematical operations that will be performed on data, and the different choices provide different information about the results. Just playing with numbers does not constitute the application of statistics; the research must be designed and carried out in such a way as to help provide answers to important questions.

Quantification is useful only to the extent that the numbers involved come from the application of reliable and valid measurements of human characteristics. Measurement consists of rules for assigning numbers to objects so that they represent quantities of attributes. A measurement method is reliable if consistent results are obtained on the same subjects by different experimenters, different versions of the measuring instrument, and under a variety of conditions. A measurement method is valid to the extent that it actually measures what it is purported to measure. Validity can be determined only by accumulating evidence regarding the extent to which the measure enhances scientific explanation.

Measures can be categorized in terms of the type of scales which they represent. Depending on the type of scale used, different information about results will be provided. The scale in which a measure is classified determines the amount of information which it provides and restricts the classes of statistics that can be employed. The major types of scales are labels (really a nonscale), categories, ranks, interval scales, and ratio scales. These are rank ordered with regard to the amount of information which is supplied and the range of statistics which can be used. Most measures in psychology and education are regarded as interval scales; this provides justification for employing nearly all of the statistical methods which are needed.

All inferential statistical methods are based on the concept of probability. A probability is any numerical value between 0.00 and 1.00 which represents an estimate of the relative frequency of events that will be of one kind rather than another. Probabilities can be obtained from (1) the principle of indifference, (2) relative frequencies found in previous research, (3) a mathematical model, and (4) intuition. Any number between 0.00 and 1.00 which is used to estimate the relative occurrence of unknown events is a probability; but the worth of any probability is determined only by subsequently gathering evidence regarding actual relative frequencies.

After probabilities are stated for simple events, rules and mathematical equations can be employed to obtain probabilities for more complex events. The field of mathematical probability is concerned with formulating such rules and deriving corresponding equations. These principles of probability underly all statistics in psychology and education.

EXERCISES

Study Questions

1 Early in the chapter, a comprehensive definition was given of measurement, and a number of essential features were discussed. Please list and briefly explain each of the major features.

2 Why are measurement and quantification so closely related?

3 List and explain some of the major advantages of standardized measures over subjective judgments.

4 Name the major types of measurement scales and give two examples of each (ones not listed in this chapter).

5 Give a definition of probability. Explain why probabilities always range between .00 and 1.00.

6 List the different ways that probabilities can be obtained and briefly explain each.

7 Explain the concept of independence with respect to probability. Give several examples of instances in which independence would not be present.

8 Explain situations in which probabilities are (a) added together, and (b) multiplied together. Give numerical examples in both cases.

SUGGESTED ADDITIONAL READINGS

Ferguson, G. A. *Statistical analysis in psychology and education*, 3d ed. New York: McGraw-Hill, 1971, Chap. 5.

Guilford, J. P., and B. Fruchter. *Fundamental statistics in psychology and education*, 5th ed. New York: McGraw-Hill, 1973, Chap. 2.

Hays, W. L. *Statistics for the social sciences*, 2d ed. New York: Holt, Rinehart, & Winston, 1973, Chaps. 3 and 4.

3

Basic Principles of Statistical Inference and Research Design

Chapter 2 discussed some of the prerequisites for the employment of statistics in research. This chapter will consider principles of research design and the way statistics can be applied to the results. The purpose of scientific theory is to provide an understandable, simple set of predictions regarding unknown events. Examples of such predictions are weather for days and months ahead, which students with test scores of a specified level will successfully complete college, the effectiveness of one method of classroom instruction over another, and the degree to which children will resemble their parents in various traits. The purpose of research is to provide evidence for or against predictions that arise from theory, whether the theory is a highly formal system of interlocking statements or a set of informal questions about natural events. The purpose of an excellent research design is to ensure that an investigation will produce results that provide clear evidence with respect to the issues. In this process, statistics has two functions: (1) to summarize the research results with descriptive statistics, and (2) to provide probability statements regarding the results with inferential statistics.

SCIENTIFIC INFERENCE

The word *inference* as used in science means quite literally to infer one thing from another. If a square table is 3 feet on each side, it can be inferred that it contains 9 square feet of surface. If a feather and a steel ball are dropped simultaneously from the same height in a vacuum, they will touch the ground at the same time. If a person has an IQ less than 90, the odds are very low that he will successfully complete college. In each of these cases, knowing one thing (event A), leads to the inference of the second thing (event B). However, the three examples illustrate different types of scientific inference, which is a matter that now will be elaborated upon.

Deductive Inference

One type of inference is concerned purely with the manipulation of symbols rather than with gathering facts about the real world. All mathematics represent this type of inference. Thus, $2 \times 2 = 4$ because the result is defined by the rules for manipulating relations among numbers. If A is greater than B, and B is greater than C, one can deduce that A is greater than C. Deductive inference of this kind is frequently spoken of as *deductive logic.*

Although most aspects of deductive logic have counterparts in the real world and are useful for the investigation of the real world, this is only a fortunate coincidence. A system of deductive logic or inference is valid if an unambiguous set of rules is stipulated for the manipulation of symbols. The only requirement is that the system be internally consistent, in the sense that contradictory deductions cannot arise. Thus, the system of making simple arithmetic operations would be inconsistent if it led to the conclusion that $2 \times 4 = 8$ but $4 + 4 = 9$.

There are two important features of deductive inference that distinguish it from other types of inference. First, it is purely concerned with the manipulations of systems of symbols which do not necessarily have counterparts in the real world. If a system of nonsense words leads unambiguously to the conclusion that if a *wuggle drang a flous,* it would be a legitimate system of deductive inference. Most mathematical systems are matched by things in the real world, but that is not the essence of the system; and the validity of the system does not depend on that correspondence.

A second feature of deductive logic that sets it apart from other types of logic is that any conclusion is either absolutely true or absolutely false. Thus, by the rules of arithmetic one can deduce that the square root of 9 is 3 and definitely is not 2. In some cases, it is very difficult to manipulate complex systems of symbols in order to make an inference (for example, in some complex calculus problems), but the answer would still be either absolutely true or absolutely false. This is not the case with other types of logic.

Inductive Inference

In contrast to deductive inference, *inductive inference* is concerned with the rules for testing theories about the world of real events. The example of the feather and the steel ball falling at the same rate in a vacuum is an example of inductive inference. The word *induce* means to make statements about relations among observable events. Whereas systems of deductive logic are useful for the planning of research and for analyzing the results, the theories being investigated and the actual gathering of data constitute aspects of inductive logic. Thus, if a steel ball is dropped from an airplane flying 1 mile high, the inductive laws of gravity infer that the ball will fall toward the earth rather than go in the opposite direction. The deductive logic of algebra can be used to express how rapidly the ball will be falling at ½ mile from the ground.

In contrast to deductive inference, an inductive inference is never finally accepted as absolutely true. Some inductive inferences are supported by so many observations that one can be extremely confident that they will hold true tomorrow. This is so for simple principles concerning gravitation, but even in such cases there is no way to actually *prove* that the principles will not change. In addition, although all the facts at the moment might support a given theoretical position, subsequent evidence might be contradictory. Even Newton's original laws of gravity have been shown to be only excellent approximations of more complex laws concerning relativity; consequently no one knows whether or not these in turn may be supplanted one day by even more precise laws.

The principle that an inductive inference is never finally accepted as absolutely true is called the *doctrine of permanent control,* meaning that the door is always open to reach a contradictory conclusion in the future. This doctrine certainly holds great weight in research in psychology and education. An experiment might indicate that a particular type of treatment relieves the anxiety of patients in mental hospitals; however, a subsequent experiment might show that the first experiment failed to take account of an important factor which influenced earlier findings. A researcher comparing two methods of instruction in foreign language might find one method to be superior to the other in his research, but a researcher at a different school would find evidence in the opposite direction. A test of readiness for the first grade might be highly predictive of actual performance in the first grade at the time the research is conducted; but if the curriculum of the first grade changed substantially, the predictiveness of the test might be markedly diminished.

Statistical Inference

Quite simply, *statistical inference* is a special form of inductive inference, one in which a principle concerning the real world must be stated in terms of probabilities rather than in terms of near certainty. For instance, even though it may be found from empirical research that 80 percent of the persons who make a particular score on a college aptitude test are successful in college, it is only a probability that any student who has that score will actually succeed. In an experiment concerning the effectiveness of two methods of memorizing materials, children in a classroom are randomly divided into two groups for the two methods of instruction. The research results show that average performance in one group is better than the average performance in the other group, but the difference could have been due entirely to chance. Although the odds are against it, the random process of assigning students could have placed most of the smarter students in the group that performed better.

A developmental study is made of the improvement in a child's ability to judge sizes of objects. It is hypothesized that this ability improves with age during the early years of elementary schooling. It is found that 19 out of 20 students make better scores in the third grade than in the second grade, and the remaining child's performance decreases. This finding strongly suggests that average performance of children increases over the time period, but is this a safe conclusion? By methods of statistical analysis that will be presented in Chapter 13, it is found that the odds are very low that a finding of 19 out of 20 cases in one direction rather than the other would have occurred by chance alone. Even the finding that one child is the exception to the rule prevents the experimenter from making an unqualified inductive inference. He is quite justified in making a statistical inductive inference to the effect that average performance increases over the age span.

SAMPLING IN RELATION TO STATISTICS

Scientific theories concern statements that are general to all objects or living things of a *specified type*. Thus, in an experiment to compare rates of memorization of words in three groups of college students, the purpose is to provide information about how well the methods would work if all college students in the country were tested. If in a study of rats it is found that removal of a particular part of the brain decreased the ability to detect odors, the experiment is intended to provide evidence about what would happen if an infinitely large number of rats were given the same treatment.

Science is concerned with generalization. Before one can estimate the extent to which the findings from any research can be generalized, it is necessary to define the population in advance. In statistics, population refers to all the members of a particular category. In some cases, as in studies of learning and perception, this represents, at least hypothetically, everyone alive. Such investigations are designed to determine what people, in general, are like. In the development of an intelligence test for United States citizens, the population includes all of the people in this country. Because of the language barrier, the test could not be applied to several other nations. Other populations consist of subdivisions of all people in the United States, such as members of trade unions, who might be asked their opinions about changes in federal legislation. In still other situations, the population in question is quite restricted, for example, in studying the attitudes of students in a particular college about athletics.

The collection of people actually investigated is called a sample. The purpose of investigating the sample is to estimate the results which would be obtained from the population as a whole. The effectiveness of this process depends upon how clearly the population is defined before obtaining a sample and the adequacy with which the sample is drawn. Although these issues are common to most research in psychology and education, it will prove useful to illustrate them with the sampling performed in public opinion polls.

Definition of Population

A population of people or other things is defined in terms of the breadth of generalizations (inductive inferences) which are being studied. In many cases, the size of the population is theoretically infinite. An example would be in a study about the effect of repetition of rapidly exposed words. Half of the subjects in an experiment are shown each word for 0.02 seconds and required to guess each word. The other half are shown the word twice, each time for 0.01 second with one-second intervals. The research concerns the question of whether duration of exposure is more or less important than number of exposures when total exposure time is held constant. If the results of the experiment clearly demonstrate that subjects in one group are more consistently accurate than those in the other group, the inference would be that everyone in the world today as well as future generations would manifest the same difference. This might not be a correct conclusion, but it is a logical one in research of that kind. If the population is theoretically infinite, or at least very large in reality, this simplifies the mathematical derivation of many methods of statistical analysis. In other words, it is mathematically convenient when the population in question is very large or theoretically infinite.

In other types of research the population is not infinite, but it is so large that it can be considered infinite for all statistical purposes. An opinion poll reporting on different television programs includes the millions of people who are watching television in this country every night. In this case, the population is so large that it can be considered infinite for all practical purposes. In other cases, the population is much more limited. For example, an investigation might be made of a new summer school program in which 1,000 students participate. After completing the program, research would be conducted on performance in school the following year, career choices, ratings of satisfaction with the program, as well as other results. For practical reasons, it would probably not be feasible to investigate a sample of more than several hundred students. In this case, the population is far from infinite, although the sample constitutes an appreciable percentage of the total population under investigation. In the most extreme case, the investigation concerns all members of the population. This would be the case, for example, in (1) taking a vote among all workers in a factory for a new schedule of hours, (2) comparing the changes in achievement test scores of students in a particular classroom from the beginning to the end of a semester, and (3) determining the percentages of students entering various professions after graduating from a particular college.

Depending on how large the population is, relative to the sample size, inferential statistics would be employed to estimate the actual results that would be obtained by studying the population. In most research performed in psychology and education, the population is either nearly infinite in size or it is very large in comparison to the sample being investigated so that inferential statistics are necessary to determine the validity of the results when applied to the whole population.

Sample Size

Many issues in the social sciences are investigated with sample surveys, in which questions are asked either of a sample or of some group in the population. The public is acquainted with sample surveys taken by commercial opinion-polling agencies, the results of which are reported in many newspapers and mentioned on radio and television. Opinion polls usually deal with issues like preferences for political candidates, matters of foreign policy, and controversial legislation. Sample surveys are also used in basic research in psychology and sociology. Surveys are made of opinions about child-rearing practices, prevention of crime, integration of races, medical care, and many other issues. Sample surveys are also used extensively in market research to determine preferences among commercial products.

The results of a sample survey may be misleading because of the small number of subjects interviewed. One frequently sees in newspapers or hears on radio the results of highly informal surveying, for example, 30 people questioned on a man-in-the-street radio program. Such small samples are totally inadequate for representing the opinions of people in general. The situation is made much worse by converting the results to percentages. For example, if 18 out of 30 persons agree with the statement that parents are too lenient with children these days, it may be reported that 60 percent of the people interviewed feel that something is amiss with the way children are being reared. If another 30 persons had been questioned, the result might have been quite the opposite.

To the extent that results vary from sample to sample, it is said that *sampling error* is present. This can be illustrated in a hypothetical case where six opinion polls are conducted with only 100 subjects in each. The question is which political candidate the respondents would vote for. The percentage of people that would vote for Smith varies from 65 to 52 over the six surveys. This range represents the sampling error. If one had the results from only one of the small surveys, he would come to a different conclusion than if he had the results of another survey. The uncertainty introduced by such variations in statistical results from sample to sample constitutes the sampling error.

The amount of sampling error is more likely to be large when only a small number of subjects are in the sample; it follows then, that the amount of sampling error decreases as subject size increases. One would have expected less variability in the percentages in the opinion poll if there had been 500 persons in each sample rather than only 100. Amount of sampling error can be determined by statistical methods which will be discussed in Chapter 9. The essence of employing inferential statistics is to determine the amount of sampling error in any case so that this sampling error will be considered in the interpretation of results. For example, if the sampling error in a voting survey is very large, there is good indication that it is due to genuine differences in voting tendencies rather than chance factors regarding the sampling of subjects. In contrast, if the difference is small in comparison to the amount of sampling error, one would place little faith in the obtained difference in percentages. This principle applies not only to the results of opinion polls but to all research results as well. Estimates of the sampling error present in all experiments in psychology and education can be obtained. To the extent that differences among treatment groups are large compared to the amount of sampling error, one can safely generalize the results obtained from an experiment to the population in question. The essence of employing inferential statistics is to determine the amount of sampling error in an experiment and judge the significance of results in relation to that sampling error.

Sample Representativeness

In addition to having a substantial number of persons, the sample must be representative of the larger group to which results will be generalized. For example, if a survey is intended to represent the opinion of all members of trade unions toward a pending item of federal legislation, the results might be misleading if all subjects are electrical workers. They might have somewhat different opinions from those of members of other trades. Then, no matter how many electrical workers were studied, the results of the survey would still be misleading.

A now famous mishap will illustrate that the sheer size of the sample studied is no guarantee of valid results. The *Literary Digest* made a very bad estimate of the voting sentiment in the 1936 presidential election. The magazine predicted a Landon victory with 370 electoral votes, but Roosevelt won 523 of a possible 531 votes. This calamitous mistake drove the magazine out of business.

A look at how the *Digest* poll operated will point up some lessons regarding the needs for representative sampling. The poll was conducted entirely by mail, with 10 million ballots being sent out for the 1936 election, of which less than 2½ million were returned. Persons who reply to mail questionnaires tend to form a select group, overweighted with people from upper-income brackets and upper-educational levels. In addition, they usually have a more direct interest in the election than those who fail to reply. In this case, it was the upper-income persons who were protesting against Roosevelt.

Worse than its dependence on mail-out ballots was the fact that the *Digest* used very poor sampling procedures. The mailing list was obtained from telephone directories and files of automobile registrations. The people in 1936 who had telephones and automobiles were, as a group, much higher on the socioeconomic scale than those who did not. At that time, the lower socioeconomic groups voted heavily Democratic and the higher socioeconomic groups voted heavily Republican. The *Digest* predicted that Roosevelt would get only 40.9 percent of the popular vote, whereas he actually got 60.2 percent.

How to obtain representative samples is not an easy matter. Theoretically, the best sample of the population in the United States would be obtained by randomly sampling a large number of persons. However, that would be nearly impossible in principle and would be prohibitively expensive in practice. One of the persons so selected might live in a remote mountain village that is snowed in most of the year. Another person might be on an oil rig standing 2 miles off the coast. Obviously, it would be extremely expensive to search out such persons for a survey. For these as well as other reasons, it is necessary to employ approximately random samples, ones that are purposefully constructed to represent the distributions of age, sex, education, and locality that exist in the country as a whole. The technical problems in constructing such samples are sufficiently complex that only experts can be trusted to perform survey research. Whole books have been written on the technical problems involved. [See Albig, (1956); Kish, (1965); and Yates (1949).]

Sampling in Actual Research

The discussion of random sampling represents the ideal situation in which a population is carefully defined, and the sample size is adequate, as well as representative of the population. Unfortunately, it is not possible to achieve these ideals in most research in psychology and education. A cardinal example concerns the many forms of research that are performed on college students. Fresh out of Ph.D. training, Professor Blum is at West Overshoe College. His speciality is the investigation of the factors that influence memory. Each semester he uses students from his course in Introductory Psychology as subjects. In a typical experiment, three groups of subjects containing 30 students each are given three different types of memorization tasks.

Obviously, Professor Blum did not conduct the investigation only to find out about the particular students, but rather to find evidence for principles that apply to some population. But what is the population at issue? Surely he hopes to make statements that are general to students other than those attending the particular college at the time or who will attend it in the future. Furthermore, does he want to generalize only to all college students or to all persons of that age group, whether or not they are in college? Would he contend that the results even held for people over eighty years of age or under seven years of age? Would he contend that they held for both males and females? Would he contend that they held for people with different IQ levels?

This should illustrate that the concept of sampling in most research in psychology and education is usually somewhat ambiguous as regards the population in question. For two reasons, this is not quite as serious a problem as it might seem. First, it is meaningful to think backward from the sample to some hypothetical population. Thus, if overwhelming evidence is found for a principle in *any* group of people, it is reasonable to infer that the principle holds for *some* population, even though one might not be able to describe that population at the time the results are obtained. Second, any research finding should be corroborated by findings in other places and with people who differ in age and other characteristics. Only after a principle is broadly investigated in this way can the generality and limitations be known with confidence. Strong statistical support for a principle in the first experiment concerning a particular issue should be viewed as only a spur to continued investigation of the issue under varying conditions and with broader samples of people.

RESEARCH DESIGN

Good research consists of much more than the simple gathering of information. It is necessary to have a careful plan, or *research design*, which ensures that valid conclusions regarding the implications of the results can be reached. Even today, it is common to find examples of so-called research that consists of a massive gathering of data without proper consideration as to whether subsequent analyses will be feasible or will make any sense. The *Literary Digest* poll in 1936 is a good example of this. Because the survey was designed poorly, only faulty conclusions could be obtained from the results. Other examples of possible flaws in research designs that render results meaningless will be given in this chapter and subsequent chapters. Principles will be stated for designing experiments which will provide valid conclusions.

Experiments and Individual Differences

Behavioral scientists study two interrelated types of data about humans and lower animals. First, they perform experiments to determine effects of different types of treatments on behavior. For example, investigations are made of the effects of magnitude of reward on the rate at which rats learn a maze. One group of rats is rewarded at the end of the maze with one food pellet, another group with three pellets, and a third group with nine pellets. The larger the reward for reaching the goal box of the maze, the faster rats learn the maze. This tells us something about the effects of rewards on learning rate.

Investigations of the thresholds for perceiving words that differ in frequency of usage in printed material provide another example of experimental treatments. Each word is shown on a screen for a fraction of a second, and the subject must report the word. Some of the words appear very frequently in printed material, others appear with moderate frequency, and still others are used very rarely. Examples of words in these categories are house, ration, and mimic. It is found that more frequently used words are more easily identified than less frequently used words. This tells us something about the influence of familiarity on perceptual recognition. In this way, we try to establish laws of behavior for mice and men.

In addition to being interested in general laws, behavioral scientists are also interested in individual differences in both mice and men. For example, a group of subjects is administered an intelligence test and a memory test. Statistical measures of correlation are made to see whether people who are high in intelligence are also high in the test of memory, and vice versa for people who are low in intelligence. Research workers investigate many types of individual differences such as ability and personality characteristics; consequently, it is important to understand the statistical methods that are employed in such investigations.

Independent and Dependent Variables

Experiments always concern one or more *independent variables* and one or more *dependent variables*. The independent variable (or variables) concerns the experimental treatment. Different levels of drug dosage, amounts of practice in a learning task, brightness of light in a study of perceptual recognition, males versus females in a study of reading achievement, and mentally ill people versus normal people in a study of anxiety are examples of independent variables. As can be seen, the independent variable might be either stated in measurable terms, such as amounts of practice, or in terms of the way people naturally differ from one another, such as males versus females.

The dependent variable (or variables) concerns the outcome of the experiment. These would be (1) the extent to which different dosages of a drug change the moods of patients, (2) differences between male and female students on a reading achievement test, and (3) different degrees of accuracy shown under different degrees of brightness of light in a study of perceptual recognition. Such variables are referred to as dependent, because if the research design were carefully planned, one can have some assurance that differences among groups in terms of the outcome of the experiment actually depend upon the way people were treated in terms of the independent variable.

Confounding Variables

A *confounding variable* is one that is (1) usually unknown to the investigator, (2) correlates, or tends to go along with, the stated independent variable, and (3) explains the outcome in terms of the dependent variable as well as the independent variable could. Several examples will be given here, and then the matter of confounding variables will be discussed in more detail later on.

An experiment that illustrates how a confounding variable operates concerns a hypothesis that a particular portion of the brains of rats is essential for discriminating differences in odors. The rat is given the opportunity of entering a dark box where one odor is present or a lighted box where another odor is present. If the rat enters the dark box, he will be rewarded with food; but if he goes to the lighted box, he will obtain no food on that particular trial. The rats are then given an operation to remove the particular portion of the brain associated with discriminating odors before the learning test is made. After the operation, each rat is placed in the same situation and measurements are made of the number of times that the rat enters the dark box with the rewarded odor rather than the lighted box with the nonrewarded odor. It is found that 78 percent of the trials for all rats combined are toward the rewarded odor in the darkened box. However, as must be perfectly obvious, it would not be safe to conclude that the rats were actually able to distinguish between the odors after removal of the particular part of the brain. The discrimination of the odor is perfectly confounded with darkness versus lightness of the box. It happens that rats, in general, like to go into dark places rather than lighted places, and this fact alone could explain the result irrespective of any abilities to discriminate odors. Consequently, no valid conclusion could be reached about the possible effects of the removed area of the brain on sensitivity to differences in odors.

A confounding variable represents a competing interpretation to that which the experimenter intended when he designed the experiment. The reader probably is saying to himself that no one would be so stupid as to let an experiment become so completely confounded as the one just described. However, it is easy to find examples almost as obvious in many experiments actually undertaken in psychology and education. For example, a confounded experiment appeared recently in a reputable journal in developmental psychology. The purpose of this experiment was to test the effect of novelty on exploratory behavior of infants. In essence, the infant was allowed to crawl into one of two partitioned chambers and play with a toy. After playing with the toy for a few minutes, the infant was then taken back and allowed a second trial. A new toy was placed in the *opposite* chamber from the one that he had entered on the first trial, and both chambers were open. It was predominantly found that the infants went into the other chamber with the different toy. The experimenter reached the conclusion that the switch in chambers was due to the fact that the child had learned something about *both* the old chamber and toy. It must be obvious that the experiment is totally confounded in the systematic placing of the new toy in the new chamber. The results may have been produced by either the new chamber or the new toy or both.

Most examples of confounding variables are much more subtle than those illustrated, and it sometimes takes years to ferret them out. An example of this is body weight for many studies of rats. Various treatment conditions employed in experiments tend to effect the body weights of rats, in addition to providing different types of situations for rat learning. Different dosages of drugs that potentially influence rates of learning or other behaviors tend to influence how much rats eat. If the dependent measure concerned how active rats were in running on a treadmill, one would not know whether the differences between the treatment groups was due to the drug itself or to the fact that fat rats move about more slowly than thin rats.

Potentially, there are always confounding variables in any type of research. Science consists, in large measure, of continously trying to weed out those confounding variables in order to determine the one essential variable that constitutes a *necessary* and *sufficient* condition for effects on the dependent variable.

Contrasted-Groups Design

One type of research design is that in which no treatment is given by the experimenter, but rather the experimenter simply compares two groups of people who differ on some basis. Examples are (1) males versus females in terms of motor skills, (2) schizophrenics versus normals in terms of perceptual abilities, (3) students in rural versus urban schools in terms of various achievement levels, and (4) groups from different ethnic backgrounds in terms of political preferences. In these cases, the so-called independent variable consists of group membership. Thus, in the *contrasted-groups design*, one makes comparisons among groups, but one does not specifically instigate the difference among the groups by any type of experimental treatment.

If the research issues concern differences among existing groups of people, there is no choice but to employ the contrasted-groups design. For example, if one wants to investigate the effects of deafness on various types of language learning, it goes without saying that one cannot take a large group of subjects and randomly deafen half of them for the sake of having a neat experimental design. Similarly, one cannot produce neuroses in people, cause brain damage, or many other things simply for the requirements that meet experimental designs. The contrasted-groups design is fraught with possible confounding variables, even when the best of efforts are made to rule them out. For example, a number of incidences have occurred in which chemical substances in the blood were found to differ between normal people and hospitalized mental patients. It was hypothesized that the chemical differences were important in causing the disease; subsequently, however, it was found that these differences were due to the confounding variable of hospital food versus the type of food that people typically eat outside the hospital. In most designs involving two or more contrasted-groups, there are potentially many confounding variables that are present, for example, differences in average intelligence, age, income, amount of schooling, geographic region, and innumerable others.

If the research issue necessarily concerns a contrasted-groups design, the best that can be done is to employ some safeguards. Essentially, this consists of matching the groups in terms of suspected confounding variables. As a simple example, one would ensure that a comparison of mental patients with normal persons would be made with an equal percentage of males versus females in each of the two groups. In a comparison of the attitudes of Catholic and Protestant adults toward college training, one would ensure that the two groups have essentially the same number of years of schooling.

For two reasons, however, efforts to match subjects in contrasted-groups designs on possible confounding variables are only partially successful. First, some knotty statistical problems are encountered concerning how the matching should be performed. [See discussion of this by Scott and Wertheimer (1967).] Second, it is never certain that all of the possible confounding variables have been controlled. The experimenter simply uses his intuition or relies on previous research findings in making efforts to control confounding variables. For instance, on any task concerning differences in learning between two types of people, the experimenter would feel sure that average IQ would need to be controlled. However, he might not have the slightest idea that differences in the ability to discriminate colors from one another might be different in the two groups and have an important impact on the learning task. In working with contrasted-groups designs, there is an endless search for possible confounding variables.

The major safeguard against the two dangers involved in employing contrasted-groups designs is to weave a network of supporting evidence for a principle. Thus, if the principle is that schizophrenics tend to be much more distractible than normal people in perceptual judgments, one could gain faith in that principle only from numerous experiments of different kinds that all led to the same conclusion. Only by weaving a network of such circumstantial evidence can a principle concerning contrasted-groups be given excellent support.

Repeated-Measures Designs

In many ways, the ideal experimental design is that in which two or more treatments are administered to the *same* subjects. An example given previously was that of a developmental study in which scores on tasks involving perceptual judgment of children in the second grade were compared after a year's lapse of time when they were going into the third grade. A second simple example would be that of studying the effects of list length on memorization in college students. On each trial, a list of randomly arranged numbers is projected onto a screen. The numbers vary from 0 to 9 and each list is drawn from those numbers. The treatment consists of the amount of numbers in each list, with there being three treatments respectively including four, eight, and twelve numbers. After an interval of 2 seconds, the subject is asked to recall as many of the numbers as he can in the order going from left to right. He is shown ten lists at each of the three levels, and items are randomly arranged by order of presentation.

In both of these examples, the experiment concerns comparisons of the same subjects—in one case at two points in time and in the other case in terms of experimental treatments. Designs concerning *repeated measures* are also frequently referred to as *within-subjects designs.* When such designs can be employed, they have a number of very attractive advantages. First, purely from a point of economy, it is necessary to seek out and deal with fewer subjects than if different subjects are used in each treatment condition. For example, in the illustrative study of memorization, 30 college students would probably provide ample data, since one has essentially 30 subjects for comparing the three treatment conditions. If, instead, different groups of subjects are used for each of the three levels of list size, one would need approximately 90 subjects to obtain the same information. A second major advantage of repeated-measures designs is that they totally rule out questions regarding any prior differences among "groups" before the experiments, as is a major problem in the contrasted-groups design.

A third major advantage is not as obvious as the other two, and a full explanation of it will be given in Chapter 11 after related matters are discussed. In essence, the advantage is that individual differences among subjects can be taken into account in employing inferential statistics. In the developmental study mentioned previously, children would differ markedly in their perceptual abilities on the first testing. Even though the average score may go up appreciably over the span of one year, individual differences on the second occasion probably would tend to correspond (correlate positively) with those on the first occasion. Thus, for each child, one could look at the amount by which he improved. Such differences in scores would be far less diverse than either of the two sets of scores taken separately, and one would thus be dealing with a much narrower range of scores. As will be discussed more fully in Part Three of the book, this would then reduce the amount of error by which the statistical significance of the change in average scores would be judged. If 100 children were tested on two occasions, this might lead to a statement of statistical significance of $p = 0.99$ that the observed difference in average scores was "real" and not due to chance factors regarding the particular groups of subjects selected for the study. In contrast, if a comparison were made of two different groups of subjects, each containing 100 students at the two grade levels, the data might only support the statement that $p = 0.85$ that the observed difference in average scores is not due to sampling error.

In spite of the attractive advantages of the repeated-measures designs, there are many cases in which they cannot be employed. In some cases, they are simply impractical because of the unavailability of subjects for a series of experimental sessions or the unwillingness of subjects to participate. An experiment might concern three types of group interactions in social psychology, in which it is necessary to apply the treatments at least two weeks apart. Obviously, it would be impossible to employ such a study on children in a summer camp in which each session lasted for only two weeks. Some experimental treatments require as much as an hour of concentrated effort on the part of each subject. It would be expecting far too much of subjects to go through three such tedious sessions in one day, and they might not be willing to participate for more than one day.

Another potential disadvantage of employing repeated-measures designs is that the different treatments might interact with one another and thus produce different results from what would be obtained if the treatments had been applied to different groups of subjects. An example is in studying the effectiveness of three different types of drugs on depressive patients. Patients could be administered drugs A, B, and C, each over a period of two weeks, and tested for anxiety, general adjustment, and other variables at the end of each two-week period. The obvious flaw in the design is that after taking the first drug for two weeks, the patient might, in essence, be a very different person. Then, on beginning therapy on drug B, the apparent effectiveness of the drug might be highly related to the earlier effects of drug A. The situation would be even more complex with respect to the effects of drug C.

Randomized-Groups Designs

When the repeated-measures design is not feasible, then by far, the most widely used and usually best research design is that in which the pool of subjects available is randomly divided into different treatment groups. An example would be in studying three types of approaches to having college students learn lists of words. The subjects available consist of 90 students in Introductory Psychology. Going down his list of student names, the experimenter would randomly assign each student to one of the three groups, the only restriction being that exactly 30 students are placed in each group. (Usually this is done with tables of random numbers like the one presented and discussed in Appendix B-1.) The random assignment of students to groups accomplishes something extremely important: it ensures that the groups, on the average, differ from each other *no more than could be expected from chance alone*. Then, it is improbable that there will be systematic differences between groups such as those that plague the contrasted-groups design. This provides a very sensible logic for the development of many inferential statistics. An example will illustrate why this is so. Imagine that 24 adults are attending a party and each writes his age to the nearest year, month, and day on a slip of paper. Next, these are placed in a hat, mixed up, and the slips are drawn by someone who is blindfolded. The first slip goes into one pile, the second slip goes into a second pile, the third slip goes into the first pile, and so on until one has two randomly selected groups of 24 slips showing ages. By methods which will be discussed in Chapter 5, one could measure the average age in each of the two groups. Any differences between the averages would be purely in terms of the chance factors of randomly selecting the slips. The same logic holds when performing experiments in psychology and education.

Only one who understands the basic principles of statistics could appreciate the beautiful logic of randomly dividing any available pool of subjects into treatment groups. In this case the logic is ironclad; no person could make a sensible argument that the groups could differ on any attribute other than by sheer chance. In Chapter 10 it will be seen how differences between such randomized groups allow one to make statistical inferences from samples of subjects to populations of subjects.

Factorial Designs

Whereas types of experimental designs discussed so far in this chapter concerned only one independent variable, it is frequently the case that two or more independent variables are manipulated in an experiment. These are called *factorial designs*, with the word factor referring to an independent variable. An oversimplified example would be studying the effects of two levels of dosage of a drug and two amounts of practice on the original learning task on memory in rats. In a randomized-groups design, the experimenter would assign each of 100 rats to the four groups involved in the design. It is typical to depict such factorial designs by diagrams like that in Figure 3-1.

The obvious advantage of factorial designs over designs in which only one independent variable is employed is that much more information is obtained about the phenomena in question. Thus, with the very simple example just described, one would obtain information in the same experiment about effects of both levels of drug dosage and amounts of practice on memory.

Whereas this example concerns only two levels on each factor, there is no end to the number of levels one can add if sufficient patience, time, and money are available for conducting the research. The experimenter could just as well have examined six levels of drug dosage and six levels of amounts of practice. Also, in factorial designs it is not necessary to have the same number of levels on each

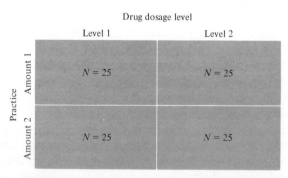

Figure 3-1. Diagram of a randomized groups design with 25 rats assigned to each of the four combinations of drug level and amount of practice.

factor, for example, one could examine six levels of drug dosage on one factor and two levels of amount of practice on the other factor. Factorial designs are not limited to two factors; rather, they can be extended to any number of factors, at least theoretically. In the same example, one could have also added on a third factor concerned with amount of time between the learning task and the tests for memory of what was learned initially.

The examples used so far all concerned randomized-groups designs; however, in practice one can employ factorial designs that mix factors of contrasted groups, repeated measures, and random assignment to groups. In an experiment on training of reading comprehension, one could compare boys and girls as a contrasted-groups factor on two methods of instruction. An equal number of boys and girls would be randomly assigned to the two types of instruction, which would make the second factor a randomized-groups factor. All subjects could be tested a year later, which would add a repeated-measures factor to the experiment. These and many other complex designs can be analyzed by statistical methods, and are used frequently in research. (Detailed discussions of the logic of applying such designs and related statistical methods are given in Winer (1971).)

Semi-Experimental Designs

Repeated-measures designs and randomized-groups designs are referred to as *true* experimental designs, because they rule out many of the ambiguities concerning the results of the so-called *semi-experimental*, or *quasi-experimental designs*. It was mentioned previously that the gremlin of research is the possible presence of a confounding variable, one which might have as much or more effect on the dependent variable as what the experimenter thought was being manipulated in the independent variable. Semi-experimental designs are ones in which the experimenter knows in advance that confounding variables might be involved. There are numerous ways in which this occurs in practice. [See discussions by Campbell and Stanley (1966).] If this is the case, it requires a great deal of cleverness on the part of the experimenter to minimize the influence of these potential confounding variables and to employ statistical methods that compensate for their effects. Unfortunately, many semi-experimental designs arise because the experimenter is unaware of true experimental designs that could be employed in the experiment. Some examples will illustrate the nature of semi-experimental designs.

All of the contrasted-groups designs mentioned previously are semi-experimental designs. Thus, one knows in advance of the experiment that comparisons of schizophrenic patients with normal people on perceptual judgment tasks are likely to be confounded by many variables other than that of being mentally ill versus normal, for example, very different kinds of experiences, age, and motivation to participate in the experiment. All experiments comparing people of different ages on any variable (for instance, vocabulary) necessarily are semi-experimental designs. One has no way of knowing whether any differences found in this regard are due to the aging process itself or to the different generations in which the subjects were reared. People above fifty years of age may perform more poorly than people in their twenties on that task, not because they are older, but because their schooling was different.

Nearly all research on the effectiveness of new programs of social action necessarily involve semi-experimental designs rather than true experimental designs. An example given by Campbell (1969) is that of investigating the effectiveness of a highway safety program in a particular state. During the year in which the program was administered, it was found that the number of accidents dropped appreciably. This could have led a naive person to the conclusion that the program was highly effective. However, it was found subsequently that accidents had been falling off at the same rate in the several previous years before the program was started. Another example is that of attempting to measure the effectiveness of a reorganized police force in a city in terms of the number of crimes reported. Typically what happens in that case is that the reported number of crimes goes up, not because the new police force is less effective in preventing crime, but because they are more accurate in reporting the crimes that occur.

Hundreds of other examples could be given of situations in which true experimental designs could not be employed; however, an investigation can be arranged in such a way as to amass very convincing evidence. One example would be that of comparing children from socially deprived neighborhoods who participate in preschool programs with children who do not participate. Several years later, it is found that the children who participated in the special program perform better on a variety of achievement tests dealing with reading comprehension, arithmetic, and other topics. Although there would be alternative interpretations of the findings, this would strongly suggest that the preschool program was beneficial.

The purpose of this discussion has been to explain that (1) some research issues necessarily require semi-experimental designs, (2) unless carefully planned, the results will be uninterpretable, (3) appropriate elaborations of the design frequently permit one to obtain excellent circumstantial information regarding the research issues, and (4) in many cases, some statistical methods are available for correcting ambiguities that otherwise would be involved in interpreting the research results. [Issues regarding semi-experimental designs are discussed in detail by Campbell and Stanley (1966).]

SUMMARY

Science is concerned mainly with the process of making inferences from the known to the unknown. There are basically two kinds of inferences involved in scientific work. The first is deductive inference, which is concerned purely with the manipulation of symbols. A cardinal example is that of mathematical inference which, for example, allows one to infer that the square root of 4 is 2. Mathematical and other forms of deductive inference are very important for elaborating theories and for analyzing the results of experiments, but they do not require support from facts in the world of real events.

The second type of scientific inference is that of inductive inference, which concerns the prediction of unknown events in the real world from known events. An example is the laws of gravity concerning the speed of falling objects. The laws have been substantiated in many previous experiments (at least to the degree of approximation that they actually hold true). Thus, they provide a basis for inferring the speed that steel balls would attain at various elevations when dropped from an airplane flying 1 mile high. The validity of inductive inferences always rests on a primitive faith that scientific laws which hold today will also hold tomorrow.

A special type of inductive inference is the statistical inference. In essence, a statistical inference is one in which the prediction of unknown events must be couched in terms of probabilities rather than in terms of near certainty. The probability that more voters will cast their ballot for one political candidate rather than another is an example of a statistical inference. This book is largely concerned with the logic and procedures for making such statistical inferences.

In order to validly make statistical inferences, it is essential that data be obtained from an adequate sample of the population in question. The purpose is to gather information that permits one to generalize from data obtained on the sample to that which would be obtained on the population as a whole. In order for this to occur, the sample must be sufficiently large to permit the precision required of the results; it is also necessary for the sample to be as representative as possible of the population in question. These characteristics are well-approximated in opinion polls and in some other types of investigations; but in most investigations in psychology and education, the characteristics are only partially realized.

In order to provide evidence for important questions, data must be gathered according to an appropriate research design. A research design consists of a set of rules regarding the application of experimental treatment conditions (independent variables), the selection of subjects, their allotment to the various conditions, and measurement of the dependent variable. There are many ways in which these and other aspects of experimentation can be performed, and it is important to specify the plan in advance. There are different possible designs for tackling essentially the same problem; some have weaknesses that others do not have, and some provide information that others do not provide. The choice among research designs for different types of scientific problems constitutes a cardinal aspect of understanding the use of statistics. It is particularly important to choose an experimental design that has no obvious confounding variables, which, if present, make the interpretation of experimental results ambiguous.

Some of the major classes of designs include (1) contrasted groups, (2) repeated measurements, (3) randomized groups, (4) factorial comparisons, and (5) semi-experimental manipulations. When there is a choice, the randomized-groups design is usually preferred. Such designs may concern only one variation in treatment conditions (for example, levels of dosage of a drug), or they may concern a factorial design in which two or more independent variables are simultaneously manipulated. Other types of designs have special advantages with particular types of experiments, such as employing the repeated-measurements design if this causes no major problems in gathering data or interpreting the results. In other cases, it simply is not possible to employ a clean experimental design; rather, it is necessary to deal with contrasted groups or with other types of semi-experimental designs. In such cases, it is important to (1) provide as many safeguards as possible, (2) make some special statistical comparisons of the results, and (3) weave a network of circumstantial evidence regarding the questions at issue.

EXERCISES

Study Questions

1 Discuss the major differences between inductive and deductive inference. Give an example of each.

2 What is the doctrine of permanent control?

3 In what way is statistical inference a special case of inductive inference?

4 Discuss the difference between a population and a sample. Give an example of each.

5 What is sampling error? Give two examples of how sampling error could occur.

6 What is meant by the terms independent variable and dependent variable? Give an example of each.

7 What is a confounded variable? Why might a confounded variable cloud interpretations of research results? Give an example.

8 Briefly discuss the features of contrasted-groups designs, repeated-measures design, and randomized-groups designs. What are the advantages and disadvantages of each design? Give an example of each.

9 What constitutes a factorial design? Give an example.

10 When are semi-experimental designs useful? Give two examples when you might use semi-experimental designs.

SUGGESTED ADDITIONAL READINGS

Blough, D. S., and P. M. Blough. *Experiments in psychology. Laboratory studies of animal behavior.* New York: Holt, Rinehart & Winston, 1964, Chap. 1.

Campbell, D. T., and J. C. Stanley. *Experimental and quasi-experimental designs for research.* Chicago: Rand McNally, 1966, pp. 34-37.

Scott, W. A., and M. Wertheimer. *Introduction to psychological research.* New York: John Wiley, 1967, Chap. 10.

Underwood, B. J. *Experimental psychology,* 2d ed. New York: Appleton-Century-Crofts, 1966, Chap. 4.

Part Two

Descriptive Statistics

4

Collecting, Scoring, and Depicting Research Results

In Part One of this book, many issues were discussed concerning how scientific theories are investigated with appropriate research designs and how the results of these are analyzed statistically; however, no matter how wise a researcher is with respect to these principles, he must dig his hands into the dirt of everyday life in order to obtain answers to scientific questions. Science consists of more than sitting in an armchair and theorizing; eventually, competing theories must be resolved in the world of facts. As was emphasized earlier, such facts are not gathered haphazardly; rather, they are based on excellent measurement methods, research designs, and preplanned methods of statistical analysis. This chapter will consider some fundamental principles regarding the gathering and depicting of research results.

COLLECTION OF DATA

The word *data* (datum in the singular) is a Latin word meaning facts. Here the word "fact" pertains to simple observations about events in the real world where there is little or no disagreement. Thus, if people in general report an eclipse of the sun by the moon on a particular day, this is an item of data. Another item of data is the observation that a student correctly spells 22 words on a test of 50 words. A third item of data is the observation of an IQ of 115 on an intelligence test. In order to qualify as good scientific data, observations must meet a variety of standards; such standards will be discussed in the remainder of this section.

Acceptable Data

Not all of the things that people talk about in daily life meet the requirement of scientific data. The requirement is that there be some public event and that nearly all people agree on what happened. The three previous examples of data all meet this standard. There are many statements that people make which do not meet the standard of public verifiability. After relatives arrive unexpectedly on Saturday morning, the lady says that yesterday she had a strange feeling that someone would visit today. A man says that he has the strong conviction that there is an afterlife beyond this worldly existence. A four-year-old child says that he looked out the window last night and saw an elephant grazing in the front yard. A lady says that she has a dreadful feeling that someone close to her will die in the near future. These types of statements cannot be objectively verified, and for that reason, they do not constitute good, usable data. Many such statements are not subject to unambiguous investigation. Thus, the lady's feeling of dread that something terrible would happen to a close associate probably would be supported in the future by *something* that happened to someone; however, this would not substantiate her powers to see in the future. Many such statements consist entirely of personal impressions that have no verifiable counterparts in the real world. This would be the case with the individual who said that he had a visitation from a deceased relative last night. This is also the case with the belief in an afterlife. There simply is no way to either refute or confirm such beliefs by scientific methods of designing research and collecting data. Rather than sit snidely in an ivory tower, however, it should be said that science is concerned with only some types of statements regarding the world, namely those that are subject to factual investigation. Science can neither disprove nor substantiate statements that are not concerned with factual evidence. This does not mean that such statements are automatically false or naive, but rather that science is concerned only with verifiable observations.

Scientific data concerns a consensus of observations by people. Thus, an eclipse of the sun is something that can be witnessed by anyone, and the sheer occurrence would be difficult to challenge. Similarly, if a student makes a mark on a sheet to indicate that one geometrical form is thought to be more pleasant in appearance than another, anyone who cares to can examine the sheet and see which of the two forms actually was marked by that student. Some people, however, are demented or intellectually perverted to the point of not accepting what seems obvious to everyone else. Even pictures taken from spacecraft headed for the moon have failed to convince a tiny minority of people that the earth is actually round rather than flat. What seems to be factual evidence always can be passed off as some form of trickery. Science is concerned with gathering evidence that is convincing to the vast majority of people. Perhaps elves dance in the forest at night, our destiny is determined by the stars, and fortune tellers divine the future, but if so, they are not open to investigation with acceptable scientific data. Science does not encompass all that is true or beautiful; it is concerned with the gathering of objective evidence which is irrefutable to nearly all persons.

Consistency of Data

In addition to the requirement that there be consistency among people regarding observations of particular events, it is also necessary for scientific data to be consistent over alternative methods of observation, from place to place in which observations of the same phenomena are made, and over periods of time. One chemist reports that when two substances are poured together they turn red, but another chemist reports that when the substances are poured together they turn blue. This obviously represents inconsistent data. Data are inconsistent if two light meters used for photography report very different amounts of illumination coming from the same visual perspective. Similarly, data would obviously be inconsistent if one clock indicates that the time is 4 P. M. and another clock indicates 4:15 P. M.

Consistency of data is referred to as *reliability*. It is not necessary for the degree of consistency or reliability to be perfect in order for data to be employed in scientific investigations. Even with relatively precise instruments such as light meters and clocks, at least a small amount of inconsistency or unreliability is present. With many of the data-gathering techniques in psychology and education, an even larger amount of unreliability is present. Thus, one would not expect perfect agreement between the scores that students make on an intelligence test if the same test is applied on two occasions four months apart. If data is totally inconsistent, there is no hope of finding any type of scientific lawfulness. If a moderate amount of inconsistency is present in the data, this tends to blur any lawfulness that can be found. The higher the level of consistency, the higher the possibility of obtaining clear-cut findings.

Scope of Data Collection

In gathering data, the rule is that it is always easy to throw away unnecessary information later, but there is no chance of recovering data that was not gathered initially. This rule holds in two ways. First, if a type of data seems to be potentially important initially, then it is wise to collect the information—if the information can be obtained easily. An example would be in a survey of attitudes concerning family planning. At the end of the questionnaire, subjects are asked to state their age, education, family size, and other vital statistics. If someone on the research staff thinks that religious affiliation may be important in attitudes toward family planning, it would be a mistake not to include a simple question of this kind. It would take the respondent only an extra few seconds to indicate his religious preference. After the results of the questionnaire are in, the experimenters may lose interest in the issue of religious preference or find that it really makes very little difference. However, if they had not obtained that information initially, there would have been no possibility of investigating the matter later. Anyone who has considerable experience in research sees many examples of potentially important pieces of information that should have been obtained in studies of learning, perception, mental testing, and other areas of investigation.

Fineness of Observation

In gathering data for research, it is almost always a mistake to classify people into gross categories when finer differentiations can be made. An example would be in a questionnaire in which people are asked to indicate their age. One way to do this would be to have each respondent make a check mark as to whether he is between ten and twenty years of age, twenty and thirty years of age, and so on. Later it is found that age is an important variable with respect to the survey results. However, the experimenter would have thrown away much valuable information by not asking the subject for his actual age to the nearest year and month.

Another example would be in a study of memory for series of digits that are presented rapidly. The subject is shown nine numbers, and immediately afterwards he is asked to recall as many numbers as he can in their proper order. The experimenter makes the mistake of scoring each series as only correct or incorrect. More information would have been obtained by scoring the number of numerals correctly recalled, ranging from 0 to 9. Fineness of observation in this regard is spoken of as *continuity* of measurement.

A measurement method is continuous if it is capable of making infinitely fine distinctions. Thus, the heights of students could potentially be measured in infinitely fine detail—at least conceivably going down to millionths of inches of height. Similarly, the spelling ability of students could be measured with a test containing thousands of items, which would permit extremely fine distinctions among individuals. In practice, however, there is always a limit to the fineness of measurement. This is because of practical problems of measurement and because, after a certain point, additional fineness of measurement provides very little new information. For example, in comparing the heights of two boys, it really is not important whether they differ by less than 0.01 of an inch. Similarly, in comparing the spelling ability of two students, it would not make a great deal of difference if one student correctly spelled 684 words in a list and another student correctly spelled 685 words. For these reasons, it is meaningful to speak of continuity as being a relative matter.

Even though a variable may be continuously measurable in theory, in practice there are always limitations on how finely the measure can be used to distinguish persons from one another. To the extent to which only gross distinctions can be made among persons, it is said that a measure is relatively *discrete* rather than continuous. An example of a very discrete measure is that of pass versus fail on an examination. In this case, no finer distinctions can be made than to indicate these two levels of performance. A relatively more continuous measure would be that of clinical psychologists rating patients on a nine-step scale ranging from "very much improved" to "very much worse." It would be possible to measure improvement at nine levels. A much more highly continuous measure is that of a vocabulary test containing 50 items. If a measurement method can be used to order people on at least 20 levels, it is meaningful to speak of it as being continuous for all practical purposes.

As a rule of thumb, if continuous measurements are logically possible but impractical in terms of extreme fineness of measurement, it is good to have data obtained on at least 12 levels of information, such as 12 levels of spelling ability or 12 levels of learning in an experiment. If data can be scored on at least a dozen levels, then almost as much information is available as would be obtained from an infinitely fine continuous measurement. However, if finer measurements are easily obtained, it is always wise to make finer distinctions. Then, if it proves convenient to deal with a smaller number of levels later, it is easy to regroup the data into fewer levels.

Experimenter Biasing of Data

There are many ways in which the experimenter can "load the dice" in such a way as to obtain misleading (biased) data. Hopefully, biasing of data is usually done unwittingly, but nevertheless, such data supply faulty answers to scientific questions. It is easy for the experimenter to unwittingly influence the results of an experiment. When college students participate in research, they make guesses about the purposes of the investigation. Even young children are usually aware that they are participating in some type of research and are on guard concerning their behavior. The pressures on subjects to behave in one way rather than another have been referred to as the *demand characteristics* of the experimental situation. An example is studying the tendency of students to cooperate in a game so that they will split monetary rewards equally. It becomes quite obvious to the students that the experiment concerns cooperation, and consequently they show their best behavior by cooperating. This may or may not be the same type of behavior that they would exhibit in more natural settings. Another example is studying the amount of time that students look at different types of pictures. The amount of time is controlled by the subject with a button which advances slides on a projector. At the start of the experiment, subjects are told to "look as long as you like at each picture." The use of the word "like" suggests that the experiment concerns what is pleasant to subjects; consequently, they might hurry through unpleasant scenes (such as a bloody automobile accident) which they would stare at in everyday life. There are many other ways in which the results of experiments can be influenced by the demand characteristics of the situation.

In some types of experiments, there is no real problem with demand characteristics influencing the results. This is the case in studies of human ability, perceptual detection, learning, memory, development of motor skills, and other tasks that concern accomplishment. In such situations, the subject is trying to do the best that he can, and the demand characteristics of the situation are attuned to the purposes of the experiment. However, in any study that concerns motivation, typical behavior, or preferences, there is always the danger that demand characteristics will erroneously influence the results. Obviously, data that is strongly influenced by such demand characteristics is worthless.

Experimental Treatments that Bias Data

There are many ways in which research is planned and conducted that can serve to bias the obtained data. An obvious example concerns the order in which subjects are tested in an experiment. It should be apparent to the reader that, when conducting an experiment, it is definitely incorrect to first study all of the subjects in one treatment group, then study all of the subjects in the next treatment group, and so on until all groups have been studied. An example would be in a simple factorial design with two types of learning as one factor and two amounts of practice as another factor. This would be a 2 X 2 design containing four groups. Eighty students could be randomly divided into four groups of twenty students each. It would be a very bad breach of scientific method to first study all of the subjects in one group, then move on serially to the other groups. Many things can change over the course of an experiment. At first, the experimenter might be quite enthusiastic and cheerful, but near the end of the experiment he becomes bored and far less patient with errors made by subjects. If the experiment lasts for several weeks, many things might happen to change the moods and outlooks of students. All of the students in one group could be tested during the week before a highly anticipated homecoming football game, and all the students in another group could be tested during the next week following a disastrous defeat on the previous Friday night. Even equipment can change somewhat over the course of an experiment. A projector that was working beautifully while the first group was being studied might start to jam during the time in which another group is being studied.

Because of these considerations, it is necessary to balance the order in which people from different treatments are studied. The safest way to do this is as follows. When preparing for research on a particular day, a table of random numbers (see Appendix B-1) is used to order the cells of a design. Each cell represents a group that is given a particular treatment. These cells can arbitrarily be numbered from 1 through the total number, starting in the upper left-hand cell of the design and working over to the right, and then coming back for the second factor, and so on. Thus, if there are six cells, one would randomly order the way in which they appeared. If it is possible to test more than one person from each cell on a particular day, the experimenter could generate another random order. If such stringent precautions prove unfeasible, one should at least obey the rule that more than one person would not be studied from any cell of the design before one person from all other cells of the design had been studied.

SCORING AND RECORDING OF DATA

If an experiment is well-planned, each observation can be recorded in terms of one of the types of measurement discussed in Chapter 2: measurement scales consisting variously of categories, ranks, interval scales, or ratio scales. Each such measurement is called a *score*. Examples of scores for the above four types of measurement scales are (1) an answer of "yes" to a survey question concerning plans to go to college, (2) a rank of 4 in a rank ordering of 15 foods in terms of preferences, (3) an IQ of 120, and (4) amount of time to push a button when a light comes on. It is useful to record most scores numerically, keeping in mind that the numbers have different mathematical properties considering the type of measurement scale being claimed for the data. It should be obvious how this is done for ranks, interval scales, and ratio scales. For categories, one can arbitrarily give numbers to the categories. In case of only two categories, a response in one category can arbitrarily be designated 1 and a response in the opposing category can arbitrarily be designated 2. Additional numbers can be used arbitrarily to record responses in more than two categories.

Planning the Scoring Method

It should be obvious that a method of scoring research results should be planned in advance rather than after mountains of data are obtained; however, one still finds atrocious examples of not doing that. This is frequently seen with respect to interviews concerning personality characteristics of mental patients, survey questions on attitudes toward government, and entire transcripts of psychotherapy sessions. When a scoring scheme is not planned in advance, the researchers frequently say to themselves, "Now that we have these mountains of data, what do we do with them?" All that can be done is to attempt to invent a scoring scheme after the data are obtained. For example, a count could be made of the number of times that patients use the word "I" or "me" in different psychotherapy sessions. As another example, graduate students in psychology could rate the apparent favorableness of the recorded responses of women toward the use of birth control. However, it is dangerous to wait until after data is gathered to develop a scoring scheme. In many cases, there is no sensible, reliable method of scoring that can be developed after the fact; or the methods that would be satisfactory otherwise prove to be unfeasible in terms of time and expense.

Decisions regarding methods of scoring eventuate in a *scoring key* for the results of applying each measurement method. For example, suppose subjects are given a questionnaire concerning attitudes toward the United Nations, in which half of the statements are favorable and half are unfavorable. The scoring key would indicate that a 1 would be given for agreement with a positive statement and disagreement with a negative statement. If, on a multiple-choice examination there is one correct alternative and three incorrect alternatives for each question, a score of 1 would be given for marking the correct alternative and a score of 0 would be given for marking any of the other alternatives. If ratings of agreement with statements in a survey are made on a six-step scale, a rating of "completely agree" would be scored 6, a rating of "mostly agree" would be given a score of 5, and so on to a score of 1 for "completely disagree." In these, and nearly all types of research, it is possible to generate a scoring key that will allow one to transform different types of responses into numerical scores.

Mechanical Aids to Scoring

Most measures in psychology and education are obtained by summing scores over items. Thus, the score on a spelling test would consist of the sum (or number) of items correctly spelled. The score on a measure of attitudes toward college would consist of the sum of ratings made of positive statements minus the sum of ratings made of negative statements. There are numerous ways of gathering data in such a way as to facilitate the obtaining of summed scores. All students are familiar with the types of answer sheets that are used for recording responses to multiple-choice examination questions, an example of which is shown in Figure 4-1. When each response is scored in one of two categories, it is very simple to punch out a stencil for manually scoring the measure. This is the case when a true-false or multiple-choice examination is given, and also when

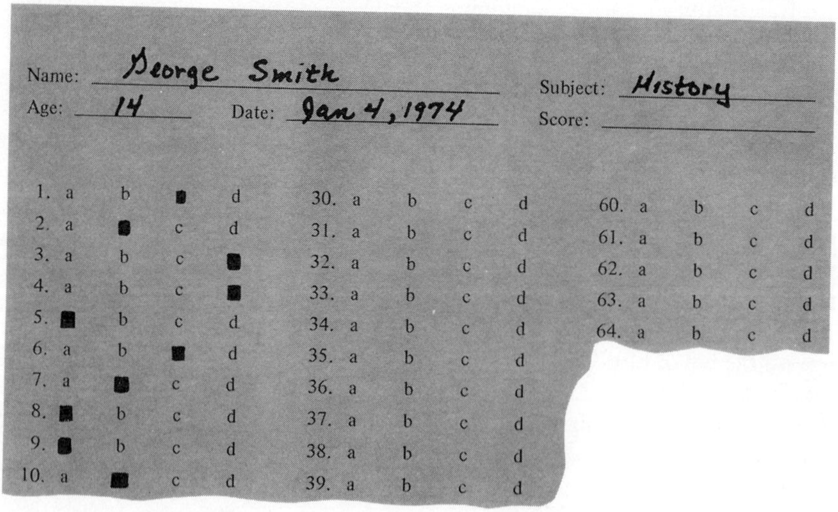
Name: George Smith
Age: 14 Date: Jan 4, 1974
Subject: History
Score:

1. a	b	■	d	30. a	b	c	d	60. a	b	c	d
2. a	■	c	d	31. a	b	c	d	61. a	b	c	d
3. a	b	c	■	32. a	b	c	d	62. a	b	c	d
4. a	b	c	■	33. a	b	c	d	63. a	b	c	d
5. ■	b	c	d	34. a	b	c	d	64. a	b	c	d
6. a	b	■	d	35. a	b	c	d				
7. a	■	c	d	36. a	b	c	d				
8. ■	b	c	d	37. a	b	c	d				
9. ■	b	c	d	38. a	b	c	d				
10. a	■	c	d	39. a	b	c	d				

Figure 4-1. Typical multiple-choice answer sheet.

measures of attitudes and interests are scored in terms of agreement or disagreement with lists of statements.

Rather than score printed answer sheets by hand, a number of commercially distributed answer sheets that can be scored by machines are available. Total scores and scores for various parts of the measure are tabulated and printed on the answer sheet.

The most advanced form of scoring and tabulating measures is through the use of high-speed, electronic computers. Many experiments can be conducted in which the subject gives his responses by punching keys on a typewriter-like console which feeds information directly into a computer. The computer can present problems to the subject, and he can reply to the computer. An example is in a study of learning. On each trial, the computer types out a list of eight alphabetical letters, and the subject is told to push either a C for correct or an I for incorrect. (Correct ones could be strings of alphabetical letters that go in a particular cycle.) The computer keeps up with the subject's correct and incorrect responses over time; after the subject is gone, the computer calculates and prints out numerous statistics regarding performance in the learning task.

With many types of measures, the subject can make his responses directly on computer data cards. For example, each item in a multiple-choice test of word knowledge can be responded to by using a stylus to punch out a hole at the proper space on a card. Other columns of the data card contain identification numbers for students and additional information about them. After the examination is over, the cards are fed directly into a computer which obtains scores over the whole test and many other important statistics regarding the results. Such special cards can probably be obtained from most of the major computer manufacturers. Facilities for performing statistical analyses are available in all major universities, central offices of public school systems, and in many commercial institutions.

For many commercially distributed tests, computerized services are available at central locations for scoring tests and providing many other statistics regarding research results. This is the case for many modern tests of aptitude and achievement (for example, a comprehensive battery of achievement tests at the fourth-grade level), where students' papers are shipped directly to a computerized scoring center somewhere in the nation. Almost by return mail, results are given in terms of the score of each student, the average score in the class, comparisons of average scores with those of schools throughout the country, percentages of students who correctly respond to each item, and many other important statistics regarding performance.

DEPICTION OF RESEARCH RESULTS

After data have been properly gathered and scored, frequently the next step is to transform the scores into various types of visual patterns which facilitate interpretation. A very simple example is that of the pie diagram, which is often seen in magazines, newspapers, and other printed material. For example, consider the percentage of students enrolled in various colleges at a university. The number of students and the relative percentage in each college are presented in Table 4-1. The commonly used pie diagram would represent these percentages as shown in Figure 4-2. The larger the slice of pie, the larger the percentage in that category. The diagram shows, at a glance, the proportional relationship (relative percentage) among the various colleges in the university. The bar graph is another simple device for visually demonstrating the same data depicted in Table 4-1. Figure 4-3 is a bar graph indicating the numbers of students enrolled in each of the colleges. The length of each bar indicates the number, which is read from the base of the graph (the X axis). For example, it can be seen there that approximately 200 students are enrolled in the nursing curriculum. Both the pie diagram and the bar graph are useful for displaying categorical data.

Table 4-1. Numbers and Percentages of Students Enrolled in Various Colleges at a University

College	Number	Percent
Liberal Arts	989	49
Nursing	197	10
Business	252	12
Journalism	53	3
Engineering	528	26
	2,019	100

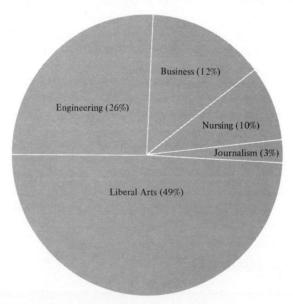

Figure 4-2. Pie diagram depicting numbers of students listed in Table 4-1.

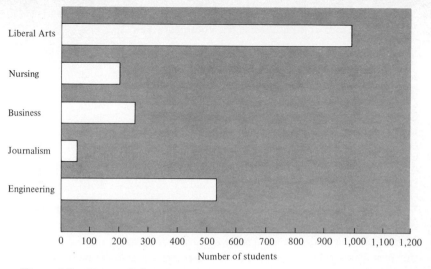

Figure 4-3. Bar graph depicting numbers of students described in Table 4-1.

Frequency Distributions

Whereas pictorial displays like those mentioned here are useful in depicting data from independent variables expressed as categories, more precise methods can be employed with rank-order scales, interval scales, and ratio scales. Although the data from some types of research in psychology and education relate to categories, more frequently they relate to the three higher forms of measurement mentioned previously.

A typical set of scores is shown in Table 4-2. The 40 scores could represent many different types of results—number of errors made in an experiment on learning, number of seconds required to solve a puzzle, or number of correct identifications of peoples' names flashed rapidly on a screen. It will be useful here to think of the numbers as representing the scores of students on a multiple-choice test of vocabulary. There are 40 items and four alternative definitions for each word. One student made only 20 correct responses; and at the other end of the continuum, one student responded correctly to all 40 items. Looking at the collection of scores in Table 4-2, it is very difficult to form a definite impression of how well students as a group performed, how widely they differed from one another in performance, and other characteristics of the results.

A first step that can be taken to provide an understanding of research results is to list the possible scores from lowest to highest, which is done in the first column of Table 4-3. It is shown that one student actually scores as high as 40 and another scores as low as 20, which says that the *range* of scores is 20 points. Range of scores will be discussed in detail in Chapter 5. Column 2 of Table 4-3 shows the number of students (frequency) that made each score. It can be seen that there are far fewer scores on the extremes than near the middle of the score

Table 4-2. Scores of 40 Students on a Vocabulary Test

Name	Score	Name	Score	Name	Score	Name	Score
John	30	Oliver	29	Gail	31	Larry	35
Mary	31	Sally	31	Averil	29	Norton	30
Charlie	24	Blaine	28	Andy	22	Mark	30
George	32	Pat	31	Buddy	20	Rick	30
Linda	26	Pete	28	Bruce	34	Tim	40
Harry	29	Hortense	27	Cindy	33	Cora	33
Cathy	32	Bob	30	David	31	Rita	29
Sam	29	Joe	33	Eva	30	Luther	34
Pauley	25	Lee	38	Sue	28	Earl	30
Gina	29	Carol	27	Eve	32	Loretta	26

range. Only one student made a score of 40 and one student made a score of 20; but six students made a score of 29. However one wants to define the term, it is apparent that the average score is somewhere in the middle of the range, in the neighborhood of 30. Statistics concerning all of these matters will be treated in detail in Chapter 5. The third column of Table 4-3 shows the percentage of students who made each score. The largest percent (17.5) made a score of 30. The fourth column of Table 4-3 shows the cumulative percentage (or frequency) who made scores up to each point ranging from 20 to 40. Thus only 2.5 percent (one person) made a score of 20, 5 percent (two persons) made a score of 22 or lower, and 80 percent made a score of 32 or lower. Such a cumulative percentage list of frequencies provides considerable information about the overall results.

In order to understand research results like those in Table 4-3, it is helpful to construct a *frequency distribution*. This is shown in Figure 4-4. Throughout the book, it will be useful to refer to the vertical axis as the Y axis and to the horizontal axis as the X axis. Frequency simply means the number of people who make scores at each level. The X axis contains the different scores possible in the research. Thus, seven people made a score of 30, and two people made a score of 26. The value of constructing such a frequency distribution is that it provides an easily understood picture of the data presented in Table 4-3. It can be seen in Figure 4-4 that (1) the scores range from 20 to 40, (2) most of the scores are in the middle of the range rather than at the extremes, and (3) however defined, the "average" is near a score of 30. Table 4-3 and Figure 4-4 supply essentially the same information, but in different ways.

When the number of persons is no greater than that shown in Table 4-3, the frequency distribution does not present nearly as clear a picture as that when many more persons are involved. With only a relatively small number of persons, the frequency distribution often appears "lumpy" and distorted in other ways. This is because of sampling error, as it was discussed in Chapter 3. Thus, purely by chance, one might select some subjects who would make scores near the extremes of the range and thus present a distorted picture of what would be ob-

Table 4-3. Frequency Distributions and Related Statistics of Scores from Table 4-2

Possible score	Frequency (number making each score)	Percent making each score	Cumulative percent
20	1	2.50	2.50
21	0	0.00	2.50
22	1	2.50	5.00
23	0	0.00	5.00
24	1	2.50	7.50
25	1	2.50	10.00
26	2	5.00	15.00
27	2	5.00	20.00
28	3	7.50	27.50
29	6	15.00	42.50
30	7	17.50	60.00
31	5	12.50	72.50
32	3	7.50	80.00
33	3	7.50	87.50
34	2	5.00	92.50
35	1	2.50	95.00
36	0	0.00	95.00
37	0	0.00	95.00
38	1	2.50	97.50
39	0	0.00	97.50
40	1	2.50	100.00

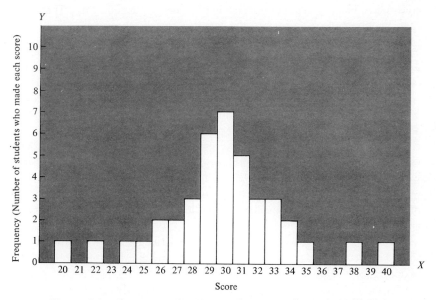

Figure 4-4. Frequency distribution for scores shown in Table 4-2.

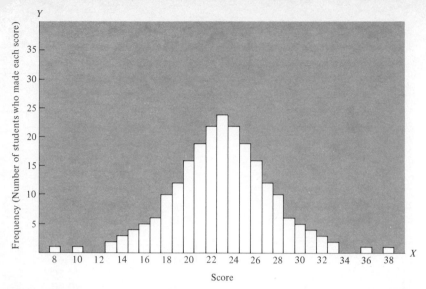

Figure 4-5. Frequency distribution of scores of 226 students on a chemistry test.

tained if much larger numbers of subjects were sampled. When large numbers of subjects are sampled, one typically finds a much more regular frequency distribution. An example is presented in Figure 4-5, which shows the scores of 226 students on a chemistry test. There are fewer gaps on the X axis in Figure 4-5 than in Figure 4-4, and the overall shape of the distribution is clearer to the eye.

Frequency distributions like those in Figure 4-4 and Figure 4-5 are routinely constructed in many types of research in psychology and education. They show some important characteristics of the data in a very direct manner.

Smoothed frequency distributions. The frequency distribution shown in Figures 4-4 and 4-5 present stair-step appearances because scores occur at regular intervals rather than in terms of finer gradations. Thus, a subject could make a score of either 15 or 16 on the test results shown in those two figures; but by the nature of the scoring key for the test, it would not be possible to make a score of 15.5. The fact that scores can occur only at particular points relates to the issue of continuity of measurement, which was discussed earlier in this chapter. If there are many more items on a test than those depicted in Figure 4-5, then the bars would be thinner. Of course, the bars would appear thinner only if approximately the same amount of space is used on the X axis. The result would be that of a smoother appearing frequency distribution rather than a jagged, stair-stepped appearance.

Figure 4-6 illustrates another method for depicting results of a study. A smoothed frequency distribution is accomplished by drawing a line through the midpoints on the blocks of the frequency distribution. The bars could be erased, leaving only the continuous line or *curve*, as it is frequently called. Frequency distributions are often depicted by such continuous curves without the bars

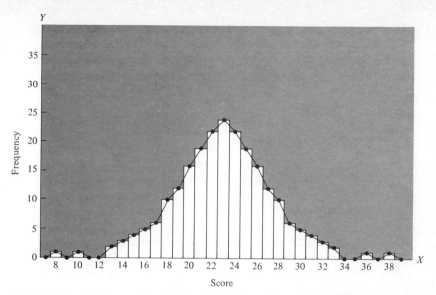

Figure 4-6. Frequency distribution from Figure 4-5 with overlaid, smoothed frequency distribution.

being present. If the test contained as many as 1,000 items, the individual bars would be so fine as to be almost invisible, and the histogram (as such stair-step frequency distributions usually are called) would start to evolve into a smoothed curve. The shape of the curve in the particular population would be well-approximated only if hundreds of persons were tested.

In some cases, measurements can be made so finely (or continuously) and there are so many subjects involved in the investigation, that an approximation of the type of smoothed curve shown in Figure 4-7 is obtained. This would be the case, for example, in the measurement of heights of 50,000 students down to a tenth

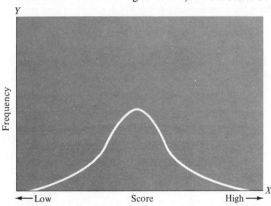

Figure 4-7. Hypothetical smoothed frequency distribution with a very large number of people and test items.

of an inch. Even if it is not feasible to make such continuous measurements and test so many subjects, it is frequently useful to think in terms of what type of smoothed curve would be obtained.

There are two major reasons that it is useful to think of data in terms of smoothed curves rather than in terms of stair-step shaped frequency distributions only. First, it is reasonable to estimate how a frequency distribution would appear if measurements were made in a highly continuous manner and there were a large number of subjects in the investigation. In most research, measures would be made more continuously if that were feasible; for example, one would employ tests with many more items than are feasible to employ in most studies. Also, if it were not for the practical problems involved, investigations would usually be made of a much larger number of subjects than is typically the case. Thus, in studying the relationship of a test of college aptitude to actual grade-point average in college, it would always be better if scores could be investigated for several thousand students rather than only several hundred. This is the case in all research; if there were no practical or ethical problems involved, the more subjects the merrier. Because of the fact that most measures are only approximately continuous and the number of subjects is limited, the frequency distribution obtained is an approximation of that which would be obtained under more ideal circumstances. A second reason that it is useful to think in terms of smoothed frequency distributions is that many of the statistical methods which will be discussed in subsequent chapters are based on the idea of such distributions rather than stair-step histograms.

Types of frequency distributions. The types of frequency distributions illustrated up to this point are ones that are found most frequently in research. Such frequency distributions (see Figure 4-7) are shaped like an elegant mountain which goes up to a central peak and tapers off smoothly from one side to the other. (In Chapter 6, a very important distribution of this general form will be shown to have many implications for both descriptive and inferential statistics. It is called the *normal distribution*.) Some frequency distributions encountered in research do not have this neat appearance. Usually this takes the form of the "tail" on one side of the curve being stretched out longer than that on the other side. Two examples are given in Figure 4-8*a* and Figure 4-8*b*. Figure 4-8*a* represents the frequency distribution for spelling ability of students in rural communities where the average performance is not very good, but some students perform very well. The frequency distribution in Figure 4-8b concerns spelling performance of children in a metropolitan area where the average student performs well, but an appreciable number of students perform very poorly. Such lopsided distributions are said to be *skewed*. If the longer tail is toward the left on the X axis, the distribution is said to be skewed left or negatively. Conversely, if the longer tail is toward the right, the distribution is said to be skewed right or positively. At least a slight degree of skewness is found in nearly all distributions in psychology and education. The examples shown in Figure 4-8*a* and Figure 4-8*b* are more ex-

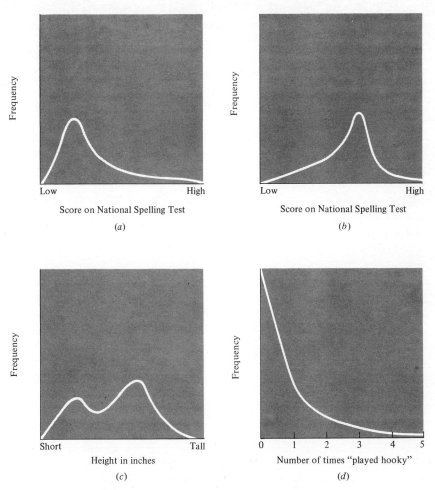

Figure 4-8. Distributions that are (*a*) skewed to the right, (*b*) skewed to the left, (c) bimodal, and (d) in the form of a J-curve.

treme than typically found.

In some cases, the skewness is so extreme that the distribution literally has only one tail. This is illustrated in Figure 4-8*d*, which shows the frequency with which students in a school system "play hooky." The vast majority were not charged with this offense at all during the school year. A moderate percentage were charged one time. At the extreme of the distribution, a tiny percentage of the students were charged five or more times for this offense. When distributions have only one tail like that in Figure 4-8*d*, they frequently are referred to as *J-curves*. Actually, the curve resembles a reversed J, but that is a minor semantic issue. Such J-curves are almost never found in measures of psychological traits or educational attainment. They are most frequently found in the percentages of times that people perform unusual acts—committing acts of truancy, breaking legs, winning lotteries, and other such rare events for people in general. On those unusual occasions when the frequency distribution constitutes a J-curve, very serious problems are posed for some of the types of statistics that will be discussed in Chapters 10 and 11.

Another typical frequency distribution is that which has two "peaks," or modes, as they are referred to. An example is shown in Figure 4-8c. Such a bimodal distribution would be found when 1,000 people are selected randomly and their heights measured; one peak or mode would correspond to the most frequent height of males and the other the most frequent height of females. An exaggeration of what might occur in this case is shown in Figure 4-8c. Bimodal distributions are very rare for actual data obtained in psychology and education; consequently, they seldom present a serious problem for the application of statistical methods.

Cumulative frequency distributions. In addition to employing frequency distributions like those illustrated, it also is useful to depict data with *cumulative frequency distributions.* Quite simply, such distributions can be constructed by showing the percentage of people who score up to each particular point on the frequency distribution. A computational example was given in Table 4-3. These results are shown graphically in Figure 4-9. Only one person made a score of 20. Because there are 40 people in the study, this transforms to 2.5 percent. This is shown as the first step on the cumulative frequency distribution in Figure 4-9.

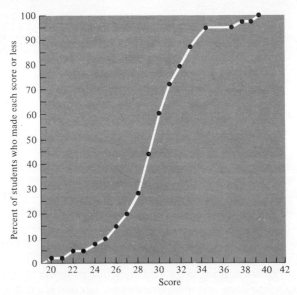

Figure 4-9. Cumulative frequency distribution of scores from Table 4-3.

The next highest score is that of 22, which was achieved by one person. Consequently, two people made a score of 22 or less, which is 5 percent of the total subjects. This percentage is shown as the second step on the cumulative frequency distribution. One keeps moving from left to right in this manner, adding the numbers of people who make scores up to a particular point and converting this number into a percentage. Of course, by the time the highest score obtained in the study is reached, the cumulative frequency necessarily must reach 100 percent. Cumulative frequency distributions provide additional insights to those that are obtained from the original frequency distributions. Also, they are very helpful in understanding and computing some important descriptive statistics which will be discussed in Chapters 5 and 6.

SUMMARY

No matter how promising a scientific theory might seem, it must be tested in real life. The raw materials for testing theories are referred to as data—observations of events. The proper collection and analysis of data are the meat of employing statistics. Before it is possible or proper to make statistical analyses, the data must have a number of desirable characteristics. First, in the proper sense of the term, the data must concern verifiable observations about the world rather than untestable private beliefs. Second, such observations should be consistent with different observers and different techniques of observing the same thing. Third, if it is feasible to do so, much more information is obtained if the data spring from well-standardized measurement methods rather than from raw observations, for example, the use of a thermometer to judge the change in temperature after a rainfall rather than making the simple observation that it is cooler.

There are a number of definite pitfalls in the attempt to collect valid data. One is for the experimenter to unwittingly determine the outcome of the data-gathering process, which sometimes occurs when human subjects "catch on" to the purpose of an experiment and slant their responses accordingly. The data can be biased by the way the research is designed, such as by testing all of the subjected in one treatment condition before subjects are tested in other treatment conditions.

After a plan is formulated for collecting data, the results must be properly recorded and scored. Generally, it is best to plan methods of scoring in advance of the investigation, because after the fact, there may be no way to obtain the desired information from the data. Usually, mechanical aids are available for recording scores in such a way as to facilitate subsequent statistical analyses. The most widely used procedure is to place scores on punch cards and have statistical analyses performed on a computer.

It is important to depict data in a way that will facilitate an understanding of the overall results and assist in the computation of descriptive statistics. The methods that can be employed for this purpose depend on the type of measurement scale involved (for example, interval scales versus ranks) and the type of information that is being sought. Two devices that are useful with categorical data are pie diagrams and bar graphs. A wider selection of methods is available for data obtained from interval scales and ratio scales, some of which are (1) stair-step frequency distributions, (2) smoothed curves, and (3) cumulative frequency distributions. These supply important supplementary information to one another about the overall results of an investigation.

EXERCISES

Study Questions

1 List and explain the essential characteristics of scientific data. Give examples in each case. Give examples of events (for example, something that someone says) that would not constitute legitimate scientific data.

2 With respect to scientific data, discuss the concepts of consistency, scope, and fineness of observation.

3 Give examples of ways in which an experimenter can bias data. What is meant by demand characteristics?

4 Give an example of a scoring method. Why is it wise to develop the method of scoring before an experiment is undertaken? Give examples of difficulties that would arise if that were not done.

5 What is a frequency distribution? Draw and label a frequency distribution, one that is different from any appearing in this chapter.

6 What is meant by continuity of measurement? Illustrate the extremes in terms of complete continuity on one hand and complete lack of continuity on the other hand. What are the advantages of having relatively continuous measurements?

7 Make drawings of the normal distribution, skewed distributions, and J-curves. Give examples of data which you think might fit each distribution.

8 Discuss a situation in which a cumulative frequency distribution would provide interesting information. Illustrate with a figure.

Problems

16	20	18	22	21	19	19	20	17	17	22	22	19
25	23	16	17	25	20	20	21	24	20	19	22	21
21	17	19	20	17	20	18	15	18	19	20	19	20
23	20	26										

These data represent the scores of 42 children on a geography test.

1 Arrange the data into a frequency distribution, supplying proper labels for the X and Y axes.

2 Construct a smoothed curve corresponding to the frequency distribution.

3 Construct a cumulative frequency distribution for the data.

4 Go back and tell what information can be obtained by looking at each of the methods described for depicting data.

SUGGESTED ADDITIONAL READINGS

Chase, C. I. *Elementary statistical procedures.* New York: McGraw-Hill, 1967, Chap. 2.

Hays, W. L. *Statistics for the social sciences,* 2d ed. New York: Holt, Rinehart & Winston, 1973, Chap. 3.

Nunnally, J. C. *Psychometric theory.* New York: McGraw-Hill, 1967, Chap. 1.

Senter, R. J. *Analysis of data.* Atlanta: Scott Foresman, 1969, Chap. 3.

5

Measures of Central Tendency and Variation

In Chapter 4, frequency distributions such as the distribution of scores on a spelling test or the distribution of scores in a study of reaction time, were discussed and illustrated. In the same sense that automobiles can be classified in terms of having two or four doors, various ranges of horsepower, and other characteristics, frequency distributions can be characterized according to three major characteristics; the first characteristic was mentioned in Chapter 4—that of the distribution shape. As was illustrated, frequency distributions might be symmetrical, bimodal, skewed, or in the form of J-curves. In addition to the distribution shape, there are two other major characteristics of frequency distributions that are important in any investigation. The first is a measure of average performance. This might be average income in a community, average performance on a test of reading comprehension, average number of words correctly recalled in a study of memory, average time taken to solve a problem, or average score made on a multiple-choice test in American history. The second important characteristic of frequency distributions is the variability about the average. Variability concerns how subjects differ from one another in terms of their performance. This chapter will be concerned with measures of average performance and variability of performance.

Symbolism and Summational Notation

Before discussing measures of average performance and variability of performance, it is necessary to consider some of the symbolism used in performing statistical operations on data. Letters late in the alphabet are used to symbolize variables. Thus, X might symbolize all possible scores obtained on a measure of intelligence; Y might symbolize all possible levels of drugs to be administered in a study of rat learning; and W might symbolize all possible scores on a measure of attitudes toward the United Nations. In any case, the symbol for the variable represents all possible scores that can be obtained, even though all possible scores might not occur in a particular investigation. For instance, on a test of correctly spelling words spoken by the teacher, scores (variable X) might potentially range from 0 to 100. However, it might be found that no student scored less than 30 and there were numerous gaps between that score and the highest obtained score of 90. The symbol for the variable (X in this case) stands for all possibilities; the frequency distribution of scores represents what actually is obtained in practice.

When an experiment is being undertaken, it is customary to refer to an independent variable as X and a dependent variable as Y. Such would be the case when X consisted of the amount of a particular drug administered to rats and Y consisted of the rate at which rats learn to turn left rather than right in a maze in order to obtain food. When there is more than one independent variable, then these can be designated by X_1, X_2, and so forth. This would be the case if the independent variables consisted of drug dosage, amounts of practice, and difficulty of the learning problem. Similarly, if there is more than one dependent variable, these can be designated by Y_1, Y_2, and so forth. This would be the case if the dependent variables in the study of rat learning consisted of numbers of correct choices, speed of making choices, and other aspects of performance.

In developing statistics, it is very useful to employ *summational notation*. The Greek letter Σ (sigma) is used to indicate the operation of summing, which can be illustrated with the amount of pay received by three clerks in an office. The clerks each work different amounts from week to week, and consequently the individual amounts and the sum of these amounts vary over time. The amounts of pay due on a particular week are $68, $92, and $54. Then $\Sigma X = \$214$. Summational notation proves very helpful in presenting computational equations in statistics. In many cases, combinations of variables are employed in research rather than individual variables; consequently, it is necessary to understand some rules regarding how such sums are obtained.

In many cases, a variable consists of an additive combination of other variables. Most frequently, this is the case with dependent variables. An example would be in research concerning the improvement of creative abilities in children. The dependent variable concerns various tests of creativity, which are added to obtain an overall measure. If there were three such tests, the composite measure could be expressed as follows

$$Y = Y_1 + Y_2 + Y_3$$

Each person would have a score on each of the separate tests and a score consisting of the sum over the three tests. The information from the three tests would then be combined into one overall variable Y. For one purpose or another, it might be useful to multiply the different variables by constants as follows

$$Y = aY_1 + bY_2 + cY_3$$

Thus, scores on the first test might be multiplied by 2.0, the second test by 1.7, and the third test by 1.5. These would then be the a, b, and c in the equation. Multiplying a variable by a constant is frequently referred to as *weighting the* variable. An example of how such weights would be applied is as follows. A student has scores of 11, 14, and 12 respectively on the three tests. His composite score would be obtained as follows

$$Score = 2.0 \times 11 + 1.7 \times 14 + 1.5 \times 12$$
$$= 63.8$$

Summational notation is useful with respect to both weighted and unweighted composites. In the example, ΣY would represent the sum of scores for all students in a group on the composite measure. It is important to see how this overall sum can be "taken apart" in terms of the variables entering the composite.

Whether or not the successive terms that are summated have different weights, an important rule is that the total sum of scores can be obtained by "running" the summation sign through the various terms that are summed. The total sum of scores for the unweighted combination given previously can be stated as

$$\Sigma Y = \Sigma(Y_1 + Y_2 + Y_3)$$
$$= \Sigma Y_1 + \Sigma Y_2 + \Sigma Y_3$$

Thus if the sums of scores for the whole group are $\Sigma Y_1 = 10$, $\Sigma Y_2 = 15$, and $\Sigma Y_3 = 25$, then $\Sigma Y = 50$. In other words, the same result is obtained by calculating the separate sums of the constituent variables and adding them together as would be obtained by summing the composite variable Y.

Another example of "running through" occurs when the variables are weighted

$$\Sigma Y = \Sigma(aY_1 + bY_2 + cY_3)$$
$$= \Sigma aY_1 + \Sigma bY_2 + \Sigma cY_3$$

The important point is that when a composite consists of the sum of a number of other variables, the summation sign either can be kept to the left of the variables in parentheses or "run through" the variables that are summed. The same result is obtained by either approach.

Another rule that applies to the sum of weighted variables is that the weights (constants) can be brought out in front of the summation signs. Thus the previous equation can also be expressed as

$$\Sigma Y = a\Sigma Y_1 + b\Sigma Y_2 + c\Sigma Y_3$$

If all variables have the same weight a, then the constant term can be brought out in front of the summation sign as follows

$$\Sigma Y = \Sigma aY_1 + \Sigma aY_2 + \Sigma aY_3$$
$$= a\Sigma Y_1 + a\Sigma Y_2 + a\Sigma Y_3$$
$$= a(\Sigma Y_1 + \Sigma Y_2 + \Sigma Y_3)$$

The foregoing operations apply only when variables are summed. If they are multiplied together, then they cannot be taken apart in that manner. An example would be when a variable consists of multiplying the numbers of errors made in a learning task by the amount of time taken to complete the task, which would be as follows

$$Y = Y_1 Y_2$$

This would provide an overall measure of difficulty in learning the particular task. In this case, the sum of scores for all persons would equal

$$\Sigma Y = \Sigma(Y_1 Y_2)$$

However, this sum could not be taken apart as

$$\Sigma Y_1 \Sigma Y_2$$

or as

$$\Sigma Y_1 + \Sigma Y_2$$

An example will serve to demonstrate this point. Table 5-1 contains the scores for John, Mary, and Fred on two tests, Y_1 and Y_2. The combined score Y is calculated by multiplying Y_1 and Y_2 together. In the equations which follow, note that the sum of Y_1 times Y_2 does not equal the sum of Y_1 times the sum of Y_2, nor is it equal to the sum of Y_1 plus the sum of Y_2.

$$\Sigma(Y_1 Y_2) = 480 + 625 + 600$$
$$= 1{,}705$$

$$\Sigma Y_1 \Sigma Y_2 = (75)(69)$$
$$= 5{,}174$$

$$\Sigma Y_1 + \Sigma Y_2 = 75 + 69$$
$$= 144$$

Table 5-1.   Scores of Students on Tests Y_1 and Y_2, and Their Composite Score Y

Student	Y_1	Y_2	$(Y_1 Y_2)$
John	20	24	480
Mary	25	25	625
Fred	30	20	600
Total (Σ)	75	69	1,705

Definitions and rules for the use of summational notation are summarized and illustrated as follows:

1 The Greek letter Σ stands for the operation of summing, which literally means to add up all of the scores obtained for an independent or dependent variable in research.

2 Variables frequently consist of additive combinations of other variables. Thus, one frequently adds over test scores to obtain a composite test score; then one frequently adds over people to obtain a sum of such composite scores. It is important for the reader to distinguish between these two approaches to summing variables — over scores that enter a composite and over people who have composite scores. Summation signs can be "run through" additive combinations of variables, for instance

$$\Sigma(Y_1 + Y_2 + Y_3) = \Sigma Y_1 + \Sigma Y_2 + \Sigma Y_3$$

3 A sum of weighted variables equals the weighted sum of those variables, or
$$\Sigma(aY_1 + bY_2 + cY_3) = \Sigma aY_1 + \Sigma bY_2 + \Sigma cY_3$$
which in turn equals
$$a\Sigma Y_1 + b\Sigma Y_2 + c\Sigma Y_3$$

4 When a composite score is obtained by multiplying two variables together rather than adding them, the composite *cannot* be "taken apart," in other words, $\Sigma(Y_1 Y_2)$ does not equal $\Sigma Y_1 \times \Sigma Y_2$. The only way to obtain $\Sigma(Y_1 Y_2)$ is to actually multiply each pair of scores and then sum the products over persons in the study.

MEASURES OF CENTRAL TENDENCY

Looking at the frequency distributions described in Chapter 4, one characteristic which stands out is the tendency for a gathering of scores toward the center of the distributions. Most people have scores near the center of the distribution, and few people have scores on the extremes. There are various measures of the middle or center of any frequency distribution. These are referred to as *measures of central tendency*. The word *average* occurs in many places in everyday life. It is said that the average man prefers football over baseball, the average young woman wants to have three children, and the average IQ in the nation is 100. As will be seen, there are various ways of defining average performance. However it is defined, the average is important for two reasons. In experiments, the average performance is important because it represents a measure of group performance for comparing the results of different treatments. An example is a comparison of scores on a reading achievement test of three groups of first-graders who have been given different types of training in reading. The test would provide an average score for each of the three groups and an average of all three groups combined. At issue would be the extent to which the average score in one group was above that in the other groups. Statistical measures would be applied to determine the extent to which such differences were because of something other than chance alone.

On the practical side, average performance is important because it determines how most organizations operate. Students who show average performance in the classroom determine in large measure how the instruction is conducted. Instruction is usually geared to students who show average performance rather than to students who are extreme in either direction. Clothes are designed to fit the tastes of the average woman; TV programs are selected to fit the tastes of the average viewer; and homes are designed to fit the needs of the average buyer. However, there are different meanings for the word average. Because there are different ways of measuring average performance, it is convenient to speak of these as measures of central tendency. The major approaches will be discussed in the following sections.

The Mode

Sometimes used as a measure of central tendency is the *mode*, which is defined as the most frequently obtained score. This can be illustrated with the frequency distribution of test scores in Figure 5-1 (which is the same data presented previously in Figure 4-4). The mode is the most frequently occurring score in the distribution, which, in Figure 5-1, is 30. The nearest competitor for the mode is a score of 29, which is obtained by six persons. The mode receives its name because it represents the high point in the distribution. It is a measure of central tendency in the sense that it represents the point at which most scores fall.

It is necessary to discuss the mode because it is a frequently mentioned statistic; however, the mode suffers from two serious faults as a measure of central tendency. First, when only a small number of scores are involved, the mode shifts about drastically from sample to sample. If another sample of subjects were measured on the test represented in Figure 5-1, the mode might be 28 instead of 30. Secondly, the mode does *not* represent a good mathematical starting point for the development of other statistics. Other things being equal, some statistical measures represent much better starting points for the development of additional statistical measures; those measures are much preferred to ones that do not lend themselves to such extensions. The mode represents something of a dead end as regards the development of other statistical methods. When very many people are being studied, the mode of the frequency distribution is usually much the same

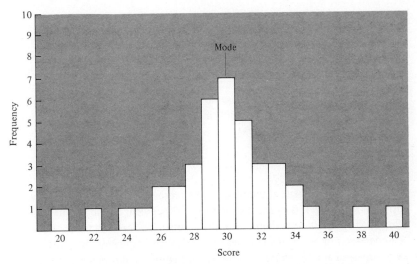

Figure 5-1. Frequency distribution of scores shown in Table 4-2.

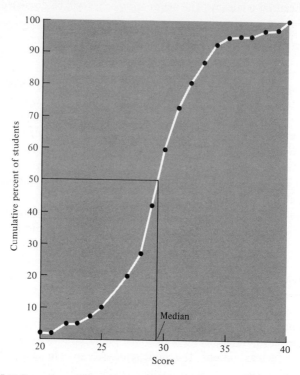

Figure 5-2. Location of the median in a cumulative frequency distribution.

as the other measures of central tendency; however, when only a small number of persons are being studied, the mode may differ considerably from other measures of average performance. The mode is introduced here not so much because it is recommended in general as a measure of average performance but because (1) it has been used for that purpose on many occasions in the past, and (2) a knowledge of the mode will help put in perspective the two measures of average performance to be discussed next.

The Median

Another measure of central tendency is the score that splits the frequency distribution in half, which is called the *median*. If 50 percent of the people make scores below 100 on an IQ test, then 100 is the median. The median probably can best be understood in terms of the types of cumulative frequency distributions that were discussed and illustrated in Chapter 4. Figure 5-2 shows where the median would lie with respect to the cumulative distribution that was shown in Figure 4-9.

The usual practice is to define the median as that point above and below which 50 percent of the persons score. However, it is almost always the case that the median represents a hypothetical point between two scores rather than an actual score. An example would be when 50 people make a score of 76 or higher and 50 people make a score of 75 or lower. Obviously, in this case the median must lie in a fractional score range which could not occur as an actual score. In such instances, the median is obtained by *interpolating* to find a hypothetical value that would break the distribution in half.

In order to interpolate, it is first necessary to discuss the exact or real limits of a score. The real limits of a score are defined as that score plus and minus one-half of one unit of measurement. For example, the upper real limit of a score of 20 would be 20.5, and the lower real limit would be 19.5. It is mathematically convenient to think of all the cases which have a particular score as being distributed evenly within the upper and lower real limits rather than all occurring exactly on the score. This convention allows one to say that the median in the above example falls at 75.5, which is the upper real limit of 75 and the lower real limit of 76. Sometimes, however, the median does not fall at such a convenient location. In that case, one calculates the median as follows. First, find the lower real limit of the score where the median falls. Second, calculate the number of cases which fall below that point and subtract that number from half the total number of cases. Third, divide this number by the number of cases which fall in the interval where the median occurs. Finally, add this value to the *lower* real limit of the interval where the median occurs. For example, Table 5-2 shows a cumulative frequency distribution of 40 scores. Notice that 17 cases fall below 29.5 and 16 cases fall above 30.5; therefore, the score which separates the top 20 and the bottom 20 scores lies somewhere between 29.5 and 30.5. There are seven cases which fall between 29.5 and 30.5, of which three must fall below the median and four above in order to divide the scoring category at the median. So the median is calculated as follows

$$\text{Median} = 29.5 + \frac{3}{7}$$
$$= 29.5 + 0.42$$
$$= 29.92$$

Rather than go through the arithmetical operations of making interpolations as described, a very close approximation to the median may be calculated directly from a cumulative frequency distribution. As shown in Figure 5-2, this is done quite simply by drawing a horizontal line from the 50 percent point on the Y axis until it touches the cumulative curve, then dropping a line vertically to the corresponding point on the X axis. Chapter 6 will discuss how this general procedure can be used to mark off numerous score levels corresponding to the different percentages of people in a cumulative frequency distribution. Circumstances in which the median is particularly useful as a measure of average performance will be discussed in Chapter 6.

Table 5-2. The Cumulative Frequency of 40 Test Scores

Score	Frequency	Cumulative frequency
25	1	1
26	3	4
27	3	7
28	4	11
29	6	17
30	7	24
31	5	29
32	4	33
33	3	36
34	3	39
35	1	40

The Mean

The most widely used and generally most useful measure of central tendency is the *arithmetic mean*. The equation for the mean is quite simple

$$M = \frac{\Sigma X}{N} \tag{5-1}$$

where M = the mean, ΣX = the sum of scores, and N = the number of scores summed.

The computation of the mean can be illustrated with the 40 test scores shown in Table 4-2. The sum of those scores is 1,196; consequently, the mean of those test scores is calculated as follows

$$M = \frac{1,196}{40}$$

$$= 29.9$$

In addition to being symbolized as M, the mean also frequently is symbolized as $\bar{X}$. In some cases it is useful to make a distinction between the mean obtained from a sample of scores and the mean of a population which is being estimated by the sample mean, for example, in comparing the mean scores on an achievement test of two groups of students that were taught French from two different books. In that case, the average score (M or $\bar{X}$) for each group is mainly useful to the extent that it provides an estimate of the mean that would be obtained if very large numbers of students across the country participated in a similar experiment. Similarly, if college students at a particular university have a mean rating of 5.5 on a seven-step scale of favorable attitudes toward disarmament, the mean is important mainly to the extent that it permits an estimate of the mean which would be obtained from testing college students across the country. When the purpose of computing a mean is to estimate the result that would be obtained from a larger population, then it is customary to symbolize the mean of the whole population as μ. It is the usual practice to designate sample statistics with letters of the

English alphabet (*M, r, s,* and others) and to designate population values with Greek letters. However, this problem will come up so seldom in this book that the reader will not have to worry about making fine distinctions in that regard.

In many cases, the intention is to obtain the mean of a relatively small group of scores rather than to estimate the mean of a large population. This would be the case, for example, in computing the average IQ of students in a classroom. The teacher wants to know how well students in her class stand in that regard, and all she needs to do is to sum the IQs of all students and divide by the number of students. The interest is in finding the average of those particular scores and not of estimating the mean of any larger population. One could refer to that mean as μ, because the whole "population" is studied. However, in such cases it is the custom to use the more conventional symbol *M*.

Properties of the mean. The arithmetic mean has a number of interesting properties which make it a very useful measure of central tendency. First, when the mean of a random sample is used to estimate the mean of a larger population, the mean of the sample is an *unbiased estimator*. What this implies is that the odds are 50-50 ($p=0.50$) that the sample mean is either above the population mean or below the population mean. Another way of saying this is that there is no reason to believe that the population mean is above or below the sample mean. An implication of being unbiased is that the same equation is used to compute the sample mean as the population mean. An example would be in determining the mean typing speed attained by students in typing courses in a large city. An essentially random sample could be obtained of 200 students in typing courses in four schools scattered throughout the city. The mean typing speed at the end of the unit of instruction could be 45.3 correctly typed words per minute. This would be obtained by summing the typing speeds of the 200 students and dividing by 200. The *M* would serve as an estimate of the mean typing speed of all students in the city who participate in typing courses during the year, say as many as 10,000 students. The mean would be obtained exactly the same way on all 10,000 students if it were feasible to study the whole population in question. This would consist of summing 10,000 scores and dividing by 10,000.

Although the mean computed on a sample of scores is an unbiased estimate of the population value, this is not the case with some statistics that will be discussed in Chapter 9. Some statistics are biased in the sense that the equation which would be applied to a sample has p greater than 0.50 of being either larger or smaller than the population value. This is the case with an important measure of variability which will be discussed subsequently in this chapter.

In addition to being unbiased, the second important property is that the sum of deviation scores about the mean is zero. A deviation score is defined as the amount a person's score differs from the mean of the distribution. This can be seen in the simplified case where a computation is made of the average score of three children in a family. The ages are 4, 6, and 8; $M = 6$. If *M* is subtracted from the three ages, deviation scores of -2, 0, and $+2$ are found. The sum of the deviations or deviates about the mean is 0 in this case, and the same necessarily occurs in every case. Any fixed characteristic such as this makes it mathematically convenient to relate one statistic to other statistics.

A third important property of the mean is that, with any particular size of sample, the mean is usually a more accurate estimate of the population mean than either the mode or median is of their respective population values. This would be evidenced in a study being made of the scores of 30,000 students on an achievement test in mathematics. As an exercise in statistics, the scores could be randomly divided into 1,000 samples with 30 students in each. The three measures of average performance would vary from sample to sample. What would be found is that the mean varies less than the median, and both of these vary less than the mode.

A fourth important property is that the sum of squared deviations about the mean is less than about any other point in a score distribution. This can again be illustrated with the ages of children of 4, 6, and 8, for which the deviations about the mean (6) were -2, 0, and $+2$ respectively. The squared deviations would be 4, 0, and 4, for which the sum would be 8. If the deviates were obtained about any number other than the mean of 6, the sum of squared deviates would be larger than 8. The reader can satisfy himself on this matter by subtracting 6.1 from the three ages and obtaining sums of squared deviates. Similarly, the sum of squared deviates will be larger than 8 if deviates are obtained by subtracting 5.9 from the three ages. Whereas the sum of the deviates is zero, the sum of squared deviates will be a positive number, except in the special case when all scores are the same, and consequently all deviates about the mean are zero. In Table 5-2, it was found that the mean of 40 scores was 29.9. If the mean is subtracted from each of the 40 scores and the resulting deviates are squared and summed, this sum will be smaller than if the deviates are obtained about any number greater than or less than 29.9.

A fifth property of the mean is that it relates to concepts of sampling error in a useful way. When the mean is used to describe the average performance in a group (for example, average IQ in a classroom), the deviates about the mean can be thought of as errors. The situation where it was necessary to make guesses about the scores of students in a group and the only information available was the mean of such scores illustrates this point. If no other information about each student were available, the best bet, in a sense, would be that each student scored exactly at the mean. It was said "in a sense" because the best bet would entail the sum of squared deviates about the mean. Thus, if the names of students are called off in turn, and no other information about the students is available, it would be wisest to bet that each student was exactly at the mean, wisest in the sense of minimizing the sum of squared deviates or errors in this situation. When a statistic minimizes the sum of squared errors in estimating the scores of individuals in a group, the mean of a population, or anything else, it is referred to as a *least-squares* statistic. The concept of least-squares will come up repeatedly in the pages ahead as a very important principle for the development of useful statistics. The usefulness of the principle lies in the fact that squared deviations are very easy to work with in calculus and other systems of mathematics. Thus, the mean represents an excellent starting point for the development of other statistics.

Because of the characteristics mentioned, the mean is a much better measure of central tendency than the mode, median, or any other measures that could be employed with most frequency distributions. There is only one exception, and this represents an incidence in which another measure is usually employed for supplementary information rather than to replace the mean altogether. This occurs when the frequency distribution is highly skewed. An example given previously will illustrate the problem. In a small town, there are 25 families. The income of the family living on a baronial estate is $60 million a year. The members of the other families work at the estate and make small yearly salaries. By adding up the total of all incomes and dividing by 25, the researcher comes to the conclusion that the average family in the community makes over $1 million a year. Of course, this would be a very misleading statistic if other statistics were not used to clarify the situation. This information could be obtained by inspecting the frequency distribution and computing the median. It is in situations of this kind that the median is particularly useful.

Location of Mean, Median, and Mode

In a perfectly symmetrical, unimodal distribution of scores, the mean, median, and mode are at exactly the same point. However, when the distribution is skewed either toward the low or high end of the score continuum, there are predictable shifts in the median and mean away from the mode. The mode is always the high point of the curve, and by definition it cannot shift from that point. When the distribution is skewed toward the high end of the score continuum (the longer tail is to the right on the X axis), the median shifts somewhat to the right, and the mean shifts even further to the right. The reverse is true when the distribution is skewed toward the lower end of the score continuum. These relationships are shown in Figure 5-3.

The reason that the median shifts toward the longer tail in a skewed distribution is that a larger percentage of people are on that side of the mode than on the other side of the mode. There is a larger amount of area in the longer tail, and the amount of area corresponds to the frequency or percentage of people making scores in that direction. The reason that the mean shifts even further toward the direction of skewness is that it depends not only on the percentages of people on either side of the mode, but also on the arithmetic value of the scores. Thus, some of the extreme scores on the skewed side of the distribution serve to "pull" the mean away from both the median and the mode. The more distinctly the distribution is skewed, the further apart would be the three measures of average performance.

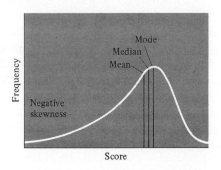

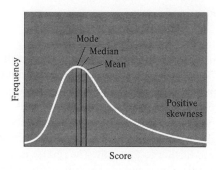

Figure 5-3. Relationship of mean, median, and mode in two skewed distributions.

Effects on the Mean of Score Transformations

Because of the wide use and importance of the mean in statistics, it is important to see what happens when all of the scores in the distribution are transformed in one way or another. If a constant number is added to or subtracted from all of the scores in a distribution, then the original mean of the distribution is increased or decreased by that amount. An example would be the mean of three scores (4, 5, and 6) which would be 5. If the number 2 is added to each of these numbers, then the new numbers would by 6, 7, and 8, and the new mean would be 7. Similarly, if a constant of 10 had been subtracted from each of the three original numbers, the mean of the new set of three scores would be −5.

All of the other laws of simple arithmetic apply to the mean when a constant term is added to all scores or all scores are multiplied by a constant. This can be illustrated in a situation in which the mean of the original distribution is 10. If all scores are first multiplied by 3, and 5 is added to each resulting score, then the mean of the transformed distribution is 35. Similarly, if 20 were first added to each score in the distribution and subsequently all of the resulting scores were multiplied by 2, then the mean of the resulting distribution would be 60.

All of the previously mentioned algebraic characteristics of the mean make it very easy to work with in the development of numerous other statistics. As an example, the mean may be calculated without dealing with negative scores. If there are some negative scores in a distribution and the largest negative score is −7, then 7 could be added to each score in the distribution. This would then make the lowest score 0 rather than −7. Also, these features permit many transformations of data without losing track of the original mean. If, in the pursuit of computing various statistics on this transformed distribution, it is found that the mean is 17, then it would be known that the mean of the original distribution was 10. As another example, distributions of scores are frequently encountered where each score ends in the same decimal, for example, 2.1, 3.1, 4.1, and so on. In performing statistics on such a distribution of scores, the numbers could be rounded, the mean of the new distribution computed, and 0.1 could be added later.

RAW SCORES AND DEVIATION SCORES

Before they are transformed in any manner, the scores obtained from measures in psychology and education are referred to as *raw scores.* These would be the number of words correctly spelled on a test, the number of errors made by rats in a maze, the sum of ratings of positive statements about the United Nations, and the amounts of time taken to correctly identify words projected on a screen. Distributions of such raw scores are symbolized by capital letters at the end of the alphabet, such as X, Y, and W. As mentioned previously, it is customary to symbolize the independent variable in an experiment by X and the dependent variable by Y. If there is more than one of either of these, they can be identified by subscripts.

In most research in psychology and education, it is necessary to make some transformations of raw scores before results can be meaningfully interpreted. An example would be the case in which a boy reports to his mother that he made a raw score of 22 in arithmetic and 48 in spelling. The mother might be inclined to say, "That is a good score in spelling, but you must improve your performance in arithmetic." Of course, this would be a groundless remark unless the mother knew much more about the situation. If there had been a relatively small number

Table 5-3. Raw Scores of Eleven Students on Tests of Arithmetic and Spelling

Student	Arithmetic	Spelling
Johnny	22	48
Fred	12	52
Mary	14	49
Bill	12	51
Jane	14	55
Susan	14	52
Michael	17	50
Sharon	19	62
Harry	11	56
Patricia	15	52
Eric	20	75
	$M = 15.45$	$M = 54.73$

of items on the arithmetic test and Johnny had performed well above average, then he actually was performing quite well in that topic. In contrast, if the spelling test was much longer and Johnny scored well below average, then he is in trouble with respect to spelling rather than with respect to arithmetic. Some raw scores illustrating these principles are shown in Table 5-3.

As a first step in transforming raw scores to a more useful form, each score can be expressed in terms of its distance from the mean. The mean of raw scores in arithmetic is 15.45, and the mean of the scores in spelling is 54.73. The transformed scores are referred to as *deviation scores* and are symbolized by lower-case letters

$$x = X - M_x$$

The equation states that each person's deviation score is obtained by subtracting the mean from his raw score. The class grades can be transformed to deviation scores as shown in Table 5-4.

Table 5-4. Deviation Scores of Eleven Students on Tests of Arithmetic (X_1) and Spelling (X_2)

Student	X_1	X_2
Johnny	6.55	-6.73
Fred	-3.45	-2.73
Mary	-1.45	-5.73
Bill	-3.45	-3.73
Jane	-1.45	0.27
Susan	-1.45	-2.73
Michael	1.55	-4.73
Sharon	3.55	7.27
Harry	-4.45	1.27
Patricia	-0.45	-2.73
Eric	4.55	20.27

The concept of deviation scores is useful in analyzing the results of experiments as well as in the interpretation of test scores. An example would be a three-group experiment which examines the influence of monetary rewards on the learning rate of mentally retarded students. One group is given no money, members of the second group are given a penny for each correct response in the learning task, and members of the third group are given 5 cents for each correct response. After the period of training is over, a test is given to all students. The mean score of the first group is 40, the mean of the second is 50, and the mean of the third is 60. The mean of all students from the three groups combined then would be 50 (assuming an equal number of students in each group). The real issue is how far apart the three groups are in terms of performance. The absolute sizes of the three means and of the grand mean (50) provide very little direct information. Consequently, for most forms of statistical analysis, the grand mean could be subtracted from the score of each student in each group. Because of principles stated earlier, the means of the three groups would be transformed to -10, 0, and +10 respectively. Also, of course, the grand mean now would be 0. For reasons that will be discussed more fully in subsequent chapters, all of the information necessary for analyzing the results of the experiment would be contained in these deviation scores and deviations of means from one another. In Chapter 6 it will be shown how transformations of the deviation scores to other types of scores help interpret data and simplify statistical equations.

MEASURES OF DISPERSION

Before a particular deviation score can be interpreted, how widely the scores are scattered above and below the mean must be learned. A deviation score of 2.00 may represent superior performance if all scores are closely packed about the mean. However, if there are numerous deviation scores as high as +100 and as low as -100, a deviation score of 2.00 would indicate near-average performance. Consequently, an index of the variation or dispersion of scores about the mean is needed in order to interpret particular deviations.

The issue of variation is important not only in the interpretation of test scores, but in all of science. Constant quantities are important to observe, but it is usually the amount of variation in phenomena that becomes a matter of concern for scientists. For example, nearly all school children have five fingers on each hand, which for all practical purposes represents a constant quantity. In contrast, school children at any one age-level vary considerably in height. This poses interesting scientific questions concerning inheritance, nutrition, and other factors that may explain such differences. Similarly in psychology and education, research is mainly concerned with variation of one type or another. If students obtain very similar scores on a measure of attitude toward disarmament, this would be an interesting finding, but not nearly as challenging to explain as would be the case if students varied considerably in that regard. Because college students vary con-

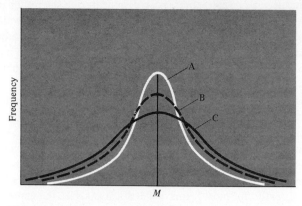

Figure 5-4. Three distributions with the same mean (M), but which have different amounts of variation about the mean.

siderably in terms of how well they perform in their coursework, this offers a challenge to develop excellent tests of college aptitude. In general, science is concerned with understanding, predicting, and controlling the variation in important natural and social phenomena. For these reasons, measures of the degrees of variation represented by frequency distributions constitute important statistics.

Figure 5-4 shows three frequency distributions that have the same mean but differ in how widely scores vary about the mean. In distribution A, scores are tightly packed about the mean; consequently, the peak of the distribution goes up higher than that for the other two curves and the tails of the distribution spread out far less. In contrast, distribution C shows wide variation about the mean, and comparatively few of the subjects are clustered around the mean value. Distribution B is between the other two distributions in the amount of variation.

The Range

There are various indices of how widely a group varies or is dispersed. One very simple index, the *range*, is obtained by subtracting the lowest score from the highest score (see Table 5-3). The highest score on the arithmetic test is 22, and the lowest is 11. This gives a range of 11. The range on the spelling test is 27, showing that the variation of scores is greater on the spelling test than on the arithmetic test. The range is a quickly obtained and often-used index of variation; however, it lacks some of the properties that are needed for an acceptable measure. It is dependent on only two scores, the highest and the lowest, If Eric had not taken the spelling test, the range in Table 5-3 would be only 14 instead of 27. Also, the range lacks the mathematical properties which permit the development of other statistics (a point to which we shall appeal quite often in choosing statistical measures).

The Average Deviation

An index of variation which is dependent on all the scores instead of just two of them and which indicates the position of an individual in a group is the *average deviation* (AD). As the name implies, it is obtained by finding how much the scores deviate on the average from the mean, as follows

$$AD = \frac{\Sigma |x|}{N}$$

The symbol $|x|$ indicates that absolute deviations are being considered, paying no attention to the signs. Thus with deviation scores of 2, 3, -4, and -2, the sum absolute would be 11. For example, using the absolute deviations for the scores on the spelling and arithmetic tests in Table 5-3, it is found that

Arithmetic	Spelling
$\Sigma |x_1| = 32.35$	$\Sigma |x_2| = 58.19$
$AD = \dfrac{32.35}{11}$	$AD = \dfrac{58.19}{11}$
$AD = 2.94$	$AD = 5.29$

The average deviation may be used to develop still other statistics; however, developing this measure further will not be worth the effort, because there are more desirable measures of variation which can be used. The range and the AD have been discussed in order to provide a background for the measure which will be presented subsequently.

The AD has a serious fault: it is based on absolute scores. It is very difficult to work mathematically with absolute scores; consequently, if the AD is used in some of the early statistical work, it severely limits the development of other measures. It will also prove unfeasible to develop a measure of variation from the deviation scores. The sum of these is always zero. Therefore, equations based on the sum of deviation scores "fall apart" and leave nothing with which the mathematician can work.

The Standard Deviation

An alternative to using either x scores or $|x|$ scores is to work with the squared deviations. These will all be positive, and it also happens that they provide an excellent starting place for the derivation of many other statistics. The squared deviations on the same two tests are shown in Table 5-5.

The *mean-square deviation* can be obtained by summing the squared deviations and dividing by the number of persons who took the test. This statistic is called the *variance* and is symbolized as σ^2

Table 5-5. Squared Deviation Scores of Eleven Students on Tests of Arithmetic (X_1^2) and Spelling (X_2^2)

Student	X_1^2	X_2^2
Johnny	42.90	45.26
Fred	11.90	7.45
Mary	2.10	32.83
Bill	11.90	13.91
Jane	2.10	0.07
Susan	2.10	7.45
Michael	2.40	22.37
Sharon	12.60	52.85
Harry	19.80	1.61
Patricia	0.20	7.45
Eric	20.70	410.87
	$\Sigma X_1^2 = 128.70$	$\Sigma X_2^2 = 602.12$

$$\sigma^2 = \frac{\Sigma x^2}{N} \tag{5-2}$$

An even more useful statistic is obtained by taking the square root of the variance, which is then called the *standard deviation*

$$\sigma = \sqrt{\frac{\Sigma x^2}{N}} \tag{5-3}$$

Applying the equation to the arithmetic and spelling tests, the following variances and standard deviations are found

Arithmetic	Spelling
$\sigma^2 = \dfrac{128.70}{11}$	$\sigma^2 = \dfrac{602.12}{11}$
$\sigma^2 = 11.70$	$\sigma^2 = 54.74$ (variance)
$\sigma = 3.42$	$\sigma = 7.40$ (standard deviation)

Subscripts can be used with the equations for variance and standard deviation to indicate which test is being studied; for example σ_1 can refer to the standard deviation of the scores on a particular test.

The standard deviation and variance can be obtained without actually going through the step of converting from raw to deviation scores. Previously, it was shown that the equation for the variance in terms of deviation scores is as follows

$$\sigma^2 = \frac{\Sigma x^2}{N}$$

Because any deviation score x equals a raw score X minus the mean M, an equivalent expression for the variance is

$$\sigma^2 = \frac{\Sigma(X - M)^2}{N}$$

By squaring the numerator of the term on the right, the following useful computational equation can be obtained

$$\sigma^2 = \frac{\Sigma X^2}{N} - \left(\frac{\Sigma X}{N}\right)^2 \tag{5-4}$$

Identical results will be obtained with all of these equations.

Since the standard deviation of the arithmetic test is 3.42, this means that one standard deviation goes 3.42 score units above the mean and another standard deviation goes 3.42 units below the mean. It is helpful to think of the continuum of raw scores as appearing like a yardstick. The mean is at a particular point on the yardstick, and standard deviations above and below the mean are marked off in pencil. The first marks above and below the mean would be 3.42 score units, the second marks indicating standard deviations would be at 6.84 score units above and below the mean, and so on for three or more standard deviations above and below the mean. The distance of 3.42 score units above and below the mean can be readily compared with the range, which is 11.

In contrast, if the variance is used as a descriptive statistic to represent the dispersion of scores, the effect of squaring the standard deviation is to create a statistic that looks very large in comparison to the range. Note that the variance for the arithmetic test is slightly larger than the range for that test and that the variance for the spelling test is over twice as large as the range. The importance of using the standard deviation is that this gets us back to the original scale of measurement for the variable, whereas σ^2 is expressed in terms of the square of the original measurement scale. Although the standard deviation is the preferred descriptive statistic regarding amount of variation, it will be seen in subsequent chapters that the variance is highly useful for calculating many statistics other than a descriptive index of variation.

Estimate of σ from a Sample

Note that in the previous discussion the standard deviation was symbolized by a Greek letter. Earlier in the chapter, it was said that Greek letters are used to symbolize population values rather than estimates of population values from samples. It was also said that the mean obtained from the sample is an unbiased estimate of the mean to be obtained from a larger population. It was explained that when an unbiased estimate is used, the same equation is applied to the sample as would be applied to the population as a whole. In contrast to the mean, the standard deviation σ is a slightly biased estimate of the population standard deviation. Thus, if one employs Equation (5-3) or (5-4) on a sample of scores, the odds are higher than $p = 0.50$ that the actual population standard deviation is *larger*. The reason for this is that in relatively small samples, the odds of obtaining scores that are very extreme on either the higher or lower end are less than when many scores are sampled. Mathematical statisticians have deduced a correction that provides an unbiased estimate of the population standard deviation from data obtained from only a sample of the population. The correction consists of using $N - 1$ rather than N in the denominators of Equations (5-3) and (5-4). The resulting statistic is symbolized as s and is called the *sample estimate of the standard deviation*. The mathematical logic for developing this measure is presented in Hays (1973). Then s would be obtained in deviation score units as follows

$$s = \sqrt{\frac{\Sigma x^2}{N - 1}}$$

(5-5)

Rather than work with deviation scores x, s can be obtained directly from raw scores. First, the square of s could be obtained with the following equation

$$s^2 = \frac{\Sigma X^2}{N - 1} \quad \frac{(\Sigma X)^2}{N(N - 1)}$$

(5-6)

Then s could be obtained by taking the square root of the above quantity.

In most uses of descriptive statistics, the difference between σ and s is quite small. For example, if $\sigma = 10$ and $N = 100$, then $s = 10.05$. Only when the number of subjects is less than 30 is there any appreciable difference between the two measures. In most uses of statistics to describe the characteristics of frequency distributions, it matters very little which of the two measures is employed. Where it becomes important to use the unbiased estimator s rather than the biased estimator σ is in the development of some inferential statistics which will be discussed in Part Three of this book. The major reason is that the statistical equations require unbiased estimators of the population variance and standard deviation. Also, in some experiments where inferential statistics are applied, the numbers of subjects in each condition is so small (perhaps 10 or less) that the bias would be substantial when employing σ rather than s.

It is very seldom the case that the population of subjects is so limited that it is possible to obtain the actual standard deviation. Usually, the standard deviation is a hypothetical statistic which is only estimated from a sample. When a hypothetical population standard deviation is being discussed, then the symbol σ_{pop} will be used to indicate that the σ is being used with respect to the population as a whole rather than the results obtained from applying the equation to only a sample of subjects.

Effects of Transformations on σ and s

After σ^2 and σ are obtained from any distribution of scores, they would be totally unaffected by adding any number (constant value) to all of the scores in the distribution or subtracting any number. Since the basic equations for σ^2 and σ are expressed in deviation score units, in all cases the mean would be zero before the calculations were performed. Thus, if the original mean of the distribution were 10, and 5 million were added to each of the scores, the mean of the distribution would still be 0 before the calculations were undertaken for σ^2 and

σ. Although this principle is not so obvious in Equation (5-4), the equation automatically equates the mean to zero in the process of calculating σ^2 and σ.

If all of the numbers in a distribution are multiplied by a constant c, then the standard deviation of the original distribution will be multiplied by that constant. This is readily proven as follows

$$\sigma(cx) = \sqrt{\frac{\Sigma(cx)^2}{N}}$$

$$= \sqrt{\frac{\Sigma c^2 x^2}{N}}$$

$$= \sqrt{c^2 \frac{\Sigma x^2}{N}}$$

$$= c\sqrt{\frac{\Sigma x^2}{N}}$$

$$= c\sigma_x$$

Thus, if the standard deviation of the original distribution is 5 and all scores are multiplied by 2, then the standard deviation of the new distribution is 10. The same proof for dividing by a constant could have been developed by inserting the reciprocal of c. If the standard deviation of the original distribution is 12, and all scores are divided by 6, then the standard deviation of the new distribution is 2. It should be noted in these cases that the variance would be multiplied or divided by the *square* of the constant.

The principles regarding effects of score transformations on the mean and standard deviation are illustrated in Table 5-6. The first column shows the scores of five students on a test. By applying the raw score equations given previously it is found that $M = 7$, $\sigma = 1.4$, and $\sigma^2 = 2$. The second column shows the deviation scores obtained by subtracting 7 from each of the scores in the first column. As is always the case, $M = 0$ for these deviation scores, but neither σ nor σ^2 are different from those of the raw scores. In the third column, 5 is added to each of the raw scores; consequently, the mean of the original raw scores is increased from 7 to 12. However, since adding a constant to the raw scores in the distribution does not change σ or σ^2, applications of the raw score equations show these values to be unchanged. In the fourth column, each of the original raw scores is multiplied by 3. This increases the mean of the original raw scores by a factor of 3, from 7 to 21. Because multiplying all of the scores in the distribution multiplies the standard deviation by that constant, the standard deviation of original raw scores is increased from 1.4 to 4.2. The variance is increased by the square of the

Table 5-6. Illustration of the Effects of Score Transformations on the Mean and Standard Deviation

Student	X	$x = X - M$	$X + 5$	$3X$	$3X - 2$
A	5	-2	10	15	13
B	6	-1	11	18	16
C	7	0	12	21	19
D	8	1	13	24	22
E	9	2	14	27	25
$M = 7$		0	12	21	19
$\sigma = 1.4$		1.4	1.4	4.2	4.2
$\sigma^2 = 2$		2	2	18	18

constant. Consequently, the variance of the original raw scores is multiplied by 9, going from 2 to 18. The fifth column in the table is obtained by multiplying the original raw scores by 3 and then subtracting 2. This does not change the σ and σ^2 from that in column 4, but the transformation reduces the mean by 2 points from 21 to 19.

All of the principles regarding σ and σ^2 also apply to s and s^2. If a constant is added to all scores in a distribution, s and s^2 are not affected. If all scores in a distribution are multiplied by a constant, s is multiplied by that constant, and s^2 is multiplied by the square of that constant.

SUMMARY

Two important types of descriptive statistics with respect to any set of research results are measures of central tendency and variation. It is necessary to understand summational notation for the development of such descriptive statistics. The Greek letter Σ is used to indicate the process of summing, and there are a number of important rules regarding how summation is undertaken.

Measures of average performance are important for both practical reasons and for the interpretation of research results. Average performance is important for practical reasons because many things in the world are tuned to what the average individual does, likes, and can understand. Average performance is important in research because the purpose of experiments is to measure the average response to experimental treatments. Thus, an experiment concerned with the effects of three different methods of instruction in reading skills would be to determine differences in average reading performance.

There are three major measures of average performance. The mode is the most frequently occurring score in a distribution. Thus, if more people make a score of 14 than make any other score, then 14 is the mode of the distribution. The median is the score point which separates the upper 50 percent of the people in a score distribution from the lower 50 percent. The term "score point" is used because the median usually is a mathematical point lying somewhere between two actual scores rather than being one of the possible scores, for example, 32.54 rather than 32 or 33.

The best measure of average performance for most purposes is the arithmetic mean, symbolized as M or $\overline{X}$. The mean consists of the sum of scores divided by the number of scores. The mean is a least-squares statistic, in the sense that the sum of squared deviations about the mean is less than that about any other point in the score distribution. In a perfectly symmetrical, unimodal distribution, the mean, median, and mode are at exactly the same point. When the distribution is skewed to the right, the mean is higher than the median, and the median is higher than the mode. When the distribution is skewed to the left, the mean, median, and mode are in the reverse rank order. Unless the distribution is extremely skewed as in a J-curve, differences between these three measures of average performance are usually trivial. Because the mean is easily computed and leads to the development of many other descriptive and inferential statistics, it is usually much preferred over the mode and median.

Without additional considerations, raw scores obtained in research usually are difficult to interpret. It facilitates the interpretation of such scores to cast them as deviates about the mean, where any deviation score x equals $X - M$. To further facilitate interpretation, it is necessary to consider the amount of variation or dispersion of scores about the mean. As is true with measures of average performance, there are a number of possible measures of variation in performance. Among these are the range, the average deviation, and the standard deviation. The standard deviation σ is by far the most useful measure of dispersion which has been proposed. It is obtained by averaging the squared deviates about the mean and taking the square root of this quantity. As is true of M, σ lends itself to many other developments in statistics.

The mean is an unbiased statistic in the sense that an estimate of the population mean from a sample entails the same equation that would be applied to the population as a whole. In contrast, the equation for σ applied to a sample is a slightly biased estimate of what would be obtained if the same equation were applied to the population as a whole. Consequently, a slight correction is required in estimating σ for the population from the scores obtained in a sample. The correction is symbolized by s and called the sample estimate of the standard deviation. The difference in the two equations is inconsequential when the number of subjects is more than about 30. The importance of the distinction will be discussed later in the book when inferential statistics are presented for the results of experiments.

The mean and standard deviation are affected in predictable ways by transformations of score distributions. If all scores in a distribution are multiplied by a constant, then the mean of the original distribution is multiplied by that constant. If a constant is added to all scores, then the mean is increased by that amount. If all scores are multiplied by a constant, then σ is multiplied by that constant; but if a constant is added or subtracted from all scores, σ is unaffected.

Both the mean M and standard deviation σ represent the cornerstones of descriptive statistics. They will be encountered repeatedly in the pages ahead.

EXERCISES

Study Questions

1 Explain what is meant by central tendency or average performance. Give three examples of average performance from daily life.

2 What are the three most widely used measures of central tendency? What are the advantages and disadvantages of each?

3 Explain and illustrate the following characteristics of the mean: (a) being unbiased, (b) the sum of deviation scores about the mean being zero, (c) being a more accurate estimate of its population value than is the case with the mode or median, and (d) having a relatively small sum of squared deviates about the mean.

4 Draw two figures showing where the mean, median, and mode would lie in a distribution that is skewed to the left and a distribution that is skewed to the right. How would interpretations differ in these two examples if one rather than the other two measures of central tendency were employed?

5 How is the mean affected by adding a constant number to all scores or multiplying all scores by a constant number? Give numerical examples of how the principles would apply separately and then jointly.

6 Give examples of raw scores X and deviation scores x. Illustrate why deviation scores are more easily interpreted than raw scores.

7 Name and illustrate three measures of variation. Which is most useful and why?

8 Distinguish between σ and its modification, s. What is the usefulness of s over σ? How are σ and σ^2 affected by score transformations—adding a constant number to all scores or multiplying all scores by a constant number? Give concrete examples. Do the same principles hold for s?

Problems

16	20	18	22	21	19	19	19	20
20	17	17	22	22	19	25	20	26
23	16	17	25	20	20	21	19	
24	20	19	22	21	21	17	20	
19	20	17	20	18	15	18	23	

These data are the scores of 42 children on a geography test.

1 Calculate the mean, median, and mode.

2 Calculate the variance σ^2 and the standard deviation σ. Transform these to s^2 and s.

3 Calculate how the mean would be affected by one of the following: (a) if all scores were multiplied by 3, (b) if 4 were added to each of the original scores, or (c) if all scores were first multiplied by 2 and then 4 added to each of the resulting scores.

4 How would σ and σ^2 be affected if the number 5 were added to each score? How would they be affected if each score were multiplied by 3?

SUGGESTED ADDITIONAL READINGS

Ferguson, G. A. *Statistical analysis in psychology and education*, 3d ed. New York York: McGraw-Hill, 1971, Chaps. 3 and 4.

Guilford, J. P., and B. Fruchter. *Fundamental statistics in psychology and education*, 5th ed. New York: McGraw-Hill, 1973, Chaps. 5 and 6.

Statistical Norms

In psychology and education, the results of most measures are meaningful only when applied to some type of *standard*. There are two major types of standards that are employed in interpreting measurement scores. The first consists of comparing performance with *values* or expectations regarding performance. For example, a track coach may expect a runner to make the 100-yard dash in less than 10 seconds. The coach knows that otherwise the runner will have little chance of successfully competing in forthcoming athletic events. The teacher in a typing course may expect all students to type at a rate of at least 30 words per minute by the end of a semester. In advance of giving a multiple-choice test, a teacher in Introductory Psychology may decide what numbers of correct responses deserve grades of A, B, and so on. In these cases, raw scores are compared directly with established values regarding the meaning of performance. Standards established in terms of values are found most frequently in educational institutions and other applied settings such as industry, government, and military. How such standards are developed and used are discussed in most books on psychological measurement and educational measurement. [See Nunnally, (1970, 1972).]

More important for this book are standards based on a second principle—those concerning *statistical norms*. Norm literally means average, and statistical norms consist of comparing scores of individuals in a group with the average response in the group. Chapter 5 discussed measures of average performance, measures of variation, and ways of interpreting measurement scores in terms of the degree of deviation about the mean. That discussion will be expanded in this chapter by (1) considering more refined statistical methods for comparing scores with the mean and (2) discussing the various principles by which groups are formed to make such comparisons. There is more than one way to make statistical comparisons among scores, and there is more than one way to formulate groups for making such comparisons.

There are two major statistical bases for establishing norms—those based on deviation scores x about the mean and those based on rank order. These will be discussed in turn.

DEVIATIONS ABOUT THE MEAN

In Chapter 5 it was shown how each raw score X could be cast as a deviation score x. This is done by (1) obtaining the arithmetic mean and (2) subtracting the arithmetic mean from each raw score. Such deviation scores can be converted into interpretable deviations about the mean by (1) obtaining the standard deviation of the score distribution and (2) dividing each deviation score by the standard deviation. In other words, the standard deviation can be used as a scale of measurement for judging the size of deviations about the mean. Deviation scores expressed in this way (x/σ_x) are called *standard scores* and symbolized by z. Before discussing standard scores in more detail, first it is necessary to discuss a mathematical distribution that proves very useful in the interpretation of z. This is called the *normal distribution*.

Normal Distribution

The normal distribution was developed in connection with games of chance, where for example, one problem is to estimate the frequencies with which certain coin tosses occur. Suppose that 10 coins are tossed on a table. What are the odds that 8 of them will be heads? If 10 coins are tossed 1,000 times, in how many tosses will all 10 be heads? What would occur more frequently, 8 heads and 2 tails or 7 heads and 3 tails? The normal distribution was derived in connection with questions such as these. The equation is a mathematical invention which can be used to estimate the frequency with which these chance events occur.

The equation for the normal distribution relates to the situation in which 10 coins are tossed many times, say 1,024 times, to choose a statistically convenient number. The expected distribution of results is shown in Table 6-1. As intuition would suggest, the distribution of results shows that the most frequently occurring result would be 5 heads and 5 tails, occurring 252 times. On the extremes,

Table 6-1. Expected Occurrences of Heads and Tails for 10 Coins Tossed 1,024 Times

Frequency	1	10	45	120	210	252	210	120	45	10	1
Heads	0	1	2	3	4	5	6	7	8	9	10
Tails	10	9	8	7	6	5	4	3	2	1	0

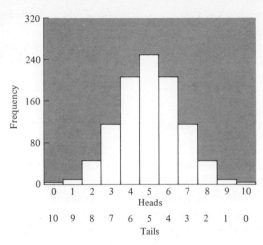

Figure 6-1. Frequency distribution of expected occurrences of heads and tails for ten coins tossed 1,024 times.

10 heads or 10 tails would be expected only once. The frequency distribution is shown graphically in Figure 6-1. Depicted there is a theoretical distribution regarding what is *expected* rather than what is sure to happen. If the expected results depicted in Figure 6-1 were compared with many actual experiments on coin tossing, in some instances the obtained distribution would be markedly different from the one in the figure.

Suppose that each toss employed 100 coins instead of 10. Then the graph would contain 101 bars, covering the range from 0 to 100 heads. Because of the larger number of bars, the graph would look less jagged, in other words, the "steps" on the graph would be much narrower. Of course, this would be the case only if approximately the same amount of space was used for portraying the X axis. If the number of coins were increased to 1,000, the steps would be so small as to be hardly visible, and the frequency distribution would begin to look like a smooth curve rather than a set of steps. Challenging the imagination further, what would the frequency distribution look like if there were an infinite number of coins tossed an infinite number of times? The normal distribution tells us what to expect, which is shown by the smooth curve in Figure 6-2.

If the normal distribution applied only to games of chance, it would be of little interest to us here. This is one of the many instances in which a mathematical invention happens to fit closely with what frequently occurs in reality. The reason that the normal distribution is so important is that many measures in psychology and education are often distributed much like the normal distribution. Each score is the counterpart of one coin, and each toss is the counterpart of one person. For example, if a well-constructed spelling test containing ten words were administered to 1,024 students, the results might approximate the frequency distribution shown in Figure 6-1. (This is because of statistical principles rather than

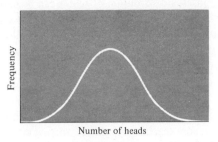

Figure 6-2. Smooth curve showing expectancies of heads for a large number of coins tossed an infinite number of times.

because the results of any good test would be due to chance factors like those in an experiment on coin tossing.) Zero heads would correspond to getting none of the spelling words correct, and ten heads would correspond to getting all the words correct. For reasons which are too technical to discuss here, the distribution of test scores obtained in practice would probably be slightly different from that shown in Figure 6-1; but if the test were well constructed, the difference between the shape of the distribution of test scores and that obtained from coin-tossing experiments would probably be relatively slight.

Instead of only a ten-item test, imagine that the test contains an infinite number of items and is administered to an infinite number of students. Because of the ways in which most tests are constructed, the results would tend to approximate the bell-shaped curve (normal distribution) shown in Figure 6-2. Of course, infinity is only a useful fiction, but the normal distribution is often well approximated when the test contains 30 items or more and is administered to 100 students or more. Approximately normal distributions of scores are also found for many other types of measures used in psychology and education, such as the research results obtained from studies of memory and perception. Because of the resemblance between many distributions of scores and the hypothetical normal distribution, it is possible to borrow some of the very useful mathematical results that follow from the normal distribution for the analysis and interpretation of research results.

When scores are obtained for relatively large numbers of persons on measures in psychology and education, one typically finds a distribution that at least resembles the normal distribution. For example, Figure 6-3 shows the distribution of scores for 200 students on an achievement test in arithmetic.

There is nothing magical about the normal distribution, and no reason that measures in psychology and education should necessarily be so distributed. Because having an approximately normal distribution opens the door to many useful mathematical procedures, tests and other measures are often developed in such a way as to approximately ensure a distribution of that form. In practice, it is not necessary to be compulsively concerned about the normal distribution. For all practical purposes, a distribution of scores can be considered a reasonable approximation to the normal distribution if the bulk of the scores cluster about the mean, if the distribution is not markedly lopsided, and if scores trail off about the mean in a way that generally resembles the curve shown in Figure 6-2.

In spite of the usefulness of the normal distribution in analyzing data, it should be clearly understood that having a normal distribution is not necessarily an indication that a measure is valid in any sense. Remember that coin tossing would provide a good approximation of the normal distribution, and, although students sometimes accuse teachers of using it, tossing coins would not provide a valid test.

Standard Scores

When the distribution of scores is approximately normal, standard scores z are very helpful aids to interpreting the location of particular scores in the distribution. This section will discuss standard scores in more detail and how they are interpreted with respect to the normal distribution. One important property of a score distribution is its standard deviation. In Chapter 5, score distributions for arithmetic and spelling which had standard deviations of 3.42 and 7.40 respectively were shown. Using the customary equation, a standard deviation could be obtained for the 200 arithmetic scores shown in Figure 6-3 and even for the distribution of "heads" shown in Figure 6-1. When the distribution of scores is approximately normal, the standard deviation has a very useful property: it indi-

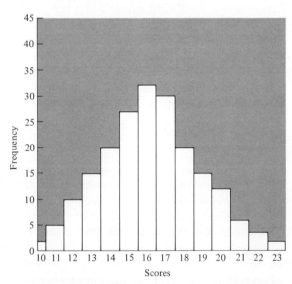

Figure 6-3. Frequency distribution of arithmetic scores for 200 students.

cates the percentages of scores that lie in various regions of the distribution.

Previously, it was said that it is difficult to interpret raw scores and that one of the ways to make scores more interpretable is to convert them to deviation scores (by subtracting the mean raw score from each raw score). It is difficult to interpret deviation scores, however, until the variation of scores is considered. One way to do this is to compare each deviation score with the standard deviation, in other words, to use the standard deviation as a unit of measurement. Scores analyzed in this way are called standard scores and are obtained by dividing each deviation score by the standard deviation of the particular distribution, as follows

$$\text{Standard score} = \frac{\text{deviation score}}{\text{standard deviation}}$$

It is customary to symbolize standard scores as z. Because deviation scores are symbolized by x and the standard deviation is symbolized by σ, the equation above more customarily is written as follows

$$z = \frac{x}{\sigma_x} \tag{6-1}$$

An example of computing standard scores is shown in Table 5-3 with respect to the arithmetic score of Johnny. The mean of the scores is 15.45 and the standard deviation is 3.42. His standard score would be computed as follows

$$z = \frac{X - M}{\sigma_x}$$

$$= \frac{22 - 15.45}{3.42}$$

$$= \frac{6.55}{3.42}$$

$$= 1.9$$

Another example would be the previously reported case of Johnny's score of 48 on a spelling test, where the mean is 54.73 and the standard deviation is 7.40. His standard score is computed as follows

$$z = \frac{48 - 54.73}{7.40}$$

$$= \frac{-6.73}{7.40}$$

$$= -0.9$$

Johnny is almost two standard deviations above the mean on arithmetic and almost one standard deviation below the mean on spelling.

The usefulness of converting raw scores to standard scores is evidenced by the standard scores of Johnny in arithmetic and spelling. Standard scores permit a direct comparison of results of two measures on which the means and standard deviations are different. Without making such a conversion, a comparison of Johnny's raw scores on the arithmetic and spelling tests would have been highly misleading.

One reason the normal distribution is important is that, if the distribution of measurement scores resembles the normal distribution, standard scores on the measure can be easily interpreted. In that case, it is very easy to determine the approximate number of persons who make scores within a specified number of standard deviations above and below the mean. A complete table showing the percentages of students lying in various regions of the normal distribution is given in Appendix B-3. A less detailed breakdown is shown in Figure 6-4. The figure shows, for example, that only about 2 percent of the students score above two standard deviations—have standard scores of 2.0 or higher. Because Johnny has a standard score in arithmetic of 1.9, most of the students score lower.

The exact interpretation of the percentage of students who score lower would require testing many more than 11 students. Among the small number of students in this example, Johnny actually has the highest score in arithmetic. When the characteristics of the normal distribution are used to estimate percentages of persons who would score above or below different levels, the expectations are based on a large hypothetical sample of persons of the same kind on which the statistics are computed rather than on the relatively small number of individuals involved in a small sample. Thus, it would be expected that about 2 percent of the persons in a large sample would score higher than Johnny in arithmetic.

Figure 6-4 shows that practically none of the persons have standard scores below – 3.0. Going upward, about 2 pecent score less than – 2.0 standard scores, 16 percent less than – 1.0, 50 percent less than 0.0 (below the mean), 84 percent less than 1.0, and 98 percent less than 2.0. When there are at least 30 test items and 100 persons, such interpretations of standard scores are fairly accurate. Even

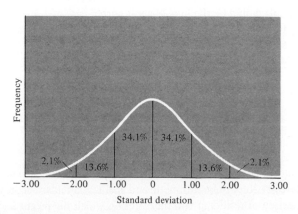

Figure 6-4. Percentages of subjects in various regions of the normal distribution. (The percentages add up to 99.6 instead of 100 because a fraction of 1 percent of the subjects lie above and below three standard deviations.)

when there are fewer items and persons, say 20 items and 30 persons, the normal distribution provides a useful approximation of the percentages of persons scoring above and below selected points on the score continuum.

Standard scores (or transformations of them) are widely used in commercially distributed tests, such as intelligence tests. Because these tests usually have many items and are administered to thousands of students, and because distributions closely approximate the normal distribution, standard scores can be interpreted rather exactly.

As mentioned previously, it frequently aids in the interpretation of test results to convert a distribution to one having a desired mean and standard deviation. Essentially, this is what is done in converting scores from raw (or deviation) scores to standard scores. Expressed as standard scores, all distributions have the same mean, which is 0; all distributions have the same standard deviation, which is 1.0. These facts follow directly from the rules stated in Chapter 5 regarding the effects of score transformations on the mean and standard deviation of any score distribution. If the mean of raw scores is subtracted from all scores in a distribution, then the mean of the transformed distribution necessarily is 0. If all scores in the resulting distribution are divided by the standard deviation, then the standard deviation of the transformed distribution necessarily is 1.0. The value of making a transformation of scores to z rather than some other transformation is that it permits a direct interpretation of scores with respect to characteristics of the normal distribution. Thus a z of 1.0 means one standard deviation above the mean, which has direct implications regarding percents of scores at above and below that level on a normal distribution.

Transformed Standard Scores

Although standard scores are directly useful to anyone who is familiar with psychological and educational measurement, people who are naive in this respect have some difficulty in interpreting standard scores. For example, a standard score of 0 is often misinterpreted as meaning zero instead of average performance on the test. Some people find it difficult to understand negative standard scores, those below the mean. For these reasons, standard scores are often transformed to a distribution having a desired mean and standard deviation. One such distribution is obtained when standard scores are transformed to a new distribution having a mean of 500 and a standard deviation of 100. Transformed scores of this kind are used with the well-known College Board tests of scholastic aptitude and other tests of this kind. An example is shown in Figure 6-5. Such transformed standard scores simply represent a convenient way of expressing the relative standings of students with respect to numbers of standard deviations above and below the mean. These transformed standard scores can be interpreted with respect to percentages of individuals at various levels, in the same way as was done for the standard deviations depicted in Figure 6-4.

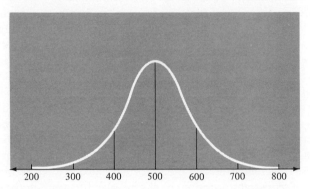

Figure 6-5. Transformed distribution with a mean of 500 and a standard deviation of 100.

Although the logic of transforming standard score distributions to other distributions could be more simply represented by equations based on either standard scores or deviation scores, it is usually more convenient to employ the following raw score equation

$$X_t = \frac{\sigma_t}{\sigma_o} X_o - \left(\frac{\sigma_t}{\sigma_o} M_o - M_t\right) \qquad (6\text{-}2)$$

where X_t = scores on the transformed scale, X_o = scores on the obtained scale, M_o, M_t = means of X_o and X_t, respectively, and σ_o, σ_t = standard deviations of X_o and X_t, respectively.

For example, it might be found that the mean of the obtained raw test scores is 40 and that the standard deviation is 5. In order to compare scores on the test with scores on another test, or in order to place the scores in an easily interpretable form, it might be desirable to transform the raw scores in such a way that the new scores have a mean of 50 and standard deviation of 10. The equation can be applied to the problem as follows

$$X_t = \frac{10}{5} X_o - \left(\frac{10}{5} 40 - 50\right)$$

$$X_t = 2X_o - 30$$

By this transformation, a raw score of 40 would be transformed to a score of 50, and a raw score of 25 would be transformed to a score of 20. Because the equation is a linear transformation, it does not change the shape of the score distribution.

SCORES BASED ON RANKS

There are two principal methods of converting raw scores to more interpretable units. One has been discussed extensively in the preceding pages. In summary, it consists of transforming raw-score distributions to distributions with prescribed means and standard deviations, or standard scores. The second method is based on ranks. As will be shown, the methods are complementary and ultimately provide much the same information.

One of the simplest methods of transforming raw scores to more meaningful units—and in many ways the most sensible—is to rank raw scores from highest to lowest. When only a relatively small number of scores are available, it is usually unnecessary to do more than rank the scores and inspect them. When very large numbers of scores are available, more refined methods of analyzing data based on ranks are needed. This would be the case, for example, in using ranking methods to establish norms for an achievement test based on the scores from a sample of 10,000 students throughout the country. It would be almost impossible to rank the scores, and the results would be difficult to interpret.

Percentiles

When the scores of individuals are being compared with scores obtained from a large sample of persons, it is useful to make transformations of ranks to what are called *percentiles*. A percentile is simply the percentage of persons who fall below a particular score. Thus, if 95 percent of the students score lower than 45 and Fred makes a score of 45, then he is at the 95th percentile. If only 20 percent of the students score lower than 18 and Mary makes a score of 18, she is at the 20th percentile.

Percentiles are very much like the ranks that would be obtained in a group of exactly 100 persons, except that in using ranks it is customary to give the highest score a rank of 1. If instead, the lowest score was given a rank of 1 and the highest score a rank of 100, these would be almost identical to percentiles. The slight difference is that percentiles are defined as the percentage of persons who score *lower* than a particular score. Thus, the person with rank 100 would receive a percentile score of 99, because 99 percent of the persons are lower. Also, the person with rank 1 would receive a percentile score of 0, because none of the persons score lower. However, the difference is so slight that it is useful to think of percentiles as representing ranks when exactly 100 scores are being studied, the largest rank (100) is given to the person with the highest test score, and the smallest rank (1) is given to the person with the lowest test score.

If there are no tied scores, percentiles are obtained by finding the percentages of persons below each raw score. For example, if in studying 200 scores, Fred makes a score of 76, no other person makes a score of exactly 76, and 160 persons make scores of less than 76, then Fred is at the 80th percentile (160 divided by 200, and the result multiplied by 100).

Because there will nearly always be tied scores, a slight modification of this method must be used to obtain percentiles. Why such a modification of procedures is necessary is illustrated by the situation in which 35 percent of the persons score higher than 45, 50 percent score lower than 45, and 15 percent make exactly the same score of 45. In this case, it would be misleading to say that any person who made a score of 45 is at the 50th percentile because of the fact that only 35 percent of the persons score higher. This ambiguity can be remedied by considering half of the persons who make the same score of 45 as scoring higher and half the persons as scoring lower. Then the first step in obtaining percentiles is to find the number of persons who score below a particular raw score plus half of the number of persons who make the particular raw score. The total is divided by the number of persons in the study, and the result is multiplied by 100. As an example, if 40 persons out of 200 score higher than 44, 140 persons score lower than 44, and 20 persons score exactly 44, 44 corresponds to a percentile of 75. The rules for reaching this quantity are as follows

	Rule	Example
Step 1	Find number of persons who score below a given raw score	140
Step 2	Add ½ the number of persons who made the given score	10 150 subtotal
Step 3	Divide by number of persons in whole group	150/200 = 0.75
Step 4	Multiply by 100	0.75 X 100 = 75th percentile

By this method, percentiles can be calculated for all scores regardless of ties in raw scores.

The following are the percentile scores for two students on the subtests of a reading achievement test

Subtest	Fred Worth	Jack Spain
Word knowledge	90	48
Reading comprehension	83	22
Reading speed	38	81

The percentiles are in relation to national norms for students in the sixth grade. Fred's score is at the 90th percentile on word knowledge; therefore, 90 percent of the students in the national sample scored lower than Fred did. Fred's score is above 83 percent of the national sample in reading comprehension, but he is above only 38 percent in reading speed. These percentile scores suggest that Fred has the capacity to learn to read more rapidly and still maintain a relatively high level of comprehension. Jack Spain is at the 48th percentile on word knowledge, very close to the average score obtained from the national sample. His reading comprehension score is only at the 22nd percentile, which contrasts strongly with his reading speed percentile of 81. This pattern of scores suggests that Jack moves too quickly through written material without fully comprehending what he reads. These examples demonstrate how percentiles are interpreted in school situations.

If distributions are essentially normal, percentiles and standard scores supply much the same information. It should be remembered from previous sections that standard scores indicate the percentages of persons who fall in various score regions of a normal distribution. For example, approximately 98 percent of the persons will have standard scores less than 2.0; approximately 84 percent will have standard scores less than 1.0; and so on for the other regions of the normal distribution. As Figure 6-6 shows, the 50th percentile is both the median and the mean of a perfectly symmetrical distribution, which corresponds to a standard score of 0.0. One of the major types of information indicated by standard scores concerns the percentages of persons making scores above and below particular points on the test continuum. Because of the ease with which standard scores can be converted to percentages of persons in various score regions, percentiles for a normally distributed variable can be estimated by converting all raw scores to standard scores and then transforming these to percentiles, using Appendix B-4. This will offer an approximation of the percentiles obtained by the more direct method described previously. However, the approximation may be rather poor unless (1) the distribution of raw scores is approximately normal, (2) there are many test items (at least 30), and (3) at least 100 persons are studied.

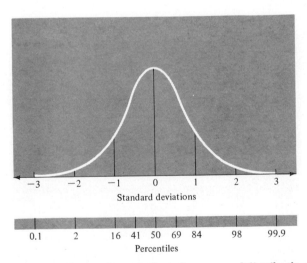

Figure 6-6.   Percentile equivalents for a normal distribution.

Cautions in the Use of Percentiles

Because tests are usually constructed so that scores conform at least approximately to the normal distribution, there are many more raw scores and ties in raw scores in the middle of the distribution than at the extremes. Consequently, when percentiles are computed, differences in raw scores near the middle of the distribution tend to be exaggerated, whereas differences in raw scores near the extremes tend to be minimized. In Figure 6-7, the distortion of distances between scores can be seen clearly. For example, 34 percent of all persons have raw scores of 20, 21, or 22; but only approximately 2 percent of the persons have scores of 24, 25, or 26. If an individual improved his test score by getting two more items correct, for instance, from 20 to 22 items correct and from 24 to 26 items correct, this would mean a much larger difference in percentile units. Thus, in interpreting percentiles, one should keep in mind that percentiles show an individual's relative position in the normative sample, but not necessarily the amount of difference in raw scores.

It is important not to confuse percentile scores with percentage-correct scores. Regarding the latter, it is sometimes useful to think in terms of the percentage of items that students get correct; however, it should be obvious that percentage-correct scores do not directly tell anything about students' standings with respect to one another. If an easy test is being given, a student can get 65 percent of the items correct and yet be in the bottom quarter of his class, thus having a percen-

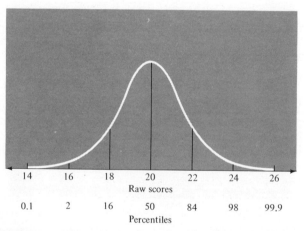

Figure 6-7. Relationship between raw scores and percentiles.

tile score of less than 25. If a difficult test is being given, a student can have a percentage-correct score of only 50, and yet be at the 90th percentile in his class.

Another caution in the use of percentiles is to be quite suspicious of interpretations of percentiles based on a relatively small number of persons, such as percentiles for a final examination in educational psychology based on the results from only 50 students. Obviously, when there are less than 100 students, there cannot possibly be even one person at each percentile level. There are usually many tied scores in such situations; consequently, there will be many "gaps" in scores corresponding to adjacent percentiles. For example, this might result in the 85th percentile being at 45 items correct and the 84th percentile being all the way down to 38 items correct. Obviously, these represent poor norms because there would be no way of knowing what interpretation to make for persons in future samples who have scores between those levels. Also, when percentiles are based on only a relatively small number of persons, the results are most unstable from sample to sample. If percentiles are developed as norms for a vocabulary test and different samples of 50 persons are administered the test, the obtained percentiles will vary considerably from sample to sample. The results from one sample might indicate that 42 items correct was the 85th percentile, and the result from another sample might indicate that 42 items correct was the 67th percentile. For the foregoing reasons, it is unwise to compute percentiles on relatively small numbers of individuals, and it is unsafe to make fine interpretations of percentiles obtained in such cases.

Comparison of Percentiles and Standard Scores

Whether one chooses to express norms in terms of standard scores or percentiles depends on the nature of the problem. For reasons that will be discussed in the chapters ahead, standard scores prove to be much more useful in performing subsequent statistical analyses than do percentiles. Whereas most of the statistical methods still to be discussed in the book could be performed directly on standard scores rather than on the original scores, percentiles do not lend themselves to such forms of analysis. For example, it will be seen in Chapter 7 that correlational analysis essentially concerns comparisons of standard scores on two measures. Most of the inferential statistics discussed in Part Three of the book assume that measures are at least approximately normally distributed; consequently, it is useful to think in terms of standard scores in employing such statistics.

Percentiles have a particular advantage over standard scores in making direct comparisons of individuals with those from a sample used to establish norms. This would be the case in comparing the score of a student on a fifth-grade test of reading speed with that of a large sample used to establish national norms. Another example would be in comparing the score that a student made on a personality test of anxiety with that of a large sample of college students throughout the country. In both cases, it is easier to interpret percentiles than to interpret standard scores (or any transformations of standard scores). In order to interpret standard scores in these cases, it would be necessary to assume that the distribution was normal and to convert standard scores to percentages of students scoring higher and lower (using Appendix B-4). Essentially what one does in making standard scores meaningful is to convert them to percentiles. Consequently, it is hard to argue against the statement that percentiles ultimately represent the best form in which to express norms for the purpose of interpreting scores of individuals.

REFERENCE GROUPS FOR ESTABLISHING NORMS

Whether statistical norms are computed as standard scores (or some transformation thereof) or percentiles, such norms are meaningful only in relation to the sample of persons used to establish norms. Two examples will illustrate the issues involved. An adult receives a standard score of -1.0 in a measure of anxiety, which suggests that he is low in anxiety. However, it is found that the normative sample consisted of mental hospital patients who were diagnosed as highly anxious. Consequently, the standard score does not provide much comfort regarding a lack of anxiety in the particular person. As a second example, a student who is applying to several prestigious universities learns that he has a percentile score of 75 on a college aptitude test with respect to a national sample. However, these institutions are so selective that nearly all of the students who are admitted have aptitude test scores at the 85th percentile or higher. In these and in other examples, a comparison of scores with norms is meaningful only in the context of the sample upon which norms are based. Different normative samples are useful for different purposes.

Diversity

One dimension upon which normative samples are meaningfully distinguished is that of the *diversity* of people represented. At one extreme, the normative sample may consist of all of the people who are members of a particular country club or all of the students in a particular classroom. Norms for members of the country club might be based on opinions about athletic activities, and norms in the classroom based on scores on tests composed by the teacher. When the normative group is so parochial, it is hardly worth the trouble to compute measures of average performance, dispersion, and make conversions to standard scores and percentiles. Norms are constructed and used when individuals are to be compared with wider collections of people. On the other extreme, norms are sometimes constructed on samples that are intended to represent everyone in a geographical region or a country as a whole. This is the case with norms established for intelligence tests. Scores made on such tests can be converted to standard scores and percentiles that are supposedly meaningful regardless of the individual's sex, age, region of the country, and other attributes.

In most cases, normative samples range between the two extremes given in relation to diversity. It is usually not worth the effort to compute elaborate statistics to compare members of a particular small group with one another; on the other hand, it is usually neither meaningful nor feasible to establish norms in relation to samples of people everywhere of every type. Usually, the normative sample is purposefully restricted in such a way as to make certain types of comparisons meaningful. For example, since males and females differ in abilities on some types of tests, separate norms are established for the sexes. Norms are frequently established on a sample for a particular reference group rather than for the population as a whole. For example, if one is studying the attitudes of farmers, obviously he would only include farmers in his sample rather than bank clerks, airplane pilots, and deep-sea divers. Frequently, samples are restricted geographically, because this provides a better basis of comparison than would be obtained from a more diverse geographic sample. This would be the case in establishing norms for a new high school course in mental hygiene. The course materials and lectures might be so different from those in other localities that only norms obtained in a particular school system would provide a meaningful comparison for the performance of individual students. The purpose of sampling subjects and administering measures is to obtain norms with respect to a *specified group*. Only after the group is specified can a meaningful plan of sampling be established and norms be constructed.

It is often useful to compare the scores of individuals with norms obtained from a number of samples relating to different populations. Thus, different types of information would be obtained by comparing the achievement test score in reading comprehension of a particular student with (1) other students in his class, (2) students throughout the local school system, and (3) students in the same grade level throughout the country. Following are some ways in which normative samples are defined in order to make meaningful comparisons in educational settings.

Age Norms

It is sometimes desirable to express norms in terms of children's ages. One such set of age norms could be obtained by testing the vocabulary of children at all ages from four to twelve. For this purpose, a list of 100 words varying in difficulty could be used. The mean score would be obtained for each age group separately. A graphic plot of these is shown in Figure 6-8. The figure indicates, for example, that the average seven-year-old child has a larger vocabulary than the average six-year-old, as would be expected.

Age norms would prove useful in interpreting the vocabulary scores of particular students. Suppose that a child is seven years old and makes a vocabulary score

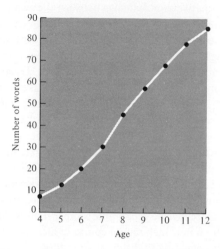

Figure 6-8. Mean vocabulary scores of children at each age from four to twelve years old.

of 25 (correctly identifies or supplies the meaning of 25 words on the list). The mean score for seven-year-olds in the normative group is 30, which indicates that the particular student is somewhat below average for his age level. To determine how much he is below average, we can find the age group which corresponds to a score of 25. Although there is no age group whose mean score is exactly 25, we can consider the curve continuous through all age levels and determine the fractional age group corresponding to that score. From Figure 6-8 we can determine that an age group of approximately 6.5 corresponds to a score of 25. Thus, the seven-year-old child has a vocabulary approximately that of the average 6½-year-old. Age norms fit in well with the way we customarily think about the progress of children and are therefore very useful in the interpretation of test scores.

Educational age. Age norms are often employed with commercially distributed achievement tests which cover most of the subjects taught in schools. After the test is administered to a broad sample (normative group), mean scores can be found for each age level. Then in all future uses of the test, scores of particular students can be compared with the age norms. If a nine-year-old child achieves an age score of only seven, this means that he is considerably behind his age group. It would then be said that he has an *educational age* (EA) of seven, as opposed to his chronological age of nine.

Mental age. Age norms are employed with some of the commercially distributed intelligence tests. By comparing a child's score with age norms, it can be determined whether he is more or less "intelligent" than the average child of his age. A score which is compared in this way with age norms is referred to as a *mental age* (MA). If a six-year-old performs as well as the average seven-year-old child, he is said to have a mental age of seven.

Grade Norms

Norms which are very similar to age norms can be obtained by finding the mean scores for children at various grade levels. If a standard spelling test is given to children in the fourth through eighth grades, the means can be plotted by grades, much as they were plotted by age in Figure 6-8. Comparing scores with grade norms gives the teacher an indication of how well pupils are progressing.

Age and grade norms are usually obtained at the end of the school year, for example, by testing children who are finishing the fourth, fifth, etc., grades. Age norms are usually very similar to grade norms, and it is difficult to argue that one type of norm is generally better than the other. The advantage of grade norms is that comparisons are made among children who have had the same amount, if not precisely the same kind, of education. The relative disadvantage of grade norms is that they tend to penalize accelerated students and overestimate the progress of retarded pupils. If a student has recently been double-promoted, he may appear only average in comparison with his classmates, who are a year older; but he would still appear superior with respect to children of his own age (using age norms rather than grade norms). Also, because children sometimes differ by as much as eight months or more of age within grades, there is some inequity in the use of grade norms. When possible, it is helpful to convert students' scores to both age norms and grade norms to utilize the slightly different kinds of information which they supply.

Sampling

A potential fault of any set of norms relates to the way in which the normative group is obtained. This concerns principles regarding the sampling of people from a defined population, matters which were discussed in Chapter 3 and will be reiterated here. The normative group is supposed to be *representative* of some defined population. As noted previously, the population may be all of the people in the United States, all the students in a particular school district, or all the students in a particular school, depending on the ways in which the norms are to be used. To obtain representativeness, it must be ensured that the normative group is *unbiased* and that sufficient numbers of students are tested.

A normative group, or sample, is unbiased if every person in the designated population has an equal chance of being selected for testing. One of the surest ways to guarantee that a sample is unbiased is to select persons randomly, for example, draw names out of a hat. Random samples can be drawn when norms are constructed locally, but for regional and national norms, approximate procedures must be employed. These approximate procedures involve selecting a sample of persons to be representative of a region or the country as a whole. Such factors as community size, socioeconomic level, public-parochial school balance, as well as many others are taken into account in selecting the sample used in establishing norms. If carefully done, these approximate sampling procedures can lead to representative results. [Discussions of methods for obtaining representative samples are presented by Kish (1965).]

In addition to being unbiased, a sample must contain sufficient numbers of persons. If, for example, there are only 20 children in the sample, luck might have it that as a group they would be much above average or much below average. Norms obtained from so small a group would provide a poor basis for the interpretation of scores. In comparison to such norms, a person who is really average might appear either superior or far below average. The only definite rule that can be given in choosing the number of students to test from a representative sample is "the more the merrier." To obtain national norms, it is wise to include at least several thousand students in the sample. If norms are to be obtained for 20,000 students in a particular school district, it would be wise to test at least 1,000 students (and, as noted previously, these should be selected by a random, or approximately random, procedure).

USES OF NORMS IN PSYCHOLOGICAL AND EDUCATIONAL RESEARCH

Now that the logic and mechanics of developing norms have been discussed, it is proper to conclude this chapter by considering how such norms are actually employed in psychological and educational research. In this connection, it is important to make a distinction between the *concept* of norms and the actual *use* of norms in research. The concept of norms is important in all aspects of the collection, scoring, and statistical analysis of data. For example, the ideas underlying standard scores and the normal distribution are indispensable for understanding most descriptive and inferential statistics. However, in employing such statistics, it is seldom necessary to actually compute such norms and make comparisons of the scores of individuals with such norms. Part Three discusses inferential statistics for determining the probability that the means of two differently treated groups are "real" rather than due to the chance factors by which people are randomly assigned to one treatment condition rather than another. Such statistical methods are derived on the assumption that the scores of the two groups in hypothetical populations are normally distributed, and that it is meaningful to interpret performance of persons in each group as standard scores. However, there is really no need to actually compute such standard scores. These computations are contained in the context of the overall statistical methods. This is the case with most of the descriptive and inferential statistics that will be discussed in the pages ahead. Concepts concerning norms are crucial for understanding the methods, but there is no need to actually go through the mechanics of computing such norms.

It is necessary to actually compute statistical norms in comparing the scores of individuals with those in a normative sample. One example would be in a contrasted-groups design in which high- and low-anxiety students are compared in terms of how rapidly they learn a particular task. The only way to select the groups would be to administer a test of anxiety and then choose the students on the basis of scores obtained from a normative sample. A more frequently occurring instance is that of interpreting the results of scores on educational achievement tests. For example, a raw score of 94 made by a student on a reading achievement test is meaningless until it is compared with results obtained from a normative sample. In applied settings, where evaluations must be made of the performance of individuals, the actual computation and use of norms is highly essential.

SUMMARY

Raw scores seldom are directly meaningful before they are compared to some type of standard. There are two kinds of standards that are important in psychology and education. The first consists of standards based on values regarding expected levels of performance. A second type of standard, which concerns statistical comparisons, is more important for this book. Such statistical comparisons relate to how well individuals perform with respect to the average. There are two general statistical approaches to making such comparisons—with standard scores and with percentiles. Standard scores z are obtained by dividing deviation scores x by σ_x. This results in using the standard deviation as a measurement scale for deviation scores about the mean. As the name implies, standard scores convert all score distributions to a form in which direct comparisons can be made among them.

The interpretation of standard scores is facilitated if the distribution is approximately normal. The normal distribution is a mathematical equation which describes the characteristics of an idealized, smoothed frequency distribution. The percentages of individuals who lie in various regions of standard scores can be deduced from the equation for the normal distribution. This is useful in the development of norms and for interpretation of individual scores.

Direct information regarding the standing of individuals in a score distribution can be obtained from percentiles. Percentiles state the percentage of individuals who fall below a particular score in a distribution. Percentiles are more useful than standard scores for interpreting the standing of individuals; standard scores are more useful than percentiles for averaging results from various tests and for performing other types of statistical analyses.

Both standard scores and percentiles are meaningful only to the extent to which they are derived from a specified sample of persons from a particular population. Some of the ways of specifying such samples are with respect to geographic regions, vocation, age groups, grade levels, and others. The choice of normative groups depends upon the research issues being investigated.

EXERCISES

Study Questions

1   What are the two major types of standards employed in interpreting measurement scores? Why is one intimately involved in statistics and the other not?

2   Why are deviation scores more easily interpreted than raw scores?

3   Because the normal distribution is purely a mathematical curve, why is it important with respect to actual distributions of measurements obtained in research? If a frequency distribution of actual data resembles a normal distribution, how does this provide useful information about research results?

4   What are the advantages of employing standard scores rather than deviation scores?

5   What are the mean and standard deviation of a set of standard scores? What is the variance?

6   How do percentiles relate to (a) standard scores and (b) scores based on ranks?

7   Why must care be used in comparing percentile scores based on a relatively small number of persons?

8   Standard scores and percentile scores provide essentially the same information. What are the circumstances in which one proves more useful than the other?

9   Why is it important to know the reference group from which standard scores are computed? Mention some misinterpretations that could be made by employing an incorrect reference group.

10   List and describe some major ways of obtaining norms, for example, the way in which reference groups are formed. Also, mention how each of these is useful in certain circumstances.

11   In what circumstances is it highly essential to have carefully obtained norms, and in what other circumstances is the gathering of norms not an important matter?

Problems

1 On an arithmetic test, Johnny made a score of 85. The mean for the class was 78.2, with a standard deviation of 8.5. What was Johnny's standard score? Approximately what percent of students scored lower, in other words, what was the approximate percentile score?

2 On the same test described in Problem 1, Mary made a score of 64. What was Mary's standard score? What was Mary's approximate percentile score?

The following IQ scores were obtained for students entering an auto mechanics class at a state vocational school

Bill	105	Bob	100	Steve	110
John	96	William	103	Keith	99
Eddie	92	Bruce	98	Joe	103
Frank	100	Tom	91	Jeff	91
Ralph	90	Don	102	Scott	104

3 Convert the above raw scores to (a) deviation scores and (b) standard scores.

4 Using the cumulative normal probabilites in Appendix B-4, convert all of the IQs in standard score form to approximate percentile scores.

5 Transform standard scores for the IQs into distributions that have (a) a mean of 100 and a standard deviation of 15 and (b) a mean of 500 and a standard deviation of 100.

SUGGESTED ADDITIONAL READINGS

Anastasi, A. *Psychological testing*, 3d ed. New York: Macmillan, 1968, Chap. 3.

Cronbach, L. J. *Essentials of psychological testing*, 3d ed. New York: Harper & Row, 1970, Chap. 4.

Guilford, J. P., and B. Fruchter. *Fundamental statistics in psychology and education*, 5th ed. New York: McGraw-Hill, 1973, Chap. 19.

7

Correlational Analysis

The discussion in Chapters 5 and 6 mainly concerned the application of descriptive statistics to individual variables. Thus, the mean test score for a group of students in mathematics concerns mathematics only and does not necessarily relate to any other variable. The percentage of people who say that they will vote for Jones rather than Smith in an election relates to the variable concerning choice of candidates and to nothing else. The standard deviation of errors for college students in a study of verbal learning concerns the variable of learning rate and nothing else. As with most of the other descriptive statistics discussed so far in this book, they concerned univariate relationships. Such measures are very useful for understanding performance on particular measures; however, science is more broadly concerned with relationships among variables rather than with variables in isolation from one another.

Investigations are spoken of as *univariate, bivariate,* or *multivariate*, based on the number of variables that are involved. Numerous examples have been given in previous chapters of univariate relationships, for example, the computation of the standard deviation for scores on a spelling test. The essence of scientific research is to find out essentially what goes together. Two broad approaches are used for this purpose. First, there is the *experimental method*, in which the investigator "causes" changes in a dependent variable(s) by manipulation of an independent variable(s). Numerous examples of such manipulations have been given in previous chapters, for example, manipulating the amount of practice and discovering the effect on the amount of learning of word meanings.

Second, and complementary to the use of the experimental method is the *observational method*, in which the experimenter does not bring about changes in an independent variable; rather, he observes the natural differences among people that exist in everyday life. Some examples are as follows: A large number of students across the country are given achievement tests in reading comprehension and mathematics. The investigator performs statistical analyses to determine the extent to which students who are high in mathematical ability also are high in reading ability. The athletic coach at a high school puts his 50 volunteers through their paces on sprints, long-distance runs, pole vaults, high jumps, and other athletic activities. He wonders to what extent some students tend to perform well in all of these activities as compared to other students who tend to perform poorly in the athletic activities. An educational researcher is investigating the relationship between years of schooling of the father and grades that students make in school. All of these represent examples of an observational approach to the answer of scientific questions, in which the experimenter really does not manipulate the variables. Indeed, in many research problems, it is meaningless to talk of which is the independent and which is the dependent variable. For example, is the arithmetic test or the reading comprehension test the independent variable in the previously mentioned investigation? However, when there is a definite direction in which predictions go, it is helpful to think in terms of independent and dependent variables. This would be the case in using a predictor test to estimate some type of success in daily life.

The observational approach is intimately related to the study of individual differences among people rather than to the manipulation of independent variables in an experiment. Such observational studies are said to concern corelationships or *correlations*, because literally they are concerned with the extent to which people are ordered alike on two or more variables. It can be said that the correlation is high if the students who make very high scores in mathematics also make very high scores in reading comprehension, and vice versa for students who make low scores in mathematics. In contrast, if the students who make very high scores in mathematics scatter all over in reading comprehension, then it can be said that the correlation between the two variables is low. Observational studies of this kind depend heavily on a particular type of statistical analysis, namely that of *correlational analysis*. Correlational analysis can be used to answer some very complex questions regarding the nature of individual differences among people, such as the extent to which ten tests of intellectual ability measure the same trait. This chapter and the following chapter will discuss some of the fundamental principles of correlational analysis (see Suggested Additional Readings at the end of the chapter for a discussion of more complex methods of correlational analysis).

Consistent Mathematical Relationships

In contrast to statistics, pure mathematics is internally neat because all relationships are entirely consistent. An example is the following equation

$$Y = aX + b$$

A graphic expression of this equation is shown in Figure 7-1. All of the points

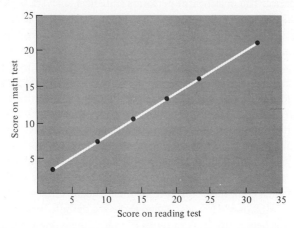

Figure 7-1. A hypothetically consistent relationship between scores on a reading test and scores on a math test.

lie neatly on a straight line, and there are no inconsistencies. Table 7-1 illustrates a perfect relationship of this kind for the scores of six students on a test in mathematics and a test in reading comprehension.

Inconsistent Mathematical Relationships

In contrast to the entirely consistent relationship shown in Figure 7-1, a much more typical set of actual data is shown in Figure 7-2, where the scores of a dozen students on a mathematics test and a spelling test are plotted. In Figure 7-2, the points do not lie neatly on a straight line, but they scatter around the line which serves to depict the general trend. (How the best-fit line is drawn will be discussed later in this chapter.) Because of the tendency for points to scatter about the trend line, figures depicting such data are referred to as *scatter diagrams.* The major questions posed by correlational analysis are (1) how closely are points

Table 7-1. Hypothetical Scores for Six Students on Two Tests

Student	Reading	Math
Joe	7	2
Susan	12	4
Connie	22	8
Pat	37	14
Steve	17	6
Charles	27	10

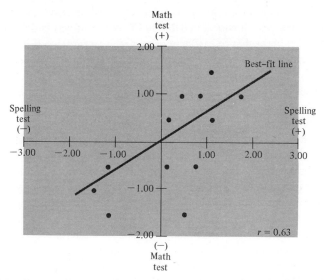

Figure 7-2. Scatter diagram of the data in Table 7-2 in standard score form.

packed about the best-fit straight line? and (2) how is the line drawn which best summarizes the relationship?

THE PRODUCT-MOMENT CORRELATION COEFFICIENT

A measure of correlation which is invaluable in the behavioral sciences will now be described. The first step in developing this measure depends upon the recognition that the similarity between raw scores people make on different variables in the behavioral sciences is highly artifactual. If comparisons of scores on two tests are being made, then the sizes of the raw scores depend to a large extent on the number of items on the two tests. If one test has 80 items and the other has 20 items, then one would expect to find much larger scores on the former test than the latter. The sizes of scores also depend on the difficulty of the items. If items on the arithmetic test are very difficult and those on the spelling test are very easy, this will change the relative sizes of scores on the two tests. Thus, average scores and standard deviations of scores tend to be artifacts of the way in which instruments are constructed in the behavioral sciences. This is also the case when measurements concern the results of experiments on people or lower animals rather than test scores. In comparing milligrams of a particular drug administered to rats and the number of errors made in running a maze, for example, the two variables would obviously be on extremely different numerical scales, and their means and standard deviations would be very different.

For the reasons mentioned, the most sensible measure of correlation is one that *relativizes* scores before comparisons are made. The relativity of scores in the behavioral sciences was discussed in detail in Chapter 6. It was said there that the two most sensible approaches to casting scores in relative form are through the computation of percentiles and standard scores. For correlational analysis, it proves much more useful to work with standard scores than with percentiles. This is purely a mathematical convenience that does not imply the superiority of one method of transforming test scores as opposed to others.

Questions regarding the relationship between two variables are answered by what is called the *product-moment* (PM) correlation coefficient. First the computational details will be described, and then the meaning of the coefficient will be discussed in detail. The computations are illustrated in Table 7-2. Deviations about the mean of any variable are referred to as *moments*. Since standard scores are deviations about the mean, then by definition they are moments about the mean. Moments prove useful in many complex statistical developments, but all that is necessary for the reader to understand here is how the term product-moment became part of the name of the correlation coefficient. The correlation consists of the mean product of these moments. The necessary calculations are illustrated in Table 7-2, which shows the scores of 12 students on two tests. A scatter diagram of this data was shown in Figure 7-2. The first two columns of numbers represent

Table 7-2. Computation of r from Hypothetical Scores on a Spelling Test (X) and a Math Test (Y)

| | Raw score | | | Standard scores | | |
Student	X	Y	z_x		z_y	$z_x \times z_y$
A	2	2	-1.47	X	-1.04	= 1.53
B	3	3	-1.15	X	-0.54	= 0.62
C	3	1	-1.15	X	-1.54	= 1.77
D	4	6	-0.83	X	0.96	= -0.80
E	5	1	-0.51	X	-1.54	= 0.79
F	6	5	-0.19	X	0.46	= -0.09
G	7	3	0.13	X	-0.54	= -0.07
H	8	6	0.46	X	0.96	= 0.44
I	9	3	0.78	X	-0.54	= -0.42
J	10	5	1.10	X	0.46	= 0.51
K	10	7	1.10	X	1.46	= 1.61
L	12	6	1.74	X	0.96	= 1.67
					$\Sigma(z_x z_y)$ =	7.56

$$r = \frac{\Sigma(z_x z_y)}{N}$$

$$= \frac{7.56}{12}$$

$$= 0.63$$

the raw scores obtained. The first step in computing the PM correlation coefficient is to convert the raw scores in each column into standard scores, employing the equations designed for that purpose. The results are shown in the third and fourth columns of numbers labeled z_x and z_y respectively. Each pair of standard scores is multiplied. Thus, student A has standard scores on the two tests of -1.47 and -1.04. The product of these is 1.53. Such products for all 12 students are shown in the fifth column of numbers. The next step is to sum the products of standard scores. The sum in this case is 7.56, which is shown at the bottom of the fifth column of numbers. The PM coefficient r is the arithmetic mean of this sum. Consequently the sum is divided by the number of subjects N, or 12 in this case. This results in a correlation of 0.63. It is customary to refer to the PM correlation coefficient as r, and to use other alphabetical letters for different measures of correlation.

Statistical Properties of r

The PM correlation coefficient r is referred to as a least-squares statistic. This principle was mentioned in Chapter 5 with respect to the arithmetic mean. The principle of least-squares applies to the PM coefficient in the sense that the best-fit line which depends on r minimizes the sum of squared deviates or points in the scatter diagram. Such deviates can be seen by looking at Figure 7-2. Some points are far above the line vertically and others are far below the line vertically. Other points are barely above the line vertically, and others are barely below the line vertically. The distance of each point above or below the line represents a deviate in the vertical plane. In correlational analysis these deviates are best visualized with respect to standard scores on the two variables, as illustrated in Figure 7-2. The size of each deviate in standard score units can be determined by subtracting the distance from the line to that point. This can be done quite simply by using a ruler to measure how far above or below the line any point is with respect to the Y axis. Thus in terms of standard scores, a point may be near the best-fit line or either far above or below the line. The PM coefficient works with the squares of such deviates above and below the line and leads to a best-fit line which minimizes the sum of these squared deviates. This can be illustrated if the reader will imagine that the best-fit line is the pointer stick on a spin-wheel game. Then the line could be spun about in circles. Wherever the line stops spinning, it would be possible to compute a set of squared deviates about the line. No matter where the line landed in such a hypothetical game, the sum of squared deviates would be larger than that determined by r unless by chance it happened to land on precisely the same place as the best-fit line which can be calculated by the use of r (discussed later in the chapter).

The characteristics of r are known from mathematical derivations in calculus. From these derivations, it is found that the best-fitting straight line drawn in a diagram of standard scores should have two properties. First, it should go through the mean (zero point) of both variables. Secondly, it should have a slope equal to r. This is shown in Figure 7-2. The best-fitting straight line shown in Figure 7-2 has a slope of 0.63. To predict standard scores in mathematics from standard scores scores in spelling as indicated in Table 7-2, the scores in spelling were multiplied by the correlation coefficient (0.63). This procedure can be stated in a simple equation

$$z'_y = rz_x$$

where z'_y = predictions of standard scores in mathematics, z_x = actual standard scores in spelling, and r = the PM correlation between z_x and z_y.
When the correlation coefficient is used to predict one variable from another, the equation is referred to as a *regression* equation. Such equations will be discussed in detail in a subsequent section of this chapter.

Limits of the Correlation Coefficient

Although r is useful in predicting one set of scores from another and in developing many other statistics, its major value is in describing the degree of relationship between two variables. No matter what the means and standard deviations of raw scores for the two variables are, r relates to a standard scale for specifying the degree of correlation, which can be directly interpreted regardless of the nature of the raw scores. The size of r ranges from 1.00 through 0 to -1.00. Thus the PM correlation cannot be greater than 1.00 or less than -1.00. Why this is so can be seen from simple verbal computation. The computational example in Table 7-2 shows that the maximum correspondence between z_x and z_y would occur if z_x were paired directly with itself, or z_y were paired directly with itself. In other words, one would be computing the correlation coefficient on two identical sets of data. The first step in the calculations in this process would be to multiply each standard score by itself. These squared standard scores would then be summed and divided by the number of scores. This is exactly the equation for the variance of any measure placed in the form of standard scores

$$\frac{\Sigma z_x^2}{N}$$

As the reader will recall from Chapter 6, the variance and standard deviation of any set of standard scores necessarily is 1.00. Obviously then, the PM correlation can never be greater than 1.00.

A similar line of argument demonstrates why r can never be less than -1.00. The strongest inverse (negative) relationship between two variables can be illustrated in the situation in which standard scores on one measure are paired with the negatives of those same standard scores. Then all positive standard scores in one column of the computations would be opposite in sign to those in the other column. Positive standard scores on one measure would correspond with negative standard scores on the other measure. The sum of products would be the same, in an absolute sense, as it would in the case where a correlation of 1.00 existed, but the sum would be negative in sign. Obviously then, it is not possible to have a negative r less than -1.00.

Correlations between 1.00 and -1.00 signify different degrees of relationship. An r of 0.00 means that there is no consistent relationship at all between the two variables. In that case, the points would spread randomly all over the scatter diagram and there would be no way of predicting one variable from the other any better than tossing dice or using another random procedure. Positive correlations mean that people tend to be ordered somewhat alike on the two variables. Negative correlations mean that people who make high scores on one variable tend to make low scores on another variable. The size of the correlation provides a handy descriptive index for the degree of relationship. Thus, a correlation of 0.70 means a stronger positive relationship than a correlation of 0.50, and a correlation of 0.50 means a stronger positive relationship than one of 0.25. Details regarding the precise meaning of sizes of r will be discussed subsequently.

CORRELATION ANALYSIS WITH DEVIATION SCORES AND RAW SCORES

Computational Methods

Although the equation for the correlation coefficient r in Table 7-2 is relatively easy to understand, it is not the easiest approach to computing the correlation. It requires a considerable amount of work to calculate standard scores and related statistics over several hundred persons rather than over only the 12 persons shown in Table 7-2. Such computations are facilitated by the use of equations for the correlation coefficient based on deviation scores or on raw scores. Some manipulations of the basic equation will show how this is done

$$r = \frac{\Sigma z_x z_y}{N} \tag{7-1}$$

It should be remembered that a standard score z_x equals a deviation score x divided by the standard deviation σ_x. Consequently Equation (7-1) could be transformed to

$$r = \frac{\Sigma(x/\sigma_x)(y/\sigma_y)}{N}$$

This same equation can be evolved in two steps to obtain Equation (7-2)

$$r = \frac{\Sigma xy}{N\sigma_x \sigma_y}$$

$$r = \frac{\Sigma xy}{\sqrt{\Sigma x^2} \sqrt{\Sigma y^2}} \tag{7-2}$$

Equation (7-2) can be used to compute the correlation coefficient from deviation scores. Next we can replace each x value in Equation (7-2) by $X - M_x$ and each y value by $Y - M_y$ to obtain the following raw-score equation

$$r = \frac{N\Sigma XY - (\Sigma X)(\Sigma Y)}{\sqrt{N\Sigma X^2 - (\Sigma X)^2} \sqrt{N\Sigma Y^2 - (\Sigma Y)^2}} \qquad (7\text{-}3)$$

It must be remembered that the correlation coefficient specifies the relationship between two sets of standard scores. Either the computations begin with standard scores as in Equation (7-1), or the standardizing is done in the computations as in Equations (7-2) and (7-3). These three equations will give exactly the same numerical value for the correlation coefficient. Thus, if the correlation is found to be 0.48 with one of the equations, it also will be 0.48 with any of the other equations for r. Although Equation (7-3) looks complicated, it is actually the easiest way to obtain the correlation coefficient if either an automatic desk calculator or a high-speed computer is available.

Prediction Equations

Prediction equations relating to the best-fit line in correlational analysis are useful for many practical problems in psychology and education, and are often referred to as regression equations. Predicting grade averages in college from a scholastic aptitude test is based on this type of equation. How such predictions are made was illustrated previously in terms of standard scores. Not only is it easier to compute the correlation coefficient from deviation scores and raw scores, but also it is often convenient to form the prediction (regression) equation from deviation scores and raw scores. The prediction equation specifies how the best-fit line is drawn.

The standard-score equation

$$z_y{}' = rz_x \qquad (7\text{-}4)$$

can be converted to the deviation-score equation

$$y' = r\frac{\sigma_y}{\sigma_x}x \qquad (7\text{-}5)$$

where y' = estimated deviation score on criterion (grades), x = actual deviation score on predictor (vocabulary), r = correlation between predictor and criterion, σ_y = standard deviation of criterion, and σ_x = standard deviation of predictor. Equation (7-5) could be used to predict students' deviation scores in college grades from their deviation scores on a vocabulary test. An example would be in the situation where a student has a vocabulary deviation score of 3.0 and the correlation is 0.50. If the standard deviations for vocabulary and grades are 2.0 and 1.0, respectively, the prediction is calculated as follows

$$y' = 0.50 \times \frac{1.0}{2.0} \times 3.0$$
$$= 0.25 \times 3$$
$$= 0.75$$

The prediction is that he will be 0.75 deviation-score units above the mean of grade averages. Let us say that he actually makes a deviation score of 1.25 in grades and that the prediction is therefore in error by 0.50 deviation-score units.

The prediction equation can also be expressed in raw-score terms

$$Y' = r \frac{\sigma_y}{\sigma_x} (X - M_x) + M_y \qquad (7\text{-}6)$$

where Y' = estimated raw score on criterion (school grades), X = actual raw score on predictor test (vocabulary), σ_y = standard deviation of criterion, σ_x = standard deviation of predictor, M_y = mean of raw criterion scores, and M_x = mean of raw predictor scores.

Although Equation (7-6) looks complicated, it is a straightforward extension of Equations (7-4) and (7-5). Equation (7-6) might predict that a person with a raw vocabulary score of 20 will make a raw grade average of 2.6.

Equations (7-5) and (7-6) can both be used to plot best-fit lines. Equation (7-5) would be used if deviation scores are plotted, and Equation (7-6) would be used if raw scores are plotted. The correlation coefficient and the three prediction equations given are the basic statistical procedures needed for the validation and use of predictor tests. The equations are also useful for many other problems concerning the estimation of one measure from another.

Of course, the correlation coefficient is not used to predict grade averages that are already known, but to forecast the grade averages of incoming freshmen. If subsequent groups of incoming freshmen are of about the same caliber as their predecessors, the correlation between vocabulary and later grades will be approximately the same. Therefore, it is safe to use the first correlation to forecast the grade averages of incoming freshmen, but only if the correlation had been obtained on a large and representative sample of students for which the prediction equation will be employed. If the sample was biased, then the obtained correlation coefficient would not be accurate in predicting grade averages from the vocabulary tests for subsequent groups of students. An example of such bias would be the case where the correlation coefficient was computed on a special group of gifted students who were being given scholarships rather than on a representative sample of incoming freshmen as a whole. Even if the correlation coefficient were based on a reasonably unbiased sample, it might not provide the proper prediction equation if this sample consisted of only a relatively small number of subjects (for instance, less than several hundred students). As with all descriptive statistics, there is some sampling error associated with the correlation coefficient, a matter which will be discussed in more detail later in this chapter.

The Symmetric Nature of the PM Correlation

It should be apparent that the correlation between any variable X and any other variable Y is symmetric in the sense that their relationship goes both ways. One could phrase the problem as how much an arithmetic test correlates with a spelling test or how much a spelling test correlates with an arithmetic test and arrive at exactly the same correlation coefficient. This can be seen by looking at the computational examples in Table 7-2. Obviously, the obtained coefficient of 0.63 would be exactly the same if the columns of standard scores were switched in their left-right positions. Also, the same correlation coefficient would be used in predicting z_x from z_y as illustrated previously in predicting z_y from z_x. [See Equation (7-4).] The equation would then be

$$z'_x = rz_y$$

The deviation score equation would appear much like that shown in Equation (7-5), but all y's would be substituted for x's and vice versa

$$x' = r\frac{\sigma_x}{\sigma_y}y$$

INTERPRETATION OF PM CORRELATION

Is a correlation of 0.78 high or low? What is a high relationship depends on the situation in which the correlation coefficient is being used. One way to think about the meaning of the correlation coefficient is in terms of the amount of scatter shown when the two sets of scores are presented graphically, as in Figure 7-2. Although it was convenient to use the scores of only 12 students to illustrate the correlation problem, it would actually be rather meaningless to apply correlational analysis to so small a group. In most important correlational problems, there are at least 100 students involved, and in some studies more than 1,000.

Correlation and Amount of Scatter

Figure 7-3 shows a typical scatter diagram relating the scores on an English achievement test to scores on a mathematics achievement test. If there were a perfect correlation between the two tests, all the points would fall exactly on the best-fit line, and there would be no scatter about the line. The more the scatter, the less correlation between the two tests. Figure 7-3 shows the amount of scatter when the correlation is 0.67. Even though it is a relatively high correlation in terms of what is often found, it can be seen that some students are real exceptions to the general trend of correspondence. Some students do very well in English and only average in mathematics. Some are only average in English and superior in mathematics.

The wider the scatter of the points about the best-fit line, the lower the correlation. When the points tend to pack tightly about the line, the correlation is high. When the points spread all over the graph and there is no visible trend of correspondence, the correlation is near zero.

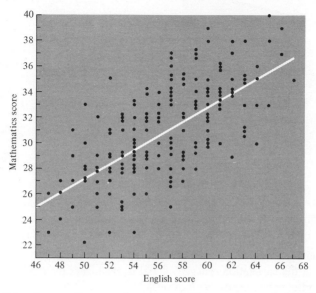

Figure 7-3. Scatter diagram of scores on achievement tests in English and mathematics.

It is easy to picture what the scatter diagram will look like as the correlation becomes larger and larger: the area of scatter will become progressively more narrow. This progressive narrowing can be seen in Figure 7-4. The three "boxes" shown in Figure 7-4 indicate the areas in which most of the points would lie for three different-sized correlations. Actually, the zones of scatter would tend to appear more like footballs of different thickness rather than boxes, but it simplifies matters to picture the amount of scatter as is done in Figure 7-4. The narrower the box on the vertical axis, the smaller would be the errors in predicting criterion scores from scores on the predictor. With a correlation of only 0.25, the box is quite "fat," and points in the scatter diagram would scatter nearly as much as possible. With a correlation of 0.70, the box would be rather "thin," and points would be confined to a comparatively small part of the possible space.

Negative Correlations

A negative correlation has the same implications regarding amount of scatter as a positive correlation of the same size. The only difference is that the best-fit line slants downward going from left to right on the graph, rather than upward, as when a positive correlation exists. A negative correlation is illustrated in Figure 7-5, which shows the relationship between a measure of interest in art and a meas-

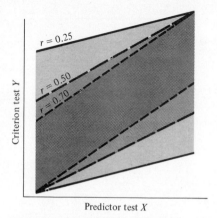

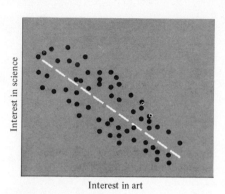

Figure 7-4. Areas of scatter for
different-sized correlations.

Figure 7-5. Negative correlation based
on the relationship between interest in
art and interest in science.

ure of interest in science. Because the two types of interests tend to be somewhat
antithetical, the correlation is negative, that is, the higher the interest in art, the
lower the interest in science and vice versa.

In many cases, the sign of the correlation is arbitrarily determined by the way
in which tests are scored. For example, a negative correlation would be expected
between the number of *errors* in a spelling test and the number of *correct* answers
in a mathematics test. Then, by reframing the problem as one of relating accuracy
in spelling (rather than errors) to accuracy in mathematics, the sign of the correlation will be reversed, or, a correlation of -0.72 would become 0.72.

Important Uses of *r*

In addition to serving as a very useful index of correspondence, correlational analysis provides a number of other important statistics. The best-fit line, which summarizes the trend of relationship, has already been mentioned. In addition, estimates can be made of the amount of error entailed in forecasting scores on one
measure from scores on another [see Nunnally (1970), pp. 86-90].

One important use of the correlation coefficient is in determining the predictive validity of aptitude tests. In a typical problem, the test is used to select students for an accelerated program of study in high school. Because the test is being used to serve a prediction function, the validity with which that function is
served is determined by correlating test results with a criterion. In this case, the
criterion would probably be grade-point averages earned in the special curriculum.
Of course, it would be necessary to wait one or more years after the test was administered in order to obtain the grade-point averages. Each student then has a
pair of scores, one on the predictor test and a grade-point average. The correlation
equations can be applied.

Another important use of correlational analysis in studies of predictive validity is with respect to college aptitude tests. Each year, millions of high school students are required to take college aptitude tests as part of the admissions requirements of colleges and universities. As predictor tests, their validity depends upon the extent to which test scores are predictive of overall grades earned later in higher education. Most typically, test scores are correlated with grade-point averages earned over four years of college.

Table 7-3 displays some typical correlations between predictor tests and various criteria of academic achievement. For example, the high correlation of 0.84 between the Academic Promise Test and the Stanford Achievement Test is what is typically found between a measure of scholastic aptitude and a comprehensive measure of achievement in the elementary grades.

The correlation coefficient is also important in psychological and educational research. As a simple example, it might be of interest to study the correspondence between muscular coordination and intelligence. Scores from a coordination test could be correlated with scores from an intelligence test. Another example would be in correlating school grades with amount of time students study. Thousands of such correlations have been computed in order to learn about psychological and educational processes.

Returning now to the primary question of "What is a high correlation?" the best guide is to compare correlations with those which are usually obtained when carefully composed tests are compared. Correlations between tests given at different times in the same class, say, American history, would be expected to be at least 0.50 but probably not higher than 0.80. Correlations between achievement

Table 7-3. Sample Predictive Validity Coefficients

Test	Criterion	Coefficient
Academic Promise Test—grade 6	Stanford Achievement Test score (battery median)	0.84
Differential Aptitude Test—Verbal Reasoning Test (administered in grade 2)	College grade-point average	0.52
Lee-Clark Reading-Readiness Test	Teacher ratings of ability to read at end of year	0.51
Metropolitan Readiness Test	Stanford Achievement Test—primary battery: Word-reading score Arithmetic	0.63 0.67
School and College Ability Test—total score for grade 5	Grade-point average—grade 5	0.68

test results and intelligence test scores run about 0.75 or higher. Two forms of a carefully constructed, commercially distributed test (such as two forms of an intelligence test) would probably correlate at or above 0.90.

Correlations between predictor tests and their criteria are usually lower than those mentioned. A typical reading-readiness test given to entering first-grade students would be expected to correlate about 0.60 with reading achievement grades at the end of the first grade. Intelligence tests and comprehensive achievement tests used to select students for honors programs and other accelerated curricula in high schools would be expected to correlate around 0.70 with overall grade-point averages. Scholastic aptitude tests used to select students for college would be expected to correlate around 0.55 with grade averages in college. Personality tests do not tend to correlate as well with school criteria as ability tests do. For example, a correlation of 0.30 between a test of social adjustment and school grades would probably be considered an interesting finding.

Correlations found in psychological and educational research tend to be even smaller than those in measuring predictive validity. For example, one would expect only rather low correlations, if any, between muscular coordination and intelligence, and between grades and amount of time spent in study. Such variables are quite complex, and it is unreasonable to expect high correlations among them. The major question at issue is whether there is a perceptible correlation. In this context, correlations as low as 0.20 are often quite interesting, and correlations as high as 0.30 or 0.40 are sometimes considered major findings.

CAUTIONS IN THE USE OF PM CORRELATION

In order for the reader to properly work with PM correlational analysis or interpret the results of others, a number of cautions should be heeded. Some of the major cautions will be discussed in this section and expanded upon in the next chapter.

Correlation and Causation

The correlation coefficient is not necessarily a measure of *causation*. For example, there is a positive correlation between the number of books in homes and the grades of students. It would be wrong to conclude from this that students make better grades because books are in the home. In well-to-do homes there are more books, typewriters, baths, golf clubs—more everything. Poor students would probably not make better grades (or not much better) if books were placed in their homes, and good students would not lower their grades appreciably if the books were removed from their homes. But even if correlations do not necessarily measure causation, they provide many clues to causative connections (using the word "cause" to mean necessary and sufficient conditions, for example, to bring about good grades).

Sampling Error

Like any other statistic, the correlation coefficient computed on a particular set of scores is only an *estimate* of the "real" correlation. Suppose, for example, that you want to learn the correlation between the height and weight of all eighth-grade students in the United States. You would probably not measure the height and weight of that many students. Instead, you would probably measure a sample of them, say 500 students from schools across the country. The correlation found in the sample is of no importance in its own right. It is important only to the extent that it is an accurate estimate of the correlation that would be found if all the eighth-graders were measured and the correlation computed. Sampling error with respect to correlation coefficients will be discussed in detail in Chapter 10.

Precision of Estimates

Even if a correlation coefficient is statistically significant, this does not mean that it is of a sufficient size to permit precise estimates of scores on one variable from scores on the other variable. A scatter diagram in which the correlation is 0.67 was shown in Figure 7-3. That is a rather high correlation in terms of what is found in most research in psychology and education. However, looking at that scatter diagram, it is easy to see that people with the same predicted score on the mathematics test vary considerably in terms of scores that they actually make. Even with much higher correlations, there is a considerable band of error about the regression line.

Correlation and Experimentation

Finally, it should be reiterated in this chapter that correlational analysis is a companion to, but not a substitute for controlled experimentation. If, for example, a strong positive correlation is found between certain types of home characteristics and grades in school, this suggests that some of those characteristics are determining the differences in grades. Whenever possible, such investigations should always be followed up with attempts to manipulate the underlying variables. For instance, if it is thought that certain types of richness of intellectual stimulation are contributing to the correlation, then it would be wise to try to manipulate these differences in controlled experiments. Only by a wedding of correlational analysis with controlled experimentation can a complete science of behavior eventually be realized.

SUMMARY

Descriptive statistics can be classified as to whether they concern univariate relations, bivariate relations, or multivariate relations. Univariate descriptive statistics were discussed extensively in previous chapters. Examples are the mean, standard deviation, and percentiles. Bivariate relations concern the extent to which two variables correspond or correlate. An introduction to the study of bivariate relationships is presented in this chapter and continues in the following chapter. Multivariate relations concern the extent to which three or more variables correspond or correlate with one another in various combinations, a topic beyond the scope of this book.

Examples of bivariate relations are those between a test of college aptitude and grade-point average in college, between a measure of intelligence and differences among subjects in performance in an experiment on perceptual recognition, and between motor coordination and reading performance in the elementary grades. Such bivariate relations concern the degree of correlation between individual differences on two measures.

In selecting a measure of correlation, it is important to realize that the absolute sizes of raw scores on the two variables are artifacts of the way measurement methods are developed. It is useful to conceptualize the problem in terms of relativized scores. For the sake of mathematical convenience, it is best to reduce the problem conceptually to that of comparing standard scores on two measures. A measure of correlation with respect to such sets of standard scores—called the product-moment (PM) correlation coefficient—has proven very useful. It is symbolized as r. Quite simply, it consists of the average product of standard scores on the two measures. All that is necessary to compute r is to (1) multiply the two standard scores for each person, (2) add these over the number of persons, and (3) divide the total by the number of persons.

As a descriptive statistic of correlation, r ranges between 1.00 and – 1.00, depending on the degree of correlation. An r of 1.00 means a perfect correlation; an r of 0.00 means that the correlation is no better than expected by chance; and an r of – 1.00 means a perfect negative correlation between the two variables being investigated. Most correlations range somewhere between either 0.00 and 1.00 or 0.00 and – 1.00. The meaning of any size correlation is relative to what can reasonably be expected in the research problem and the size of the correlations typically found in the past. Thus, what would be considered a disappointingly low correlation in one type of research problem would be an encouragingly high correlation in another research problem.

In addition to serving as a very useful descriptive statistic for bivariate relationships, the correlation coefficient enters into the development of many other descriptive and inferential statistics. Regarding descriptive statistics, one of the most important uses of r is in developing equations for predicting one variable from another (sometimes referred to as regression equations). Such prediction equations allow one to place a best-fit line in the scatter diagram depicting the relationship between two variables. The line is "best-fit" in that it minimizes the sum of squared departures of points above and below the line. Such prediction equations can be used in forecasting success of students in college based on the results from scholastic aptitude tests, and to make predictions in other applied settings.

PM correlation should be considered in the context of a number of cautions. First, correlation does not necessarily mean causation. It is easy to think of numerous examples in which two variables correlate highly, not because either is causing the other, but because they incidentally relate strongly to a third variable. Second, as is true with all descriptive statistics, the actual r found in any study is not important in its own right, but only to the extent to which it correctly mirrors the r that would be obtained from a whole population of people. If the sample on which r is based is biased in one way or another, the obtained r will be misleading no matter how many persons are involved in the study. Even if the sample is reasonably unbiased, then there will be considerable sampling error if N is small, for instance, no more than 100 subjects. Third, it is necessary to consider the the precision with which a correlation of a particular size allows one to make estimates of one variable from another. Even when the correlation is higher than that found in most studies (say, 0.70 or higher), there is still considerable scatter about the best-fit line. Rather low correlations may be important with respect to issues in basic research, but unless correlations are quite high, they leave much room for error in predicting performance in applied settings. Fourth, it is important to realize that correlational studies are companions to, but not substitutes for controlled experimentation. Correlational studies provide hints that can be followed up in many cases by controlled experiments. The two approaches constitute useful companions for a complete behavioral science.

EXERCISES

Study Questions

1   Briefly explain the difference between univariate and multivariate relationships. Give an example of each.

2   Why is there a need for correlational analysis in psychology and education? Consider the nature of consistent and inconsistent relationships.

3   Although there are computing formulas that employ raw scores or deviation scores, correlational analysis is basically concerned with the correspondence between two sets of standard scores. Why is it necessary to conceptualize correlational analysis in terms of the correspondence between two sets of standard scores?

4   What are the two major questions posed by correlational analysis? What do the answers to these questions indicate about the data?

5   Explain why a correlation may never be above +1.00 or below −1.00.

6   If variable A correlates 1.00 with variable B, can it be said that variable A causes variable B? Why?

7   What does the sign (+ or -) of a correlation indicate? Give examples of situations in which one might expect to find one rather than the other.

8   Give at least two examples of situations in which prediction (regression) equations based on the correlation coefficient would be useful.

9   How is the size of the correlation coefficient related to the amount of scatter in the graph of relationship between two variables? Draw outlines of the scatter that you might expect for correlations of 0.20, 0.60, and 0.90.

10   What are some important cautions in the use of the correlation coefficient? Give at least one example (different from those in this chapter) of how failure to heed these cautions would result in misinterpretation of research results.

Problems

A school psychologist wishes to determine if IQ and grades are related in a small classroom. He has the following data from which to work

		IQ	Grade Average
	A	85	1.5
	B	90	1.1
	C	95	2.2
	D	100	2.7
Student	E	105	2.1
	F	110	3.1
	G	115	3.3
	H	120	2.7

1   Compute the correlation between IQ and grade averages. Obtain the correlation coefficient with Equations (7-1), (7-2), and (7-3).

2   Using Equation (7-6), compute the predicted grade average for each of the students.

3   Construct a scatter diagram for these data and draw in the regression line employing Equation (7-6).

SUGGESTED ADDITIONAL READINGS

Guilford, J. P., and B. Fruchter. *Fundamental statistics in psychology and education*, 5th ed. New York: McGraw-Hill, 1973, Chap. 6.

Hays, W. L. *Statistics for the social sciences,* 2d ed. New York: Holt, Rinehart and Winston, 1973, Chap. 15.

Nunnally, J. C. *Psychometric theory.* New York: McGraw-Hill, 1967, Chaps. 4 and 5.

8

Special Issues in Correlational Analysis

In Chapter 7, fundamental principles of PM correlational analysis were discussed. In order not to obscure those basic principles, some important auxillary issues were left for discussion in this chapter. First, PM correlational analysis was illustrated with approximately continuous variables, such as test scores in school topics. In many problems requiring correlational analysis, however, one or both of the variables is highly limited in terms of the number of different scores that can be obtained. For example, one variable may be measured on only two score points such as correct or incorrect on a test item, while the other variable might be measured on many score points such as total scores of students on a true-false test containing 100 items.

A second issue involves the extent to which the best-fitting straight line (using r) adequately describes the relationship between the two variables. The prediction (regression) equations given in Chapter 7 based on the PM correlation all produce *straight* lines, but it is not necessarily the case that a straight line is the most appropriate one for summarizing the relationship. There are many possible irregularities in the relationship that might either make the PM correlation inappropriate or require cautions in the intepretation of r.

A third issue concerns some of the factors that influence the size of r. For example, if the two variables have very differently shaped distributions of scores, this limits the possible size of r. These and other special issues concerning correlational analysis will be discussed in this chapter.

FACTORS THAT INFLUENCE THE SIZE OF THE PM COEFFICIENT

The size of the PM correlation can be misleading unless (1) the two distributions being correlated have similar shapes, and (2) the standard deviations of the two samples of scores are close in size to the standard deviations in the population as a whole.

Shapes of Distributions

The PM coefficient r cannot be as high as 1.00 or as low as – 1.00 unless the two distributions being correlated have exactly the same shape (mirror images of one another in the case of a negative correlation). More importantly, if the two distributions have very different shapes, the correlation will be lower than it would be if they had the same shape. This holds true regardless of the size of r in the latter instance. The most extreme example occurs when one of the variables is relatively *continuous* and the other one is *dichotomous*. Why there cannot be a perfect relationship between a dichotomous variable and a continuous variable is illustrated in Figure 8-1. For the dichotomous variable, all of the scores are on two points. To have a perfect correlation it would be necessary for all of the scores at those two points to fall exactly on two points of the other variable; however, since the other variable is continuous, this is not possible if scores are distributed widely over the continuum as in an approximately normal distribution. Consequently, scores at either of the two points on the dichotomous variable must correspond to a range of points on the continuous variable.

Figure 8-1 was composed in the following way. First, an approximately normal distribution of scores was obtained for the continuous variable. An example would be the distribution of scores on an intelligence test or the number of words correctly memorized in a study of human memory. Fifty percent of the scores were allocated to each of the two categories of a dichotomous variable, which is illustrated by passing or failing on some test item or other kind of performance. Scores on the continuous variable were placed into the pass and fail categories in such a way as to make the highest possible PM correlation. This was done quite simply by taking the top half of the people on the continuous variable and placing them in the pass category and likewise placing the lower half of the people into the fail category. Even though this is the best possible relationship that could be obtained, the points can be seen to scatter considerably.

Figure 8-1 illustrates the general principle that the sizes of correlations are restricted when the two variables have differently shaped distributions. Distributions can differ in shape not only when one of the two being compared has more possible data points, but even when they are both approximately continuous. For example, if one variable is highly skewed toward the high-score end and the other variable toward the low-score end, this will tend to limit the size of the correlation. This is illustrated in Figure 8-2. The variable X is highly skewed toward the

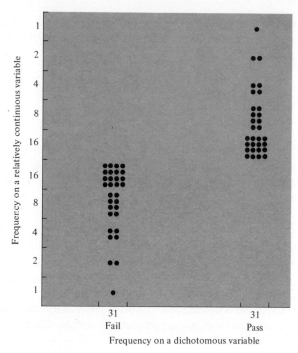

Figure 8-1. . Scatter diagram of the maximum possible correlation between a dichotomous variable with a 50-50 split of pass-fail and a variable with an approximately normal distribution.

low end, and the variable Y is highly skewed toward the high end. An effort was made to depict the highest correlation possible by pairing high scores on X with high scores on Y and vice versa for low scores. Why a perfect correlation is not possible is obvious when one tries to place the top eight people on X. For there to be a perfect correlation, all eight would have to lie at the highest level on Y. But since there are only two persons at the highest level on Y, it is necessary to place six of the eight persons at lower levels on Y. Not only is the correlation less than 1.00, but also the relationship is curvilinear, which is the usual accompaniment of correlating differently shaped distributions.

The restriction of the correlation depends on (1) how high the correlation would be if the distributions had the same shape and (2) how different in shape the distributions are. Regarding point 1, in an attempt to obtain a perfect correlation, differences in shapes of distributions have an effect regardless of the size of the correlation. Suppose, for example, two variables have the same-shaped distributions and the correlation is found to be 0.50. Also assume that the relationship is linear, in other words, the points cluster symmetrically about a straight line. If

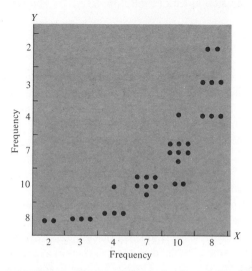

Figure 8-2. A scatter diagram for two differently shaped distributions of scores.

the form of one distribution is then artificially altered, the correlation tends to be less than 0.50. An example would be one in which the distribution is transformed by squaring each score. How much the correlation is lowered depends on the size of the correlation when the distributions are of the same shape. For a correlation of 1.00, a change in shape of one distribution might lower the correlation by 10 or 20 points. As the correlation between the same-shaped distributions becomes less and less, altering the shape of one distribution has less effect. Although no equations are available for forecasting the amount of change, experience indicates that changes in the shape of one distribution seldom alter a correlation of 0.50 by more than five points. For correlations of 0.30 or lower, even drastic changes in the shape of one distribution, for example, changing a normal distribution to one that is distinctly bimodal, tend to have very little effect. Thus, in most studies in psychology, results of correlational analysis would be much the same whether distributions were shaped similarly or differently. Correlations as high as 0.70 are rare, and the average of all correlations reported in the literature probably is less than 0.40.

Because it is known that altering the shape of one of two distributions has very little effect on moderately sized correlations, the investigator need not be compulsive about the precise resemblance of the two distributions being correlated. Unless the difference between the two distributions is so marked as to be obvious to the naked eye, the investigator can move securely ahead to correlational analysis. If one of the distributions is highly skewed or both are skewed in different directions, some transformations of the scores in the two distributions can be performed in such a way as to make the shapes of the distributions more compatible. [See discussion in Kirk (1968), pp. 63-67.]

Effect of Variation

The PM correlation concerns the extent to which two tests or other measures *covary*, that is, the extent to which the two measures rank order people the same in terms of scores. Consequently, only to the extent to which there is considerable variance in the two measures being compared can the correlation be large. The most extreme example occurs when all people make exactly the same score on the two measures. In that case there is no variation in either measure, and *r* perforce is 0. A slightly less extreme example is that of correlating the number of fingers that people have on their left hand with those that they have on their right hand. One could sample 1,000 people and actually obtain an *r* in this case. Although some people will have missing fingers, thus causing a tiny amount of overall variation, this variance is so small that *r* necessarily would be close to 0. High correlations can be obtained only when there is a large amount of variability in the measures being compared. There is nothing strange about this principle, because the idea of the correlation coefficient is to show the strength of relationship in accordance with the amount of variation that is present in the two measures.

Because the correlation coefficient tends to be influenced by the sizes of the standard deviations of the variables being compared, it is important that the standard deviations in the sample being investigated are approximately the same as those in the population to which the results will be generalized. This is done by obtaining a reasonably representative sample of subjects from the population in question. A good example is a predictor test which is being correlated with some measure of successful performance. This would be the case in correlating scores on a test of interest in engineering with grades subsequently made in a college of engineering. If the standard deviations of scores on the test and on grades are either less or more than they would be in the population as a whole (students in engineering colleges across the country), the correlation coefficient would then be either an under or overestimate respectively of the *r* which would be found in the population as a whole. [Some statistical corrections that can be made in this case are discussed in Guilford and Fruchter (1973).]

The influence of the standard deviation on test validity relates to an interesting and often misunderstood observation: intelligence tests become less successful predictors as higher educational levels are reached. The tests correlate around 0.70 with elementary school grades, 0.60 with high school grades, and 0.50 with college grades; in addition, they tend to correlate only slightly with the grades of students in graduate school. The reason for the progressive decline in validity is that the variation of intellectual ability is gradually being decreased. The less able students tend to be eliminated at each successive level of schooling. At the graduate school level, there is relatively little variation in intellectual ability. Tests can "commit suicide," if, as is often the case, they are used at various educational stages to determine who should continue in school or in some vocation. Theoretically, a test could reach the stage where it correlates 0 with the criterion which it has been so successful in predicting over the years. This situation is much like that of the physician who advises his patients so successfully on how to remain well that he finds himself with no ailments to treat.

IRREGULARITIES IN THE SCATTER DIAGRAM

In the previous chapter, PM correlation was illustrated with scatter diagrams that tend to fit neatly about a straight line. It is fortunate that this approximates the case in most basic research and applied work; however, since there is no reason that such neat relationships should occur, definite exceptions are sometimes found in practice. One type of irregularity was hinted at in the discussion of Figure 8-2, where it was shown that very differently shaped distributions not only limit the size of the correlation but lead to nonlinear (curvilinear) trends. Two major types of irregularities that occur in applying PM correlational analysis will now be discussed.

Homoscedasticity

In Chapter 7, it was mentioned that, unless the correlation is either +1.00 or −1.00, points will scatter above and below the best-fitting straight line. What was not mentioned there is that the amount of scatter may be greater at some points along the line than at others. An example of unequal variation is shown in Figure 8-3, which concerns the degree to which a predictor test actually is predictive of a criterion variable. The variation (scatter) about the best-fit line is considerably more at the higher end of the predictor test than at the lower end in Figure 8-3. *Scedasticity* means scatter or variation. Thus, if the variation is approximately the same all along the best-fitting straight line, relationship is said to be *homoscedastic*; if the variation is substantially different along the line, then the relationship is *heteroscedastic.*

If the relationship is heteroscedastic, substantially more precise predictions can be made at some points on the best-fitting straight lines than at others. This is illustrated in Figure 8-3. There would be much more precision in predicting criterion scores for persons who made low scores on the predictor test than for persons who made high scores. Precision here refers to the total amount of error in predicting scores on one variable from scores on the other variable. Another way of looking at it is from the perspective that the predictor test is a better test for people who make low scores than people who make high scores. This relates to how tests are constructed initially. [See discussion in Nunnally (1967), Chap. 8.]

For two related reasons, investigators do not want to find marked heterosce-

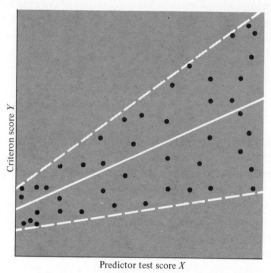

Figure 8-3. **Scatter diagrams in which the variation on Y increases as X grows larger.**

dasticity in a correlation scatter plot. First, as already alluded to, in applied situations a test would be more effective with people at some levels of ability than at others. Second, in basic research, the presence of a heteroscedastic relationship limits the extent to which the investigator can generalize from his results. Thus, he might report that the correlation between reaction time on a speed-of-movement test correlated 0.50 with speed of detecting rapidly presented visual objects; however, if the relationship were markedly heteroscedastic, the investigator would have to hedge his generalization and warn the reader that this relationship held better for people at some parts of the two measurement continuums than at other parts. In other words, he would have to limit his generalization. Because scientists always hope that their research results will support the widest possible generalizations, marked heteroscedasticity in the scatter plot is about as welcome as ants at a picnic. Fortunately, such marked heteroscedasticity as illustrated in Figure 8-3 seldom occurs in practice. Also, unless several hundred persons are being studied, there are not enough data points in the scatter plot to permit the investigator to observe and analyze anything other than extreme departures from homoscedasticity.

The presence of homoscedasticity is usually spoken of as one of the *assumptions* in employing r. Unless readers of research reports are informed to the contrary, they will assume that there was no strong tendency toward heteroscedasticity in the relationship.

Nonlinearity

A second assumption in computing *r* is that the best-fitting line in the scatter plot indeed is straight, or linear. In Chapter 7, issues concerning correlational analysis were illustrated with scatter diagrams where a straight line did a good job of describing the relationships. The prediction equations presented there all put straight lines in the scatter plots; however, there is no necessity for relationships found in the real world to be linear. *Nonlinear* relations are illustrated in Figures 8-4 through 8-7.

In Figure 8-4, the best-fitting straight line is a convex curve. Thus, in predicting scores on *Y* from *X*, the highest scores on *Y* would be predicted for people who have average scores on *X*. Lower scores on *Y* would be predicted for persons who either have low scores on *X* or high scores on *X*. Relationships like that in Figure 8-4 are spoken of as *convex curves,* or more simply as *inverted U-shaped curves.* The opposite situation is depicted in Figure 8-5. This would be referred to as a *concave curve* or more simply as a *U-shaped relationship.*

A really unusual possibility is depicted in Figure 8-6. The best-fitting line has two humps in it. Although it is possible for such a relationship to exist in psychology or education, the writers of this book have never seen a reported relationship that so obviously conformed to a two-humped pattern.

What is more frequently found than a distinctly U-shaped relationship is that the best-fitting straight line simply levels off at either the higher or the lower end of the *X* axis as in Figure 8-7. This means that scores on *Y* tend to increase with scores on *X* up to a point, but after that point scores on *Y* tend to level off with increasing scores on *X*. In comparing a predictor test with a criterion, this would

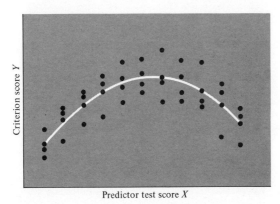

Figure 8-4. A scatter diagram in which the best-fitting curve is convex.

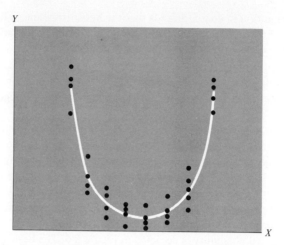

Figure 8-5. A scatter diagram in which the best-fitting curve is concave.

mean that scores on X are predictive of scores on Y only up to a point. Similarly, in basic research, a curve like that depicted in Figure 8-7 would indicate that the relationship holds up only to a point on each of the two variables. As was true with respect to heteroscedasticity, the presence of a distinctly nonlinear relationship limits the generalization that can be made about research results. If the relationship is obviously nonlinear—whatever the form of the relationship—the reader

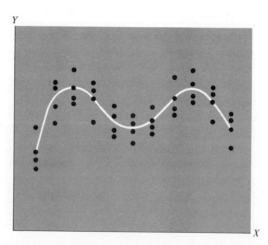

Figure 8-6. A scatter diagram in which the best-fitting curve has two humps.

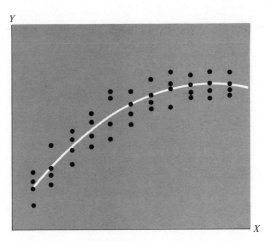

Figure 8-7. A scatter diagram in which the relationship levels off at the higher scores on X.

of research reports should at least be told about this, even if nothing is done to analyze the precise nature of the relationship.

It should be emphasized that the various equations discussed in Chapter 7 for computing r measure the degree of correspondence as though the relationship is linear, whether it actually is or not. Also, the prediction equations discussed in Chapter 7 place the best-fitting straight line in the scatter plot whether or not the relationship actually is linear. In other words, r is a measure of the degree of linear correlation only. This is illustrated in Figure 8-8 which shows a curvilinear scatter plot containing both the best-fitting line for the actual curve and the line that would be plotted in employing the prediction equations based on r discussed in Chapter 7.

Frequently, investigators compute r without even looking at the scatter plot. Consequently, the shape of the best-fitting line may never be known, and the actual degree of correspondence between the variables might be grossly underestimated. Of course, it is wise to actually make scatter plots when it is feasible; however, in massive projects where the investigator is intercorrelating 50 or more variables, this is simply unfeasible in most instances. In many research projects of this magnitude, there is the possibility that some nonlinear relationships might go undetected.

When the relationship is nonlinear, then r *underestimates* the degree of relationship. It should be obvious that it is possible to have a perfect nonlinear relationship, as depicted in Figure 8-9. The degree of nonlinear relationship can be computed with statistics which are similar in principle to r, but which require different equations. Essentially what these do is to measure the amount of varia-

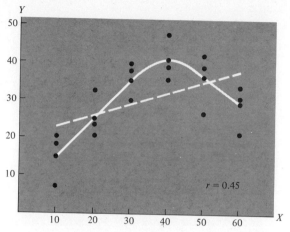

Figure 8-8. A scatter diagram in which the best-fitting straight line (dotted line) underestimates the true relationship (solid line).

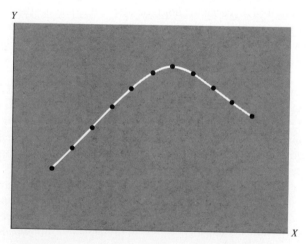

Figure 8-9. A perfect curvilinear relationship.

tion about the best-fitting line, whatever the shape of the line. If this variation is small with respect to the variable being predicted, then the correlation is high; similarly, the correlation is low if the variation is high. The basic measure of correlation for nonlinear relationships is referred to as the *correlation ratio*. An introduction to this and related statistics is given in the Suggested Additional Readings. Fortunately, most investigations in psychology and education concern relationships that are at least approximately linear.

There are numerous instances in which the slope of the best-fitting straight line tends to level off somewhat either at the upper or lower end of the X continuum, but distinctly U-shaped relationships are very rare indeed. Even if there is a mild departure from a strictly linear relationship (as depicted in Figure 8-7), r still does a good job of describing the trend. As is true of the other factors that limit the size of r, the limitation on r is slight unless the departure from linearity is quite marked, as illustrated in Figures 8-4 and 8-5. When such marked departures from linearity are found, research reports should state the nature of the relationship, and the statistical methods which are discussed in the Suggested Additional Readings should be applied.

PM CORRELATIONS WITH NONCONTINUOUS DISTRIBUTIONS

As mentioned in the first part of this chapter, it is frequently necessary to correlate two variables when one or more of them is not continuous. First, one of the variables might be continuous and the other dichotomous. An example would be the correlating of sex status with scores on a vocabulary test, in which case females would receive a score of 1 and males would receive a score of 0, or vice versa. Any other two numbers would serve equally well to identify group status. Which group was given the higher number would serve merely to determine the sign of the correlation, in other words, whether it was positive or negative.

Second, both of the variables being correlated might be dichotomous. An example would be the correlating of sex status with passing or failing a particular item on a vocabulary test. Another example would be the correlating of brain damage versus the absence of brain damage with being above or below the median in an experiment on memory.

A third case in which correlational analysis must be performed with noncontinuous distributions is that in which both variables are in the form of ranks. An example would be the correlating of the rank orderings that two persons make for 20 foods. From Chapter 2, the reader will remember that rank orderings such as these provide no direct information about the distance between the objects or persons which are ranked. Consequently, correlating two such sets of ranks raises some special issues over the more usual case in which the distributions are at l least approximately normal in shape and it is sensible to treat the distributions as though they constituted interval scales or ratio scales.

The three measures of correlation that are most useful for the above three types of situations respectively are *phi*, *point-biserial*, and *rho*. There is apparently some confusion in the minds of nonspecialists about these coefficients. It is frequently assumed that these coefficients are different from one another and that they are all different from the PM correlation. [See Equation (7-1).] Both assumptions are incorrect. All three of these coefficients are the same, and they are all the same as the regular PM coefficient *r*. Such "other" coefficients are sometimes thought to be different because the computations look different; however, this is entirely because of the type of data to which they are applied rather than because of a different mathematical rationale. Some shortcut equations have been developed for cases where one or both of the variables are not continuous. These are only special cases of the PM equation, and aside from the convenience of working with such shortcut equations when computers are not available, the PM equation could be used to obtain exactly the same result that would be obtained from phi, point-biserial, or rho.

Phi

When both distributions are dichotomous, a shortcut version of the PM coefficient which is called phi, is available. Phi can be illustrated in the situation where two test items are being correlated.

	Item 1	
	fail	pass
Item 2 pass	17	30
fail	33	20

The preceding diagram shows the scores for 100 students on two items. It indicates, for example, that 30 students pass both items and 33 fail both items. It is convenient to symbolize the four quadrants as follows

	Item 1	
Item 2	b	a
	c	d

A shortcut version of the PM coefficient is obtained as follows

$$\text{phi} = \frac{ac - bd}{\sqrt{(a + b)(c + d)(b + c)(a + d)}} \tag{8-1}$$

As mentioned previously, although the equation for phi looks different from the PM equation, the former is only a special case of the latter. When correlating two dichotomous distributions, exactly the same results as obtained from phi would be obtained by standardizing scores and placing them in the PM equation. If half the persons pass one item and passes are scored 1 and failures scored 0, all persons passing would have a standard score of +1 and all failing would have a standard score of - 1. Such standard scores may look rather strange, but that does not disturb the mathematics of the problem.

Before the advent of high-speed computers, phi was frequently applied to artificially dichotomized variables. For example, in item analysis dichotomous item scores can be correlated with artificially dichotomized scores on the test. One way to dichotomize total scores is to make all scores below the median 0 and all scores at or above the median 1. Phi could then be used to correlate each item with total scores. Unless computational labor is a very important consideration, it is unwise to articifially dichotomize one or both of the variables being investigated. If both variables are continuous, it is best to apply the regular PM equation. If one variable is inherently dichotomous (for example, pass-fail on test items) and one is continuous, it is best to apply point-biserial, which will be discussed subsequently. Information is always lost when a continuous variable is dichotomized. As a shortcut version of the PM coefficient, phi is the preferred measure of relationship when variables are inherently dichotomous.

Point-biserial

When one dichotomous variable is to be correlated with a continuous variable, a shortcut version of the PM equation called point-biserial r_{pb} is available. The most frequent occasion for employing this equation is in correlating a dichotomous test item such as pass-fail with essentially continuous total scores on a test. The shortcut equation is as follows

$$r_{pb} = \frac{M_s - M_u}{\sigma} \sqrt{pq} \qquad (8\text{-}2)$$

where M_s = mean score on continuous variable of "successful" group on dichotomous variable, M_u = mean score on continuous variable of "unsuccessful" group on dichotomous variable, σ = standard deviation on continuous variable for total group, p = proportion of persons falling in "successful" group on dichotomous variable, and $q = 1 - p$.

As with phi, r_{pb} was sometimes employed when one of two continuous variables was artificially dichotomized before the days of high-speed computers. For example, rather than apply the regular PM equation to the continuous scores on two tests, scores on one of the two tests were dichotomized, the "cut" most frequently being done at the median. Then the shortcut equation was applied. This is very poor practice, however. The computational time saved is not great, and fuller information would be obtained by correlating the two continuous variables. Point-biserial is the preferred measure of correlation when one variable is continuous and the other is inherently dichotomous, as with pass-fail or male-female. As mentioned previously, the numerical result obtained by applying the regular PM equation is exactly the same as that which would be obtained from the short-cut version r_{pb}.

Rho

For correlating two sets of ranks, a shortcut version of the PM equation called rho is available. The equation could be used, for example, to correlate the rankings of two judges concerning the extent to which 20 patients had improved in the course of psychotherapy. The equation is as follows

$$\text{rho} = 1 - \frac{6\Sigma d^2}{N(N^2 - 1)} \tag{8-3}$$

where N = number of objects or persons ranked, and d = algebraic difference in ranks for each object or person in two distributions of ranks.

Results obtained by applying rho are exactly the same as those obtained by applying the regular PM equation to two sets of ranks.

Table 8-1 presents the rankings by a man and his wife of their preferences for 15 fruits. Also the table shows the difference between these ranks (d) and the square of these ranks (d^2). Rho is quickly calculated by adding the d^2 column and then placing the results into Equation (8-3). As shown in the equation which follows, there is a correlation of 0.93 between the two sets of ranks.

$$\text{rho} = 1 - \frac{6(38)}{15(225 - 1)} = 1 - \frac{228}{3360}$$

$$= 0.93$$

Table 8-1. Rank-Order Preference of 15 Fruits by a Man and His Wife

Fruit	Man	Wife	d	d^2
Apple	1	2	1	1
Pear	2	1	1	1
Grape	3	3	0	0
Plum	4	5	1	1
Orange	5	4	1	1
Banana	6	7	1	1
Watermelon	7	6	1	1
Strawberry	8	9	1	1
Raspberry	9	11	2	4
Blackberry	10	10	0	0
Blueberry	11	8	3	9
Apricot	12	15	3	9
Pineapple	13	14	1	1
Coconut	14	12	2	4
Mango	15	13	2	4
				$\Sigma d^2 = \overline{38}$

There are three possible reasons for employing rho. First, two continuous distributions can be converted to ranks and rho applied to save computational labor. This is a poor reason, for the computational time saved is not great. In this instance, rho applied to the ranks would usually be very close to the regular PM equation applied to the continuous variables, particularly if both continuous variables are approximately normally distributed.

A second reason for applying rho is to estimate what the PM correlation between two distributions which are markedly different in shape would be if the two were rescaled to have approximately the same shape. If, for example, one distribution is highly skewed to the left and the other is highly skewed to the right, the PM correlation will be less than it would be if both distributions had the same shape (for reasons that were discussed previously in this chapter). If both distributions were transformed to have the same shape—usually normal distributions—the correlation would increase somewhat. [Methods for transforming skewed distributions to ones that are more nearly normal are discussed in Kirk (1968) and in Winer (1971).] Before going to the labor of transforming the two distributions, it might be useful to estimate how much the variables would correlate after the transformation. This can be done with rho. By ranking scores on the two variables and applying rho, one will obtain a correlation that closely approximates the correlation that would be obtained from the two normalized variables.

The third and best reason for employing rho is to correlate two distributions that are inherently expressed as ranks, for example, if 20 patients were ranked by two psychiatrists with respect to improvement during the course of therapy. When measurement is in the form of rank order, rho provides a useful index of correlation. Because rho is a PM equation and PM equations are often said to "require" interval scales, some would call this an "illegitimate" use of rho. It is hard to see much sense in such arguments. Since rho ranges between +1 and -1, it serves to describe the degree of relationship between two sets of ranks. Tests of statistical significance are available when both variables are inherently in the form of rank order. [See McNemar (1962).] As a shortcut version of the regular PM equation, rho is the preferred measure of relationship when both variables are inherently in the form of ranks.

Estimates of PM Coefficients

Previously in this section it was mentioned that rho is usually a good estimate of the PM coefficient obtained when both distributions being correlated are changed back from ranks to approximately normal distributions. In this sense, it can be said that rho is an estimate of r obtained between two normal distributions.

Whereas rho is a good estimate of r that would be obtained between two approximately normal distributions, this is not the case for phi or point-biserial. The reason is that when two distributions have grossly different shapes, the size of the PM coefficient is restricted. (Remember that both phi and point-biserial are based exactly on the same logic and computations as *r*.) When employing point-biserial, it is obvious that a dichotomous variable must have a very different shape from a continuous variable. An example given previously in this chapter illustrated how this situation necessarily leads to a spread of scores in predicting a continuous variable from a dichotomous variable, thus restricting the correlation over that which could possibly occur when both variables are approximately continuous. It also is possible for two dichotomous variables to have different "shapes." This occurs when the percentage "splits" on the two dichotomous variables are different, for example, if half of the students in the group passed one item and 80 percent of the students in the group passed a second item. In essence, these represent differences in shapes of the two dichotomous distributions; consequently, the correlation cannot reach 1.00 in any case. It is generally expected that the correlations obtained using phi and point-biserial in the special cases where they apply will be considerably less than would be found in the case where *r* could be applied to continuous distributions. [Principles concerning the amount of this restriction and the equations used to estimate *r* in the general case are discussed in Nunnally (1967), Chap. 4.]

Two correlation coefficients are used to estimate *r* when one or both variables is dichotomous. Neither of these is recommended for general use, and the reader should not bother to seek a full understanding of them. However, because their names appear so much in literature in psychology and education dating up to about 1955, the coefficients and their uses will be briefly discussed.

The *tetrachoric* correlation coefficient can be used to estimate from two dichotomous variables what the *r* would be in a population if the variable underlying each dichotomous variable were normally distributed. Thus, the tetrachoric coefficient could be used to estimate what the correlation would be between two test items that are scored only as pass-fail if the two items could actually be scored relatively continuously over numerous points. The tetrachoric correlation is employed with the same type of data as phi (for instance, with two dichotomous distributions), but the two coefficients are very different mathematically and usually produce substantially different results when applied to the same data.

The *biserial* correlation concerns one dichotomous variable and one continuously distributed variable. It is used to estimate what the correlation would be if both variables were normally distributed. An example would be in correlating pass-fail scores on a test item with the total scores on the test. Biserial *r* could be used to estimate what the correlation would be if both variables were normally distributed; in other words, it would be possible to score the pass-fail item on many points.if an approximately normal distribution of scores resulted. Although biserial *r* serves in essentially the same situation that point-biserial does, the two coefficients should definitely not be confused. They are based on different mathematical principles, and usually produce markedly different results when both are applied to the same data.

For a variety of reasons, biserial, tetrachoric, and other estimates of *r* should not be employed in most research. These coefficients frequently provide very poor estimates of the *r* that actually would be obtained when both distributions are approximately normal. Numerous instances have been found in which the estimate was off by as much as 20 points of correlation. Equations concerning these estimates of *r* and additional cautions regarding their actual use are given in Nunnally (1967), Chap. 4.

MULTIVARIATE CORRELATIONAL ANALYSIS

All of the discussion of correlational analysis to this point has concerned bivariate correlational analysis, that is, in situations where a correlation coefficient is obtained between two variables. A possibility not mentioned previously is that the correlational problem may concern more than two variables, in which case it is said that *multivariate correlational analysis* is employed. An introduction to methods applied in this case is given in the Suggested Additional Readings. Multivariate correlational analysis is mentioned here because statistics of this kind are very useful in the analysis of research results, and applications of such multivariate statistics are frequently mentioned in research reports.

A situation in which multivariate corrrelational analysis would be needed is that in which two or more aptitude tests are used to select students for graduate training in psychology. Tests concerning word knowledge and mathematics are typically used for that purpose. The problem is that of combining scores on the tests in such a way as to obtain a composite that correlates most highly with grade-point average in graduate training. One way to do this would be to simply average standard scores on the tests. This would produce a new variable consisting of the composite of the predictor variables. This new variable could then be correlated with grade-point averages, employing the usual PM equation. In other words, the process of averaging predictor variables essentially consists of producing a bivariate correlational problem from a multivariate correlational problem. In most cases, however, one does not simply average the scores from the predictor variables. Rather, the composite would be more predictive of grade-point averages if different weights were applied to the standard scores on the two predictor tests before they were added together. It is usually found that the most predictive combination in the preceding example is obtained by giving a higher weight to the vocabulary test than to the mathematics test, for example, giving the vocabulary test a weight of 2, and leaving the mathematics scores as they are. This is the same as saying that before the standard scores are averaged, standard scores in vocabulary are doubled and standard scores in mathematics are left as they are —weights of 2 and 1 respectively. What one could learn from multivariate correlational analysis is the precise weights that would produce the most predictive composite in any particular problem. The interested reader should consult Ferguson (1971) and Guilford and Fruchter (1973). A more extensive discussion of this topic may be found in Nunnally (1967).

SUMMARY

Basic principles of PM correlational analysis were discussed in Chapter 7; in this chapter special issues that arise from this type of analysis were discussed. Among these issues are (1) factors that influence the size of correlations, (2) irregularities in the scatter diagram, and (3) computing equations that are useful in special cases.

The PM coefficient r cannot be as high as 1.0 or as low as -1.0 unless the two distributions being correlated have exactly the same shape (mirror images of one another in the case of a negative correlation). More importantly, if the two distributions have very different shapes, the correlation will be lower than it would be if they had the same shape. This holds regardless of the size of r in the latter instance. If the correlation were very high in same-shaped distributions but the shapes actually are quite different, then the correlation in the latter case might be reduced considerably. The amount of restriction is usually rather slight when the correlation in same-shaped distributions is no higher than about 0.50. The most extreme example of restriction in correlation because of differences in shapes occurs when one of the variables is approximately normally distributed and the other is in the form of a dichotomy (for example, pass-fail on a test item correlated with total scores on a 50-item vocabulary test). If both sets of scores are in the form of dichotomies (for example, pass-fail on two test items), the possible correlation will be restricted unless the same percentage of subjects passes each item.

The size of r is also restricted by the extent to which a group being investigated varies with respect to the two measures. If the amount of variability is reduced by the method of sampling subjects, this would make the correlation less than if there had been no restriction in this regard. An example would be correlating scores on two different IQ tests from a sample of subjects in a college honors program rather than from a broader sample of students.

One possible irregularity in a scatter diagram is heteroscedasticity, or lack of homoscedasticity. This means that the amount of scatter is larger at some score levels than at other score levels. The presence of heteroscedasticity requires the investigator to qualify any generalizations he might make about the results. Another irregularity that might be present in the scatter diagram is nonlinearity of the best-fitting line. Such nonlinear relations range from best-fit lines that level off at some score level to those that are definitely U-shaped. If there is only a mild departure from nonlinearity, the regular PM equation r can still be applied; however, if there is a marked tendency for the relationship to be U-shaped, special correlational equations must be applied. Fortunately, most bivariate relationships found in applied work and in basic research are at least approximately linear, and distinctly U-shaped distributions are very rare.

When one or both variables is *not* continuously distributed, some special versions of the PM equation can be applied. These situations occur when (1) one distribution is relatively continuous and the other is in the form of a dichotomy, (2) both distributions are in the form of dichotomies, and (3) both distributions are in the form of ranks. The three equations that apply in those cases are called point-biserial, phi, and rho, respectively. It should be emphasized that these are only different-appearing forms of the PM coefficient, and exactly the same result would be obtained by applying the usual equation for r. In previous days, the use of these equations was justified mainly in terms of computational time; however, if high-speed computers are available, it is much simpler to apply the regular PM equation in all three of these special cases. The reader needs to be familiar with these coefficients because their names appear in the literature dating back over half a century.

EXERCISES

Study Questions

1. How is the size of the correlation coefficient affected by the shapes of the two score distributions involved? Consider the situation in which two relatively continuous distributions are differently shaped and the situation in which one or both of the distributions are dichotomous.

2. How is the size of the correlation coefficient affected by the amount of variation in the sample relative to the amount of variation in the population?

3. Draw outlines of scatter plots in which the bivariate distributions are (a) heteroscedastic and (b) nonlinear. How do such factors influence the interpretation of research results?

4. With what types of score distribution would one employ the following variations of the PM correlation coefficient: (a) phi, (b) point-biserial, and (c) rho?

5. For what purposes in the past have investigators used the tetrachoric correlation coefficient and the biserial correlation coefficient? What is the major reason that these coefficients are not recommended for general use in research?

6. Compose an example of how multivariate correlational analysis could be used. What advantage would this have over simply averaging predictor variables?

Problems

1. Calculate the phi coefficient on the following set of data from two items on a test. A 1 means pass, and a 0 means fail.

	Item 1	Item 2
1	0	1
2	0	1
3	1	0
4	1	1
5	1	1
Student 6	0	0
7	0	1
8	1	1
9	1	1
10	1	0
11	1	0
12	0	1

2   Calculate the point-biserial correlation between the following scores on item 1 of a test and the total test score.

	Item 1	Total test score
1	1	12
2	1	10
3	0	3
4	0	4
Student 5	1	5
6	0	7
7	0	5
8	0	6
9	1	6
10	1	12

3   Calculate a rho correlation on the following set of ranks obtained from two teachers. The teachers ranked 10 students in terms of their merit for a scholarship.

	Teacher 1	Teacher 2
1	2	3
2	1	2
3	3	4
4	6	1
Student 5	5	5
6	4	8
7	7	7
8	8	9
9	10	10
10	9	6

SUGGESTED ADDITIONAL READINGS

Ferguson, G. A. *Statistical analysis in psychology and education*, 3d ed. New York: McGraw-Hill, 1971, pp. 303-308, 348-351, 356-358, and Chap. 26.

Guilford, J. P., and B. Fruchter. *Fundamental statistics in psychology and education*, 5th ed. New York: McGraw-Hill, 1973, Chaps. 14, 15, and 16.

Nunnally, J. C. *Psychometric theory.* New York: McGraw-Hill, 1967, Chap. 5.

Part Three

Inferential Statistics

9

Statistical Inference

Part One of the book concerned general principles regarding the nature and application of statistics. Part Two discussed the major descriptive statistics. Part Three will be concerned with inferential statistics. As preparation for a discussion of the more widely used inferential statistics in psychology and education, the nature of statistical inference itself will be discussed in this chapter.

THE PLACE OF INFERENCE IN SCIENCE

Some fundamental principles about the nature of scientific inference were discussed in Chapter 3. That discussion will be summarized in this section, and additional principles will be considered. Science is concerned with two types of inference, or with two kinds of logic—deductive inference and inductive inference. Deductive inference is concerned with the drawing of conclusions from mathematics and other systems of formal logic. Thus, it is deduced, or deductively inferred, that a box which is 4 feet on each side contains a total of 64 cubic feet. Similarly, it can be inferred that if Bill is taller than Fred and Fred is taller than Joe, then Bill is taller than Joe. Much more complex forms of deductive logic are only expansions of the same logical procedure involved in these simple examples.

In contrast to deductive inference, inductive inference is directly concerned with the nature of everyday events. Inductive inference is literally a leap into the unknown—an estimation of what unknown events will be like from data that has been obtained. Such inferences range in generality from the recurrence of specific events to principles regarding the behavior of vast domains of natural phenomena.

An example of inference regarding a specific event is the prediction (by most of us) that the sun will rise tomorrow. For countless centuries, the old fiery ball has been known to appear at predictable times on the eastern horizon. On the basis of observing the recurrence of such natural phenomena, men (perhaps some lower animals as well) make the assumption that things in the universe will behave as they have in the past. For the same reason, it is expected that a steel ball dropped from the hand will fall to the ground rather than rise into the heavens, water will flow downhill, and all people will die someday. These are all simple inductive inferences, simple in the sense that they concern only the recurrence of a much observed regularity in nature. Note, however, that such inferences depend very much on what has been actually observed in daily life and not on any form of deductive logic. Thus, in the same sense that there is no way to prove that $2 + 2 = 4$ by referring to the real world, there is no way to prove that the sun will rise tomorrow with any form of deductive logic, mathematical or otherwise.

Rather than being primarily concerned with recurring specific events, science is more broadly concerned with principles regarding such events. Thus, the laws of gravity not only lead to the conclusion that a steel ball will fall toward the earth, but in addition, the laws predict how rapidly the ball will fall and other things about the nature of gravitational attraction.

Statistical Inferences

The inductive inferences just discussed concerned situations in which there was little or no uncertainty about the outcome of particular events. While it is amusing to discuss the possibility that the sun will not rise tomorrow, it would be difficult to find people who took the matter seriously. This is the case with many of the inductive inferences made about the occurrence of specific events in the real world; however, many of the more general inductive inferences or principles about the real world are based on probability rather than on certainty. This holds true even with respect to the numbers of atomic particles that are emitted from radioactive substances in any period of time. It can be determined how many such particles will be emitted on the average, but the amount varies over time. Thus, one must deal with probabilities and discuss the matter in a statistical sense. In education and psychology, it is even more obvious that most inductive inferences concern probabilities rather than certainties. An example with respect to a specific event would be in predicting whether or not a student with a college aptitude test score of one standard deviation above the mean would complete college training. From previous investigations, it has been found that 80 percent of the students who made scores that high or higher successfully obtained college degrees. Thus, $p = 0.80$ that the student in question would successfully complete college.

An example of employing probability statements with respect to more general inferences rather than specific events concerns correlations between aptitude test scores and success in colleges across the country. The typical correlation actually obtained in investigations of this kind is in the neighborhood of $r = 0.50$ to $r = 0.65$. Such correlations serve to summarize the relationship between aptitude test scores and college grades. Thus, one may make inferences from the test scores to college grades, but only with respect to the probabilities associated with the correlation between the two.

Measured amounts of any homogeneous substance correlate almost perfectly with the weights of those amounts. This would be the case in an experiment where different-sized boxes filled with sand were weighed. If the experiment was carefully undertaken, the correlation between the size of the box and the weight of the box would be close to 1.00. Thus, the inductive inference that amounts of a homogeneous substance are proportional to weights of the substance is a near certainty. In contrast, many inferences in psychology and education concern correlations that are far less than 1.00, and thus are true only in a statistical sense.

SAMPLING DISTRIBUTIONS

Characteristics of Sampling Distributions

Notably in Chapter 5, but also in other chapters of the book thus far, numerous examples of frequency distributions of scores obtained in research were given, for example, distributions of IQs or number of correct responses in an experiment on verbal learning. The three major properties of such score distributions are the shape, central tendency, and dispersion. What is very important to realize is that descriptive statistics computed on such distributions of scores also have frequency distributions of their own. A frequency distribution for a descriptive statistic computed over many samples is referred to as a *sampling distribution.* An example would be computing the mean height in inches of 1,000 samples of students, each containing 50 boys. There would then be 1,000 frequency distributions of scores, each with its own mean and standard deviation. The mean and standard deviation for any sample would serve as a basis for estimating what the mean and standard deviation would be if those descriptive statistics were computed on a frequency distribution containing all 50,000 boys. Of course, the mean, standard deviation, and other descriptive statistics would be somewhat different from sample to sample. Considering the mean, it would be possible to actually construct a frequency distribution for the 1,000 samples, the result of which would constitute a sampling distribution for the mean. Each descriptive statistics, or relationship among descriptive statistics, has a characteristic sampling distribution. The mean has a normal distribution; the correlation coefficient has a distribution that is somewhat flatter than the normal distribution; and the differences among means of three or more samples drawn simultaneously have a characteristic sampling distribution which is quite different from the normal distribution in most cases.

Of course, in employing inferential statistics, it is almost never the case that the sampling distribution for the descriptive statistic in question is obtained by a process of actually drawing thousands of samples as in the hypothetical case concerning the heights of boys. What is usually done instead is to work the other way around and use the descriptive statistics obtained from a sample to estimate the same descriptive statistics that would be obtained from the population. Also, the descriptive statistics obtained from the sample permit one to estimate the sampling distributions of such descriptive statistics that would actually be obtained in a large-scale sampling experiment.

It should be emphasized that sampling distributions for descriptive statistics are almost always different in some important ways from the typical distribution of scores within samples. The distribution of sample means is expected to have the same (normal) distribution of that of the scores in each sample from a normally distributed population; however, the standard deviation of the sampling distribution of means is expected to be *less* than that of the standard deviation of scores in each sample. As the number of subjects is made larger and larger in each sample, the standard deviation of the sampling distribution of means is expected to become smaller and smaller in proportion to the typical standard deviation of scores in each sample. As previously mentioned, the shapes of some sampling distributions are very different from the shapes of the individual samples. The important points are (1) descriptive statistics and combinations of descriptive statistics have sampling distributions, (2) characteristics of a sampling distribution can be estimated from the characteristics actually found in a sample of subjects, and (3) the estimated sampling distribution can be used to make probability statements regarding the mean, standard deviation, and other characteristics of the population as a whole.

Amount of Variation in a Sampling Distribution

All inferential statistics are concerned with variation in the phenomena being investigated. Such variation constitutes *error* in estimating the characteristics of particular people as well as the results of experiments. A hypothetical example would be guessing the IQs of recruits in the Army. For this example, let it be assumed that recruits constitute a random sample of young men, although in actuality it is known that there are selection factors that tend to favor the recruitment of certain types of persons rather than others. Assume that the recruits are taking an IQ test for which national norms are available. The population mean is 100 and the standard deviation is known to be a particular amount. The experiment concerns guessing the IQs of recruits as they enter the door where testing is to be conducted. Because the population mean is known to be 100, the best bet, without any other information about each recruit, would be that each recruit had an IQ of precisely 100. (This strategy would follow from the principle of least-squares.) Of course the recruits will vary considerably about the population mean, with the variation in this sample being estimated by the known standard deviation of test scores. In this case, the population standard deviation of test scores would constitute a measure of the amount of error in guessing IQs of randomly selected people when no other information was available about them. Using tables of the normal distribution presented in Appendix B-4, probabilities could be asserted for persons walking in the door and having IQs above or below any particular level, for example, having IQs that are two standard deviations above the mean.

It is more difficult to understand the meaning of error in other instances, so that special equations are needed to investigate the error. A good example of this would be in determining the amount of error with respect to the finding from an opinion poll that 55 percent of the persons in a polling sample say that they will vote for candidate Jones rather than candidate Smith. If all of the eligible voters in the country were studied rather than only a sample, what is the probability of finding that less than 50 percent of the voters would say that they will vote for Jones rather than Smith? Another example is found in comparing the effects of three methods of reading instruction on scores obtained from achievement tests of reading comprehension. Ninety students are randomly divided into three experimental groups. After the course of training, it is found that the three groups differ in average achievement test scores; however, one should wonder whether these differences are "real." They might be due to various types of error associated with the random process of assigning students to groups and chance factors that permit some students to learn more than others or to make higher scores on the test. It would be necessary to determine amounts of error and use this to assert probabilities regarding results of the experiment.

Statistical Estimates

It has been mentioned numerous times in this book that statistical results obtained from samples of subjects are important only to the extent that they provide estimates of the values that actually would be obtained from studying a population as a whole. The experimenter can usually choose one from several available descriptive statistics which concern much the same characteristics of the data. This can be illustrated with the mean, median, and mode. Essentially, all are concerned with average performance in a sample of subjects. They are computed by different approaches, and they provide somewhat different information about central tendency. The same is true of most descriptive statistics: there are alternative equations which provide somewhat different information about the data. Thus, there are alternative descriptive statistics for measuring amount of variation and correlation. Some descriptive statistics and their corresponding equations have proven to be more useful than others. Reasons that this is so were discussed with respect to the general preference for employing the mean rather than any other measure of central tendency, the standard deviation rather than any other measure of variation, and the product-moment coefficient rather than any other meas-

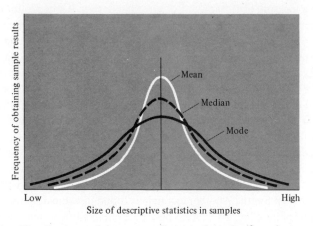

Figure 9-1. Distributions of means, medians, and modes for a large number of samples.

ure of correlation. In addition to the advantages discussed previously, there are other features that make some descriptive statistics more desirable than others.

One desirable feature of any descriptive statistic is that the error of estimating population characteristics from sample data is the smallest possible. This is illustrated in comparing the mean, median, and mode. A hypothetical example is shown in Figure 9-1. The X axis shows the range of measures of statistical results that would be obtained by drawing many samples from a population, such as heights of boys or scores on an achievement test. Because scores are normally distributed, the mean, median, and mode would fall at exactly the same point, as indicated in Figure 9-1. If many samples were drawn from the population, the descriptive statistic (for instance, the mean) would vary from sample to sample. It is expected that each measure of central tendency would be normally distributed over many samples, but with different standard deviations. Illustrative distributions for the three measures of central tendency are shown in Figure 9-1. Each distribution shows the frequency of values expected over a very large number of samples. As would be expected, the distributions are normally distributed about the population value. What is important to note in Figure 9-1 is that the three measures of central tendency differ in terms of the extent to which the sample estimates are expected to vary around the actual population value. The mean varies least, and the mode varies most.

If one actually gathered mountains of data from many samples as illustrated in Figure 9-1, it would be possible to compute a standard deviation for each of the three measures of central tendency. In that case, the standard deviation would constitute a measure of the amount of error in estimating the population value from the statistic. The standard deviation of sample values is referred to as a *standard error*, which denotes a measure of the amount of error in estimating a descriptive statistic in a population from a descriptive statistic obtained from a sample of that population (for example, the standard error of the mean). Generally, the amount of error in employing all descriptive statistics is phrased in terms of the standard deviation or variance of the expected distribution of errors. Different equations are required for estimating the amount of error involved with different statistics. Thus, in later chapters equations will be presented and illustrated with respect to the mean σ_M and the correlation coefficient σ_r. To reiterate, a desirable feature of any statistic is that the amount of error be as small as possible. Thus, σ_M is smaller than the standard error of other measures of central tendency, as illustrated in Figure 9-1.

Another important characteristic of any descriptive statistic is that it be *unbiased*. Essentially, a descriptive statistic is unbiased if there is no reason to believe that the estimate of the population value obtained from a sample is either greater or less than the actual population value. The arithmetic mean has this characteristic. If, on the average, a random sample of young women say that they want to have 2.3 children, then this statistic is unbiased in the sense that there is no reason to believe that the number would either be more than or less than 2.3 if all the women in that age group in the country were studied.

In contrast to the mean, some other statistics are slightly biased in the sense that the result obtained from a sample is expected to be higher or lower than the population value. It was mentioned in Chapter 5 that this is the case with the standard deviation. Consequently, the equation for σ must be slightly altered (by computing s) in order to obtain an unbiased estimate. The problem of bias that occurs in some descriptive statistics is usually so slight that it can be ignored *unless* only a small number of subjects is being studied (say, less than 30). For the inferential statistics which will be discussed in subsequent chapters of Part Three, corrections for the small amount of bias automatically are taken care of in the computational equations.

The Law of Large Numbers

A fundamental principle in statistics is that the amount of error associated with the estimate of any population value from a representative sample is inversely related to the number of individuals in the sample. Thus, if a study concerns the percentage of people who will vote for one political candidate rather than another, more faith can be obtained in the percentage arrived at from 100 people rather than 10, from 1,000 people rather than 100, and from 100,000 people rather than 1,000. A similar test could be applied in the situation where a gambler is curious about whether or not a pair of dice is biased in the direction of "coming up" with higher numbers more often than lower numbers. The possible sums of numbers range between 2 and 12. He could toss the dice 100 times and note the frequency with which each sum appeared. Because of factors regarding the sampling of events, there would be some error in generalizing to the infinite possible tosses of the dice. More faith could be placed in the percentage of occurrences associated with 1,000 tosses than with 100, and even more faith could be placed in many thousands of tosses. In all situations that involve sampling of occurrences, the precision of estimates (inversely, the lack of error) is positively related to the number of observations that are sampled.

It should be strongly emphasized that the *law of large numbers* applies only if samples are representative of some population. As already mentioned at numerous points so far in this book, if samples are biased in one way or another, results obtained from even thousands of persons will provide a poor estimate of population characteristics.

It should also be strongly emphasized that the law of large numbers concerns the amount of error that would be *expected* from using representative samples of different sizes to estimate any characteristic of the population; however, there is no assurance at all that the law of large numbers would be obeyed in any particular case. Thus, the mean obtained from a sample of only 50 persons might turn out to be exactly the same as the population mean; the mean obtained from a sample of 300 persons might differ considerably from the population mean; however, it is improbable that this would be the case. Probability and associated inferential statistics apply *in general* to cases of a particular kind (for instance, variation in percentage of persons who say that they will vote for one candidate rather than another from sample to sample). Inferential statistics concern general rules for gauging the probability of some types of outcomes in research and the improbability of others.

In every day language, the law of large numbers is referred to as the "law of averages." Although this popular phrase is often misconstrued, it does take account of the primary principle in statistics concerning the increased confidence in estimates of population values obtained from larger and larger samples. Although elaborate statistical methods have been developed for estimating population values from relatively small samples, these are not substitutes for obtaining large enough amounts of data for precisely estimating such population values. Statistical methods of estimating population values are mainly useful when it is unfeasible to actually obtain the large amounts of data that would be required for obtaining highly precise estimates. In other words, the more data that can be obtained practicably in an experiment, the better. There is no magic whereby statistical methods can obtain more precise information about the real world from smaller samples of data than from larger samples of data.

The Inverse-Square Law

Not only are larger samples of data more precise than smaller samples of data in estimating population values, but with most of the descriptive statistics discussed in this book, the expected amount of error is inversely proportional to the square root of the number of subjects in the sample, giving rise to the *inverse-square law.* By "amount of error" we mean the standard deviation (standard error) of the sampling distribution for the particular descriptive statistic. As will be discussed more fully later, it is known that the standard error for the mean is as follows

$$\text{Standard error of mean} = \frac{\sigma_{pop}}{\sqrt{N}} \tag{9-1}$$

where N = the number of persons in the sample, and σ_{pop} = the standard deviation of scores in the population as a whole.

Although larger random sample are always expected to provide better estimates than smaller random samples, the advantage in this regard tends to diminish as larger and larger amounts of data are obtained. For example, whereas the standard error of the mean would be reduced considerably by increasing the sample size from 100 persons to 1,000 persons, going from 1,000 to 2,000 persons would not result in a similarly large decrease in the standard error. For this reason, it is frequently not worth the trouble to increase the sample size from an already large sample to an even larger sample. The sample size needed in any experiment depends on how precisely population characteristics must be estimated. Such judgments regarding sample size partly depend upon general experience with the type of research problem and partly upon the intuitions of the experimenter (which may prove to be incorrect). Regarding the former consideration, it is usually found in polls of the public that preferences for one political candidate over another are less than 65 percent. Consequently, it makes a great deal of difference, for example, whether the population value is actually 53 percent or somewhat lower. This requires a relatively large sample to ensure that the population value is precisely estimated.

In estimating the required numbers of subjects for an experiment, an experimenter might estimate on the basis of intuition, that 20 college students would be required in each of two groups for an experiment on memory. He would base this on his general experience regarding many previous studies of a similar nature. Subsequently, it might be found that the size of the difference between the means of the two groups was sufficiently large in comparison to the error (as indicated by the variability within groups) to leave little doubt that a difference would be found in the population as a whole. On the other hand, the experimenter's intuitions might have been incorrect to the point where the amount of error was so large in comparison to mean differences that no firm conclusions could be reached about differences that would be found in the population as a whole.

Degrees of Freedom

It would be more precise to say that the inverse-square law applies to what is called the *degrees of freedom* rather than to the number of persons sampled N. Strictly speaking, the degrees of freedom (df) is a concept that arises from mathematical derivations of inferential statistics. In analyzing the mathematical models used to derive inferential statistics, it is found that the effective sample size frequently is slightly less than the actual number of persons sampled. An example would be in the case where the estimate of the population standard deviation s is computed on a sample of 100 persons. In that case, it is found that the effective sample size df is actually 99 rather than 100. In computing the PM correlation between two tests on 100 subjects, it is found that the effective sample size df is 98 rather than 100. Thus, the inverse-square law applies to the df rather than to the actual N of the sample. Some intuitive support for this principle can be obtained by considering the way in which the PM correlation is calculated. If the correlation is computed for only two persons on any two measures, then the correlation is either 1.00 or -1.00 (except in the unusual case where both subjects make the same score on one or both measures). Thus, it can be said that the first two points must be thrown away, or not regarded as degrees of freedom. Only when at least a third person is included can the correlation be different from 1.00 or -1.00. Consequently, in computing the error for the correlation, the effective sample size is $N - 2$ rather than N. A similar logic underlies the computation of df for all other inferential statistics. Mention will be made of df at numerous points in the following chapters, and the statistical distributions presented in Appendix B are organized in terms of df rather than N. The concepts of df is particularly important when employing inferential statistics with respect to the significance of difference among the means of three or more differently treated experimental groups (which will be discussed in Chapters 11 and 12).

Experimental Independence

Because the number of subjects is related to the precision with which results obtained from a sample can be used to estimate population values, it is important to make a qualification: the number of subjects can be entered into statistical equations only if experimental results for them are *experimentally independent.* Results obtained from subjects are experimentally independent if the result obtained for one subject has no influence at all on the result obtained for any other subject. Results would not be independent if the dependent variable consisted of an achievement test and students were seated so close together that they could copy each others' answers. If the situation were so flagrant that students could actively discuss each question and unanimously arrive at an answer, then it would be more appropriate to say that only one subject was involved in the experiment rather than the number seated in the room.

A subtle example of experimental dependence would be in an experiment comparing two methods of learning number skills. In each of two groups being compared, the students who have difficulty in learning number skills are strongly influenced by students who find it very easy to acquire number skills. Students talk and learn from one another, and the general morale of the classroom influences study habits regarding the topic. If students who are very bright with respect to the topic progress rapidly, then there is a strong tendency for students weaker in that regard to improve markedly also.

The inverse-square law applies to the number of *independent* observations. In the two examples given, the requirement of independence was broken in either a flagrant or subtle manner. In all cases, it would be incorrect to employ the number of subjects studied in the experiment as the number of independent observations. To do so would be to underestimate the amount of error, or overestimate the degree of precision in going from the obtained results of the experiment to those expected with much larger groups of students. Whenever possible, experiments should be designed in such a way that independence of observations is ensured. The inferential statistics which will be discussed in the remaining chapters of this book are based on the assumption that such independence has been obtained.

Sources of Error

The most prominent source of error in most experiments is due to the sampling of subjects. At least as an ideal, the subjects in any experiment can be thought of as randomly drawn from a defined population. Even so, there is obviously considerable chance associated with which subjects actually appear in a sample. There are numerous other sources of error in any experiment. If the research results consist of rankings by students of their preferences for an occupation, then there is error in the sense that students probably would give somewhat different rankings if asked to do so at a future point in time. If the equipment used in a study of reaction time is functioning erratically, this could either raise or lower the scores of subjects. If, from session to session, the experimenter varies instructions given to subjects, this can constitute a source of error. Thus, it is useful to think not only of subjects being randomly sampled for an experiment but also of each subject being studied under a random set of myriad influences. All of these sources of error go together to form a general amount of error for investigating the results of an experiment. Methods will be discussed in subsequent chapters for determining this overall amount of error and for interpreting results of experiments in the light of the overall error.

A DEMONSTRATION OF SAMPLING DISTRIBUTIONS

Much of what has been said so far in this book regarding inferential statistics can be illustrated with an experiment. This will be an experiment into the nature of statistics based on imaginary data. The problem is that of estimating the average (mean) number of years of training held by all of the United States astronauts.

Although the numbers of individuals in most populations is usually very large (infinite, for all practical purposes), in this case the population consists entirely of 48 persons. The distribution of years of training is shown in Figure 9-2. One of the astronauts has just been recruited and has zero years of training, two astronauts have one year of training, three astronauts have two years of training, five astronauts three years of training, and so on up to ten years of training. This is a symmetrical distribution roughly approximating the normal distribution.

For one fanciful reason or another, it is not possible to contact all of the astronauts and question them about years of training. Rather, it is necessary to estimate the average number of years of training in the group as a whole from samples of the astronauts. Of course, the reader of this book knows that the mean of this population is precisely 5.00, but this could only be estimated from each sample. Stretching the imagination further, the samples are drawn randomly by 80 different persons investigating the phenomena. Twenty persons draw samples of size 4, twenty persons draw samples of size 8, twenty draw samples of size 12, and twenty draw samples of size 24 (1/12, 1/6, 1/4, and 1/2 of the total N of the population). The experiment could be undertaken by making up a deck of 48 cards, in which one of them has the number 0 written on it, two of them have the number 1 on them, and so on. After the deck was thoroughly shuffled, a sample of four astronauts could be obtained by taking the four top cards from the deck and writing down their years of training. A second sample could be obtained by replacing the four cards in the deck, shuffling the deck thoroughly, and dealing out four more cards. In the same way, samples of any size could be ob-

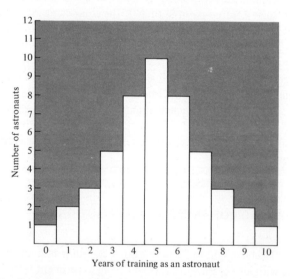

Figure 9-2. Population distribution for years of training for United States astronauts.

tained. The results shown in Table 9-1 are from a computer simulation of the experiment using years of training for astronauts.

Because of the complexity of the table, some explanations are required. The four pairs of columns in the body of the table show the mean M and sample estimate s of the population standard deviation σ_{pop}. The first column in each pair shows the 20 means obtained from the 20 computerized samples. The second column in each pair shows the 20 estimates of the population standard deviation, computed with the raw-score equation for s presented in Chapter 5. [See Equation (5-6).] Below the body of the table are various summary statistics. The first row shows the sum of means and the sum of s values for each sample size. Each of these is divided by 20, which provides the means shown in the second row below the table. For example, the mean of the means for a sample size of 4 is 5.02, and the mean of the s values for a sample size of 4 is 2.28. The third row shows the

Table 9-1. 20 Sample Values of M and s for each of Four Different N's Concerning Years of Training For a Population of 48 Astronauts

	$N = 4$		$N = 8$		$N = 12$		$N = 24$	
	M	s	M	s	M	s	M	s
	5.00	0.82	4.00	1.20	4.33	1.97	4.29	2.85
	6.25	1.71	4.62	2.50	5.00	2.41	4.21	2.15
	4.75	2.63	5.75	2.25	6.00	2.45	4.83	2.73
	5.50	2.08	3.88	2.42	5.67	2.23	4.83	2.32
	5.75	2.06	6.38	2.92	4.83	1.34	4.50	1.25
	4.00	3.56	4.75	2.66	6.08	2.35	5.13	2.44
	3.25	0.50	5.50	2.39	5.08	1.68	4.83	1.74
	5.50	0.58	4.75	2.19	6.25	1.66	5.37	2.36
	4.25	1.71	4.38	2.07	4.33	1.87	5.46	2.21
	5.75	2.22	3.75	2.05	5.75	1.66	5.37	2.02
	4.75	3.30	4.62	2.83	4.50	2.32	4.58	2.12
	6.00	2.94	5.37	2.07	4.58	2.43	5.42	2.12
	4.25	3.30	4.25	2.38	4.42	2.07	5.96	2.37
	4.75	2.06	5.00	2.51	5.33	2.19	5.04	2.29
	2.75	2.75	4.75	1.49	4.83	1.90	4.71	1.83
	6.75	3.59	5.88	2.17	5.08	2.35	5.50	2.67
	7.00	2.45	6.25	1.75	4.08	2.78	4.87	1.57
	5.75	2.75	5.63	2.26	5.58	1.62	5.46	2.11
	5.00	3.27	4.87	1.73	4.50	2.65	4.71	1.73
	3.50	1.29	4.75	2.76	4.50	2.20	5.00	1.91
Sum =	100.50	45.58	99.12	44.58	100.75	42.11	100.08	42.77
Mean =	5.02	2.28	4.96	2.23	5.04	2.11	5.00	2.14
s of means =	1.14		0.76		0.66		0.45	
σ_M =	1.08		0.76		0.62		0.44	
s_M =	1.14		0.79		0.61		0.44	

Population M (μ)　= 5.00
Population σ (σ_{pop}) = 2.16

results of applying the equation for s [Equation (5-6)] to the 20 means for each sample size. Thus, s for the 20 means in the sample size of 24 is 0.45. The numbers in the two rows labeled σ_M and s_M are theoretical values rather than actual computations of the data in the table. They will be explained subsequently. In the center at the very bottom of the table are the actual mean μ and standard deviation σ_{pop} of the population of 40 scores: 5.00 and 2.16 respectively.

Table 9-1 illustrates a number of important principles regarding inferential statistics. First, both the means and s values within each of the four sample sizes vary about the population mean of 5.00 and population standard deviation σ_{pop} of 2.16. Second, while the means and s values in each sample size vary about the actual population mean and standard deviation, the averages in each sample size are much closer to the population mean and standard deviation. This is a direct illustration of the law of large numbers. Third, the law of large numbers is exemplified by the fact that the s of the means in a sample size decreases progressively in going from sample sizes of 4 to sample sizes of 24. Thus, the range of the means for sample sizes of 4 is from 2.75 to 7.00 while the range for sample sizes of 8 is 3.75 to 6.38. Going to sample sizes of 12, we find a range of 4.08 to 6.25, and finally with sample sizes of 24, a range of 4.21 to 5.96. This clearly demonstrates that as sample size increases, the amount of error decreases. These are vivid illustrations of the "law of averages" at work in an actual statistical experiment.

Fourth, the need to use unbiased estimates of population values is directly evidenced. The mean of each sample is computed in exactly the same way as it was for the population. The average means for the four sample sizes are very close, and they all are very close to the population value of 5.00. In contrast, it was necessary to employ a slightly different equation to estimate the population standard deviation σ_{pop}. The reader will remember from Chapter 5 that the equation for the standard deviation is as follows

$$\sigma = \sqrt{\frac{\Sigma x^2}{N}} \qquad (9\text{-}2)$$

However, when this equation is applied to a sample, the results obtained are somewhat biased. To offset this bias, the correct equation to be employed with a sample is

$$s = \sqrt{\frac{\Sigma x^2}{N-1}} \qquad (9\text{-}3)$$

If this correction were not made, the expectation would be that the average value of the four sampling conditions would underestimate σ_{pop}. The underestimation would be negligible with an N of 30 or more, but it would be important with an N of less than 30.[1]

[1] Because of technical reasons much too difficult to be discussed here, the estimate of σ_{pop}, or s, using $N-1$ rather than N is still slightly biased for samples less than 10; however, s^2 is an unbiased estimate of σ_{pop}^2. [See Hays (1973), pp. 284-285 for a complete discussion of this topic.]

Fifth, the experiment demonstrates the validity of methods in mathematical statistics for estimating the standard error of a statistic computed on a sample. As shown in Equation (9-1), the standard error for estimating a population mean from the mean of a sample is

$$\sigma_M = \frac{\sigma_{pop}}{\sqrt{N}}$$

Because σ_{pop} can be computed directly in this special example, it can be found that

$$\sigma_{pop} = 2.16$$

Then σ_{pop} can be divided by the square root of the sample size in each of the four samples (4, 8, 12, and 24, respectively) to produce the four values of σ_M shown in the table. For example, when σ_{pop} of 2.16 is divided by the square root of 4, one obtains a σ_M of 1.08 for a sample size of 4. This is the standard deviation of the sampling distribution of means for a sample size of 4 from a population with σ_{pop} of 2.16. Note that σ_M grows progressively smaller as sample sizes grow larger. Each result in the row labeled "σ_M" can be compared with the result immediately above it in the row labeled "s of means." For a sample size of 4, s of means is 1.14 and σ_M is 1.08. Note for the four sample sizes how closely σ_M approximates the actual standard deviation of means obtained from the computerized experiment. This shows in a very direct way how a mathematically derived statistic (for example, σ_M) can provide an excellent estimate of the actual sampling distribution of a descriptive statistic (in this case, M). In the pages ahead, many mathematical equations which are known to provide excellent estimates of sampling distributions found in practice will be presented.

Of course, σ_{pop} is almost never known; consequently, it must be estimated from the values obtained from a sample. The s in any sample can be substituted for σ_{pop}, so that Equation (9-1) for the standard error of the mean can be transformed to

$$s_M = \frac{s}{\sqrt{N}} \tag{9-4}$$

Because σ and s differ only in the subtracted 1 in their computational equations, Equation (9-4) for computing s_M can be expressed as

$$s_M = \frac{\sigma}{\sqrt{N-1}} \tag{9-5}$$

What this indicates is that the standard error of the mean can be computed by employing the *equation for σ applied to the sample* and dividing by the square root of $N - 1$ or by employing the equation used to obtain s and dividing by the square root of N.

Values of s_M are shown in the fifth row at the bottom of Table 9-1. A value of s_M could have been found for each sample size. Thus, for sample size 8, the first s in the column of 1.20 could have been divided by the square root of the sample size. Twenty such estimates of s_M could have been obtained for each sample size. In order to obtain a better overall estimate of s_M, the equation for s_M was applied to the mean of the 20 estimates of s for each sample size. For example, the average s of 2.14 for sample size of 24 was divided by the square root of 24, producing an s_M of 0.44. In a similar way, an s_M was obtained for the other sample sizes.

It can be seen that s_M obtained from the average s in the experiment is very close to σ_M obtained from the known σ_{pop}. Both of these in turn are close to what is found when the equation for s is applied to the 20 means obtained for each sample size in the experiment. To repeat, a mathematically derived statistical equation (σ_M) provides a good estimate of the standard deviation of sample values for a descriptive statistic (in this case, M); however, because this mathematical equation is based on a characteristic of the population which is usually unknown, namely σ_{pop}, it is necessary to develop an equation for the standard error of the statistic based on the values of s obtained in particular samples. Because the values of s in each column of the table vary considerably, one would come up with a different value of s_M depending upon the particular sample obtained in any experiment; however, when values of s are averaged over as many as 20 samples and s_M is computed on this average, one obtains an excellent approximation of both s_M and the actual s of the 20 means obtained in the experiment. Thus, one can compute various characteristics of sampling distributions when scores are available only for a sample rather than for the population as a whole. What is important to note, however, is that any particular s_M obtained from a sample might grossly misrepresent σ_M obtained from an actual knowledge of σ_{pop}. These discrepancies, however, would average out over many experiments such as those predicted in Table 9-1. Thus, in the general case, s_M would provide a good estimate of σ_{pop} and can be used to estimate characteristics of sampling distributions.

CHARACTERISTICS OF SIGNIFICANCE TESTS

During the last 30 years, a great deal of attention in psychology and education has been given to testing the statistical significance of research results. A discussion of such tests consumes a major portion of most introductory texts in statistics. Essentially, any observed differences among treatment groups in an experiment are said to be statistically significant if the odds are low that the differences could be attributable entirely to error. Such sources of error were discussed previously in this chapter, where it was said that sampling error is one of the major components of the overall amount of error in any experiment.

Tests of significance were introduced initially to substitute for the impressionistic interpretation of research results that had been prevalent in the past. Thus, if in an experiment with two groups the mean of one group is higher than the mean of another group, it is tempting to interpret the difference as being "real" and to go on from there to an elaborate discussion of the implications of the finding. In fact, many such observed differences are entirely attributable to chance, and as a result, they will not be borne out in subsequent experiments. If the chance element that is prevalent in nearly all research in psychology and education is not taken account of, many unreliable findings would be reported in the scientific literature and subsequently have impacts on both theory land applied professional activities. Statistical tests of significance act as a hurdle to prevent such unreliable findings from being taken seriously.

How Significance Tests Are Determined

In the chapters ahead, numerous examples will be given of significance tests for inferential statistics. Here, it is important to discuss how such significance tests are developed. They do not depend upon intuition, nor do they depend upon the gathering of facts. Rather, they all are based upon statistical *models.* They represent mathematical derivations. An example of such a model is the standard error of the mean, which was already discussed and will be discussed again in Chapter 10

$$\sigma_M = \frac{\sigma}{\sqrt{N}}$$

This equation was obtained by postulating a model and then making mathematical derivations. Each model embodies a set of assumptions. One such assumption is that the different samples drawn from the population are independent of one another in the sense that the mean obtained from one sample is in nowise influenced by the mean obtained from another sample. Another assumption is that scores in the population as a whole are normally distributed. All of the significance tests discussed in the following chapters are based on mathematical models concerning probability distributions. The significance tests which are derived mathematically from these models are intuitively appealing in most cases. Efforts will be made to make these significance tests as understandable as possible; however, it should be understood that these significance tests are derived mathematically rather than following directly from common sense or being based on empirical research. The only way to understand these models is to study them directly. Because a detailed discussion of such models would be inappropriate in an introductory text of this kind, appropriate significance tests will be "talked out" rather than presented in the form of mathematical derivations. When an equation is presented as being the appropriate significance test for a particular statistic, the reader will have to take the equation on faith or refer to the Suggested Additional Readings and specific references.

Examples of Significance Tests

Significance tests are available for nearly all statistics that are used frequently. An example is that of testing the PM correlation for significance. An exploratory investigation is made of the correlations among different types of athletic skills, such as high jump, pole vault, sprints, and others. The sample consists of 200 boys drawn from three high schools in a particular city. After the computations are completed, the correlations are found to range from near 0 up to 0.70. Rather than interpret these findings directly, the investigator should apply inferential statistics in order to determine the probability that each coefficient differs from 0 simply as a result of sampling error. Similarly, such tests of significance should be employed before interpreting differences between sizes of the coefficients. Another example would be in comparing high school achievement test scores of students who participated in an honors program with students who participated in the usual curriculum. On the average, differences favor the honors students, but tests of significance of difference should be applied before the observations are taken seriously. The third example concerns a study of the changing interests of college students toward the humanities and away from science over the course of college training. Again, any observed differences should be tested for statistical significance before they are taken seriously.

It is common practice in the work-a-day world of research to examine all statistical results for significance shortly after they are obtained. If the results stand up well with respect to such tests of significance, the investigator is encouraged to probe the implications of the data in more detail. If the data do not pass these tests of significance, the investigator is understandably discouraged; and unless additional data produce significant findings, the original observed findings should not be taken seriously at all.

The Null Hypothesis

In the formal language of mathematical statistics, tests of significance are said to concern the *null hypothesis*. Thus, in the comparison of two differently treated experimental groups, initially the investigator is willing to consider the possibility that any observed differences will be due entirely to error. If that were actually the case, differences between means would be no greater than what would be expected by chance. The difference between means is compared with the appropriate standard error (to be discussed in Chapter 10). If the difference is very large in comparison to the standard error, then it is improbable that the difference could be due entirely to chance factors. This probability can be stated in the usual way, for example, $p = 0.05$ or $p = 0.01$. If the probability is low, the null hypothesis is improbable; thus, it is said that the hypothesis is rejected at the probability value stated. For these reasons, statistical significance is usually stated in terms of the *improbability* of observed results being due to error—sampling error and the other types of error discussed previously. It actually makes more sense to turn the question around and ask about the probability that an observed difference is real and thus not due to error. If the statistical significance is at the 0.05 level, it is more informative to talk about the *statistical confidence* as being at the 0.95 level. This means that the investigator can be confident with odds of 95 out of 100 that the observed difference will hold up in future investigations. The null hypothesis is introduced here because (1) it relates directly to the way in which probabilities regarding significance tests are reported, and (2) the reader will encounter language relating to the null hypothesis in textbooks and research reports.

Acceptable Levels of Statistical Significance

A question that has not been answered to this point concerns the level of statistical significance that is used as a general rule for accepting findings as real rather than more likely due to error. This is partly a matter of practical considerations. If it is very easy to gather data with respect to a particular problem, then it is reasonable to expect the investigator to obtain enough data to leave little doubt about the statistical reliability of the results. Thus, rather than report that a result was significant at the 0.05 level, it would be more appropriate for the investigator to continue gathering data to the point where the significance either was at the 0.01 level or, in the other direction, the significance approached 0.50 (pure chance). In a situation where it is extremely difficult to gather data, much more respect must be shown to the significance levels of any data that are at hand. An example would be in comparing test scores of two groups of people with different, unusual types of brain damage. Assume that it is feasible to obtain no more than 10 persons in each group, and the difference between groups is significant at the 0.05 level rather than any lower level. Because of the rarity of the data, however, the result would be appreciated by the scientific community.

Levels of statistical significance usually required in research reports vary somewhat as a matter of fashion. Up until about 20 years ago, it was not uncommon to see major research reports in which most of the differences were significant only at the 0.05 level. Now, such results are not taken very seriously, and it is more customary today to see results reported only if they reach the 0.01 or even lower probability levels (higher levels of significance).

In choosing an acceptable level of statistical significance, the investigator walks a fence between two possible mistakes. If the probability level is set relatively high (say the 0.05 level), then there is a danger of accepting a statistical result as real when it is actually due only to error. If the probability level is placed very low (say the 0.001 level or less), the investigator runs the risk of making the opposite mistake—rejecting a finding as being due to error when it is actually real. For these reasons, a good compromise is to employ the 0.01 level in most experiments. If the results are significant only at the 0.05 level, this is provocative and gives encouragement for further investigation. If the results are significant at the 0.001

level or beyond, this means that a great deal of faith can be placed in the reality of the finding.

Computation of Significance

The mechanics of applying inferential statistics consist of transforming some relationships among descriptive statistics into a form that allows one to make probability statements. The various equations employed with inferential statistics merely serve to make the transformation from the descriptive statistics. An example would be in comparing differences between two means. After the difference between the two means is divided by the standard error of differences between means, the result can be transformed into a probability by using one of the tables in Appendix B. These tables show probabilities corresponding to various sections of the characteristic sampling distributions for the mean, standard deviation, correlation coefficient, and other descriptive statistics.

The probability distribution which is used most frequently in making tests of significance of difference is the normal distribution. A table for making such conversions is presented in Appendix B-3. The table could be employed, for example, in the case where it is found that the mean achievement test score in arithmetic for fourth-grade students in a particular school is two standard errors above that for students at the same level in the country as a whole. In this case, there was no definite hypothesis that students in this particular school would be above the population mean; consequently, a *two-tailed test* would be appropriate. That is, one should consider the percentage of persons in a normal distribution that lie both above two standard deviations above the mean and below two standard deviations below the mean. Appendix B-3 shows that approximately 5 percent of the persons in a normal distribution are in those two regions and the remaining 95 percent are within the bounds of two standard deviations above and below the mean. This is another way of saying that (1) the difference of the sample mean from the population mean is significant at the 0.05 level, (2) the null hypothesis is rejected at the 0.05 level, or (3) the investigator can have 95 percent confidence that the sample mean actually differs from the population mean rather than the apparent difference being due only to sampling error. All of these are different ways of saying the same thing. If there had been a definite hypothesis regarding the superiority in arithmetic of the particular students in the sample in comparison to students intthe country as a whole, the probability in each of these three types of statements would have been divided in half.

In contrast to the mean, the significance tests for some other statistics are related to probability distributions which are different from the normal distribution. Depending on the statistic, some of the probability distributions are highly skewed, and others are even J-curves. At the introductory level, it is not necessary for the reader to understand in detail how these probability distributions are derived for different statistics. The important points to grasp are (1) appropriate probability distributions are available for all statistics which are used widely, (2) appropriate equations are available for comparing relations among observed statistics with the amount of error, and (3) appropriate tables are available for computing probabilities concerning significance of differences. These matters will be discussed in detail in the remaining chapters, and the necessary tables for computing probabilities are presented in Appendix B.

Directionality of Predictions

What has not been mentioned so far is that the probability associated with a statistical test depends on the predictions or hypotheses that are made before the experiment is undertaken. A two-tailed test is said to be made when neither theory nor common sense would lead to a definite prediction regarding the outcome of the experiment. For example, in obtaining an exploratory correlation of a test of anxiety with a test of athletic fitness, there may be no good reason to predict in advance that the correlation would be positive rather than negative. Similarly, in comparing a novel method of instruction in spelling with the conventional method, there may be no basis for making a firm prediction as to which will work better. In these, and all other cases where a two-tailed prediction is made, the investigator must consider the probability associated with *both* tails of the probability distribution which relates to the significance test. An example is shown in Figure 9-3. The mean difference for the novel instructional group is found to be 1.96 (to choose a convenient number) standard errors above the mean of the conventional teaching method. This indicates that the probability is only about 0.025 of finding a larger difference purely by chance; however, the fact that the difference might have been reversed, with the group scoring higher actually scoring lower in a hypothetical infinite repeating of the experiment with other subjects must be taken into account. Thus, the probability in the lower tail of the distribution, which is about 0.025, must also be taken into account. Then, one must add together the two probabilities, which sum to approximately 0.05. Therefore, in a two-tailed statistical test, it should be said that the results are significant at the 0.05 level.

In many experiments, either common sense or a definite hypothesis specifies the expected direction of a statistical result. One example would be in correlating a measure of motor skills with reading speed. Because it is almost unheard of to find any human abilities that correlate negatively with one another, the expectation is that the correlation will either be positive or near 0. In that case, imagine that a correlation of 0.40 is actually obtained. Then, one would make a *one-tailed test*, considering only the improbability of finding a correlation that high purely by chance. Thus, the significance would be based only on the upper tail of the distribution. The probability associated with statistical significance for a one-tailed test is always half of that for a two-tailed test in the same situation. Thus, if an unpredicted difference between two means is found to be significant at $p = 0.05$

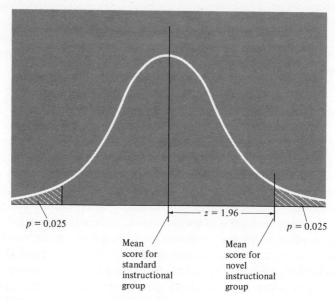

$p = 0.025$

$z = 1.96$

$p = 0.025$

Mean
score for
standard
instructional
group

Mean
score for
novel
instructional
group

Figure 9-3. Expected distribution of differences between two means of many pairs of samples from the same population.

with a two-tailed test, then the same comparison would have shown $p = 0.025$ with a one-tailed test.

The reader should be left with three principles in mind regarding the directionality of statistical tests. First, the matter is rather technical, and it would be difficult for the reader of an introductory text to understand the issues fully. It is necessary to mention it here because the matter is brought up in some textbooks and research reports. Second, questions of directionality and the appropriate statistical tests are discussed in detail in Chapters 10 and 11 and properly indicated on probability distributions presented in Appendix B. Third, unless there is a very definite hypothesis regarding the direction of the outcome of an experiment, it is always prudent to assume that a two-tailed test is being made. It is easy for investigators to fall into the trap of making one-tailed hypotheses after all statistical results are known. It is usually the case that neither common sense nor theory is wise to be skeptical about the employment of one-tailed tests for most experiments.

Usefulness of Significance Tests

As already mentioned in several places in this book, tests of statistical significance are mainly important in determining whether or not the results of experiments should be taken seriously. Statistical significance should not be confused with the more general use of the word significant. In studies where a very large number of subjects is investigated, even very tiny correlations and differences between means are frequently statistically significant, As another consideration, the results may be statistically significant but not be of any practical significance. Statistical significance means just that: the odds are low that the result is due purely to random errors inherent in the sampling of subjects and other chance factors in the experimental situation. Tests of statistical significance are mainly important in the negative sense. If the research results do not pass the minimal hurdles provided by these tests, then, of course, they should not be interpreted in any way.

CONFIDENCE INTERVALS

It is definitely a mistake to consider tests of statistical significance as important beyond providing an initial hurdle to weed out totally untrustworthy findings. After passing that initial hurdle, the results should be examined in other ways regarding the exact nature of the findings and the importance for theory and daily life. At the simplest level, this consists of inspecting the results (for instance, correlations of differences between means) and considering how important such findings are for theory and practice. In addition, confidence intervals can be used to determine the limits in which sizes of correlations and sizes of differences between means can be safely interpreted.

In many ways, *confidence intervals* supply much more information than obtained from tests of statistical significance alone. Also, it will be shown why tests of statistical significance really represent only a special case of confidence intervals. In spite of the importance of confidence intervals in statistics, it is beyond the scope of this book to discuss the matter in detail. The interested reader will find a detailed discussion in Hays (1973), Chaps. 9 and 15.

Confidence intervals can be illustrated in a simple experiment in which IQs of sixth-grade boys are correlated with physical fitness. A standard test is used to measure IQ. Physical fitness is measured by a variety of exercises, the scores from which are combined to obtain an overall measure. The two measures are correlated, employing the usual PM coefficient. With a sample of 300 boys, it is found that $r = 0.38$. First, the investigator should test the correlation for statistical significance by the use of equations to be discussed in Chapter 10. It is found that the correlation is significant at the 0.001 level (employing a two-tailed test). Second, after the result passes this minimal hurdle, the experimenter should think about the importance of the correlation coefficient. Although such a correlation is not large in an absolute sense, the unexpectedness of the finding has important implications for theories concerning intelligence and physical fitness. Third, to help the investigator interpret the finding, it would be wise to apply confidence intervals. How this is done is illustrated in Figure 9-4. Methods for computing such intervals can be found in Hays (1973), Chap. 15. The 95 percent confidence interval stretches from $r = 0.28$ to $r = 0.47$. Essentially what this means is that the experimenter can feel 95 percent sure that the correlation of the populations of boys that age is somewhere within this interval. In other words, in taking many samples from the population, the expectation is that in only about 5 percent of the samples will the correlation be either higher than 0.47 or lower than 0.28. The confidence interval for the 99 percent level stretches from $r = 0.23$ to $r = 0.51$; the interval for 99.9 percent confidence stretches from $r = 0.21$ to $r = 0.53$.

In most correlational problems, it is more important to consider the lower bound of the confidence interval rather than the upper bound. This tells the investigator how far above 0 the correlation can be safely interpreted. The 99 percent confidence level is usually taken as a useful compromise between being too lenient and being overly severe when interpreting results; consequently, it would be safe to conclude in this case that the correlation is at least as high as 0.23. Used in this way, confidence intervals provide very helpful guides concerning the interpretation of research results. They can be employed with many types of statistics in addition to correlation coefficients. Why tests of statistical significance are only special cases of confidence intervals is illustrated in the instance where the lower arm of the confidence interval crosses 0 correlation. This means that the obtained correlation is not statistically significant at the level specified by the probability of the confidence interval. In Figure 9-4, it is noted that the 99 percent confidence interval extends to 0.23. If this interval had crossed 0, then the results would not be statistically significant at the 0.01 level. Because the 0.01 level serves as a useful hurdle for statistical significance, the results would not have been taken seriously unless supporting evidence was obtained in subsequent investigations. Confidence intervals can be employed with respect to most of the statistics used in psychology and education. They have not been used nearly as much as they should have in the past; they should be used much more widely in the future.

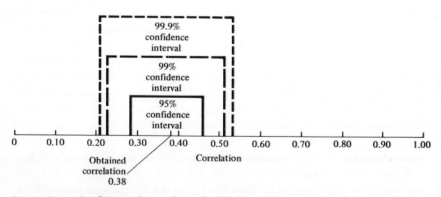

Figure 9-4. Confidence intervals at the 95, 99, 99.9 percent levels for an obtained sample correlation of 0.40.

SUMMARY

Science is concerned with two types of inference—deductive inference and inductive inference. Deductive inference consists of drawing conclusions from mathematics and other types of symbolic logic. Such inferences depend entirely upon the manipulation of symbols within a system. Any inference is either absolutely true or absolutely false, and no amount of evidence from the real world is necessarily involved. In contrast, inductive inferences concern statements about regularity in the real world. The truth of inductive inferences depends upon the gathering of facts; and no matter how much factual evidence may support a particular inductive inference, there is always the possibility that different evidence will be obtained tomorrow. A statistical inference is a particular type of inductive inference, one in which expected events in everyday life must be accompanied by probability statements, for instance, the probability that a person with an IQ of 115 will successfully complete college training.

A descriptive statistic obtained on a sample of subjects is important only to the extent to which it is useful in estimating the same descriptive statistic that would be obtained from some population of subjects. Any descriptive statistic (such as M or r) can be thought of as having a sampling distribution; that is, if successive random samples were drawn from the population and such descriptive statistics were computed on each sample, one would find a frequency distribution of each statistic analogous to the way in which one finds a frequency distribution of test scores in any one sample. This sampling distribution can be thought of as a distribution of errors in the sense that the wider the distribution, the more the descriptive statistic varies from sample to sample. Because many such distributions of errors are approximately like the normal distribution, it is meaningful to describe such distributions of errors with the standard deviation—called the standard error in this case. The standard error is relatively small when the number of subjects that are sampled is large, and vice versa when the number of subjects is relatively small. This principle is called the law of large numbers. In particular, the standard error with respect to many descriptive statistics is inversely related to the square root of the number of subjects in the study. This principle is called the inverse-square law.

Strictly speaking, the inverse-square law applies to the degrees of freedom (df) rather than to N itself. The concept of df arises from mathematical models that are used to derive various inferential statistics. Some intuitive support for the concept can be obtained by noting the number of subjects that must be "thrown away" before real information is obtained regarding an estimate of the population descriptive statistic from the descriptive statistic obtained on a sample. This is exemplified by r, whose df is $N - 2$.

The nature of sampling distributions, degrees of freedom, and standard errors was illustrated in the chapter with a hypothetical experiment concerning years of training by astronauts. A distribution of years of training was composed for a total of 48 individuals, with a known M and σ_{pop}. A computer was used to draw 20 samples from this distribution for each level of N equaling 4, 8, 12, and 24 respectively. Computed for each sample was M, s, and various statistics summarizing the overall results. Among other things, the computerized experiment demonstrated (1) actual sampling distributions for M and s, (2) mathematical statistics (such as s_M) used to estimate actual characteristics of empirically obtained sampling distributions, and (3) a number of instances of the law of large numbers at work.

These characteristics of sampling distributions and their associated standard errors permit the development of various tests of statistical significance. Essentially, significance tests concern comparisons of descriptive statistics obtained on a sample (or differences between such descriptive statistics) with appropriate standard errors. For example, there is a standard error for the difference between the means obtained from two samples of subjects. A comparison of such results from descriptive statistics with the appropriate standard error can be translated into a probability by employing the appropriate table for making such transformations. If the probability is very low, say, 0.01 or less, it can be safely concluded that the obtained results regarding descriptive statistics on the samples are probably *not* due to sheer chance but probably relate to some real difference between the samples of subjects. Probability statements made in this way are said to relate to the null hypothesis, meaning that originally, the experimenter should make no assumption that the samples really are different until the significance of the difference is shown by the obtained probabilities. It is usually more meaningful to turn the matter around, subtract the significance level from 1.00, and state the probability that the finding is "real" rather than due to chance, for instance, a significance level of 0.05 means that one can have 0.95 confidence that the finding is real.

Significance tests are primarily useful in determining if obtained research results pass an initial hurdle concerning whether or not they should be taken seriously; otherwise, such significance tests provide only meager information. If that initial hurdle is passed, the investigator should then go on to examine his results in other ways. One important approach requires the use of confidence intervals to determine the zone in which results can be safely trusted. Such confidence intervals should be employed much more widely in research than they have to date.

EXERCISES

Study Questions

1 With what two types of inference is science concerned? Compose two examples of each. Briefly mention the place of these two types of inference in psychology and education.

2   In what way is statistical inference a special case of inductive inference? Give an example.

3   What is a sampling distribution? Give an example.

4   In what sense is the standard error a special case of the standard deviation?

5   In what way is the law of large numbers related to sampling error? How does the inverse-square law apply?

6   What is the most prominent source of error in experiments in psychology and education? What can be done to reduce this? What are some other sources of error?

7   Discuss relations among (a) σ_{pop}, (b) the equation for σ applied to a sample, and (c) s. Why is the df used with s? What are σ_M and s_M?

8   What is the null hypothesis? Give an example regarding a hypothetical research problem. What does it mean to reject the null hypothesis? How does the rejection of the null hypothesis relate to confidence in the reality of research results obtained from a sample?

9   Distinguish between one-tailed and two-tailed tests of significance. Compose examples of hypothetical experiments in which each would be appropriate. If the probability for a two-tailed test is $p = 0.02$, then what would be the corresponding probability with respect to a one-tailed test in the same instance?

10   What are confidence intervals? Give examples from hypothetical experiments with respect to the mean and the correlation coefficient. What information do they add in addition to significance tests concerning the null hypothesis?

Problems

Following are the scores of 25 students on an IQ test

90	110	104	94	106
95	103	107	100	97
95	98	101	99	100
120	92	115	93	100
106	94	105	100	97

On the basis of these scores, answer the questions and solve the problems which follow.

1   Assume that the study is concerned purely with these students and with no larger group. In other words, this is the population in question. Compute σ_{pop} and the mean of the sample (in this case μ rather than M). Would there be any sampling error for either statistic?

2   As in the more general case, assume that this is only a sample from a larger population to which the results will be generalized. Apply the same equation for σ_{pop} to this sample, in which case it is customary to symbolize the statistic as σ rather than σ_{pop}. Compute σ_M. What would σ_M have been if σ were the same and N were 101 rather than 25?

3   Because the concepts of degrees of freedom should be employed when using results of samples to estimate population values, it would be more proper to compute s and s_M rather than σ and σ_M. Compute s and s_M for the 25 scores.

4   Compare the results obtained from Problem 3 with those obtained from Problem 2. Which statistic applied to a sample will always be larger in a numerical sense? When is the difference relatively large and when is it relatively small?

SUGGESTED ADDITIONAL READINGS

Ferguson, G. A. *Statistical analysis in psychology and education*, 3d ed. New York: McGraw-Hill, 1971, Chaps. 9 and 10.

Guilford, J. P. and B. Fruchter. *Fundamental statistics in psychology and education*, 5th ed. New York: McGraw-Hill, 1973, Chap. 8.

Hays, W. L. *Statistics for the social sciences*, 2d ed. New York: Holt, Rinehart and Winston, 1973, Chaps. 2, 7, 9, and 10.

10

Inferences Regarding Measures of Central Tendency, Variation, and Correlation

As was discussed in Chapter 5, there are three important types of descriptive statistics which serve to summarize the results of experiments. The first is a measure of central tendency, for which the arithmetic mean is used most widely. Thus, in comparing two differently treated groups in an experiment, the most important descriptive statistics in most cases would be the means of the two groups. Assuming that differences among means are statistically significant, the larger these differences, the larger the effects of experimental treatments on the dependent variable. Even if differences among means are statistically significant but very small in an absolute sense, the treatments have little effect on the dependent variable.

The second type of descriptive statistic which is important in research is a measure of the variability of scores within samples, for which purpose the standard deviation is the most widely used measure. An example would be in comparing male and female high school students on a test of driving proficiency after a course in driver training. It is found that male and female students do not differ on the average substantially; however, female students show a much wider dispersion of performance scores than males. Some female students have very high scores on the performance tests, and at the other extreme, some female students have very low scores. In contrast, male students tend to cluster more closely about their mean, neither having scores that are extremely high or extremely low.

A third type of descriptive statistic that is employed very frequently in research is the PM correlation coefficient, which was discussed in detail in Chapters 7 and 8. A typical research problem is that in which a test of motor skills is correlated with grades in typing classes in high school.

Of course, in any research project, the results obtained from comparing two or more treatment conditions are informative only to the extent that they mirror the results that would be found in studying much larger numbers of persons; consequently, it is necessary to employ inferential statistics with respect to results obtained from an experiment. In this way, it is possible to make probability statements about the extent to which the results obtained from an experiment would be substantiated in the investigation of much larger numbers of persons. This chapter will consider the simple case in which means, variances, and correlations are tested for significance when only two groups are involved in the research. Chapters 11 and 12 will consider cases in which more than two groups are involved in the research project.

INFERENCES ABOUT MEASURES OF CENTRAL TENDENCY

In a simple experiment comparing treatment effects of only two groups, the most important inferential statistics usually concern the significance of differences between means on the dependent measure. This would be the case in comparing the average scores of two differently treated groups in any study of learning, perception, or methods of instruction in athletic skills. The standard error of the mean s_M was mentioned in Chapter 9. This is the expected standard deviation of means from any size sample that would be obtained from a very large number of samples, for example, samples of student performance on a test concerning the ability to detect alphabetical letters rapidly presented on a screen. In Chapter 9, it was also said that the standard error of the mean concerns two descriptive statistics in the sample—the number of subjects in the sample N and the estimate of the population standard deviation obtained from the variability actually found in the sample s. The standard error of the mean was stated in Equation (9-4)

$$s_M = \frac{s}{\sqrt{N}}$$

Whereas s_M is important theoretically, the standard error of the difference between two means rather than with the standard error of only one mean is usually of more concern in actual research. In relation to the example given previously, one such difference would be between the scores of male and female students on a test of perceptual accuracy. Even more common would be the differences between means in the many experiments that are performed on two groups of subjects in which the total group available is randomly divided. Standard errors of the mean could be obtained for each of the two samples, these being symbolized as s_{M_1} and s_{M_2}. For the moment, let it be assumed that N is the same in both groups. In this case, a general principle of statistics is that the error associated with the difference between two sample values equals the square root of the sum of the squared standard errors for the samples taken separately

$$s_{MD} = \sqrt{s_{M_1}^2 + s_{M_2}^2}$$ (10-1)

where s_{MD} = the standard error of the difference between two means, s_{M_1} = the standard error of the mean of Group 1, and s_{M_2} = the standard error of the mean of Group 2.

The difference between two means is then compared with s_{MD} as follows

$$t_{(df)} = \frac{M_1 - M_2}{s_{MD}}$$ (10-2)

Probability values corresponding to t are found in Appendix B-6. The normal distribution z was discussed in Chapter 6. The *t distribution* is another important statistical distribution. More properly, t refers to a set of distributions that vary somewhat in terms of df; consequently, in Equation (10-2) the term on the left is presented as $t_{(df)}$. The df for the standard error of the mean s_M in any sample equals the number of subjects in the sample minus 1. The df for the standard error of the difference between two means s_{MD} equals the sum of df for the two samples. As an example, if in employing Equation (10-1) there are 30 subjects in each group, then the df for s_{MD} would equal 58. Then, in Equation (10-2), there

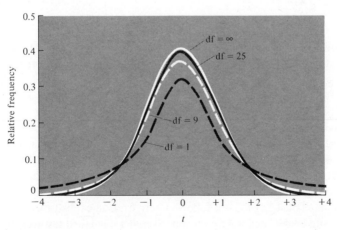

Figure 10-1. Distribution of t for various degrees of freedom.

would be 58 df for t, and consequently one would show $t_{(58)}$. The result obtained from Equation (10-2) would then be referred to Appendix B-6 with regard to a df of 58. When the number of df is small (less than 30), the t distribution is flatter than the normal distribution. As the df grows larger, the t distribution becomes very similar to the normal z distribution. The relationships are illustrated in Figure 10-1, which shows t distributions for samples with 1, 9, 25, and infinity (∞) df respectively.

Any value of t obtained from a comparison of two sample means can be tested for significance with the probability values shown in Appendix B-6. An example is as follows. Two experimental groups each contain 30 students. The members of each group are tested on their ability to recognize words that are rapidly presented on a screen. The members of Group 1 are familiarized with the words before the experiment, but no familiarization is given to Group 2. In the test of perceptual accuracy, it is found that the members of the first group have a mean of 25 correct responses, and the members of the second group have a mean of 20 correct responses. The unbiased estimates of the population standard deviations from the two samples s_1 and s_2 are 11.5 and 9.85 respectively. Employing Equation (9-4), a standard error of the mean can be obtained by dividing those values by the square root of 30. In turn, these two standard errors can be placed in Equation (10-1) to obtain s_{MD}. Following Equation (10-2), the t value would then be obtained as follows

$$
\begin{aligned}
t_{(58)} &= \frac{25 - 20}{\sqrt{4.41 + 3.20}} \\
&= \frac{5}{\sqrt{7.61}} \\
&= \frac{5}{2.76} \\
&= 1.81
\end{aligned}
$$

There are 30 subjects in each group. Thus, each group has 29 df. The df in the t test for differences between two means equals the sum of df for the two groups; consequently, this t has 58 df. In Appendix B-6, probability values are shown for df of 40 and df of 60 but for nothing in between. The probability values at these df levels are so similar that it really would not matter much which one was chosen. This is because beyond df of 30, probability values for different levels of t are very much the same at all levels of df and very much the same as those obtained from the normal distribution. Looking across the row corresponding to 40 df, it can be seen that the t of 1.81 in the previous equation is less than the value of 2.02 required for significance at the 0.05 level in a two-tailed test. If, as in most experiments, a one-tailed test did not follow closely from an explicit theory, then the result would be declared not significant. Even if a one-tailed test were justified in this circumstance, the obtained t would be only slightly larger than the t of 1.684

required for significance at the 0.05 level. The best conclusion would be that the results are, at most, suggestive of possible differences that would be found with larger groups of subjects; however, the lack of more obvious statistical significance would rule out any claims for definite findings in the experiment.

Unequal Sample Size

Equation (10-1) applies for all large samples and for small samples (N less than 30) where the N is the same in both groups. In many controlled experiments, an equal N in each group is the case. For example, in comparing two differently treated groups in a study of learning, the common practice is to randomly divide the available subjects into two groups of equal N.

When only small samples are obtained and the N's are not equal in the two groups, a precise test of significance entails the use of a special equation. The standard errors of the two groups must be differentially weighted before they are combined to obtain an estimate of the standard error of the difference s_{MD}. The necessary approach to obtaining s_{MD} for small groups with unequal N's is given in Equation (10-3)

$$s_{MD} = \sqrt{\frac{N_1 s_1^2 + N_2 s_2^2}{N_1 N_2}} \qquad (10\text{-}3)$$

where s_1^2 and s_2^2 = unbiased sample estimates of the population variances obtained from the two samples, and N_1 and N_2 = the numbers of subjects in the two samples.

This equation then becomes the denominator to Equation (10-2). Thus, if the N in one group is 14 and the N in the second group is 8, the special correction presented in Equation (10-3) should be applied. How Equation (10-3) is employed is illustrated in Table 10-1.

The experiment for which the data in Table 10-1 applies concerned the number of hours per week children watch television. It was conducted to determine if a change in television-viewing time occurred when children entered the first grade. From the data given, it is found that $t = 1.95$. In Appendix B-6, it is found that with 32 df it is necessary to have a t of at least 2.04 for significance at the 0.05 level. The t of 1.95 obtained from the data in Table 10-1 is slightly below that level; consequently, the mean difference in the experiment is not quite significant at the 0.05 level. Since this level of significance is usually considered the minimum for which results can be taken as strong evidence, at most, the results can be suggestive of possible differences that might be found in future research. Thus, there is little evidence from this experiment to indicate that a change occurs in television-viewing time when children enter the first grade.

Equation (10-1) leads to a good estimate of the s_{MD} unless the N is small in one or both groups, the N's are very different in the two groups, and the variances are markedly different in the two groups. Fortunately, these three circumstances

Table 10-1. Statistical Results and Computation of t for a Study Comparing Hours of Viewing Time for Kindergarten and First-Grade Children

Kindergarten	First graders
$N_1 = 14$	$N_2 = 20$
$M_1 = 22.4$	$M_2 = 20.7$
$s_1^2 = 6.8$	$s_2^2 = 5.9$

$$s_{MD} = \sqrt{\frac{(14)(6.8) + (20)(5.9)}{(20)(14)}}$$

$$t = \frac{M_1 - M_2}{s_{MD}}$$

$$= \sqrt{\frac{95.2 + 118.0}{280}}$$

$$= \frac{22.4 - 20.7}{0.87}$$

$$= \sqrt{0.76}$$

$$= \frac{1.7}{0.87}$$

$$= 0.87$$

$$= 1.95$$

Not significant at 0.05 level

$$df = N_1 + N_2 - 2$$
$$= 32$$

are seldom present simultaneously in comparing differences between two means. If the N in one group is 35 and the N in the other group is 38, it would usually not be necessary to apply the special correction presented in Equation (10-3). Differences of this kind frequently occur because of the loss of subjects in one or both groups. An example would be in randomly assigning students from three sections of the fourth grade in a particular school to two different methods of instruction in spelling. Initially, this might result in 35 students being placed in each group. At the end of the term, when dependent measures are administered, there would probably be some missing subjects in each group because of children having transferred to other schools or having been absent on the day of testing. This might result in 28 subjects being tested in one group and 31 subjects being tested in the other group. Because the difference in each sample is so small, Equation (10-1) would provide an excellent estimate of the proper s_{MD}, particularly if s_1 and s_2 were not markedly different.

In other cases, the N in each group is so large that it would not be necessary to employ Equation (10-3) even when rather large differences in N were present. An example would be an experiment in which 150 students are selected in a relatively random manner from a college to test a new type of dormitory life. The sample is selected from a total college enrollment of 3,000 students. At the end of the school year, dependent measures consist of school records and responses to questionnaires by the special group of 150 students and 200 other students randomly drawn from the college enrollment. Significance tests are then computed on mean differences obtained from the different dependent measures. Because the N's are large in both groups, it would not be necessary to apply Equation (10-3), rather, it would be justifiable to apply Equation (10-1) as an estimate of s_{MD}.

Paired Observations

Equation (10-1) concerns the situation in which subjects are independently assigned to two groups. Thus, subjects are randomly assigned to the two groups rather than purposely placed in the groups because of any personal characteristics. In some experiments, however, it is definitely wise to purposely pair up subjects before randomly assigning each member of the pair to experimental treatments, so that *paired observation* can be made. This is done in the situation where (1) it is known in advance of the experiment that subjects vary considerably with respect to an attribute that is likely to be important in relation to the dependent measures, and (2) it is possible to match subjects before the experiment in terms of this attribute. An example would be in comparing any special method of instruction with the usual method. Scores on the dependent measure of achievement would probably correlate highly with the initial IQs of the students in each of the two groups. If IQs vary widely in the school, as is usually the case, this variability will constitute a source of error which would be evidenced in s_{MD}. This error can frequently be reduced markedly by matching (pairing) subjects according to IQs. This is illustrated in the situation where there are 60 students available for the study. Measures of IQ would usually be obtainable from tests administered routinely in the school. The first step in assigning students to matched groups would be to rank them from highest to lowest according to IQ. Then, a coin flip could be used to determine whether the top person in terms of IQ is placed in Group 1 or Group 2. The second person in this regard would automatically be placed in the second group. Students ranking further down on the list would be assigned in the same way, ensuring that an equal number of students would be placed in each group. A quicker and simpler approach would be to assign students according to a table of random numbers like that presented in Appendix B-1. Each student on a list of available subjects would be associated with one of the numbers appearing in the table. It does not matter how the students appear on the list, for instance, in alphabetical order. The experimenter can also start at any point in the table. A frequently used practice is for the experimenter simply to close his eyes and make a pencil point somewhere in the table. Then, going down any column of numbers, the student is assigned to one experimental treatment if his name corresponds to an even number or assigned to the other experimental treatment if his name corresponds to an odd number. The only restriction would be that an equal number of students be placed in each of the two groups.

There are many other cases in which the standard error of the difference between means can be reduced by pairing subjects. One example is in studying the effects of drugs on the maturation of the brains of rats. Because there are hereditary differences in size and other features of brains in rats, the error that would be entailed in that regard can be reduced by picking pairs from the littermates of several offspring born to mothers. Of course, the members of each pair should be either both male or female rather than cross-sexed.

The classic example of pairing subjects is in a study of identical twins. A special method of training in motor skills is applied to children beginning at the age of eight months and lasting for two years. One twin in each pair is given the special course of training, and the other is left to develop on his own. Children in the experimental group are given exercises such as climbing stairs, arranging objects, and other activities relating to the development of motor skills. Because of the time and expense required for training the experimental group, it is important to use all of the statistical power possible in assessing the significance of differences between the two groups. The use of identical twins provides an opportunity to greatly reduce the experimental error by pairing subjects. Identical twins are very much alike with respect to all personal characteristics; consequently, they would differ only slightly on the dependent measures unless the treatment had a real effect.

The ultimate in paired observations is that in which individuals are compared with themselves before and after an experimental treatment. Such designs are referred to as *own control* or repeated-measures designs. In some instances, such designs have a very important advantage over comparing randomly selected groups. [Some cautions regarding the use of repeated-measures designs are discussed in Campbell and Stanley (1968).]

When subjects are matched before being randomly assigned to groups, or when subjects receive both treatment conditions, a special set of equations can be used for testing the significance of difference. These are illustrated in Table 10-2.

The purpose of the experiment is to determine whether subjects are better at detecting a light stimulus onset rather than a stimulus offset. Ten subjects are required to press one button for the occurrence of a stimulus onset and another button for the disappearance of another stimulus. Scores in the form of fractions of a second for button pushing are presented in Table 10-2. The score for each subject represents the average reaction time over numerous trials. Thus, a score of 33 corresponds to 0.33 of a second. The table shows reaction times in the two circumstances, differences between reaction times, and other relevant statistics. Note that N refers to the number of score pairs, either the number of pairs of individuals when subjects are matched or the number of subjects in a repeated-measurements design.

The first step is to compute the difference in scores D either for the individual in the two treatment conditions or between the matched individuals in the two treatment conditions. The estimated standard deviation of these difference scores in the population is obtained as follows

$$s_D = \sqrt{\frac{\Sigma(D - M_D)^2}{N - 1}} \qquad \qquad (10\text{-}4)$$

In this case, s_D is analogous to s_1 and s_2, the two estimates of population standard deviations of scores for the two types of experimental tasks. What is different, however, is that s_D is an estimate of the population standard deviation of difference scores for the two types of treatments. Once obtained, s_D can be converted to a standard error when it is divided by the square root of the number of score pairs

$$s_{MD} = \frac{s_D}{\sqrt{N}} \qquad \qquad (10\text{-}5)$$

Table 10-2. Comparison of the Reaction Time of Ten Subjects to the Onset of a Stimulus Light and to the Offset of a Stimulus Light

Subject	Light onset	Light offset	Difference (D)	$D - M_D$	$(D - M_D)^2$
1	33	41	8	$-$ 0.5	0.25
2	37	52	15	6.5	42.25
3	41	37	$-$ 4	$-$12.5	156.25
4	28	41	13	4.5	20.25
5	47	50	3	$-$ 5.5	30.25
6	38	51	13	4.5	20.25
7	48	47	$-$ 1	$-$ 9.5	90.25
8	28	39	11	2.5	6.25
9	29	41	12	3.5	12.25
10	37	52	15	6.5	42.25

$N = 10 \qquad M_1 = 36.6 \quad M_2 = 45.1 \qquad \Sigma D = 85 \qquad \qquad \Sigma(D - M_D)^2 = 420.50$

$$s_D = \sqrt{\frac{\Sigma(D - M_D)^2}{N - 1}}$$

$$= \sqrt{\frac{420.50}{9}}$$

$$= \sqrt{46.72}$$

$$= 6.84$$

$$\text{df} = N - 1$$

$$= 9$$

$$s_{MD} = \frac{s_D}{\sqrt{N}}$$

$$= \frac{6.84}{\sqrt{10}}$$

$$= \frac{6.84}{3.16}$$

$$= 2.16$$

$$M_D = \frac{85}{10}$$

$$= 8.5$$

$$t = \frac{M_D}{s_{MD}}$$

$$= \frac{8.5}{2.16}$$

$$= 3.93$$

Significant beyond the 0.01 level

Then, M_D (same as $M_1 - M_2$) can be divided by s_{MD} to form a t ratio. From the data in Table 10-2, it is found that $t = 3.93$. When making a comparison of matched groups, the df consists of the number of *pairs* minus 1. This is either the number of paired subjects when matching procedures are employed or the total number of subjects when each person participates in both experimental treatments. If a total group of 20 subjects is divided into 10 matched pairs for an experiment, then df = 9. If instead, 10 subjects underwent both treatments, the df also would equal 9. In Table 10-1 there are 10 subjects who received both experimental treatments; consequently, df = 9. The t of 3.93 with df of 9 is then referred to Appendix B-6. With a two-tailed test, this is found to be significant beyond the 0.01 level. The implication is that the apparent difference is probably real and not due only to chance factors with respect to the way subjects were selected or other elements of error in the experimental situation.

INFERENCES REGARDING VARIANCES

In some cases, it is important to test for the significance of difference between two variances. An example would be in comparing the scores of male and female college students on a measure of sociability—the tendency to be socially outgoing rather than retiring. In a study, it is found that average scores of males and females are very similar, but is is also noted that the dispersion of scores appears to be larger for males than that for females. The estimated population standard deviation for males s_1 is 4.8, and the result for females s_2 is 4.1. The variances are $s_1^2 = 23.04$ and $s_2^2 = 16.81$. The test which is applied to the significance of differences between two variances is simultaneously a test of the significance of the difference between the two corresponding standard deviations. The significance test for the difference between two variances is formed by dividing the larger variance by the smaller variance as follows

$$F = \frac{s_1^2}{s_2^2} \qquad\qquad (10\text{-}6)$$

In this example, $F = 1.37$. The *F ratio* is another important sampling distribution, in addition to the normal distribution and the t distribution discussed previously. A table of values for the F distribution is presented in Appendix B-7.

What is needed to determine the p value for two variances is the F ratio and the df for each of the two variances. The df equals $N - 1$ for each sample. In this case, there are 25 males and 51 females. Then $df_1 = 24$ and $df_2 = 50$. The probability is found by first looking along the top of the table for the df corresponding to the variance in the numerator of the F ratio and looking down the side of the table for the df corresponding to the denominator of the F ratio. The table shows three p values relating to each combination of df, corresponding respectively to the 0.05, 0.01, and 0.001 levels. For the special case of testing the significance of the difference between two variances, it is necessary to *double* the probabilities found in Appendix B-7. This is because the larger variance is arbitrarily placed in the numerator of the F ratio in Equation (10-6). The table is designed for the more frequent situation in which the problem specifies which variance becomes the numerator and which variance becomes the denominator. This matter will be discussed extensively in Chapters 11 and 12. Appendix B-7 holds for all the cases that will be discussed regarding ratios of variances, except the special case of comparing variances of two samples.

For the previous example, the F ratio for 24 and 50 df is 1.74 at the 0.05 level and 2.18 at the 0.01 level. In the example, the F ratio is 1.37. This means that the difference in variance is not statistically significant even at the 0.10 level (as mentioned previously, twice the probability value shown in the table).

Paired Observations

The F test just described is used to compare two different samples. Such comparisons of different samples are illustrated with differences in variances of males and females in terms of test scores. Another case of comparing different samples would be that of variances of achievement test scores in two schools. In some cases, it is important to compare variances of two measures based on paired observations. Examples of various types of paired observations in conjunction with significance tests for the mean were given previously. Some examples given were persons paired according to IQ, family membership, and, in the extreme case, individuals paired with themselves on two measures. With such paired observations, it is possible to compute a correlation coefficient between the two sets of scores. Thus, in comparing the scores that students make on two tests of motor skills, it might be found that the two measures correlate 0.63. Because there almost always will be a positive or negative correlation between two sets of paired observations, Equation (10-6) for the F test cannot be applied. Instead, a special equation is available for testing the significance of the difference between two variances based on paired observations. The equation is presented and discussed in Guilford and Fruchter (1973), pp. 169-170.

INFERENCES REGARDING CORRELATION COEFFICIENTS

Another important use of significance tests is with respect to correlation coefficients. There are many cases in which the PM correlation is computed on a small number of persons, for example, the scores of 15 students on two tests of personality. It might be found in this case that the correlation is 0.40, which could lead the experimenter to reach important conclusions about the result; however, unless correlations are based on substantial N's (say, 100 or more cases), they are beset with considerable sampling error. Consequently, it is important to perform significance tests to provide evidence as to whether or not correlations are significantly different from 0 and whether observed differences in two or more correlations are statistically significant.

The Significance of a Correlation

By far the most widely occurring problem in applying inferential statistics with respect to correlation coefficients is that of testing the significance of the difference of an observed correlation from 0. In undertaking a correlational analysis, the interest is usually in estimating the relationship between two variables in a whole population of people. Consequently, the correlation obtained from a sample is important only to the extent to which it permits such an estimate of the population value.

The effect of sampling error on the correlation coefficient can be illustrated in the circumstance where an experimenter is trying out a new measure of aptitude for reading. Rather than deal directly with verbal material, the test consists of problems concerning relations among geometrical forms and among pictures of objects from real life. The purpose of the test is to predict how rapidly students will learn to read in the primary grades. The worth of the test is determined by correlating scores obtained in kindergarten on the reading aptitude test with the scores obtained two years later on a reading achievement test at the end of the second grade. The scores of 312 children on the reading aptitude test administered in kindergarten and achievement test scores obtained later are investigated. In this case, it is found that the correlation is 0.57; however, the first question that the experimenter must ask himself is whether or not the correlation is real rather than due only to sampling error.

Even if the population correlation is 0, the correlation found for a particular sample probably would not be exactly 0. An experiment could be undertaken in which a large number of samples is drawn, each containing 100 persons, and the correlation computed. Then, it would be expected that these correlations would range around 0. There would be no reason to expect more positive than negative coefficients, or vice versa. The dispersion of the coefficients about 0 would be dependent on the N, or sample size; that is, the correlations obtained from successive samples would crowd nearer to 0 when the sample size was large—assuming again that the population correlation was exactly 0. (Such a sampling of correlation coefficients is analogous to the sampling of means discussed earlier in this chapter.) The distributions of a large number of coefficients that would be obtained for different sample sizes would probably look like those shown in Figure 10-2. Because the true correlation is 0 for the three sizes of N shown in Figure 10-2, all of the nonzero coefficients are due to chance. With an N of only 10, correlations greater than +0.50 and less than −0.50 would occur appreciably often purely by chance. With an N as large as 400 it would be rare to find chance correlations that varied even 10 points above or below 0.

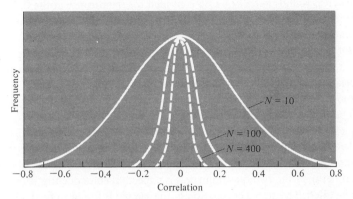

Figure 10-2. **Distributions of sample correlations when the population correl-ation is 0.00 (N is the sample size).**

The statistical significance of the difference of a correlation from 0 can be tested with the same t distribution used for testing the significance of the difference between two means. The equation used to obtain t in this situation is

$$t_{(df)} = r\sqrt{\frac{N-2}{1-r^2}} \qquad (10\text{-}7)$$

The df for the PM correlation coefficient is equal to the number of subjects minus 2. Significance values for the t test can be obtained from Appendix B-6. Two examples of employing this equation are as follows.

An experimenter has developed two new tests of creativity. They concern producing words that relate to specified pairs of words and determining rules whereby lists of alphabetical letters are ordered. Because the tests are in an ex-perimental phase, any information at all about the possible correlation would be helpful to the experimenter. He has scores on the two tests from only 10 subjects, but he is quite curious as to whether the data suggest a substantial positive cor-relation. By employing the usual PM equation for the correlation coefficient, a value of 0.60 is obtained. With the use of Equation (10-7), the significance of this correlation could be tested with the t statistic as follows

$$t_{(df)} = r\sqrt{\frac{N-2}{1-r^2}}$$

$$= 0.60\sqrt{\frac{8}{0.64}}$$

$$t_{(8)} = 2.124$$

Because $N = 10$, the df $(N - 2)$ is 8. This value is then referred to Appendix B-6. In this case, it would be sensible to employ a one-tailed test because the measures are thought to concern the same attribute and should correlate positively. In this instance, it is found that a t of 1.86 is needed for significance at the 0.05 level for a one-tailed test. Consequently, even though N is only 10 in this case, the experimenter has enough evidence to encourage him for further study of the two tests. Of course, it is usually a waste of time to compute a correlation coefficient when the N is no larger than 10 because, in such cases, very wide departures from 0 correlation are obtained frequently by chance.

A more substantial investigation of the correlation between two variables would be that in which an experimenter compares the scores of 100 students on two questionnaires concerning personal problems. On each questionnaire, students are asked to mark problems that they have in daily life. A total score is obtained by summing the number of problems that are marked. In this case, a positive correlation between the two questionnaires is expected; consequently, a one-tailed test is justified. The actual correlation in the sample is found to be 0.35. Equation (10-7) could be applied as follows

$$t_{(df)} = r \sqrt{\frac{N - 2}{1 - r^2}}$$

$$= 0.35 \sqrt{\frac{98}{0.88}}$$

$$t_{(98)} = 3.710$$

Using the table for t in Appendix B-6 with 98 df for a one-tailed test, it was found that a t of 3.71 was well beyond the 0.001 level of significance.

Rather than find the significance level of the correlation coefficient by converting the obtained value to t, the significance can be obtained directly from Appendix B-5 for any case in which the df is not considerably larger than 100. All that is necessary is to find the proper df $(N - 2)$ on the left-hand column and then look across the corresponding row at the various levels of significance. Unless the exact df is present in the table, the proper approach is to compute the significance level in terms of the next *lower* df appearing in the table. Unless there is a definite hypothesis regarding the significance test, it is almost always wise to employ a two-tailed test. One example would be a correlation of 0.38 with 20 df. The correlation here would be significant between the 0.10 and the 0.05 level. Unless the correlation reaches at least the 0.05 level, then it is usually not considered sufficiently significant to be taken seriously. Another example would be a correlation of 0.32 with an N of 96. The resulting df of 94 should be referred to the row for 90 df. This shows that the correlation is significant beyond the 0.01 level.

Although it is important to test for the statistical significance of a correlation co-efficient, passing that hurdle is only a minor matter. It is much more important to obtain subsequent information regarding how faithfully the size of the correlation can be interpreted. An example would be in correlating an aptitude test with college grades, in which case it might be found that $r = 0.50$. With an N of 100 students, it is found from Appendix B-5 that the coefficient is significant beyond the 0.01 level; however, with an N of no more than 100, the actual correlation that would be found with larger numbers of subjects could be very different from 0.50. After determining that a correlation is significantly different from 0, an important next step is to determine how high above or below 0 one can safely estimate the population correlation coefficient as being.

Issues regarding the *level of confidence* with which correlations can be safely interpreted as different from 0 are illustrated in Figure 10-3. This is a graphic portrayal of information obtained directly from Appendix B-5. The X axis shows the df of different sized samples ($N - 2$). The Y axis shows possible correlations obtained in particular investigations, such as the r mentioned above of 0.50 in correlating an aptitude test with college grades. The curves above and below the X axis indicate the 0.01 significance levels for a two-tailed test of the difference of a PM correlation from 0. Any correlation either above the line in the upper half of the graph or below the line in the lower half of the graph is significant beyond the 0.01 level and thus can be said to be in a "safe zone." The safe zones are indicated by shading. The zones are safe in that the experimenter can feel relatively sure (with 99 percent confidence) that the population correlation is different from 0. Between the two safe zones are two unsafe zones above and below the X axis. Correlations falling in either of these two areas are not significant at the 0.01 level or less (although they might be significant at the less stringent level of 0.05 or less). Looking up or down the scale on the Y axis and then moving to the right, information regarding how safely the correlation obtained from a sample can be considered different from 0 is obtained. Some examples will illustrate how this is done.

First, consider a positive correlation of 0.40 obtained in a particular investigation. If the df is no more than 10, the correlation is far down into the unsafe zone. If the df in that particular investigation is as much as 50, the correlation falls into the safe zone, but it is only slightly above the unsafe zone. This should give some caution to the experimenter in interpreting how high the correlation actually is above 0. Out as far as df of 200, a correlation of 0.40 is not only significant beyond the 0.01 level, but also the investigator can feel sure (with 99 percent confidence) that the correlation in the population is no less than 0.18. All the way out at 1,000 df, a correlation of 0.40 could be given a rather precise interpretation in relation to the 0 level, because the level required for significance is only 0.08.

Similar information about negative correlations is obtained from Figure 10-3.

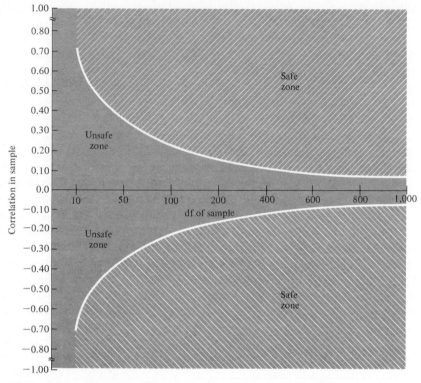

Figure 10-3. Negative and positive correlations that are significantly different from 0 (in the two safe zones) for different sizes of samples. Any negative or positive correlation in the shaded zone is significantly different from 0.

A correlation of −0.60 falls into the safe zone with df slightly above 10 and is far down into the safe zone by the time that df = 50. By the time that df passes 400, it is safe to conclude that the population correlation is at least 50 points below 0.

It should be made clear with respect to these examples that principles relating df to statistical significance concern potentially different samples that vary in terms of *N*. Of course, there is no way in which to change the df regarding a particular correlation after a sample has been drawn and an *r* is computed.

The inferential statistics depicted in Figure 10-3 provide information not only concerning whether or not a sample correlation is significantly different from 0, but more importantly, how far away from zero the population correlation probably is. Without considering such inferential statistics regarding the possible distance of the population correlation from 0, the sheer finding of statistical significance for a sample correlation provides only meager information regarding the results of an experiment.

Comparison of Two or More Correlations

A less frequently occurring problem than that of testing the significance of one correlation coefficient is that of testing the significance of difference between correlations. An example would be in testing the significance of difference between the correlations of two different college aptitude tests with college grades. The two tests are administered to a sample of students, and each is later correlated with grade-point averages. The correlation for one test is 0.65, and the correlation for the other test is 0.50. It is tempting to conclude that the first test is better than the second; but before reaching this conclusion, the significance of the difference should be determined. In another sample of subjects, the second test might actually have a higher correlation with GPA than the first test would.

In other instances, one of the two correlations is hypothetical rather than being an obtained sample value. This is the case when an obtained correlation is compared with some theoretical value. It might be prohibitively expensive to employ a test unless it correlated at least as high as 0.40 with a measure of performance in some occupation. If an obtained value is actually above the theoretical point, then a statistical test can be made to determine whether it is significantly above that point. A thorough discussion of significance tests for differences among correlations as in the given examples would be too technical for inclusion in this book; however, the reader should be aware of these problems and know that the proper statistical methods are available. [See Guilford and Fruchter (1973).]

SUMMARY

There are three types of descriptive statistics which are most important for interpreting the results of research. These are measures of central tendency, variability, and correlation. The preferred measures in these cases are (1) the arithmetic mean, (2) the standard deviation, and (3) the PM correlation coefficient. In most investigations, because these descriptive statistics are computed on a sample of subjects which is small in comparison to the size of the population involved, it is necessary to employ inferential statistics to determine the extent to which results from the sample can be properly generalized to the population.

There are many instances in research where it is necessary to test for the significance of difference between two treatment groups. If the probability is low (significance high) that the difference in average performance of the two groups is not due to chance alone, then it is safe to interpret the finding as a difference that probably would be found in the population as a whole. The difference between the means of the two groups can be assessed for significance by the well-known t test. The t distribution shows what would be expected in a random sampling of means from a particular population. In that case, the means of samples would differ from one another only by chance. When the sample size is large (for example, several hundred), the t distribution is almost indistinguishable from the normal distribution. In contrast, when the sample size is small (30 or less), the t distribution is markedly flatter. In that instance, there are more cases expected above or below two standard deviations in the t distribution than would be expected in the normal distribution. A table which permits the transformation of t to various probability levels concerning statistical significance of results is given in Appendix B-6.

While it may be found that two groups being compared in an investigation do not differ with respect to average performance, they may differ with respect to variability of performance. A statistical test can be made to determine whether or not two standard deviations are significantly different from one another. Actually, what is done is to square the standard deviations (obtained variances) and divide the larger by the smaller. The ratio of two such variances concerns another widely employed statistical distribution—the F distribution. As is true of the normal distribution and the t distribution, values of F can be transformed into probabilities regarding the statistical significance of results of experiments (using the table given in Appendix B-7).

The size of a PM correlation coefficient obtained from a sample can be tested for statistical significance with an equation that relates to the t distribution. All that need be known for employing the equation are (1) the size of the correlation obtained from the sample and (2) the number of subjects involved. Even this small amount of computation can be circumvented in the case where df is no more than 100 by referring the PM correlation directly to the table of significance values presented in Appendix B-5.

Regardless of how simple or complex the research design, results are usually reported in terms of arithmetic means, standard deviations, and PM correlation coefficients. These are excellent descriptive statistics, but results from a sample are meaningless unless they faithfully mirror the results that would be found in a population as a whole. Evidence to support this is obtained by employing proper tests of statistical significance.

EXERCISES

Study Questions

1 Give one example each of instances in research in which significance tests would be applied to measures of central tendency, variation, and correlation. What information would such significance tests supply?

2   What is the difference in the use of s_M and s_{MD}? For each, give one example of situations where they could be applied. Why is s_M usually only of theoretical interest?

3   What is the t distribution? How does it relate to the normal distribution? When would they be very much the same, and when would they be different?

4   Compose an example of an instance in which it might be necessary to compute s_{MD} when the N's in the two samples are very different. In what circumstances would it be necessary to apply Equation (10-3) rather than (10-1)?

5   Give an example of a hypothetical experiment in which it would be useful to have paired observations rather than independent samples. How can this potentially result in obtaining more precise information (less error) from any particular number of subjects than would be the case if the same number of subjects were randomly divided into independent groups?

6   Compose an example of a research problem in which one would apply the F ratio to differences between two variances. [See Equation (10-6).]

7   Design a research problem in which it would be useful to apply the t test to the size of a correlation coefficient obtained from a sample of subjects. Discuss on an intuitive level why df = $N - 2$ for the correlation coefficient.

8   Explain why confidence levels are particularly important with respect to correlation coefficients obtained from a sample of subjects. Give an example making up numbers rather than actually computing statistical results.

Problems

1   A researcher is interested in discovering the effects of a particular drug on learning ability in monkeys. On a learning task, it has been found in many previous studies that in normal monkeys the average is 40 percent correct responses during the first day of testing. It is hypothesized that the drug will enhance learning rate. The drug is administered to 11 monkeys, the results of which are as follows

		Percent correct		Percent correct
	1	62	8	94
	2	21	9	87
	3	46	10	38
Subject	4	31	11	81
	5	81		
	6	83		
	7	98		

Apply s_M to the results, and test the null hypothesis with the t distribution. What conclusion would be reached?

2   Sixteen college students were randomly divided into two groups of eight each for a study of effects of distraction on memorization of a list of 20 words presented serially. Group 1 had distracting sounds placed in their ears through earphones. Group 2 was not distracted in this way. Following are the number of words correctly remembered by subjects in each of the two groups

		Group 1	Group 2
	1	8	15
	2	7	18
	3	4	6
Subject	4	9	12
	5	2	15
	6	6	10
	7	10	9
	8	12	16

Employing s_{MD} and the t distribution, what would the one-tailed probability be in this case? Although a one-tailed test would be appropriate in this case, what would have been the probability for a two-tailed test?

3   A study is being made of the effects of drugs on the speed with which rats will run down a long runway to obtain a pellet of food. Running speed is determined before and after the drug is administered. Following are the running times in seconds

		Seconds before drug	Seconds after drug
	1	20	15
	2	24	12
Subject	3	21	13
	4	29	14
	5	19	12
	6	22	13

Using tests for paired observations (repeated-measurements), test the significance of difference between the two means with Equations (10-4) and (10-5). Cite the probabilities associated with both one-tailed and two-tailed tests. In this case, because the study was rather exploratory and no definite hypothesis was formulated, the two-tailed test would be more appropriate. What conclusion would be reached about the results of the experiment?

4   A researcher hypothesizes that variances will be different in two experimental treatment groups. The experiment concerns the detection of rapidly flashed lights on a screen. One group of subjects is given a warning signal before the flashes occur, and the other group is given no warning. It is hypo-

thesized that subjects in the former group will vary much more in performance than subjects in the latter group. The reasoning is that the warning signal will markedly facilitate performance of some subjects but will greatly
hinder other subjects because of differences in mental approaches to the
task. With 25 subjects in each group, it is found that $s^2 = 7.45$ for the first
group and 3.12 for the second group. Assess the significance of these results
with Equation (10-6) and the table of probabilities presented in Appendix
B-7. What conclusion would be reached in this case?

5   It is found that a test of reading achievement correlates 0.50 with a test of
mathematical achievement in a sample of 125 subjects. Compute t for this
result with Equation (10-7). What is the associated probability of this correlation being significantly different from 0?

6   Rather than employ the t test, the probability associated with the significance of difference of a correlation from 0 can be sought directly in Appendix B-5. From that table, list probabilities associated with the following sized correlations and number of subjects in the sample: (a) $r = 0.25$
and $N = 48$, (b) $r = 0.52$ and $N = 96$, (c) $r = -0.33$ and $N = 25$, and (d)
$r = 0.08$ and $N = 79$.

SUGGESTED ADDITIONAL READINGS

Ferguson, G. A. *Statistical analysis in psychology and education*, 3d ed. New
York: McGraw-Hill, 1971, Chap. 11.

Guilford, J. P. and B. Fruchter. *Fundamental statistics in psychology and education*, 5th ed. New York: McGraw-Hill, 1973, Chaps. 8 and 9.

Hays, W. L. *Statistics for the social sciences*, 2d ed. New York: Holt, Rinehart
& Winston, 1973, Chaps. 14 and 15.

Senter, R. J. *Analysis of data.* Glenview, Illinois: Scott Foresman, 1969, Chap. 9.

11

Simple Analysis of Variance

A topic that was considered prominently in Chapter 10 was that of performing inferential statistics regarding differences in mean scores in an experiment concerning two groups, for example, two groups of students that had been given different types of instruction in mathematics. It is frequently the case that more than two groups are involved in experiments. An example of this would be in studying the effects of different drugs on social interaction among depressive patients in a mental hospital setting. It has been hypothesized that when people become depressed, they communicate much less with other people than they would when in a normal state. One measure of amount of communication is the sheer number of words that an individual speaks to others in any given period of time. Thus, number of words spoken to others is recorded and used as the dependent measure in the experiment. It is of interest to compare the effects of different drugs on the amount of communication as evidenced in the dependent measure concerning verbal communication. One approach would be to take two drugs at a time and compare them when available patients are randomly assigned to one of two groups. Rather than compare only two groups given two different drugs, however, it is more frequently the case that three or more groups would be compared, each given a different drug. Much more information is obtained from an experiment in which three or more treatments are compared than in the case where only two treatments are compared. Thus, whereas it may be found that drug A increases communication more than drug B, there would still be questions regarding the relative effects of drugs C and D. Another example would be in studying the effects of different amounts of practice on the reading speed of students. A simple comparison of two groups that were given different amounts of practice would testify to the effectiveness of the procedure, but it would not provide very detailed information about the effects. Much more information could be obtained by providing five different groups with five different amounts of practice and subsequently measuring the effects on reading speed. Many experiments in psychology and education necessarily concern the comparison of three or more groups rather than two groups only.

When there are three or more groups, why not begin the analysis of results by making t tests between all pairs of means? For example, if there are five means, one could make ten t tests among all possible pairs of means. With this approach, one might find evidence that some means differed significantly at a particular probability level and others did not differ significantly at that level. There is a primary reason that it is unwise to begin the analysis of results from three or more groups by making such pair-wise significance tests among means. Such pair-wise tests among means should be made only after an overall test of significance among means is undertaken. (Later in the chapter, methods for making such pair-wise comparisons among means after the overall statistical analysis is completed will be mentioned.) As the first step in such analyses, an overall measure of significance is available which simultaneously tests whether treatment conditions produce different effects. Thus, rather than ask simply whether mean A is greater than mean B and whether mean B is greater than mean C, statistical methods are available which will allow, all at once, a test of significance regarding whether the means taken together are significantly different from one another. This chapter is devoted to a discussion of elementary principles and procedures regarding the application of such simultaneous tests to the effects of more than two treatments.

Inferential statistics regarding the significance of difference among three or more groups can be derived from the procedures discussed in Chapter 10 concerning the F test for comparing two variances. Such methods for analyzing experimental results from three or more groups are referred to as *analysis of variance* (ANOVA).

There are numerous forms of ANOVA that can be employed for even the most complex of experiments in psychology and education. It would be far beyond the scope of this introductory text to go into an elaborate discussion of ANOVA; however, it should be possible here to (1) describe the general procedures that are involved, (2) discuss principles and computational routines for simple experimental designs, and (3) provide the reader with sufficient background to understand the more detailed discussions of ANOVA cited in this chapter. Analysis of variance for simple experimental designs will be discussed in this chapter; more complex designs will be discussed in Chapter 12.

COMPONENTS OF VARIANCE

A simple F test for comparing two variances was discussed in Chapter 10.

$$F = \frac{s_1^2}{s_2^2}$$

It was said that this test could be used to compare the difference in variance of two samples of subjects, for example, intelligence test scores of two classrooms of students. Also described was how the F value obtained in this way could be referred to Appendix B-7 to determine the significance of difference in the variances involved. The same logic used to compare two variances can be extended to compare differences in means among three or more groups of differently treated subjects. Thus, the means of the differently treated groups will vary about the grand mean, and this variance can be tested for statistical significance.

In order to understand the logic and use of a simple analysis of variance, the reader should inspect Table 11-1, which shows the scores of three groups of people with five persons in each group. The numbers in Table 11-1 have purposely been made extremely simple in order to illustrate principles underlying ANOVA. More realistic examples will be used subsequently to illustrate the actual computation and use of ANOVA. There are five persons in each group shown in Table 11-1. Scores in the first group are 1, 2, 3, 4, and 5. Scores in Group 2 overlap to some extent with those of Group 1 and Group 3. The intention here is to portray the scores of 15 people in three differently treated groups. These can be thought of as scores in a study of competition in group situations, interpretation of facial expressions, or any other experimental situation.

Each group in Table 11-1 has received a different treatment. There appears to be a tendency for the scores in Group 2 to be higher than the scores in Group 1, and for the scores in Group 3 to be higher than those in Group 2. Of course, no one would ever find such a neat set of scores, but these scores will prove useful in illustrating the nature of ANOVA. At the bottom of the table the means for the three groups are shown: $M_1 = 3, M_2 = 6$, and $M_3 = 9$. The mean of all scores in Table 11-1 M_{tot} is equal to 6. What is needed is a statistical test to provide evidence as to whether or not the differences among means reflect real differences or if they are due only to chance factors regarding the sampling of subjects and other sources of error in the experimental situation. The general logic of employ-

Table 11-1. Scores of Five Subjects in Each of Three Differently Treated Groups and Means for Each Group

Group 1	Group 2	Group 3
1	4	7
2	5	8
3	6	9
4	7	10
5	8	11
$M_1 = 3$	$M_2 = 6$	$M_3 = 9$
	$M_{tot} = 6$	

ing the F test to make comparisons among two variances can be used to compare the means of the three groups.

Sampling of Means

You may recall that the F test requires two variances s_1^2 and s_2^2. In the following sections, the two sources of these necessary variances will be described. If experimental treatments actually have no effect at all and the observed differences in Table 11-1 were due only to chance, then the variability of the means should be no more than what would be expected by chance. Imagine that the numbers in Table 11-1 were obtained from a random sampling of scores from the same population of persons. Then, the difference in means of the groups would be due to chance alone. Suppose one could repeatedly gather samples of five subjects and calculate the mean score of each sample. Some of the means would be higher, some lower, and some in between those means in Table 11-1. If many more samples were calculated, then a distribution of these means could be plotted. Just as it makes sense to calculate an estimate s^2 of the population variance from deviates about the means of a sample of subjects, it is also meaningful to compute such an estimate based upon the distribution of these sample means. Although in actual research there would not be a distribution of means based on a large number of samples, an estimate of the population variance may be calculated upon the means that are at hand. This can be readily demonstrated with the means in Table 11-1.

The first step in determining the estimated population variances s^2 using the means of the three groups is to calculate an average of these means. The average of the three means M_{tot} is equal to 6. The next step is to calculate the deviates about M_{tot}. Both M_1 and M_2 deviate by 3 score units from M_{tot}. Normally, the next two steps in calculating a variance are to square and sum the deviates; however, for reasons which are discussed later in this chapter, there is one important additional step. After M_{tot} has been subtracted from a group mean and the resulting deviate squared, it is necessary to multiply this squared deviate by the number of subjects in the group from which the mean was calculated. For example, when M_{tot} is subtracted from M_3 and the resulting deviate squared, this squared deviate must be multiplied by 5, or the number of subjects in Group 3. The same procedure would be followed for M_1. This procedure is referred to as *weighting the squared deviate* by the sample size. After each of the deviates is squared and weighted, they are added together. The resulting sum of squared deviates in our example equals 90.

It should be remembered from Chapter 5 that an unbiased estimate of the population variance is obtained by dividing the sum of squared deviates by the number of scores minus 1. In this case, there are three scores (three means); consequently, one should divide by 2 rather than by 3. In other words, the degrees of freedom equal 2. Then, an estimate of the population variance is obtained by dividing 90 by 2, which, of course, is 45. This is an unbiased estimate of the population variance that would be obtained if differences among means were due only to chance.

How does one decide whether the population variance estimated from differences among means is important or unimportant? The answer is to compare the variance estimate obtained from the means with a different estimate of the population variance. Such an estimate may be calculated from the variances within each of the three treatment groups. If the scores within the groups had ranged from 0 to 1 million, then the variance estimate of 45 obtained from the means would look rather small; in contrast, if the variance within groups is no larger than it appears to be in this case, then the variance estimate obtained from the means appears important.

What is needed is a comparison between the variance estimate obtained from the means and the variances within groups. The variance of a sample is an estimate of the population variance; therefore, pooling (or averaging) the variances from all of the groups also provides an estimate of the population variance. The procedure for this is illustrated in Table 11-2. The mean of each group is subtracted from each score in the group. In this case, the scores are conveniently arranged so that the computations can be easily visualized. In Group 1, M_1 (which equals 3) is subtracted from each of the scores in the group, leaving deviates of -2, -1, 0, $+1$, and $+2$ respectively. The numbers are conveniently arranged so that the same deviates occur in Group 2 and Group 3. To obtain an s^2 value in each group, the squares of these deviates must be added and then divided by the number of subjects minus 1 (4 in each case). The sum of squared deviates in each group is 10, and the df in each group is 4. Thus, s^2 in each group is 2.5. An average s^2 could then be computed over all the groups by summing the three values and then dividing by 3. In this particular example, all three of the s^2 values are the same, and all are equal to 2.5. Thus, the average s^2 within groups equals 2.5.

A simpler procedure is to sum the squared deviates about the mean in each group, add these, and divide by the total number of subjects minus the number of groups. In other words, rather than divide the number of squared deviates in each group by 4 and average these, it would be more convenient to simply sum the squared deviates over all groups and divide by the number of subjects (15 in

Table 11-2. Deviation Scores for Group Means and Squared Deviation Scores Within Groups

Group 1		Group 2		Group 3	
x	x^2	x	x^2	x	x^2
-2	4	-2	4	-2	4
-1	1	-1	1	-1	1
0	0	0	0	0	0
1	1	1	1	1	1
2	4	2	4	2	4
$\Sigma x^2 = 10$		$\Sigma x^2 = 10$		$\Sigma x^2 = 10$	

this case) minus the number of groups (3 in this case). In this way, it can be seen that the df for the measure of variation within groups equals the total number of subjects minus the total number of groups.

The estimate of the population variance from the weighted deviates of treatment means about the grand mean is spoken of as the *mean-square between groups*, and is symbolized as MS_{bg}; that is, after the deviates are properly weighted, the sum of these is then divided by the proper df, resulting in a mean-square. Conversely, the estimate of the population variance from squared deviates within groups is referred to as the *mean-square within groups* and is symbolized as MS_{wg}. In this case, deviates are formed about the within-groups means. These are squared and summed across groups; and the resulting sum is divided by the appropriate df.

The F Test

After computations are completed, the real issue is the extent to which the estimate of the population variance from the between-groups means is greater than the same estimate obtained from the variability of scores within groups. Saying it another way, the issue hinges on whether MS_{bg} is large in comparison to MS_{wg}. If there are no real differences for the treatment groups in the population in question, then the expectation is that MS_{bg} would be approximately the same as MS_{wg}. These would be only two ways of estimating the same population variance. (Keep in mind that this does not mean the distribution of scores in the population is determined by chance factors only. What it means is that the supposed effects of the treatments are due only to the chance allocation of subjects to the different experimental groups.) In Chapter 10, the F test was discussed as a means of testing the significance of difference of two variances. The same F test can be used in ANOVA designs to test for the significance of difference of three or more means. In this simple ANOVA design, the F test would be made as follows

$$F = \frac{MS_{bg}}{MS_{wg}}$$

In the case mentioned previously, the result is as follows

$$F = \frac{MS_{bg}}{MS_{wg}}$$

$$= \frac{45}{2.5}$$

$$= 18.00$$

If the differences among means were due only to chance factors, the expected F ratio would be approximately 1.0, but we see that it is 18.00. This looks like a very large F ratio; let us see how this relates to statistical significance.

Significance Levels

The significance level for any F test can be obtained directly from Appendix B-7. It was mentioned in Chapter 10 that in comparing two variances obtained from an investigation, it is necessary to multiply the probabilities in Appendix B-7 by 2. This is *not* the case in employing ANOVA, because, as mentioned previously, it is decided in advance that the MS_{bg} will be divided by the MS_{wg}. Thus, the obtained F can be compared directly with the F distribution to determine the significance level. The steps for doing this are much like those for determining the significance of a t test. Recall that for the t test what is needed is the df associated with the obtained t. In ANOVA, the F test has two df values associated with it. These are the df for MS_{bg} and the df for MS_{wg}. In the example, the df value for between groups is determined by subtracting 1 from the total number of groups. The total number of groups will be represented by J; hence, the df value is represented as $J - 1$. The df value for within groups is calculated by first determining the total number of people in the study or N_{tot} and subtracting from N_{tot} the number of treatment groups or J. Thus the df for within groups may be represented as $N_{tot} - J$. In the example presented in Table 11-1, these values are df-between = 2 and df-within = 12.

In the F table the df values for MS_{bg} are listed across the top of the table, one for each *column* of numbers. Down the left side of the table, the df values for MS_{wg} are listed, one value for each *row*. The numbers inside the table are the values of F necessary to be significant with the associated df. Note that there are three F values corresponding to each pair of df. The upper value is the size F necessary to be significant at $p = 0.05$, the middle value at $p = 0.01$, and the lower value at $p = 0.001$.

In order to determine if the obtained F is significant, turn to the F table and look for the column with a 2 over it and slide a finger down the column to the row that has a 12 beside it. By doing this, we find that an $F = 18$ with 2 and 12 df is significant beyond the $p = 0.01$ level; that is, the obtained F is larger than the F in the table, which is 6.93. In this way, one can obtain assurance as to whether two or more of the groups simultaneously differ from one another in a statistically significant manner. If the overall F test is not statistically significant, it would be hazardous to make comparisons among the different groups, even if some of the differences appeared to be substantial. An overall test of this kind gives the experimenter confidence that it is safe to go in and make comparisons among groups. Without this assurance, it is quite hazardous to make any interpretations at all of the apparent trends in the data.

The generality of the problem of ANOVA is amply demonstrated in Tables 11-1, 11-2, and the accompanying discussions. If all were governed by randomness, the means of differently treated groups would vary in a predictable manner. The MS_{bg} would not be expected to be any larger than the MS_{wg}. Many samplings would have an expected mean of 1.00 for the F distribution, and the sampling distribution would be predictable from the results presented in Appendix B-7. Even the most complex of experimental designs and related ANOVA approaches are based on this simple principle.

PARTITIONING OF SUMS OF SQUARES

The hypothetical scores shown in Tables 11-1 and 11-2 illustrate a very general principle in ANOVA, which is that the total sums of squared deviates about the overall mean can be broken down into additive components. It should be remembered from Chapter 5 that a variance is computed as follows

$$\sigma^2 = \frac{\Sigma(X - M)^2}{N}$$

$$= \frac{\Sigma x^2}{N}$$

Each x is a deviate about the mean, such as a deviate about the mean IQ of a group or a deviate about the number of problems solved in a study of learning. Of course, the sum of these is, by definition, the sum of squared deviates. When the sum of squared deviates is divided by the appropriate degrees of freedom, an estimate of the population variance for any set of scores is obtained.

The total sum of squared deviates for a study is determined by subtracting the overall mean M_{tot} from the score of every subject, squaring this deviation score, and summing all the squared deviates. In ANOVA, the total sum of squared deviates can be *partitioned* into two sources, depending upon whether they represent variation within treatment conditions or variation between treatment conditions. The total sum of squared deviates is equal to the sum of squared deviates between groups plus the sum of squared deviates within groups.

The procedure for partitioning the total sum of squared deviates may be easily understood by examining the score for one subject in one group. In a general fashion, the score for any one person in any group may be written as X_{ij}. This is the the score of the ith person in the jth group. The first subject in the first group of a study makes score X_{11}. This score is read as the score of the first subject in the first group. The deviation of X_{ij} from M_{tot} is $X_{ij} - M_{tot}$. This deviation score may be partitioned into two deviation scores; the deviation score of X_{ij} from M_j (mean of group j) and the deviation of M_j from M_{tot}. This partitioning is represented as follows

$$(X_{ij} - M_{tot}) = (X_{ij} - M_j) + (M_j - M_{tot}) \tag{11-1}$$

For example, from Table 11-1, X_{53} or the score of subject number 5 in Group 3 may be partitioned as follows

$$(X_{53} - M_{tot}) = (X_{53} - M_3) + (M_3 - M_{tot})$$
$$(11 - 6) = (11 - 9) + (9 - 6)$$
$$5 = 2 + 3$$

This simple step is of primary importance because it allows the partitioning of the total variance into that attributable to variation within groups and variation between groups.

The next step in partitioning is to square both sides of Equation (11-1). This results in the following

$$(X_{ij} - M_{tot})^2 = (X_{ij} - M_j)^2 + (M_j - M_{tot})^2 + 2(X_{ij} - M_j)(M_j - M_{tot})$$

This equation is the square of Equation (11-1), which is the result of the squared partitioning for one subject. The next step is to add the squared deviation scores for all the subjects in each group. This may be represented with a Σ or summation sign as depicted in Equation (11-2). In this equation Σ is read as the sum of the scores of all i subjects in group j

$$\sum_i (X_{ij} - M_{tot})^2 = \sum_i (X_{ij} - M_j)^2 + \sum_i (M_j - M_{tot})^2 + 2(M_j - M_{tot}) \sum_i (X_{ij} - M_j) \quad (11\text{-}2)$$

There are two important aspects of Equation (11-2). First, the last part of the equation $2(M_j - M_{tot}) \sum(X_{ij} - M_j)$ is simply the summation of deviation scores multiplied by a constant. It was pointed out in Chapter 5 that the sum of deviation scores (not squared) about a mean is equal to 0. Thus, this part of the equation necessarily equals 0; consequently, the related symbols may be omitted. A second important point is that the value $(M_j - M_{tot})$ is a constant; that is, it is the same value for every subject in Group j. Therefore, $\Sigma(M_j - M_{tot})^2$ may be written as $N_j(M_j - M_{tot})^2$, where N_j is the number of subjects in Group j. Thus, the squared deviation of a group mean M_j from M_{tot} is multiplied by the number of subjects in the j group or N_j. This step, of course, produces the same result as repeatedly adding the constant $(M_j - M_{tot})$.

Earlier in this chapter, it was said that the deviation of a group mean from M_{tot} must be weighted by the number of subjects in each group. The reason for weighting is thus demonstrated; as one sums the squared deviation for each subject, this constant value is repeatedly summed. Equation (11-2) can then be reduced to the following

$$\sum_i (X_{ij} - M_{tot})^2 = \sum_i (X_{ij} - M_j)^2 + N_j(M_j - M_{tot})^2$$

The final step in partitioning sums of squares is to sum the values for each of the groups. This is demonstrated using two summation signs as follows

$$\sum_j \sum_i (X_{ij} - M_{tot})^2 = \sum_j \sum_i (X_{ij} - M_j)^2 + \sum_j N_j(M_j - M_{tot})^2 \quad (11\text{-}3)$$

When two or more Σ's are used in an equation, the procedure is to begin with the "inside" Σ and work out. Thus, first sum the scores of all the i subjects in each group and sum these over the j groups.

Equation (11-3) is the final step in partitioning the total sums of squared deviates into its two components. Another way of writing Equation (11-3) is as follows

$$SS_{tot} = SS_{wg} + SS_{bg}$$

The *total sum of squared deviates* (SS_{tot}) is equal to the *sum of squared deviates within groups* (SS_{wg}) plus the *sum of squared deviates between groups* (SS_{bg}).

The results of Equation (11-3) can be checked with the data from Table 11-1. This consists of nothing more than subtracting 6 from each score in the table. The results are shown in Table 11-3. These scores are the deviates about M_{tot} that would be obtained by pooling the scores from all subjects in Table 11-1, irrespective of their treatment conditions. In this case, it can be found that the total sum of squared deviates about $M_{tot} = 120$. In Table 11-2, it was shown that the sum of squared deviates within groups equals 30. Referring to Table 11-1, it was reported in the text that the weighted sum of squared deviates of the three means about the grand mean equals 90. Keep in mind that SS_{bg} is obtained by weighting the actual deviates of means about the grand mean by the number of subjects in each group. Thus, it can be seen that for the data presented in Table 11-1, SS_{wg} plus SS_{bg} precisely equals SS_{tot}.

What has been demonstrated here is a very general principle in ANOVA, namely that SS_{tot} can be broken down into additive components concerning variation within groups and between groups. (Keep in mind that SS_{bg} requires a weighting of the actual deviates of means about the grand mean.) This principle holds not only for the case of a very simple ANOVA concerning three groups, but also for any number of groups and for much more complex ANOVA designs. Chapter 12 will discuss ANOVA when subjects are classified in more than one way, for instance, different types of training and different amounts of practice. In all such cases, the SS_{tot} can be neatly subdivided into those attributable to the various circumstances of treatment and those attributable to the variability within groups.

When a sum of squared deviates is divided by its proper degrees of freedom df, it is referred to as a mean-square MS. This is because it literally represents an average sum of squared deviates, taking into account the df required to obtain an unbiased estimate of a population variance. A mean-square is an estimated population variance. If there were no treatment effects, MS_{bg} would equal MS_{wg} and each would be equal to MS_{tot}. (Notice, however, that MS_{tot} does not equal the sum of MS_{bg} and MS_{wg}.) A comparison of MS_{bg} and MS_{wg} can be subjected to the F ratio test discussed previously. If there are significant differences among

Table 11-3.   Deviation Scores About M_{tot} and Their Squares

Group 1		Group 2		Group 3	
x	x^2	x	x^2	x	x^2
-5	25	-2	4	1	1
-4	16	-1	1	2	4
-3	9	0	0	3	9
-2	4	1	1	4	16
-1	1	2	4	5	25
	$\Sigma x^2 = 55$		$\Sigma x^2 = 10$		$\Sigma x^2 = 55$

the treatment means, then MS_{bg} will be larger than MS_{wg}. In complex experiments, numerous such ratios can be examined for their statistical significance.

This method of breaking down SS_{tot} into parts and into the respective mean-squares is the basis of all ANOVA. The designs actually employed in research may become quite complex, but the basic idea of breaking SS_{tot} into its component parts and computing mean-squares lies at the root of all of these forms of analysis.

Assumptions of ANOVA

As with many other statistics, there are some assumptions which are made when applying ANOVA techinques to research findings. For the simple ANOVA, there are three basic assumptions. First, it is assumed that an individual's score is independent of any other score. Thus, each subject's score is assumed not to be influenced by the scores of other subjects. Second, the variance within each treatment group is assumed to be equal to the variance of each of the other treatment groups in the study. Third, the populations from which the samples were randomly drawn are assumed to be normally distributed.

The experimenter should make every effort to see that these assumptions have been met; however, it is sometimes difficult to ensure that all of these assumptions have been met exactly. Fortunately, ANOVA results are not overly sensitive to minor violations of these assumptions. What must be done when these assumptions cannot be met is for the experimenter to exercise greater care when interpreting the results. Additional discussion of these assumptions and basic tests for determining if these assumptions have been met may be found in Hays (1973), and in Winer (1971).

COMPUTATIONAL PROCEDURES

The procedures for employing a simple ANOVA are amply demonstrated in Tables 11-1 through 11-3 and the accompanying computations; however, actual computations of statistics are usually more easily performed on raw scores than on deviation scores. Whereas it is more meaningful to talk in terms of deviation scores or standard scores, it is more convenient to actually compute statistics from raw scores; consequently, it is useful to present some equations for computing the necessary components for simple ANOVA from raw scores rather than from deviation scores. An example worked through in this regard will use the data presented in Table 11-4.

The data in Table 11-4 represent four treatment groups, each of which received a different teaching method for doing long division. After all groups had completed the course, a general test with 40 problems was administered to each group. The data in the table represent the scores on the test. At the bottom of the table are

Table 11-4. Raw Score Example for Calculational Equations

	Subject scores on test (X_{ij})		
Group 1	Group 2	Group 3	Group 4
$X_{1,1} = 37$	$X_{1,2} = 36$	$X_{1,3} = 32$	$X_{1,4} = 30$
$X_{2,1} = 37$	$X_{2,2} = 28$	$X_{2,3} = 24$	$X_{2,4} = 32$
$X_{3,1} = 30$	$X_{3,2} = 36$	$X_{3,3} = 38$	$X_{3,4} = 32$
$X_{4,1} = 36$	$X_{4,2} = 22$	$X_{4,3} = 29$	$X_{4,4} = 32$
$X_{5,1} = 39$	$X_{5,2} = 34$	$X_{5,3} = 38$	$X_{5,4} = 39$
$X_{6,1} = 36$	$X_{6,2} = 22$	$X_{6,3} = 28$	$X_{6,4} = 33$
$X_{7,1} = 35$	$X_{7,2} = 36$	$X_{7,3} = 39$	$X_{7,4} = 35$
$X_{8,1} = 33$	$X_{8,2} = 17$	$X_{8,3} = 21$	$X_{8,4} = 31$
$X_{9,1} = 32$	$X_{9,2} = 39$	$X_{9,3} = 36$	$X_{9,4} = 32$
$X_{10,1} = 33$	$X_{10,2} = 18$	$X_{10,3} = 20$	$X_{10,4} = 31$
$\sum_i X_{i1} = 348$	$\sum_i X_{i2} = 288$	$\sum_i X_{i3} = 305$	$\sum_i X_{i4} = 327$
$\sum_i X_{i1}^2 = 12{,}178$	$\sum_i X_{i2}^2 = 8{,}930$	$\sum_i X_{i3}^2 = 9{,}771$	$\sum_i X_{i4}^2 = 10{,}753$
$N_1 = 10$	$N_2 = 10$	$N_3 = 10$	$N_4 = 10$
	$N_{tot} = 40$		

values calculated on each group. In the following section, a simple ANOVA will be calculated on this data.

Before calculating SS_{tot}, SS_{wg}, and SS_{bg} by the following computational methods, there are three values which need to be calculated for each group. These are (1) the number of subjects in each group, (2) the sum of the raw scores (X_{ij}) in each group, and (3) the sum of the squared scores $(X_{ij})^2$ of each group. Notice that Step 3 does not concern finding deviates, but only squaring each subject's score and summing these for each group. These values are at the bottom of Table 11-4. For example, the number of subjects in Group 1 is 10. The sum of all scores in Group 1 is 348. The sum of squared scores in Group 1 is 12,178. Using these values for each group, three additional scores may now be calculated. These are as follows

$$A = \sum_j \sum_i X_{ij}^2$$

$$= \sum_i X_{i1}^2 + \sum_i X_{i2}^2 + \sum_i X_{i3}^2 + \sum_i X_{i4}^2$$

$$= 12{,}178 + 8{,}930 + 9{,}771 + 10{,}753$$

$$= 41{,}632.0$$

$$B = \sum_j \sum_i X_{ij}$$

$$= \sum_i X_{i1} + \sum_i X_{i2} + \sum_i X_{i3} + \sum_i X_{i4}$$

$$= 348 + 288 + 305 + 327$$

$$= 1{,}268.0$$

$$C = \sum_j \frac{(\sum_i X_{ij})^2}{N_{ij}}$$

$$= \frac{(\sum_i X_{i1})^2}{N_1} + \frac{(\sum_i X_{i2})^2}{N_2} + \frac{(\sum_i X_{i3})^2}{N_3} + \frac{(\sum_i X_{i4})^2}{N_4}$$

$$= \frac{(348)^2}{10} + \frac{(288)^2}{10} + \frac{(305)^2}{10} + \frac{(327)^2}{10}$$

$$= 40,400.2$$

In these computational equations, A is the total of the sum of squared scores for each group. Thus, after performing Step 3, the values obtained for each group are summed. A similar procedure is followed to find B, except that B is the total of the sum of raw scores from each treatment group. The procedure for finding C is somewhat more complicated. First, the total of the raw scores for each group is squared and then divided by the number of subjects in that group. Notice that this procedure requires that scores first be summed and then squared, which is symbolized by the square sign being outside the parentheses or $(\sum X)^2$ rather than $\sum X^2$. Next, after these values are obtained for each group, they are added together to yield C.

Using the values A, B, and C, there are three general computational equations that permit the determination of SS_{tot}, SS_{bg}, and SS_{wg} without first finding all the various deviation scores. These equations are as follows

$$SS_{tot} = A - \frac{B^2}{N_{tot}}$$

$$SS_{bg} = C - \frac{B^2}{N_{tot}}$$

$$SS_{wg} = A - C$$

It is now a matter of simply filling in appropriate numbers to obtain all the SS values

$$SS_{tot} = A - \frac{B^2}{N_{tot}}$$

$$= 41,632.0 - \frac{(1,268)^2}{40}$$

$$= 41,632.0 - 40,195.4$$

$$= 1,436.6$$

$$SS_{bg} = C - \frac{B^2}{N_{tot}}$$

$$= 40,400.2 - 40,195.4$$

$$= 204.8$$

$$SS_{wg} = A - C$$

$$= 41,632.0 - 40,400.2$$

$$= 1,231.8$$

It is always wise to check to see if SS_{bg} added to SS_{wg} equals SS_{tot}, and in this case it does.

The next step is to divide SS_{bg} and SS_{wg} by their df values to obtain the respective MS values. Recall that earlier in the chapter the df for SS_{bg} was defined as $J - 1$, where J is the number of groups in the study. The df for SS_{wg} is $N_{tot} - J$. So MS_{bg} and MS_{wg} are found as follows

$$MS_{bg} = \frac{SS_{bg}}{J - 1}$$

$$= \frac{204.8}{3}$$

$$= 68.2$$

$$MS_{wg} = \frac{SS_{wg}}{N_{tot} - J}$$

$$= \frac{1,231.8}{36}$$

$$= 34.2$$

With these two MS values, the F test is then calculated

$$F = \frac{MS_{bg}}{MS_{wg}}$$

$$= \frac{68.2}{34.2}$$

$$= 1.99$$

The final step in performing the ANOVA is to determine if the obtained F is statistically significant. In Appendix B-7 the F value is sought for 3 and 36 df. A problem which is encountered is that there are no values for 3 and 36 df specifically. When this happens, the general practice is to look up the next lower df values below our specific values. In this case, it turns out that there are F values in the table for 3 and 35 df. To be significant at the $p = 0.05$ level requires an F of 2.87. The obtained F is less than 2.87; therefore, there are no statistically significant differences among the means in this example. This is another way of saying that no strong evidence came from the experiment regarding differences in effects of the four treatments on development of skill in long division.

REPEATED MEASUREMENTS

So far in this chapter, simple ANOVA has been illustrated in the situation in which comparisons are made of *different* groups of subjects; however, there are many instances in which all experimental conditions are imposed upon the same group of subjects. As discussed in Chapter 3, when the same subjects are employed in all experimental conditions, this is referred to as a repeated-measurements or within-subjects design. An example would be that in which all subjects are given different amounts of exposure to words, and the dependent variable concerns recognition of the words. Four amounts of exposure time could be used, and the major question would be to what extent the amount of exposure time influenced the accuracy of recognition. In this case, all subjects would be present in all four conditions (exposure times).

Another example of a repeated-measurements design would be that concerning the tendency of students to look longer at complex geometric forms rather than simple geometric forms. There are five levels of complexity involved. Three figures are employed at each level of complexity. Students are allowed to push a button in order to turn off each geometric form as it appears. The longer students wait to push the button, the more appealing is the appearance of the geometric form. A different random order of presentation is used for each student. The dependent variable consists of the amount of time spent viewing each geometric form. Then, each student would have three scores at each of five levels of complexity.

In examples such as these, the same subjects are employed in all treatment conditions. In Chapter 3, some of the pros and cons of employing a repeated-measurements design rather than a design in which different subjects appear in each treatment condition were discussed. For example, it was mentioned that in studies of drugs it usually would not be feasible to use a totally within-subjects design, because the drugs might interact adversely with one another.

When a repeated-measurements design can be employed, it allows the experimenter to use the same subjects over and over again. Thus, it brings about a real economy in terms of the use of subjects. In other words, one obtains a great deal more information from each subject when it is feasible to place each subject in all treatment conditions. This results in a modification of the equations required for ANOVA and the associated F test. These equations are discussed and illustrated in Hays (1973), Kirk (1968), and Winer (1971).

MULTIPLE COMPARISONS

Suppose that the overall F test from an ANOVA is statistically significant. What does one conclude about the differences among the various treatment conditions? An example would be the previous one in which students were allowed to view geometric forms of five levels of complexity. Because of a highly significant F value, could it be concluded that the highest level of complexity was viewed longer than the next highest level of complexity, and so on down the line? The purpose of ANOVA is to obtain an overall probability level for the differences among the means as a group. This is a necessary and important first step, but it does not indicate that adjacent levels of a set of treatments are different from one another. This would be the case with different levels of dosage of a drug, different amounts of exposure time to words, or different amounts of time that students look at geometric forms. All that is told by a significant F value for the ANOVA is that *something* occurred significantly different from chance. Beyond that, it is necessary to pick apart the different treatment effects in terms of what are called *multiple comparisons*. These constitute a special use of statistics, which would be beyond the scope of this book to discuss in detail. In short, multiple comparisons are methods used in going back and comparing the different treatments with one another. These are discussed in detail in Kirk (1968), pp. 69-99. The reader should be skeptical of any research reports in which such multiple comparisons are not used as a follow-up to an overall ANOVA. The reader should also seek out these specialized statistics when analyzing results of his own experiments.

SUMMARY

When an experiment concerns only two groups of subjects which are given different treatments, the preferred test of significance is the t test; however, most experiments in the behavioral sciences concern the simultaneous comparison of more than two treatment groups. When this is the case, it is inappropriate to perform t tests among all possible pairs of means as a first step in an analysis of experimental results.

The proper statistical test to employ when there are more than two treatment groups is the F test. The F test follows from the logic of comparing two variances. What one does essentially in employing the F test for making comparisons among three or more groups is to obtain two estimates of the population variance, one from the variability within groups and one from the variability of group means. When the latter is divided by the former, an F test can be used to assess the probability of the observed differences among means being due entirely to chance, rather than to any systematic effects of treatments. When the F test is employed in that way, it is referred to as analysis of variance and abbreviated as ANOVA.

The F tests are based on the concept of mean-squares. The simplest example is that of the estimate of the population variance from a sample. This was discussed in considerable detail in Chapter 10 with regard to the descriptive statistic of s^2. This is the simplest and most basic type of mean-square. More complex mean-squares can be obtained in the use of ANOVA. Thus, one mean-square MS_{wg} represents the estimate of the population variance from the cumulative squared deviates of scores in cells about their cell means. A conceptually more complex mean-square is that obtained from the variability of group means about the grand mean, which is referred to as mean-square between groups or MS_{bg}. Mathematical models can be employed to derive an estimate of the population variance of scores from this source of variability.

If there were really no differences among treatment groups, so that all could be considered random samples from the same population of scores, then MS_{wg} and MS_{bg} should differ no more than would be expected by chance. By dividing MS_{bg} by MS_{wg}, an F test can be used to test for the significance of difference. All that is required is to refer the obtained F and the corresponding df to the probabilities listed in Appendix B-7. If the obtained probability is very low (at least 0.05, but especially beyond 0.01), this provides strong evidence that the average scores in the several treatment conditions are not due to a random sampling of people from a homogeneous population; rather, this is very strong evidence that some of the differences among treatment effects are real.

EXERCISES

Study Questions

1 When there are three or more treatment groups, why is it more proper to begin the analysis with an ANOVA rather than make t tests among all pairs of means?

2 In Chapter 10, the F ratio was introduced as a means of testing the significance of difference of two variances of individual differences in scores. What is the logic of applying the same F ratio to variances among means of treatment groups?

3 What is a mean-square? In a simple, one-way ANOVA, are both the mean-square within groups and the mean-square between groups variances in the usual sense of the word? Why is it necessary to weight the actual sums of squares of treatment means about the total mean?

4 If there is no difference at all in the population among experimental treatment groups, then what would be the expected F ratio? Why?

5   In intuitive terms, explain the df associated with mean-square within, mean-square between, and mean-square total.

6   From Appendix B-7, list the probabilities associated with the following F ratios and df: (a) $F = 1.00$, df $= 600$, (b) $F = 18.42$, df $= 57$, and (c) $F = 3.18$, df $= 87$.

7   What does it mean to partition sums of squares in ANOVA? Why do sums of squares for between- and within-factors add up to the total sums of squares?

8   List the two major assumptions in the use of ANOVA. Give examples of how these could be violated in actual research.

9   What are the potential advantages of repeated-measurements or within-subjects designs over randomized-groups designs?

10   Why is it important to follow up an ANOVA with an investigation of multiple comparisons? Compose an example illustrating how such multiple comparisons would provide important additional information.

Problems

Following are the results of a hypothetical experiment concerning three randomly selected groups of convicted juvenile delinquents. Group 1 is simply placed on probation without any subsequent treatment—a control group. Groups 2 and 3 are given different types of training when probation starts. A social behavior checklist is employed by social workers to assess how well the former juvenile delinquents are performing in society six months after being placed on probation. The higher the score, the better the person is performing in society.

		Group		
		1	*2*	*3*
	1	2	8	14
	2	4	10	16
	3	6	12	18
Subject	*4*	8	14	20
	5	10	16	22
	6	12	7	11
	7	5	9	7
	8	7	4	9

Perform a complete ANOVA on these experimental results. Employ the raw score computational formulas presented in the chapter. Show all calculations. End up with a table showing sums of squares, df, mean-squares, F ratio, and the probability associated with that F ratio. What interpretation would be placed on the results of the experiment?

SUGGESTED ADDITIONAL READINGS

Ferguson, G. A. *Statistical analysis in psychology and education*   3d ed. New York: McGraw-Hill, 1971, Chap. 15.

Guilford, J.P., and B. Fruchter. *Fundamental statistics in psychology and education*, 5th ed. New York: McGraw-Hill, 1973, Chap. 13.

Hays, W. L. *Statistics for the social sciences*, 2d ed. New York: Holt, Rinehart and Winston, 1973, Chap. 12.

Kirk, R. E. *Experimental design procedures for the behavioral sciences.* Belmont: Brooks/Cole, 1968, Chap. 2.

12

Factorial Designs

Chapter 11 concerned experimental designs in which there is only one independent variable, such as amount of practice in an experiment on learning. It is frequently the case that experimental designs concern two or more independent variables rather than only one. An example is in comparing the effects on mental patients of three types of drugs and three different dosage levels of the drugs. The three types of drugs would constitute one independent variable and the three dosage levels would constitute another independent variable. The dependent variable in this case would be accuracy in detecting geometrical forms flashed on a screen for a fraction of a second. Another example would be in comparing male and female high school students in three schools in terms of performance on a mathematics achievement test. The student's sex would constitute one independent variable, and the three schools would constitute a second independent variable.

When only one independent variable is involved in an experiment, it is referred to as a single-classification or a *single-factor* design. Similarly, when more than one independent variable is involved in the experiment, it is spoken of as a *factorial design*. The number of independent variables, or factors, may be as little as two or as many as six or more factors involved. An effort will be made in this chapter to acquaint the reader with (1) the fundamental concepts involved in employing all factorial designs, (2) computational procedures for relatively simple designs, and (3) references to sources for obtaining detailed explanations and computional procedures for more complex designs.

Table 12-1 illustrates the assignment of subjects in a design involving two factors. In this simple illustration, there are only two independent variables, or factors, and there are only two treatment conditions in each factor. Factor A could be thought of as concerning a comparison   two schools, and Factor B could be

Table 12-1. A 2 × 2 Factorial Design with Factor A Representing Two Schools and Factor B Representing a Comparison of Male and Female Students

Factor A: School

		A_1	A_2
Factor B: Male versus female	B_1	$N_{11} = 20$	$N_{12} = 20$
	B_2	$N_{21} = 20$	$N_{22} = 20$

$$N_{tot} = 80$$

thought of as concerning male and female students. The dependent variable could be scores on a mathematics achievement test. Table 12-1 shows how subjects would be allotted to each of the four "cells" of the design. Thus, A_1 would represent students from one school and A_2 would represent students from the other school. Row B_1 would represent female students and B_2 would represent male students. There would be 20 male and 20 female students from each school, resulting in a total of 80 subjects (N_{tot}). The effects due to a particular treatment or factor of a factorial design are generally referred to as *main effects*. Thus, in this example, one would speak of the main effects due to sex and school.

In referring to each cell, it is convenient to use double numerical subscripts as in Table 12-1. Conventionally, the first subscript represents the row of the table and the second subscript represents the column of the table. Thus, N_{12} symbolizes the number of subjects in the cell corresponding to the first row and the second column of the design. This use of numerical subscripts will prove convenient later in discussing statistical results in factorial designs.

Table 12-1 illustrates a design for only two factors and only two groups on each factor; this is the simplest of all factorial designs. It is frequently the case that there are numerous treatment levels on each factor, for example, six amounts of practice in a learning task or six dosages of drugs administered to rats. In addition, factorial designs are often employed when there are numerous factors rather than only two. An example would be three strains of rats, three different drugs, four levels of dosage of each drug, and six days of administering the drugs. A dependent variable in this case could be amount of exploration in an especially equipped apparatus called an open field. It is convenient to refer to the different factors of the design with capital letters. Thus, the fourfold design previously mentioned would be referred to as an $A \times B \times C \times D$ design. The X is read as "by." Deciding which alphabetical symbol should be assigned to which factor is arbitrary. The number of treatment levels on each factor can also be similarly designated. In the example given, this would be referred to as a 3 × 3 × 4 × 6 design.

In some cases, the levels of a factor in a factorial design are quantitatively ordered, and in some cases they consist of qualitative differences. Examples of quantitatively ordered factors would be amounts of practice, dosage levels of a particular drug, and years of schooling. Qualitatively ordered factors would be different drugs, male versus female students, and types of instruction in mathematics. The same procedures of ANOVA apply whether all factors are quantitatively ordered, qualitatively ordered, or whether there is a mixture of the two in the same design. The major difference is in follow-up statistical investigations after the ANOVA is completed. Thus, if a factor in the design proves to be statistically significant, one can subsequently employ some follow-up statistical procedures on quantitatively ordered factors which could not be performed on qualitatively ordered factors.

The reason for employing a factorial design with two or more factors rather than only a single-factor design is that much more information is obtained. For example, in comparing male and female students in two schools, there is not only the opportunity of finding whether or not the two schools differ in mathematics achievement, but also whether or not male and female students differ from one another in that regard. There are two major reasons that it is better to employ a number of factors in a factorial design rather than investigate each one of them separately in a single-factor experiment. The first is that when one is preparing for an investigation, it is much easier to go ahead and collect information about a number of factors in one experiment rather than investigate the factors one after another. This frequently results in a considerable savings in terms of time and expense. Secondly, it is better to investigate a number of independent variables (factors) simultaneously rather than in separate experiments because there are usually subtle differences in the circumstances surrounding the different experiments. If nothing else, the sheer difference in time when the separate factors were investigated might bring about different results than would be obtained if the independent variables were investigated simultaneously. There are many other subtle influences that could differ from experiment to experiment, such as participation of different experimenters, changes in apparatus for measuring the dependent variable, or slight changes in the instructions given to subjects; consequently, a great deal more faith can be placed in the comparability of results obtained in a multi-factor experiment than in comparing results from a number of different experiments each of which manipulated only one factor.

BASIC PRINCIPLES IN FACTORIAL DESIGNS

Methods of ANOVA for studying factorial designs represent extensions of the principles discussed in Chapter 11 for analyzing single-factor designs. In both cases, the methods are based upon the general principle of comparing different sources of variance with one another and referring them to the table of F values presented in Appendix B-7. Basic principles concerning factorial designs can be discussed with respect to the simplified example given in Table 12-2. Factor A concerns different levels of dosage of a drug which tends to activate animals—

Table 12-2. Factorial Design, Scores on Exploration, and Means for Rats Reared in Two Types of Environments (Factor B) and Given Three Dosage Levels of a Drug (Factor A)

Factor A: Drug dosage

		A_1		A_2		A_3	
Factor B: Rearing condition	B_1	2 3 4 5 6	$M_{11} = 4$	4 5 6 7 8	$M_{12} = 6$	6 7 8 9 10	$M_{13} = 8$	$M_{B_1} = 6$
	B_2	4 5 6 7 8	$M_{21} = 6$	6 7 8 9 10	$M_{22} = 8$	8 9 10 11 12	$M_{23} = 10$	$M_{B_2} = 8$
		$M_{A_1} = 5$		$M_{A_2} = 7$		$M_{A_3} = 9$	

$$M_{tot} = 7$$

make them more energetic. The smallest dosage level is A_1 and the largest dosage level is A_3. Factor B consists of comparing two groups of rats reared in different conditions. The dependent measure in this case was the amount of exploration in an open field. An open field consists of a large box with grid lines on the floor. The more the rat moves around across the grid lines, the higher the measure of exploration.

Table 12-2 shows the scores for three levels of dosage of a drug in two different types of circumstances. Rats in Group B_1 were raised in isolation from other rats; rats in B_2 were raised in the usual circumstance, with other rats in the immediate environment. The scores in Table 12-2 were chosen in such a way as to present a grossly oversimplified but easily understood example of statistical procedures involved in factorial designs. Later in the chapter, a realistic example will be given, and the complete computational equations will be presented. There is one score for each of five different rats in each cell of the factorial design shown in Table 12-2. Thus, in the cell corresponding to A_1 and B_1 of the factorial design, the five scores for five different rats are 2, 3, 4, 5, and 6 respectively. These scores correspond to amounts of exploration in the open field discussed previously. The mean scores in each cell are shown in the table. Thus, the mean for the first row and the first column $M_{11} = 4$, and the mean for the second row and the third column $M_{23} = 10$.

Shown on the rows and columns are the respective overall means. Thus, for all three groups of rats raised in condition $B_1, M_{B_1} = 6$. For the rats raised in condition $B_2, M_{B_2} = 8$. Because there are three different levels of drug dosage, there are

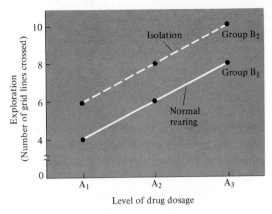

Figure 12-1. Effects of three levels of drug dosage on groups of rats given normal rearing (B_1) and groups of rats raised in isolation (B_2).

three different column means: $M_{A_1} = 5$, $M_{A_2} = 7$, and $M_{A_3} = 9$. The grand mean M_{tot} for all scores in Table 12-2 is 7.

It is apparent from the means of rows and columns that there are differences relating to both factors in the design. These differences are portrayed in Figure 12-1, where it can be seen that the two groups of rats not only tend to differ from one another in terms of overall amount of exploration, but also the amount of exploration in each group tends to be influenced by the level of drug dosage. By interpreting the scores in this way, the conclusion can be reached that both the rearing of animals and amount of drug dosage appear to have influenced amount of exploration.

Although there are apparently mean differences due to both factors in the experimental design depicted in Table 12-2, the question to ask is whether or not the differences are statistically significant. The appropriate statistical tests for this and other factorial designs can be obtained by an extension of the principles stated in Chapter 11 concerning one-factor designs. In the latter case, there were only three sums of squares—SS_{bg}, SS_{wg}, and SS_{tot}. After dividing each by the appropriate df in each cell, three mean-squares were obtained. When the MS_{bg} was divided by MS_{wg}, the resulting ratio could be referred to the general table for the F statistics presented in Appendix B-7. A modification of this procedure allows a general approach to testing for significance in factorial designs involving more than one factor.

As is true in one-factor experiments (like those discussed in Chapter 11), the sums of squares in multi-factor designs can be partitioned into additive components. The first step is undertaken by determining either the sum of squared deviates for means on rows of means on columns. The same result is obtained by starting with either approach. The method will be illustrated in Table 12-2 by starting with the means of the columns. The column means are 5, 7, and 9. As is necessarily so, the mean of the column means is the same as M_{tot}, which is 7. The departures from M_{tot} of the column means are -2, 0, and 2 respectively. As explained in Chapter 11, these deviations of column means about M_{tot} must be squared and then weighted by the number of raw scores contributing to each mean. Since each column mean is calculated by adding over 10 scores, each deviation of a column mean about M_{tot} must be weighted by 10. Thus, the three squared and weighted deviations are 40, 0, and 40 respectively. The sum of squared deviates then for Factor A $(SS_A) = 80$.

Effects due to these column means can be subtracted from the scores in all cells of the design. Quite simply, this may be done by subtracting the mean of each column from each score in the column. The results of this procedure are shown in Table 12-3.

Since the means for columns were subtracted from all scores within columns, the residual mean in each column of Table 12-3 is 0. Also, because the average column mean is the same as M_{tot}, then M_{tot} in Table 12-3 is 0; however, note that row means M_{B_1} and M_{B_2} are not 0; rather, they are -1 and 1 respectively. Thus, there are effects leftover after the means attributable to Factor A (drug dosage) are subtracted.

Analysis can now be made of Table 12-3 to assess effects attributable to the different environments in which the rats were reared. This can be done by finding the sum of squares relating to Factor B (SS_B), which is the sum of squared deviates for M_{B_1} and M_{B_2}. This is, of course, accomplished with the data in Table 12-3 by

Table 12-3. Scores Remaining from Table 12-2 After the Mean of Each Column Is Subtracted from Each Score in that Column

Factor A: Drug dosage level

	A_1	A_2	A_3	
B_1	-3 -2 -1 0 1 $\quad M_{11} = -1$	-3 -2 -1 0 1 $\quad M_{12} = -1$	-3 -2 -1 0 1 $\quad M_{13} = -1$	$M_{B_1} = -1$
B_2	-1 0 1 2 3 $\quad M_{21} = 1$	-1 0 1 2 3 $\quad M_{22} = 1$	-1 0 1 2 3 $\quad M_{23} = 1$	$M_{B_2} = 1$
	$M_{A_1} = 0$	$M_{A_2} = 0$	$M_{A_3} = 0$	

Factor B: Rearing condition

$$M_{tot} = 0$$

Table 12-4. Residual Scores After Means Have Been Subtracted for Factor A, and Subsequently Residual Means Have Been Subtracted for Factor B

Factor A: Drug dosage

Factor B: Rearing condition	A_1		A_2		A_3		
B_1	−2, −1, 0, 1, 2	$M_{11} = 0$	−2, −1, 0, 1, 2	$M_{12} = 0$	−2, −1, 0, 1, 2	$M_{13} = 0$	$M_{B_3} = 0$
B_2	−2, −1, 0, 1, 2	$M_{21} = 0$	−2, −1, 0, 1, 2	$M_{22} = 0$	−2, −1, 0, 1, 2	$M_{23} = 0$	$M_{B_2} = 0$
	$M_{A_1} = 0$		$M_{A_2} = 0$		$M_{A_3} = 0$		

$M_{tot} = 0$

squaring, weighting, and then summing the means M_{B_1} and M_{B_2}. The reason that this may be done is that M_{B_1} and M_{B_2} are already in deviation score form, since M_{tot} is equal to 0. Thus, SS_B is equal to 30. The squared deviates of the two means were weighted by 15 since there were 15 rats in condition B_1 and 15 rats in condition B_2.

The next step in analyzing the factorial design presented originally in Table 12-2 is to subtract the row means in Table 12-3 from the scores in each row. These are presented in Table 12-4. Note that in Table 12-4, the means of all cells are precisely 0. Thus, there are no systematic effects at all left. All that remains is the within-cell variance of individuals about the 0 means. This represents a pure error term concerning individual differences in response to treatment combinations in the various cells.

The original scores were chosen in such a way as to make the example very neat. By simple calculations it can be found that the sum of squared deviates in each of the cell is 10; consequently, the sum of squares within groups in the whole design is 60. The total sum of squares can be calculated from Table 12-2 in the same manner explained in Chapter 11. SS_{tot} proves to be 170. As is true in the analysis of one-factor designs, the sum of squares from the various sources add up to the total sums of squares, as follows

$$
\begin{aligned}
SS_A &= 80 \\
SS_B &= 30 \\
SS_{wg} &= 60 \\
SS_{tot} &= 170
\end{aligned}
$$

Before going further, the reader should be alerted to the fact that the neat division of sums of squares shown here occurs only in highly artificial examples of this kind where the cell means are all precisely 0 after the influences of the main effects are subtracted. Later, it will be shown how a modification is required to take account of the situation in which cell means are not precisely 0 after the influences of the main effects are subtracted.

Mean-Squares

Corresponding to any source of variation is a mean-square. This is obtained by dividing the appropriate sum of squares by the related degrees of freedom. The total df in Table 12-2 equals the total number of subjects minus 1 ($N_{tot} - 1$), which is 29. On both columns C and rows R, the df equals the number of means minus 1, which is $C-1$ for columns and $R-1$ for rows. In this example, the df for columns is 2 and for rows is 1. The df for residual within-cells is equal to $RC(n-1)$, where n is the number of subjects in each cell. In this case, the df for within-cells is 24. It should be apparent that these last three df values do not sum to the total df ($N_{tot} - 1$). The two remaining df are attributable to a source of variance which will be discussed later in this chapter. Shown in Table 12-5 is a breakdown of the sum of squares, degrees of freedom, and related mean-squares. The F ratios for Factors A and B are also presented.

The principle stated in Chapter 11 with respect to the implications of mean-squares holds with complex factorial designs as well as with one-factor designs. If scores in all cells of the design are randomly sampled from the same population, then the mean-square attributable to any factor of the design would provide an estimate of the same overall population variance. In that case, MS_A would be expected to equal MS_B and both in turn would be expected to equal MS_{wg}. Such a result would be expected only from a random drawing of persons from a total population in which none of the treatment factors had any real effect; however, to the extent to which the mean-square for any treatment condition differs markedly from the residual mean-square within cells, *then* it is reasonable to reject the hypothesis that the observed differences related to treatment conditions are only because of chance. To the extent to which the mean-square for either or both treatment conditions is markedly different from the residual MS_{wg}, *then* the ex-

Table 12-5. ANOVA Summary for Data Depicted in Table 12-2

Factor	Sum of squares	df	Mean-square	F Ratio
A: Dosage levels	80.0	2	40.0	16.0
B: Group of rats	30.0	1	30.0	12.0
Individual differences within cells	60.0	24	2.5	
Total	170.0	29		

perimenter can have some faith in the "reality" of the observed findings.

Each of the two ratios of mean-squares shown in Table 12-5 can be referred to the table of F values given in Appendix B-7. It is found there that the main effect for Factor A with 2 and 24 df is significant beyond the $p = 0.001$ level, and Factor B with 1 and 24 df is significant beyond the $p = 0.01$ level.

The results of the ANOVA support the hypothesis that both factors influence rats' exploratory behavior. Exploration grows larger as drug dosage levels are increased, and exploration is greater for rats reared in a normal home cage than in isolation from other rats.

INTERACTION IN FACTORIAL DESIGNS

The data presented in Table 12-2 represent a factorial design in which effects are *additive*. This additivity can be seen in Figure 12-1. Note that the two curves are parallel over the three drug dosage levels. The additivity inherent in Table 12-2 was demonstrated by first subtracting the column means from the scores in each column and then subtracting the residual mean on each row from the scores in each row. After the column means and residual row means were subtracted in this way, the remaining cell means were all precisely 0, as shown in Table 12-4. Of course, since the means for all six cells are 0, then the row means and column means necessarily are 0 also. In other words, taking out the effects due to the two factors completely erases all systematic differences of the independent variables. All that was left in that case was a residual within-cell variance, which served as a source of error for judging the significance of Factors A and B in that design. Since effects due to columns and rows could be subtracted out in that way, one could easily work backwards from Table 12-4 and add in effects due to rows and columns, which would bring us back to the original set of data shown in Table 12-2.

The scores in Table 12-4 could be transformed back to those in Table 12-3 by adding on the two row means shown in the latter. In a similar manner, the scores in Table 12-3 could be transformed back to the original table by adding on to the scores in each column the respective column means in Table 12-2. This is another way of showing that the main effects in the design depicted in Table 12-2 are additive. This is illustrated in three ways. First, when effects due to row means and column means are subtracted, the mean of each cell is precisely 0. Second, one can add main effects to the table of error scores and arrive back at the original table of data. Third, when this additivity is achieved, a graphic plot of cell means presents a series of parallel curves.

Regarding the last point mentioned, additivity results in parallel curves regardless of whether or not one or both factors of the design are quantitatively or qualitatively ordered. An example in which both factors are qualitatively ordered is in Figure 12-2 where mean achievement test scores in reading comprehension of girls and boys in three different schools are shown. Because schools constitute a

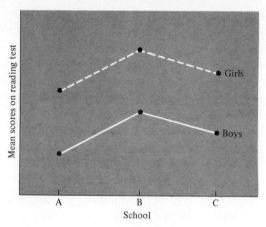

Figure 12-2. Comparison of boys and girls in three schools on a reading comprehension test.

qualitative factor rather than a quantitative factor, it is entirely arbitrary which school is designated by which alphabetical letter. By changing the order in which schools B and C occur in the graph, the mean scores will take on the appearance shown in Figure 12-3. Even if the two figures present different appearances, the curves are parallel in both cases, that is, boys and girls are the same distance apart

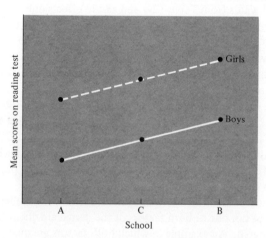

Figure 12-3. A rearrangement of the order in which schools B and C occurred in Figure 12-2.

254 · *Factorial Designs*

in the three schools. As discussed, when the curves are parallel in this way, then effects are additive. This is the case regardless of how many levels there are on each factor and how many factors there are in the design.

Nonadditivity

In actual research, results frequently depart markedly from the principle of additivity. When this occurs, it is said that the factors in the design *interact*. An *interaction* between factors can be illustrated by a slight alteration of Table 12-2. This is done by adding six score units to each of the five scores in the cell corresponding to Level A_3 of drug dosage and Group B_2 of rats (those reared in the normal condition). In this example, none of the scores in the other five cells would be changed. This results in the data shown in Table 12-6. Again, scores have been selected in such a way as to make all cell means, row means, and column means integers, which would almost never occur in practice.

Before taking apart the data shown in Table 12-6, it would be useful to depict the nature of the interaction, as shown in Figure 12-4. Note that the two curves for drug dosages shown in that figure are definitely not parallel. They are parallel for dosage Levels A_1 and A_2, but the two curves depart markedly for Level A_3. At the highest level of drug dosages, rats raised in the normal condition manifest much more exploratory behavior than those raised in isolation. Thus, the two factors interact, in the sense that the differences in means scores for one factor are larger at some rather than other levels of the second factor. The same departure from additivity would have been evident by plotting the two groups of rats on the

Table 12-6. A Modification of Table 12-2 by Adding Six Score Units to the Scores in the Cell Corresponding to the Third Column and Second Row

Factor A: Drug dosage

		A_1		A_2		A_3	
Factor B: Environment of rearing	B_1	2 3 4 5 6	$M_{11} = 4$	4 5 6 7 8	$M_{12} = 6$	6 7 8 9 10	$M_{13} = 8$ $M_{B_1} = 6$
	B_2	4 5 6 7 8	$M_{21} = 6$	6 7 8 9 10	$M_{22} = 8$	14 15 16 17 18	$M_{23} = 16$ $M_{B_2} = 10$

$M_{A_1} = 5$ $M_{A_2} = 7$ $M_{A_3} = 12$

$M_{tot} = 8$

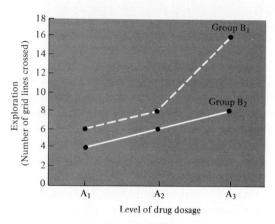

Figure 12-4. An interaction created by adding six score points to all scores in the cell corresponding to the third column and second row of Table 12-2.

X axis and the three levels of drugs on the Y axis. This would have resulted in three curves in which case the curve for Level A_3 would have been much steeper than that for the other two levels of drug dosage. By either method of inspecting the data, the curves are not parallel, and thus the effects of the two treatment conditions are nonadditive.

The Meaning of Interactions

It is almost never the case that main effects in factorial designs are precisely additive, as in the data depicted in Table 12-2. If results are presented graphically, there will almost always be an observable departure from strict parallelism of the curves. This might be either because the interaction is "real" in the population being studied, or because of sampling error and other sources of error in conducting the experiment. In analyzing factorial designs, it is important to determine the statistical significance of observed interactions. As will be shown later in the chapter, the size of the interaction can be tested for significance in the same way that main effects are tested.

The implication of an interaction with respect to behavior is that the treatments literally combine in complex ways. An example would be in comparing three amounts of practice on two methods of instruction in mathematics. One method of instruction would be consistently better than the other for the first two levels in terms of amounts of practice; however, for the third level of practice, students undergoing the superior method of instruction "catch on" and rapidly move far ahead of students undergoing the other method of instruction. Another example would be in comparing memory for rapidly presented words and geometrical forms. The independent variable concerns four levels of exposure time when the stimulus materials are presented on a screen. For the higher levels of exposure time, performance on the words is consistently better than that on the geometrical forms; however, at the lowest level of exposure time, performance falls off much more on the geometrical forms than on the words.

STATISTICAL PROPERTIES OF INTERACTIONS

As a prelude to discussing the statistical nature of interactions, it would be useful to see how interactions are manifested in actual research results. For this purpose, it is instructive to reinspect Table 12-6, which was obtained by adding six score units to one cell in Table 12-2. These two tables should be carefully compared with respect to the changes in row means and column means. Let us see what happens when column effects and row effects are systematically subtracted in the same way as was done for Table 12-2. To further illustrate the principle, it also will be instructive to first subtract the effects due to rows and subsequently the effects due to columns, which is the reverse order from that which was done with respect to Table 12-2. This will provide a graphic demonstration of the principle that the results are the same no matter which factor is removed first from the original table of data.

The row means in Table 12-6 are 6 and 10 respectively. When these are subtracted from scores in the respective rows, the results are as shown in Table 12-7. The residual column means in Table 12-7 are then subtracted from scores in the

Table 12-7. Residual Scores from Table 12-6 After the Mean for Each Row Was Subtracted from Each Score in the Row

Factor A: Drug dosage

	A_1		A_2		A_3	
B_1	-4 -3 -2 -1 0	$M_{11} = -2$	-2 -1 0 1 2	$M_{12} = 0$	0 1 2 3 4	$M_{13} = 2$ $M_{B_1} = 0$
B_2	-6 -5 -4 -3 -2	$M_{21} = -4$	-4 -3 -2 -1 0	$M_{22} = -2$	4 5 6 7 8	$M_{23} = 6$ $M_{B_2} = 0$

Factor B: Environment of rearing

$$M_{A_1} = -3 \qquad M_{A_2} = -1 \qquad M_{A_3} = 4$$

respective columns, resulting in Table 12-8. As is necessarily so, row means and column means in Table 12-8 are all 0. After effects due to both factors are removed, row means and column means must be 0 regardless of whether or not there is an interaction in the data.

The most important thing to note in Table 12-8 is that all cell means are *not* 0. Thus, there are effects left in the cells that cannot be attributed either to the row means or the column means. The residual means in the cells after effects due to rows and columns are removed demonstrate the interaction as depicted in Figure 12-4. Because there was no interaction in the data presented in Table 12-2, all cell means were precisely 0. Thus, the leftover sum of squares was a pure measure of error against which the significance of the two main effects could be tested for statistical significance. In discussing the data in that example, it was said that an idealized case was being presented. In all actual instances in which factorial designs are analyzed, it is necessary to remove the sum of squares attributable to interactions before the remaining sum of squares can be turned into a measure of error variance. The sum of squares in Table 12-2 was broken down into three additive components— SS_A, SS_B, and SS_{wg} which added to SS_{tot}. In actual practice, it is necessary to partition SS_{wg} into a component attributable to the interaction and a remaining component due to error. The *sum of squares due to interaction* is usually symbolized as $SS_{A \times B}$. Whereas A and B signify the individual factors or main effects, A X B symbolizes the interaction of the factors. After sums of squares due to main effects and interactions are removed, the remaining sum of squares frequently is symbolized as SS_E, signifying a *sum of squares attributable purely to error*. It must be kept in mind that SS_E consists of the sum of squared deviates in the table

Table 12-8. Residual Scores from Table 12-7 After Means from Column Were Subtracted from Each Residual Score in Each Row

Factor A: Drug dosage

		A_1		A_2		A_3	
		-1		-1		-4	
		0		0		-3	
	B_1	1	$M_{11} = 1$	1	$M_{12} = 1$	-2	$M_{13} = -2$	$M_{B_1} = 0$
		2		2		-1	
		3		3		0	
		-3		-3		0	
		-2		-2		1	
	B_2	-1	$M_{21} = -1$	-1	$M_{22} = -1$	2	$M_{23} = 2$	$M_{B_2} = 0$
		0		0		3	
		1		1		4	

Factor B: Environment of rearing

$M_{A_1} = 0$ $M_{A_2} = 0$ $M_{A_3} = 0$

after main effects and interactions have been removed.

Calculation of $SS_{A \times B}$

The $SS_{A \times B}$ is determined by the variation of the cell means about M_{tot}. In Table 12-8, the six residual cell means are dispersed about a grand mean of 0; consequently, a sum of squared deviates of the cell means about the grand mean can be obtained by simply squaring, weighting, and summing the six cell means. In the case of calculating the $SS_{A \times B}$, the weighting factor is equal to the number of subjects in each cell. This is just as in the case for the rows and columns effects, that is, the weighting factor equals the number of scores contributing to each cell mean. In this example, each squared cell mean is weighted by 5, the number of scores in each cell. Thus, $SS_{A \times B}$ is equal to 60. If there were no interaction between the two factors of the design, the residual cell means in Table 12-8 would be dispersed very little about a grand mean of 0. To the extent that this dispersion is small, there is very little interaction in the data; conversely, to the extent that this sum of squares is large, *then* there is a marked interaction of factors.

In a similar way to which a mean-square can be obtained for main effects, a mean-square can be obtained for the interaction. The df for interaction equals the df for the number of rows minus 1 multiplied by the df for number of columns minus 1. In this particular case, df for the interaction equals 2. If the number of levels in each row is stated as R and the number of columns is stated as C, then the df for interaction equal $C-1$ multiplied by $R-1$. This df can be derived mathematically as the appropriate divisor for converting $SS_{A \times B}$ into the mean-square for interaction ($MS_{A \times B}$). This method of obtaining the df for interaction can be made intuitively appealing as follows. Table 12-8 resulted from removing the main effects attributable to Factors A and B. Because there are two groups on Factor B, df = 1 for SS_B. Similarly, df = 2 for SS_A. Because the interaction evidenced in Table 12-8 represents a residual joint effect of Factors A and B, then SS_A has df equal to the product of those related to the systematic factor $(R - 1)$ $(C - 1)$.

Table of Variance Components

With these considerations in mind, a breakdown of sums of squares, df, and mean-squares for the data presented in Table 12-6 is shown in Table 12-9. Note that the sums of squares for the four components add up to the total sum of squared deviates about the grand mean. Also note that the df for the various components add up to the total df(29). The total mean-square is not shown because it is not required in computing F ratios.

F ratios for the three components of variance are obtained by dividing each of the three mean-squares by the residual MS_E. Thus, the F ratio for MS_A is obtained from dividing 130 by 2.5, resulting in 54.0. Probability values relating to

Table 12-9. ANOVA Summary Table of the Data Presented in Table 12-6

Factor	SS	df	MS	F
A	260.0	2	130.0	54.0
B	120.0	1	120.0	48.0
A X B interaction	60.0	2	30.0	12.0
Within-cell residual				
error variance	60.0	24	2.5	
Total	500.0	29		

each F ratio can be obtained in the usual way from Appendix B-7. For the main effect of Factor A, an F ratio of 54.0 with 2 and 24 df is significant beyond the $p = 0.001$ level. For factor B, which has 1 and 24 df, an F ratio of 48 is also significant beyond the $p = 0.001$ level. The interaction of Factors A and B has 2 and 24 df. The interaction F ratio of 12.0 is significant beyond the $p = 0.001$ level.

Interpretation of Probability Values

As is true in all tests of statistical significance of differences among treatment effects, the probabilities associated with F ratios in factorial designs relate to the odds of observed differences being due only to error—sampling error and other sources of error in the experimental situation. If the probability associated with the F test is low (0.01 or less), it is improbable that the observed results are due to pure chance. Saying it in another way, it is highly probable that the observed differences are "real."

COMPUTATIONAL PROCEDURES

As has been mentioned at numerous places in this book, the computational approaches that provide the most insight into statistical methods are not frequently the most feasible for calculating the same statistics in actual research. Also, while it is useful to employ highly simplified examples in order for the reader to grasp the workings of statistical methods, the reader should also be acquainted with more complex-appearing but realistic examples. For these reasons, this section will discuss a realistic example of a two-factor design, and the appropriate raw-score equations will be presented and illustrated in detail.

The computational procedures are much the same as those described in Chapter 11. Several extensions are required because it is necessary to calculate two main effects and an interaction. To facilitate discussion, we shall again use the Σ notation developed in Chapter 11. Recall that it was said there that ΣX_i meant to add up the raw scores for the i subjects. This notation was extended to $\sum_{j} \sum_{i} X_{ij}$ which means to sum the scores of all the i subjects in all the j groups. For

Table 12-10. A Simple 2 × 2 Factorial Design with only Two Scores in Each Cell

Columns (A)

Rows (B)	$X_1 = 1$ $X_2 = 2$	$X_1 = 3$ $X_2 = 4$
	$X_1 = 5$ $X_2 = 6$	$X_1 = 7$ $X_2 = 8$

the present discussion, it is necessary to extend the notation again. Since there are two factors involved (A and B), it is necessary to make a distinction between summing "across" rows and summing "across" columns. To speak of summing across columns implies to sum all the scores in each row. To sum across rows indicates that the operation is to sum all the scores in each column. Table 12-10 will be useful in clarifying the distinction between summing across rows or columns.

Table 12-10 represents a simple 2 × 2 factorial design with two scores in each cell. As was indicated earlier in this chapter, the cells of the factorial design are numbered from left to right for columns and from top to bottom for rows. It is also conventional to label the cell for rows and then columns. Thus, the first subject's score in row 1 column 2 is 3. Another way to label this score is X_{112} or more generally as X_{ijk}. In this general notation, i represents the subject number, j the row number, and k the column number.

Now it is easy to employ the symbols in explaining the two directions of summation. The symbol $\sum_k \sum_i X_{ijk}$ means to sum across columns. For example, where j is 1 (the first row) the sum from Table 12-10 is as follows

$$\sum_k \sum_i X_{i1k} = 1 + 2 + 3 + 4$$

and where j is 2 (the second row)

$$\sum_k \sum_i X_{i2k} = 5 + 6 + 7 + 8$$

In a like manner, to sum across rows is symbolized as $\sum_j \sum_i X_{ijk}$. Again from Table 12-10, summing the first column across rows where k is 1 is as follows

$$\sum_j \sum_i X_{ij1} = 1 + 2 + 5 + 6$$

The only other notation which is necessary is the triple summation sign, $\sum_k \sum_j \sum_i X_{ijk}$. This triple summation notation simply means to add up all of the scores in all of the cells.

If the reader understands this discussion of summational notation, it will be a rather straightforward matter to present the computational procedures required for a factorial design. [The procedures which will be presented assume that there is an equal number of subjects in each cell of the design, which is the case in most experiments. In those unusual cases where there are different numbers of subjects in the cells, special computational procedures are required, as discussed in Kirk (1968) and in Winer (1971).] Numbered steps will be followed in presenting the computational procedures. Before anything else is done, the data should be arranged in tabular form as in Table 12-2. In this way, the row and column to which each subject's score belongs can be kept clear. When this is completed, there will be a table of raw scores with R rows and C columns. The total number of cells in the design is RC. In each cell there are n scores. The total number of scores is N_{tot}, which is equal to RCn. The number of scores in each row is Cn, and there are Rn scores in each column. In Table 12-10, for example, $R = 2$, $C = 2$, $n = 2$, and $N_{tot} = 8$. There are Rn or 4 scores in each column and Cn or 4 scores in each row. With these points in mind, the steps for computing an ANOVA on a two-factor design are as follows

Step 1. Find ΣX_i (the sum of the raw scores) for each jk cell in the factorial design. This sum of raw scores for each cell will be employed later, so it should be written into each cell. Place it in each cell just as the means were written into Table 12-2.

Step 2. Square each of the cell totals found in Step 1 and sum these squared values. Call this value E.

Step 3. Find $\sum_k \sum_j \sum_i X_{ijk}$, that is, add up all of the raw scores. Call this value T. This may be done by simply adding the totals of each cell from Step 1.

Step 4. Find $\sum_k \sum_j \sum_i X_{ijk}^2$, that is, square each raw score and then sum over all subjects. Call this value S.

Step 5. For each row, sum the cell totals found in Step 1 $\left(\sum_k \sum_i X_{ijk}\right)$ across columns. Keep each row total separate and write the value on the outside end of each row in the data table.

Step 6. Repeat the Step 5 procedure except now find $\left(\sum_j \sum_i X_{ijk}\right)$, the sum of each column across rows. Again, this may be accomplished by adding the cell values obtained in Step 1. Write these values at the bottom of each column.

Step 7. Square the values at the end of each row found in Step 5 and sum these squared values across columns. Call this sum J.

Step 8. Square the values at the bottom of each column found in Step 6 and sum these. Call this sum K.

In sigma notation, Steps 5 and 7 may be symbolized as $\sum_j (\sum_k \sum_i X_{ijk})^2$, and in a like manner Steps 6 and 8 may be symbolized as $\sum_k (\sum_j \sum_i X_{ijk})^2$. With the values found in Steps 1 through 8, we can now calculate the SS values for the various treatment and interaction effects by employing the following simple equations

$$\text{SS total} = S - \frac{T^2}{N_{tot}}$$

$$\text{SS}_A \text{ or SS columns} = \frac{K}{Rn} - \frac{T^2}{N_{tot}}$$

$$SS_B \text{ or SS row} = \frac{J}{Cn} - \frac{T^2}{N_{tot}}$$

$$SS_E \text{ or SS within error} = S - \frac{E}{n}$$

$SS_{A \times B}$ or SS interaction $= $ SS total $-$ SS row $-$ SS column $-$ SS within error

Each of these SS values should be entered in an ANOVA summary table like Table 12-5. In this summary table, a df value should be listed next to its respective SS value. The df values are $(R - 1)$ for rows, $(C - 1)$ for columns, $(R - 1)(C - 1)$ for interaction, $RC(n - 1)$ for within error, and $(N_{tot} - 1)$ for total. Recall that the sum of the various df values should equal $(N_{tot} - 1)$. Next in this summary table, the MS values should be calculated, which simply requires dividing each SS by its respective df value as follows

$$MS_A = \frac{SS_A}{C - 1}$$

$$MS_B = \frac{SS_B}{R - 1}$$

$$MS_{A \times B} = \frac{SS_{A \times B}}{(R - 1)(C - 1)}$$

$$MS_E = \frac{SS_W}{RC(n - 1)}$$

With these four MS values, the appropriate F ratios may be calculated. They are as follows

$$F_A = \frac{MS_A}{MS_E}$$

This F for the column main effect has $(C - 1)$ and $RC(n - 1)$ df.

$$F_B = \frac{MS_B}{MS_E}$$

The F for the row effect has $(R - 1)$ and $RC(n - 1)$ df.

$$F_{A \times B} = \frac{MS_{A \times B}}{MS_E}$$

This F for interaction has $(R - 1)(C - 1)$ and $RC(n - 1)$ df. These three F values also may be entered into the ANOVA summary table.

To exemplify the use of these calculational equations, it will be useful to ex-

Table 12-11. Data Summary Table for Example Problem of Two-Factor ANOVA

Factor B: Minutes of visual deprivation

Factor A: Number of sides of figures (complexity)		5	10	15	
20	data	4.2, 5.1, 9.3, 11.2, 10.3, 7.5, 10.2, 8.7, 11.0, 4.5	6.1, 5.3, 12.0, 11.5, 7.6, 11.2, 10.6, 9.6, 1.2, 9.9	9.2, 11.2, 12.0, 7.9, 5.1, 8.9, 7.3, 9.6, 9.8, 11.2	
		$\sum_i X_{i11} = 82.00$	$\sum_i X_{i12} = 85.00$	$\sum_i X_{i13} = 92.20$	$\sum_k\sum_i X_{i1k} = 259.20$
		$M = 8.20$	$M = 8.50$	$M = 9.22$	
		$\sum_i X^2_{i11} = 738.90$	$\sum_i X^2_{i12} = 828.72$	$\sum_i X^2_{i13} = 888.64$	$\left(\sum_k\sum_i X_{i1k}\right)^2 = 67{,}184.64$
		$\left(\sum_i X_{i11}\right)^2 = 6{,}724.00$	$\left(\sum_i X_{i12}\right)^2 = 7{,}225.00$	$\left(\sum_i X_{i13}\right)^2 = 8{,}500.84$	
40	data	8.3, 6.6, 12.2, 13.3, 6.9, 7.1, 10.5, 10.3, 11.2, 10.5	10.0, 11.4, 12.3, 5.8, 6.1, 10.4, 9.7, 10.2, 9.5, 8.7	9.7, 7.1, 7.6, 9.2, 11.5, 10.1, 11.1, 6.7, 8.6, 9.8	
		$\sum_i X_{i21} = 96.90$	$\sum_i X_{i22} = 94.10$	$\sum_i X_{i23} = 91.40$	$\sum_k\sum_i X_{i2k} = 282.40$
		$M = 9.69$	$M = 9.41$	$M = 9.14$	
		$\sum_i X^2_{i21} = 988.23$	$\sum_i X^2_{i22} = 924.33$	$\sum_i X^2_{i23} = 859.26$	$\left(\sum_k\sum_i X_{i2k}\right)^2 = 79{,}749.76$
		$\left(\sum_i X_{i21}\right)^2 = 9{,}389.61$	$\left(\sum_i X_{i22}\right)^2 = 8{,}854.81$	$\left(\sum_i X_{i23}\right)^2 = 8{,}353.96$	

Table 12-11. (Continued)

11.7	$\sum_i X_{i31} = 115.20$	13.2
10.2	$M = 11.52$	9.8
10.2		11.7
12.7	$\sum_i X^2_{i31} = 1,360.02$	10.2
10.3		9.6
7.9	$\left(\sum_i X_{i31}\right)^2 = 13,271.04$	8.5
14.2		16.7
13.6		14.7
11.5		12.5
12.9		11.8

$\sum_i X_{i32} = 118.70$

$M = 11.87$

$\sum_i X^2_{i32} = 1,466.09$

$\left(\sum_i X_{i32}\right)^2 = 14,089.69$

19.1	$\sum_i X_{i33} = 145.20$
12.1	$M = 14.52$
14.5	
12.3	$\sum_i X^2_{i33} = 2,156.80$
16.4	
15.7	$\left(\sum_i X_{i33}\right)^2 = 21,083.04$
13.3	
15.6	
14.7	
11.5	

$\sum\sum_{k\ i} X_{i3k} = 379.10$

$\left(\sum\sum_{k\ i} X_{i3k}\right)^2 = 143,716.81$

$\underset{j\ i}{\sum\sum} X_{ij1} = 294.10$

$\left(\underset{j\ i}{\sum\sum} X_{ij1}\right)^2 = 86,494.81$

$\underset{j\ i}{\sum\sum} X_{ij2} = 297.80$

$\left(\underset{j\ i}{\sum\sum} X_{ij2}\right)^2 = 88,684.84$

$\underset{j\ i}{\sum\sum} X_{ij3} = 328.80$

$\left(\underset{j\ i}{\sum\sum} X_{ij3}\right)^2 = 108,109.44$

$\underset{k\ j\ i}{\sum\sum\sum} X_{ijk} = 920.70$

$M_{tot} = 10.23$

$\underset{k\ j\ i}{\sum\sum\sum} X^2_{ijk} = 10,210.99$

$N_{tot} = 90.00$

amine the results of a study concerning visual exploratory behavior. In this experiment, visual exploratory behavior consisted of having the subject look at visual displays. Each subject was shown a series of pictures. The subject had control of how long each picture remained on the viewing screen. Thus, the dependent variable was the mean amount of time spent viewing each picture. The score on the dependent variable was obtained by recording the number of seconds the subject spent viewing each slide in the series and finding the average viewing time of all the slides.

It was hypothesized that visual exploration would be influenced by two variables. The first variable is the complexity of the visual figures. The figures employed were random geometric figures. Complexity was measured by the number of sides in the figure. Three levels of complexity were employed: 20-, 40-, and 60-sided figures.

The second variable thought to be important was the amount of time a subject was forced to look at a blank screen before he was allowed to view the materials in the stimulus display. The three time periods employed were 5, 10, and 15 minutes. This factor is referred to as *visual deprivation*.

The three levels on each of the two factors resulted in a 3 X 3 factorial design. Ninety subjects were selected from a group of college students. These were then assigned randomly to each of the nine cells, with the usual provision that the same number of subjects occurred in each cell.

The data for this experiment are arranged in Table 12-11. In addition to the raw scores, there are four other values in each cell of the design. These are (1) the sum of the raw scores in that cell, (2) the mean for that cell, (3) the sum of the squared raw scores in that cell, and (4) the square of the sum of raw scores. At the end of each row there are two values: (1) the sum of the raw scores from each cell in that row summed across columns and (2) the square of that value. Similar values are entered at the end of each column except that these values are a result of summing across rows.

With the data nicely arranged in the table, one can proceed quickly to the determination of the SS values. Note that several of the steps have been completed already, so the values T, S, J, K, and E may be found easily.

$$T = \sum_k \sum_j \sum_i X_{ijk}$$

$$= 4.2 + 5.1 + 9.3 + \cdots + 15.6 + 14.7 + 11.5$$

$$= 920.70$$

$$T^2 = 847{,}688.49$$

$$S = \sum_k \sum_j \sum_i X_{ijk}^2$$

$$= (4.2)^2 + (5.1)^2 + (9.3)^2 + \cdots + (15.6)^2 + (14.7)^2 + (11.5)^2$$

$$= 10{,}210.99$$

$$J = \sum_j(\sum_k\sum_i X_{ijk})^2$$

$$= (259.20)^2 + (282.30)^2 + (379.10)^2$$
$$= 67,184.64 + 79,749.76 + 143,716.81$$
$$= 290,651.21$$

$$K = \sum_k(\sum_j\sum_i X_{ijk})^2$$

$$= (294.10)^2 + (297.80)^2 + (328.80)^2$$
$$= 86,494.81 + 88,684.84 + 108,109.44$$
$$= 283,289.09$$

$$E = \sum_k\sum_j(\sum_i X_{ijk})^2$$

$$= (82.00)^2 + (85.00)^2 + \cdots + (118.70)^2 + (145.20)^2$$
$$= 6,724.08 + 7,225.00 + \cdots + 14,089.69 + 21,083.04$$
$$= 97,491.99$$

These values T, S, J, K, and E may now be substituted into the equations for the appropriate SS values as follows

$$SS_{tot} = S - \frac{T^2}{N_{tot}}$$
$$= 10,210.99 - \frac{847,688.49}{90}$$
$$= 10,210.99 - 9,418.76$$
$$= 792.23$$

$$SS_A = \frac{K}{Rn} - \frac{T^2}{N_{tot}}$$
$$= \frac{283,289.09}{30} - 9,418.76$$
$$= 9,442.97 - 9,418.76$$
$$= 24.21$$

$$SS_B = \frac{J}{Cn} - \frac{T^2}{N_{tot}}$$
$$= \frac{290,651.21}{30} - 9,418.76$$
$$= 9,688.37 - 9,418.76$$
$$= 269.61$$

$$SS_E = S - \frac{E}{n}$$

$$= 10,210.99 - \frac{97,491.99}{10}$$

$$= 10,210.99 - 9,749.20$$

$$= 461.79$$

$$SS_{A \times B} = SS_{tot} - SS_A - SS_B - SS_E$$

$$= 792.23 - 24.21 - 269.61 - 461.79$$

$$= 36.62$$

The next step is to divide SS_A, SS_B, $SS_{A \times B}$, and SS_E by their respective df. This procedure leads to the following results

$$MS_A = \frac{SS_A}{C - 1}$$

$$= \frac{24.21}{2}$$

$$= 12.10$$

$$MS_B = \frac{SS_B}{R - 1}$$

$$= \frac{269.61}{2}$$

$$= 134.80$$

$$MS_{A \times B} = \frac{SS_{A \times B}}{(R - 1)(C - 1)}$$

$$= \frac{36.62}{4}$$

$$= 9.15$$

$$MS_E = \frac{SS_E}{RC(n - 1)}$$

$$= \frac{461.79}{81}$$

$$= 5.70$$

The final step in evaluating the results of the experiment is to calculate the appropriate F values and then find the corresponding probability values (significance levels) in Appendix B-7. The three F ratios are as follows

$$F_A = \frac{MS_A}{MS_E}$$

$$= \frac{12.10}{5.70}$$

$$= 2.123$$

$$F_B = \frac{MS_B}{MS_E}$$

$$= \frac{134.80}{5.70}$$

$$= 23.649$$

$$F_{A \times B} = \frac{MS_{A \times B}}{MS_E}$$

$$= \frac{9.15}{5.70}$$

$$= 1.605$$

After these calculations are completed, one moves to the final step of comparing the F ratios with the appropriate probability values in Appendix B-7. Again, recall that the df for MS_W are listed down the side of the table and the df for treatment effects are listed across the top of the table. Thus, to determine if F_A is significant, look along the top of the table for the column with a 2 over it and then look down that column to find the df which is closest to 81. As a general rule, unless the df is very close to that appearing above or below that in the table, it is wisest to employ the next lowest value. In this case, the next lowest value is 60. The F ratio of Factor A with 2 and 81 df is found not to be significant. The F of Factor B with 2 and 81 df is found to be significant beyond the 0.001 level. The F for interaction with 4 and 81 df is not significant. Thus, one can make the very simple statement that only levels of complexity had an effect on length of visual exploration. All of the ANOVA results are summarized in Table 12-12. Such a table makes it easy to keep track of results and easy to communicate these results to others.

INTERPRETATION OF INTERACTIONS

If the interaction proves to be statistically significant, there is a question of what to do about it. Not mentioned previously is the fact that the interaction may take

Table 12-12. ANOVA Summary Table for Data Presented in Table 12-11

Factor	SS	df	MS	F
Deprivation (A)	24.21	2	12.10	2.123
Complexity (B)	269.61	2	134.80	23.649
A × B	36.62	4	9.15	1.605
Within error	467.79	81	5.70	
Total		89		

on a multitude of different forms. The first step in analyzing the nature of a significant interaction is to make a graphic plot of the treatment means, as illustrated in Figure 12-1, where no interaction was present. In Figure 12-4, a statistically significant interaction was present, but it was of a form that constituted no major difficulties for interpretation; however, some of the interactions that are found in research results do present difficult problems for interpretation. Examples will be discussed in the following paragraphs.

Different Types of Interactions

The simplest type of interaction is that in which one or more curves depicting main effects differ in slopes from other curves. These and other possibilities will be illustrated with the experiment depicted in Figure 12-1 and Table 12-2. The difference in slope may be because of a sudden change in the effect of one variable at one level. This was illustrated in Figure 12-4, in which case the difference

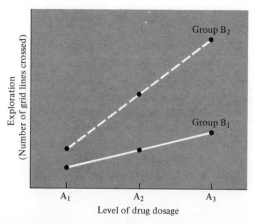

Figure 12-5. An interaction consisting of a difference in slope of two curves.

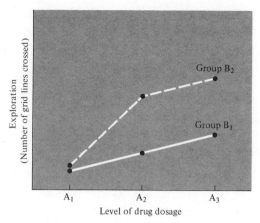

Figure 12-6. An interaction consisting of no difference at one point on a treatment effect but differences at two other points.

between the two groups of rats that had been observed at drug dosage Levels A_1 and A_2 became accentuated at Level A_3.

An overall difference in slope is illustrated in Figure 12-5. Both curves are straight lines, but the slope for rats in Level B_2 is noticeably steeper than that for the rats in B_1. This constitutes an interaction.

A second possibility is that treatment conditions at some level on one factor differ with respect to another factor, but differences at other levels are not significant. This situation is illustrated in Figure 12-6. At the lowest level of drug dosage, mean scores on exploration are almost identical. At the two higher levels, the drug has a definite effect on average amount of exploration in the two groups of rats.

A third possibility is that two or more curves actually cross over. This is evidenced in Figure 12-7. At the lowest level of drug dosage, the rats in Group B_2 actually show less exploratory behavior on the average than the rats in Group B_1. The two higher levels of drug dosage have a dramatic effect on the rats in Group B_2; consequently, they move far above the rats in Group B_1 in terms of average exploratory behavior. This results in an actual crossover of the two curves. Even more bizarre types of crossover interactions are possible, for example, when the curves cross two times rather than once.

The Meaning of Different Types of Interactions

If significant interactions are found in a factorial design, this necessarily restricts any generalizations that can be made about the main effects. When no significant

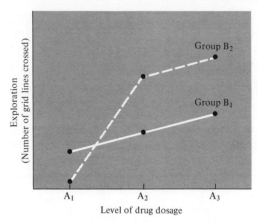

Figure 12-7. A crossover interaction.

interactions are present, the generalizations can be rather simple. For example, with respect to the results depicted in Figure 12-1, the generalization is that both drug dosage and method of rearing systematically affect amount of exploratory behavior. There is no need to further qualify this generalization; and without further qualifications, it can be assumed that the effects are essentially additive. When a significant interaction is found, it is necessary to qualify such simple generalizations. The type of qualification depends upon the nature of the interaction.

In the first type of interaction mentioned here, only a slight qualification is necessary with respect to findings regarding the main effects. Either an overall difference in slope or a difference in slope at a particular level does not require a major change in the way that the overall results would be interpreted. Of course, the interaction should be mentioned in a research report, but no elaborate explanation would be required. Indeed, slight interactions of this kind are more the rule than the exception.

The second type of interaction mentioned does constitute a definite problem for interpretation. In that case, the two groups of rats differed at two drug dosage levels but not at the lowest level; consequently, it is not proper to make an overall statement that the drug has a different effect on amount of exploration in the two groups of rats. What is required instead is a more complex generalization to the effect that at some levels of drug dosage the groups of rats are differentiated in terms of amount of exploratory behavior, but at other levels there is no difference between the two groups of rats. Also, when an interaction of this type is obtained, there is a question as to what would occur at intermediate levels of a factor. The rats are different at drug Level A_2 but not different at Level A_1. A natural question that arises concerns the point between A_1 and A_2 at which the two groups of rats would be differentiated. An interaction of this kind can be clarified only by additional research in which intermediate levels of one or more of the factors in the design are investigated. When there is either no interaction or an interaction because of differences in slopes of curves, it is reasonable to believe that an overall difference exists due to the factor. When a marked interaction is found, questions naturally arise as to what the result would be if more levels were employed on one or more of the factors.

The third type of interaction mentioned presents even more problems than the first or second. When the curves actually cross over as in Figure 12-7, no simple generalization is possible. This means that an independent variable which has one effect at one level, has the opposite effect at another level. In other words, there is no simple lawfulness regarding the relations between factors of the design. When this occurs, it indicates that (1) relations between the independent variables are complex, and (2) considerably more research is required, employing additional levels on one or more of the factors in the design. Fortunately, crossover interactions of this kind are rarely found in research results.

ADDITIONAL CONSIDERATIONS CONCERNING FACTORIAL DESIGNS

In keeping with the introductory level of the book, only rather simple factorial designs have been discussed in detail. The principles which have been discussed are general to all factorial designs; consequently, the reader should be able to understand statistical results relating to factorial designs presented in research literature. However, in the actual conduct of research, much more complex designs are frequently employed and some important follow-up types of statistics are required after the probability values associated with F ratios are obtained. These additonal considerations regarding factorial designs are discussed in detail in the Suggested Additional Readings at the end of this chapter. Two major considerations that are important in understanding factorial designs will now be discussed.

Repeated-Measurements Designs

The factorial designs discussed in this chapter concern comparisons of *different* groups. Thus, the initial example of a factorial design shown in Table 12-2 concerned six different groups of rats. The data depicted in Figure 12-2 concerned three groups of girls and three groups of boys. In no case was an example used in which the same subjects appeared in more than one cell of the design. In actual research, however, it is frequently the case that subjects do appear in more than one cell of the design. As mentioned at numerous points in this book, it is economical to employ subjects in more than one treatment condition if that is feasible.

In some cases, all subjects appear in all cells of the factorial design. Such designs are referred to as totally within-subject or repeated-measurements designs, as contrasted with between-groups designs. An example of the former would be in studying the amount of looking time at geometrical figures which varied in terms of complexity and in terms of amount of preexposure. Geometrical forms are constructed at three levels of complexity. Subjects are shown half of the forms at each level for a period of 10 seconds. Subsequently, subjects are shown geometrical forms in pairs on a screen. In each case, the subject has been familiarized with one of the two forms but not the other. A camera is used to measure the amount of time spent looking at each of the two figures. The hypothesis is that prior familiarization reduces amount of time looking at the familiarized figures as opposed to amount of time looking at unfamiliar figures. This represents a 3 X 2 design. Factor A consists of three levels of complexity, and Factor B consists of familiarized as opposed to unfamiliarized designs. In this case, all subjects receive all six treatment conditions.

In other cases, a mixed design is used where one or more factors of the design constitute repeated measurements and the other factor or factors concern comparisons of different groups. This can be illustrated quite simply by adding a comparison of male and female students onto the study of looking behavior. There would still be the two within-subject factors of complexity levels and familiarization. There also would be a between-groups factor of males versus females. In some very complex factorial designs, there may be as many as two or more between-groups factors and two or more within-subject factors. A complete discussion of such complex factorial designs would be far out of keeping with the intended level of this text; however, the reader should be aware of these possibilities when reading research reports. Also, the detailed statistical methods should be sought out if the reader is required to employ complex factorial designs embodying within-subject factors as well as between-groups factors.

Multiple Comparisons

As is true with single-factor designs, it is sometimes necessary to make follow-up analyses of factorial designs to determine the statistical significance of the different cell means from one another. This involves what are referred to as *multiple comparisons.* How to perform such multiple comparisons is discussed in detail in advanced texts on statistics, such as those listed in the Suggested Additional Readings at the end of this chapter. The problem can be illustrated with some of the figures shown previously in this chapter. For the data depicted in Figure 12-4, it is found that there is an overall difference for Factor B (two groups of rats) with respect to amount of exploration; however, the difference is larger at drug level A_3 than at the other two drug levels. The question arises as to whether or not the differences at each drug level are statistically significant. Thus, if a t test were made between the two groups at drug Level A_1, would this difference be statistically significant? Another issue regarding multiple comparisons is evidenced in Figure 12-5. Whereas at the highest levels of drug dosage the difference between the two groups is very large, at the lowest level of drug dosage the difference is very small. The question arises as to whether or not the difference at the lowest level is statistically significant. Another type of problem regarding multiple comparisons is exemplified by the data depicted in Figure 12-7. The figure shows a crossover interaction. It must be determined whether the observed difference in exploration at each drug level is statistically significant.

One approach to making multiple comparisons is to employ the t test discussed in Chapter 10 with respect to cell means. As discussed in Chapter 10, such t tests can be used to compare any two means whether they concern repeated measurements on the same subjects or different groups of subjects. In some cases, the use of the t test in this way offers a reasonable approach to making multiple comparisons if interpretations are made only of differences that are highly significant— beyond $p = 0.01$ or less.

The problem in using the t test to make multiple comparisons is that there is an opportunity to "take advantage of chance." Thus, simply by fishing around among all possible differences in cell means of a complex design, some of the t tests would be "significant" purely because of the number of possible comparisons. This could be the case even if there are no real differences at all in the population of subjects in question. The opportunity to take advantage of chance in this way grows with the number of possible comparisons of means. One could imagine what would happen in a three factor repeated-measurements design with five levels on each factor. There then would be 125 cells in the design. This results in a total of 7,750 possible comparisons of the means, two at a time. Obviously, if all of the data were obtained from a table of random numbers, some of the mean differences could be significant by chance alone. Where there are many possible comparisons of means in a factorial design (for example, more than a half dozen), special methods of multiple comparison are required. These are conservative in the sense that they take account of the opportunity to take advantage of chance. The reader should be suspicious of statistical analyses that do not employ these methods of multiple comparison, and these methods should be sought out if the reader conducts research concerning complex factorial designs. These are discussed in detail in Kirk (1968) and Winer (1971).

Analysis of Trends

It was mentioned previously that in many research designs some or all of the factors are quantitatively ordered. When the factors are quantitatively ordered, it is important to perform follow-up analyses after overall F tests are made which determine the exact shapes of the curves (trends). Examples of quantitatively ordered factors are drug dosage levels, amounts of practice, or grade levels of students. The usual analysis of variance tells whether or not the separate factors and their interactions are statistically significant, but it does not specify the exact form of the relationship. Thus, the relationship between a quantitatively ordered factor and the dependent variable might be an ascending straight line, a descending straight line, an inverted U-shaped relationship, or other type of curve. After significance tests are made with analysis of variance, it is important to make subsequent analyses of the trends involved. Such analyses provide highly important information in addition to significance tests relating to the main effects and interactions of the factorial design.

SUMMARY

Factorial designs involving two or more independent variables represent straightforward extensions of one-factor designs discussed in Chapter 11. The advantage of multi-factor designs is that they provide an opportunity to learn much more from a research project than could be obtained from single-factor designs alone. Regarding two-factor designs, one could simultaneously learn about effects of methods of instruction and amounts of practice, species of rats and levels of drug dosage, and other such simultaneous manipulations of two variables. In some research projects, there are many factors manipulated simultaneously, although after a point, the sheer complexity of such designs can become confusing.

Factorial designs can be investigated with methods of ANOVA based on the concept of mean-squares. When there are two or more factors to the design, then there are as many mean-squares as independent variables. Thus, in a two-factor design, there is a MS for columns and a MS for rows. In addition, when there are two or more factors in the design, it is possible to analyze the interaction of factors. If effects due to columns and rows are additive, then there is no significant interaction; however, in most investigations in psychology and education, the several factors of a design usually interact at least to some extent. It is important to understand the various types of interactions that occur. Slight departures from additivity are the rule rather than the exception; however, it is seldom found that an interaction is so marked as to result in an actual crossover of effects.

The use of the F test in factorial designs is most easily understood in terms of deviation scores. In this chapter, it was shown how a 2 X 2 factorial design could be taken apart in terms of sums of squares relating to such deviation scores. This resulted in four sums of squares: SS_A, SS_B, SS_E, and $SS_{A \times B}$. The four constituent sums of squares add to SS_{tot}. After each of these sums of squares is divided by the proper df, mean-squares are obtained. The significance of MS_A, MS_B, and $MS_{A \times B}$ can be assessed with an F test by dividing each of these by MS_E. Related probability values can be obtained from Appendix B-7.

Whereas it is easier to understand the analysis of factorial designs in terms of deviation scores, in actual practice it is more convenient to apply raw-score equations. A set of equations was presented which can be employed in practice. Two topics were mentioned which are beyond the scope of this book but with which the reader should have a speaking acquaintance. These are repeated-measurements designs and the analysis of trends.

EXERCISES

Study Questions

1   What are the relative advantages of performing an experiment relating to a factorial design rather than performing a number of experiments investigating the treatment variables separately? Compose an example.

2   Do the sums of squares in a factorial design from all sources add up to the total sums of squares? What principle is involved here that applies to even highly complex factorial designs involving three or more factors?

3   What is the error term in a factorial design? Is this the same error term that is used in a one-factor or simple ANOVA?

4   What is the interaction term in ANOVA? Give an example. In what sense is it another source of variation that can be tested for significance?

5   Discuss the concept of additivity with respect to the different treatments in a factorial design. How does this relate to the concept of interaction? Compose an example.

6   Compose examples of different types of interactions that might occur in research. Draw figures to illustrate. Discuss how each of these would affect the interpretation of experimental results.

7   Can factorial designs be employed with repeated-measurements? Give an example.

8   Why would one want to make multiple comparisons after the ANOVA for a factorial design is completed?

9   How would an analysis of trends provide additional information over the results of a factorial ANOVA? Compose an example.

Problems

The table here represents a modification of Table 12-6 concerning the effects of drug dosage and environmental rearing on exploration in rats. The modification consisted of taking out the column in Table 12-6 corresponding to drug dosage Level A_2. In this table, drug dosage A_2 is the same as A_3 in Table 12-6. This modification changes most of the computational results over that found for the data in Table 12-6 but still leaves the computations very simple.

		Factor A: Drug dosage	
		A_1	A_2
Factor B: Environment of rearing	B_1	2	6
		3	7
		4	8
		5	9
		6	10
	B_2	4	14
		5	15
		6	16
		7	17
		8	18

Compute a complete ANOVA for these experimental results. Employ the raw score computing routines given in the chapter. Show all major computational steps. Summarize the results with an ANOVA table like that in Table 12-9. Interpret the results.

SUGGESTED ADDITIONAL READINGS

Ferguson, G. A. *Statistical analysis in psychology and education*, 3d ed. New York: McGraw-Hill, 1971, Chap. 16.

Guilford, J. P., and B. Fruchter. *Fundamental statistics in psychology and education*, 5th ed. New York: McGraw-Hill, 1973, Chap. 13.

Hays, W. L. *Statistics for the social sciences*, 2d ed. New York: Holt, Rinehart & Winston, 1973, Chap. 12.

Kirk, R. E. *Experimental design procedures for the behavioral sciences.* Belmont: Brooks/Cole, 1968.

Winer, B. J. *Statistical principles in experimental design*, 2d ed. New York: McGraw-Hill, 1971.

Part Four

Nonparametric Statistics

13

Analysis of Categories
and Ranks

The statistical methods discussed in Part Three of the book are based on two major assumptions. First, it is assumed that the data relate to interval or ratio scales (rather than to ranks or categories). Second, it is assumed that scores are sampled from populations that are at least approximately normally distributed, for example, as in correlating two sets of test scores which are assumed to be sampled from normally distributed populations of test scores. These assumptions are required in using the significance test for the product-moment correlation, the t test for difference between two means, and F tests relating to analysis of variance. It was mentioned that all of these tests are "robust" in the sense that even marked violations of the assumption of normality of distributions have little influence on descriptive statistics or probabilities obtained from significance tests; however, in some experimental situations, it is quite obvious that the obtained scores do not fit the normal distribution. This is the case when scores are inherently in the form of either categories or ranks. An example of categories would be the percentages of students in a confidential survey who say that they have or have not ever smoked marijuana. Their responses are obviously in relation to categories rather than in relation to higher forms of measurement. Another example of categories would be the numbers of students in high school who say that they will undertake various courses of training in college.

Data obtained in the form of ranks also do not meet the assumption of a normal distribution of population scores. An example would be in studying psychologists' rankings of improvement of patients undertaking different types of psychotherapy. Each therapist ranks 12 patients from 1 (most improved) to 12 (least improved).

Even though the research data may not inherently be in the form of either ranks or categories, the assumption of a normal distribution of scores in the population under consideration might be grossly violated. An example would be in studying the number of days in a semester that students are absent from school. Rather than being normally distributed, the distribution would more nearly resemble a J-curve. Most of the students would be absent no more than one or two days, and, on the extreme, a few students would be absent more than ten days. (Such frequency distributions were discussed in Chapter 4.) Even though number of days absent would constitute a perfectly sensible ratio scale, the extreme departure from a normal distribution of research results would prevent the application of inferential statistics which are based on the assumption of at least an approximately normal distribution being present.

It is necessary to apply *nonparametric statistics* rather than the statistical methods discussed in Part Three of this book when data are (1) in categorical form, (2) in the form of ranks, or (3) from interval or ratio scales but have a grossly nonnormal distribution. The term *parameter* is used in mathematics with respect to any fixed characteristic of a measurement problem. For example, the circumference of a circle is said to be a parameter of a circle. All circles have a circumference, and the circumference describes one useful characteristic of a circle. In statistics, the most important parameters are those relating to the characteristics which describe a distribution of scores. These are the mean, standard deviation, and functions concerning the distribution shape. When data are either in the form of categories or ranks, then it is meaningless to talk about these three important parameters of a frequency distribution; consequently, the nonparametric statistics must be employed. Also, if data obtained from interval scales and ratio scales are markedly divergent from the normal distribution, it would be necessary to convert them to either categories or ranks before making statistical comparisons. In either case, it is necessary to employ the types of inferential statistics that will be discussed in this chapter rather than the parametric statistics. The nonparametric statistics are so named because they make no assumption about the mean, standard deviation, or shape of the underlying distribution of scores.

There are far too many nonparametric statistics available to permit a discussion of more than a fraction of them here. Some of them are highly specialized and are used very rarely. Extensive discussions of these nonparametric statistics are provided in the Suggested Additional Readings at the end of the chapter. The purpose of the discussion in this chapter will be to convey some general principles regarding the use of nonparametric statistics and to illustrate some of the more widely used methods.

Three situations in which it is absolutely necessary to employ nonparametric statistics rather than their parametric counterparts were described previously. These occur when the data are (1) in the form of categories, (2) in the form of ranks, and (3) from interval scales or ratio scales but distributed in a manner that is markedly different from the normal distribution. In the early 1950s, some behavioral scientists argued that nonparametric statistics should be used quite generally even in those cases where the data were not obviously in the form of categories or ranks and when distributions were approximately normal. Such arguments were based on the premise that even normally distributed variables in psychology and education could *not* be sensibly construed as relating to interval scales or ratio scales. For two reasons, very little credence is given to that argument these days. First, very good arguments can be given to show that most of the measurements in psychology and education intended to be either interval scales or ratio scales can be legitimately analyzed as such. [See discussion in Nunnally (1967), Chap. 1.] Second, when dealing with interval scales or ratio scales, most of the parametric statistics are very robust in the sense that the results are usually very much the same under various distortions of the distribution shape. For example, significance tests that depend upon the assumption of a normal distribution produce very much the same probability values when the distribution is markedly skewed, flattened, or otherwise different from the normal distribution. Unless the divergence from normality is so extreme as with a J-curve, the assumption of normality is usually not a major problem; consequently, there is no great harm in employing parametric tests even if the assumption of normality of distributions is somewhat violated. However, the reader needs to be aware of some general principles regarding nonparametric statistics and obtain an acquaintance with some widely used techniques for two reasons. First, one of the three circumstances mentioned that necessitate the use of nonparametric statistics occurs frequently in research. Second, even when one of those circumstances prevailed and it would have been wiser to employ parametric statistics, the reader will encounter research reports extending back many years where nonparametric statistics were employed.

ANALYSIS OF CATEGORICAL DATA

Much research in psychology and education relates to data in the form of categorical responses rather than to measures concerning ranks, interval scales, or ratio scales. Numerous examples of categorical data have been given previously. Examples would be the numbers of students who study various foreign languages in high school or the number of women in a survey who say that they employ some type of birth control. There are then two types of categorical response concerning subjects who say yes and those who say no.

In discussing categorical data, it is important to make a distinction between the situation where the final data is in the form of categories and the situation in which a total score is obtained by adding up categorical responses to test items. In the two examples given, the final data consisted of categorical responses, in these cases, responding either yes or no to a survey question. In many cases, subjects are required to make categorical responses to a number of test items and a total score is obtained by summing over these items. This would be the case in any type of true-false test in which the total score would consist of the number of correct responses. This also would be the case in a scale of attitudes toward the United Nations in which the total score would consist of the number of agreements with positively worded statements. When test scores consist of the sum of responses one way or the other to dichotomously worded items, then such scores frequently meet all of the requirements for the employment of parametric statistics, such as the t test for differences between means. This section is concerned with the situation in which the final data is in the form of categorical responses for which it is necessary to employ nonparametric statistics.

Descriptive Statistics for Categorical Data

As has been mentioned at numerous places in this book, it is important to make a distinction between descriptive statistics and inferential statistics. By far the most widely used and meaningful way to describe categorical data is in terms of percentages. In one example given previously, it would be very informative to describe the results of a survey concerning number of students studying different foreign languages by casting the data in the form of percentages. Thus, it might be found that 30 percent of the students completing high school had studied no foreign language, 20 percent had completed at least one semester of Spanish, and so on for the other languages. With the example concerning birth control, it would be meaningful to report that 78 percent of the women sampled said that they employed some type of birth control, and the remaining 22 percent said that they did not. Such percentage figures are used widely in daily life and they represent a very useful way of communicating results from samples of categorical data.

Percentages are not only useful in describing the overall results of an investigation, but they can also be used to break down the data in numerous ways. One example would be to show separately the percentages of male and female students who have studied the various foreign languages or the percentages in different occupational groups who say that they will vote for one candidate rather than another.

Another descriptive statistic that is useful with a special type of categorical data is the phi coefficient, which was discussed in Chapter 8. Phi is useful for correlating two sets of categories where there are two categories in each. It is most useful in correlating data obtained from test items that may be scored only on a pass-fail basis. An example would be correlating scores from two items on a multiple-choice test of vocabulary. The student either chooses the correct alternative and thus passes, or he chooses one of the incorrect alternatives and thus fails. In order to investigate the extent to which all items on the test tend to measure the same thing, it is helpful to employ the phi coefficient for correlating each item with all other items on the test. Thus, if there are 20 items on the test, one would have as many phi coefficients as there are possible pairings of items. An analysis of these coefficients provides valuable information about the extent to which the items "hang together" and thus measure the same thing. [See discussion in Nunnally (1967), Chap. 8.]

Inferential Statistics for Categorical Data

Although it is most meaningful to describe categorical data in terms of percentages, it is easier to perform related tests of statistical significance on the frequencies from which the percentages are obtained rather than on the percentages themselves. A very general test for performing inferential statistics on such frequencies is referred to as *chi square*, symbolized by the Greek letter χ^2 .

Most frequently, chi square is employed in what is called a *test of independence*; that is, it is used to test the null hypothesis that the numbers of individuals appearing in different categories are no different from what would be expected by chance alone. This is similar to the way in which the null hypothesis is employed in testing for the significance of the correlation coefficient, the t test for difference between two means, and the F test for differences among more than two means.

A simple example of the use of chi square is in testing whether a flipped coin is biased or fair. If a coin is flipped 60 times, the most probable result is 30 heads and 30 tails. Chi square permits a test of whether departures from this expected 50-50 split are significantly different from chance. For example, suppose the result is obtained of 35 heads and 25 tails. Is this a significant departure from expectancy? The equation for chi square is a follows

$$\text{chi square} = \Sigma \frac{(f_o - f_e)^2}{f_e} \tag{13-1}$$

where f_0 = the frequency of the observed occurrences, and f_e = the frequency of the expected occurrences.

The computational steps for this example are shown in Table 13-1.

Chi square is one more probability distribution in addition to the normal distribution z, t, and F. After a value of chi square is obtained from the results of an experiment, it can be converted to a probability. Probability values relating to various levels of chi square are given in Appendix B-8. In this example, the df equals 1. A general rule for calculating the df for chi square is presented

Table 13-1. Use of Chi Square with Respect to the Fairness of a Coin

Frequencies and computations

		f_o	f_e	$(f_o - f_e)$	$(f_o - f_e)^2$	$\dfrac{(f_o - f_e)^2}{f_e}$
Coin	Heads	35	30	5	25	0.83
	Tails	25	30	-5	25	0.83

$$\chi^2 = \Sigma \frac{(f_o - f_e)^2}{f_e}$$

df = 1

Not significant

$$= \frac{(35 - 30)^2}{30} + \frac{(25 - 30)^2}{30}$$

$$= \frac{(5)^2}{30} + \frac{(-5)^2}{30}$$

$$= \frac{25}{30} + \frac{25}{30}$$

$$= 0.83 + 0.83$$

$$= 1.66$$

later in this chapter. Utilizing Appendix B-8, it is found that a chi square of 1.66 with 1 df is not sufficient to reject the null hypothesis at the 0.05 level. It is shown that a chi-square value of 3.84 is needed to reject the null hypothesis at the 0.05 level. Thus, there is no compelling reason for rejecting the coin as being fair. Saying it another way, there is no convincing evidence that the coin is unfair.

An example of the use of chi square with respect to a simple 2 × 2 table of data in the behavioral sciences is in the study of differences between male and female high school students regarding plans for college education. In the school system of a large city, a survey is conducted on the opinions of students about present and future schooling. One of the questions is "Do you have definite plans to enter college training after graduating from high school?" The sample consists of 600 students who were contacted in study halls at four schools scattered over the metropolitan area. (The investigator assumes that this method of gathering data represents a relatively random sampling of students in the school district.) It happens that 280 of the subjects obtained in this way are male and 320 are female. In this sample, the number of yes answers to the above question was 187 for males and 161 for females. The investigator asks himself whether or not these differences appearing in the sample probably represent real differences in the population of all students in the school system. The chi-square test can be employed directly on the frequencies; this procedure represents a test of significance of difference for the corresponding percentages as well.

A method for calculating expected frequencies in this example and in all other cases is described as follows. The procedure will be illustrated with respect to the 187 males in Table 13-2 who respond yes to the question. The first step is to locate the row total and column total corresponding to the particular cell, which in this case is 280 and 348 respectively. Second, these totals are multiplied. Third, the expected frequency is obtained by dividing this quantity by the total number of responses N shown in the table, in this case 600. Thus, the expected frequency is $(280)(348)/(600) = 162.4$. The expected frequencies for the other three cells in the table are calculated by the same procedure.

A simple rule to obtain df for chi square is to multiply the number of rows minus one $(R - 1)$ times the number of columns minus one $(C - 1)$. Thus, in this example, the df would be calculated as follows

$$(2 - 1)(2 - 1) = 1$$

Utilizing Appendix B-8, it is found that chi square of 10.83 with 1 df would be significant at the 0.001 level; consequently, the chi square of 16.64 found in this example is significant beyond that level. This supports the conclusion that the two categories (sex and stated desire for continued education) are probably

Table 13-2. Use of Chi Square in Comparing Differences in Plans for College Training Between Male and Female High School Students

		Obtained frequencies		
		Do you plan to go to college?		
		Yes	No	Total
Sex	Male	187	93	280
	Female	161	159	320
	Total	348	252	600

		Frequencies and computations		
f_o	f_e	$(f_o - f_e)$	$(f_o - f_e)^2$	$\dfrac{(f_o - f_e)^2}{f_e}$
187	162.4	24.6	605.16	3.73
93	117.6	-24.6	605.16	5.15
161	185.6	-24.6	605.16	3.26
159	134.4	24.6	605.16	4.50

$$\chi^2 = 16.64 \qquad \Sigma \frac{(f_o - f_e)^2}{f_e} = 16.64$$

df = 1   Significant at less than 0.001 level

not independent. Stating the matter in another way, the odds are higher than 999 out of 1,000 that a larger proportion of male students in the school district plan to attend college than do female students.

A more complex use of chi square in research is illustrated in Table 13-3. In this example, a researcher wishes to determine whether teachers in small, medium, and large elementary schools think that a current reorganization has had a beneficial effect on the educational process. The null hypothesis would be that there is no difference between size of school and opinions concerning the evaluation of the administrative reorganization. The necessary computational steps are shown in Table 13-3. In this example there are three rows and four columns. Thus, the df may be calculated as follows: $(3 - 1)(4 - 1) = 6$

Table 13-3. Use of Chi Square in a Study Comparing Attitudes of Teachers From the Different Sizes of Schools Regarding a Planned Administrative Reorganization

		Opinion				
		Beneficial	Harmful	No change	No opinion	Totals
Size of school	Small	61	40	10	10	121
	Medium	111	90	9	6	216
	Large	161	212	33	6	412
	Totals	333	342	52	22	749

Frequencies and computations

f_o	f_e	$(f_o - f_e)$	$(f_o - f_e)^2$	$\dfrac{(f_o - f_e)^2}{f_e}$
61	53.8	7.2	51.84	0.96
40	55.2	-15.2	231.04	4.19
10	8.4	1.6	2.56	0.30
10	3.6	6.4	40.96	11.38
111	96.0	15.0	225.00	2.34
90	98.6	-8.6	73.96	0.75
9	15.0	-6.0	36.00	2.40
6	6.3	-0.3	0.09	0.01
161	183.2	22.2	492.84	2.69
212	188.1	23.9	571.21	3.04
33	28.6	4.4	19.36	0.68
6	12.1	-6.1	37.21	3.08

$$\chi^2 = \Sigma \frac{(f_o - f_e)^2}{f_e}$$

$$= 31.82$$

df = 6   Significant at less than 0.001 level

The resulting chi square of 31.82 is greater than that shown in Appendix B-8 for the 0.001 level corresponding to 6 df, which is 22.46. Differences among the three sizes of schools are therefore significant at less than the 0.001 level. Thus, the most reasonable conclusion is that size of school and attitude toward the administrative reorganization are not independent. It can be seen that this lack of independence is due to the fact that there is an inverse relationship between a school's size and the proportion of people who say that the reorganization is beneficial. Well over half of the respondents from small schools say that the reorganization is beneficial, but considerably less than half of the respondents from large schools say that the reorganization is beneficial.

Thus far, the examples of the use of chi square have been analogous to one-factor experimental designs employed in analysis of variance. Chi square can also be used for the analysis of multifactor investigations concerning categorical data. An example would be a research project concerning the effectiveness of three types of marriage counseling. In addition to being categorized according to the type of counseling that they undertake, couples are also categorized according to whether or not they have children and into one of six occupational groupings concerning the work of the husbands. This results in a 3 X 2 X 6 experimental design, analogous to those employed in analysis of variance. The dependent measure consists of 0s and 1s, with a 2 signifying that the couple is still married two years after the end of the counseling sessions. Chi square can be used to "take apart" the significance of difference of the three factors in this design. An overall discussion of how to employ chi square with complex factorial designs is given in Hays (1973) and Siegel (1956). Although other statistical methods have been developed for the analysis of categorical data, all of them boil down to essentially the same logic as chi square. [See a detailed discussion of these matters in Ferguson (1971), Chap. 13.]

The use of chi square requires two assumptions. First, as is true with all statistics relating to between-groups designs, it is assumed that scores in one category (or cell) are experimentally independent of one another. Essentially, this means that the response of one individual is in nowise influenced by the response of another individual. Numerous examples have been given in this book of how non-independence could occur in research.

The second assumption in using chi square is that the frequencies obtained in each category from sampling the population in question are normally distributed about the population value. Thus, if 32 percent of the population in question fall into a particular category, the assumption is that the percentages (and thus, relative frequencies) obtained from samples would be normally distributed about that quantity. This is nothing more than the usual assumption of sampling errors being normally distributed about a particular population value for a statistic, which is a very reasonable assumption *except* in the situation where the population percentage in any category is very small. For example, if the population percentage in any category is less than 5, then it would not be expected to find a normal distribution of percentages obtained from a large number of samples, but rather one would expect a distribution skewed toward the higher percentage end of the continuum; consequently, it is unsafe to employ chi square when the percentages expected in any category are very small, say, less than 10. When it is necessary to employ chi square with such small expected frequencies in any category, a special statistical correction is required. [See discussion in Siegel (1956), Chap. 4).]

Placing Higher-Order Measures into Categories

Analysis of categorical data (for example, with chi square) sometimes is performed on scores that could be reasonably considered as ranks, interval scales, or ratio scales. Unless there are compelling reasons for doing this, however, such analyses fail to take advantage of the much richer information available in the higher-order scales. The major reason for making such transformations is that the original data from interval or ratio scales are so highly skewed that it would not be appropriate to apply the parametric statistics discussed in Part Three of the book. It has been mentioned a number of times that the parametric statistics (for instance, analysis of variance) are very robust in the sense that good approximations to significance tests are obtained even if score distributions are obviously nonnormal; however, when the distributions are extreme in this way, it is not appropriate to apply the parametric statistics. By extreme is meant score distributions that approximate J-curves, such as those illustrated in Chapter 4. Such curves are more frequently found in comparing intact groups of subjects rather than in comparing experimental treatments. An example of the former would be in comparing the number of days male and female high school students are absent during a semester. Most students would be absent no more than several times, some students would be absent seven or eight times, and way out on the extreme, some students would be absent most of the semester. Thus, most of the scores (days absent) would be bunched up near zero, and there would be a very long "tail" stretching out toward larger numbers of days absent. In such extreme cases, it would be inappropriate to apply statistical tests such as the t test. One approach to performing a significance test would be to combine scores for males and females and dichotomize, or cut them at some level. (It is most useful in this regard to make the cut near the median of the combined distribution.) Then, the data from a ratio scale (days absent) would be transformed to categorical data. If, in this case, the cut were made at two days of absence, then frequencies in the categories male and female would consist of the number of individuals who had been absent more than two days. The frequencies for males and females could be analyzed by chi square in the same way that any other frequencies relating to categories could.

Although it is not wise to purposefully degenerate data from ratio scales and interval scales into categories, this practice is sometimes necessary with respect to comparisons of two or more experimental treatments. An example would be in a study of the effects of three amounts of illumination on the ability of subjects to visually detect alphabetical letters projected onto a screen. After the results are obtained, it can be seen that the task was very easy under the highest level of illumination, so much so that half of the subjects make correct responses in all cases. Under the lowest level of illumination, the distribution of scores is approximately normal. Under the middle level of illumination, the task is rather easy, and, consequently, the distribution is markedly skewed toward the low-score end of the continuum. It would not be sensible in this case to apply analysis of variance. What could be done instead is to combine the scores from the three groups into one overall frequency distribution, cut the scores near the median, and then apply a chi square analysis in the same way as was illustrated above for comparing male and female students in terms of numbers of absences; however, it is never a happy circumstance for the experimenter when he must degenerate data on an interval scale or a ratio scale into dichotomous scores. Much more information and much more powerful statistical analyses could be performed if the score distributions in each experimental treatment are at least roughly normal. Recasting data from higher-order scales into categories is an unpleasant necessity after it is found that the distribution shapes are of a type that do not permit more powerful analyses.

ANALYSIS OF RANKS

The statistical analysis of ranks constitutes an uncertain middle ground between the analysis of higher-order scales and the analysis of categories. If the data can be construed sensibly as relating to interval scales or ratio scales (which is usually the case) and the obtained frequency distributions even approximately resemble the normal form, then it is far wiser to apply powerful parametric descriptive statistics and inferential statistics rather than resort to nonparametric statistics concerning ranks. At the other extreme, as discussed in the previous section, there are cases when the data necessitate being analyzed as categories or it is necessary to degenerate data from interval scales or ratio scales into categories in order to perform the necessary analyses. For a number of reasons, the analysis of ranked data constitutes a more controversial issue. The first point of consideration regarding analysis of data in terms of ranks is that if data meet the requirements for parametric statistics (that is, interval scale and normal distribution), then there is very little to be gained from degenerating such data into ranks. An example of degenerating higher-order scales to ranks is as follows. A comparison is made of the number of correct responses by 20 students in memorizing two types of word-pairs. The two types of word-pairs are mixed together in the same list, and students are given five minutes to memorize as many pairs as they can from a sheet containing the words. The question is whether one type of word-pair is more easily remembered than the other. There would then be two distributions of scores, one for each of the two types of word-pairs. After plotting frequency distributions for the two types of words, the experimenter sees that the assumption of normality is reasonable. This would be an excellent case in which to use the t test for matched scores, the scores being matched in the sense that all subjects appear in both treatment conditions. This test was discussed in Chapter 10.

Another approach to analyzing data in this example is to first pool the scores from the two distributions and rank them from highest to lowest. One could then find the average rank for the two lists of words. In this way, it might be evident that one list appeared easier on the whole than the other. One could then go on to perform statistical analyses of a type to be mentioned later on the data expressed as ranks; however, this is almost always a mistake. As previously mentioned, most parametric analyses provide richer information than the nonparametric analyses.

The second point of consideration regarding analysis of data in terms of ranks is that although there are some important exceptions, there is usually little, if any, time saved in employing them over comparable parametric statistics. Some nonparametric analyses which are very quickly undertaken will be mentioned later; however, time is seldom saved by employing statistics concerning ranks, particularly in the case where higher-order scales have been degenerated into ranks. Even in those few cases where nonparametric analyses can be undertaken very quickly by hand, the small saving in time frequently encourages one to be penny-wise and pound-foolish. The time taken to perform statistical analyses usually represents a very trivial part of the overall time spent in performing research; consequently, it would be a shame not to wring every possible bit of statistical information out of a set of data just in order to save some time in statistical computations.

A third point of consideration regarding the analysis of ranked data concerns the source of the data itself. Whereas it is not wise to degenerate higher-order measures into ranks as previously discussed, sometimes the data are inherently in the form of ranks. This would be the case if four clinical psychologists ranked ten patients in terms of the amount of improvement in psychotherapy. This also would be the case if teachers ranked eight students in terms of receiving a special merit award for school achievement. When the actual measurement methods themselves relate specifically to ranks, then the results must obviously be analyzed as ranks; however, in most research in psychology and education, the data are either obviously in the form of categories or they can sensibly be considered as either interval or ratio scales. Ranking can be a very tedious process; and if subjects are required to rank more than 20 items, they frequently become confused, make errors, and get irritated. This is the reason that most data concerning human impressions is in the form of ratings (for example, rating books on a seven-step scale concerning like-dislike responses). Such data can reasonably be considered as constituting an interval scale; and if assumptions are met for the parametric statistics, it is much better to employ them than to perform nonparametric analyses of ranks.

The fourth point of consideration regarding analysis of ranked data concerns whether descriptive or inferential statistics are under consideration. Whereas it has been stated that it is best to avoid the analysis of ranks in most uses of inferential statistics, there are some very useful descriptive statistics that relate to ranks which will be discussed subsequently.

To summarize: (1) inferential statistics regarding ranks have been oversold; (2) nevertheless, the reader should become acquainted with the issues and some of the methods; (3) there are some quick and easily understood methods which can be employed for special purposes; and (4) some descriptive statistics applied to ranked data provide very useful information.

Descriptive Statistics for Ranks

As should be remembered from previous chapters, correlational analysis provides very useful information about the extent to which two sets of scores are ordered alike rather than differently. Such correlational analysis always concerns a number of score pairs. The PM correlation coefficient was advocated in Chapters 7 and 8 as a general approach to measuring the degree of correspondence between two sets of scores, such as scores of the same subjects on two tests of intelligence. It was mentioned that the PM correlation can be performed on two sets of ranks rather than on interval data, in which case the coefficient is called rho. This is only a different-appearing version of the product-moment correlation, and the same results are obtained from using the latter rather than the former on ranked data. Rho constitutes a useful measure of correlation between two sets of ranks and is generally advocated for that purpose.

A very useful measure of correlation between sets of ranks which can be employed not only in the case of two sets of ranks but in the case of three or more sets of ranks as well is available. This is referred to as the *Coefficient of Concordance,* usually symbolized as *W.* The method is illustrated with the data shown in Table 13-4, which depicts the results from having 6 (m) clinical psychologists rank the same 8 (N) patients in terms of judged amount of improvement in psychotherapy. Each psychologist interviews the patients, examines various types of test scores, and observes the patients under other circumstances. The question is that of the extent to which the psychologists as a group tend to agree with one another about the rankings of the patients. Rho could be applied to the ranks for any two psychologists, and an average rho could be obtained for all possible pairings of psychologists in this regard; however, the Coefficient of Concordance can be used to obtain an overall index of the amount of agreement. The computational steps are shown at the bottom of Table 13-4. The first step is to sum the m (in this case 6) therapists' ranks for each patient

Table 13-4. Use of the Coefficient of Concordance (W) for Determining the Overall Amount of Agreement Between Six Therapists Regarding Rating of Improvement of Eight Patients

		Patients (N)							
		A	B	C	D	E	F	G	H
	1	6	4	3	2	7	1	8	5
	2	7	3	1	4	8	2	6	5
Therapist	3	8	2	1	4	5	3	7	6
(m)	4	8	4	1	3	6	2	5	7
	5	5	3	4	1	8	2	7	6
	6	7	1	4	2	5	3	6	8

$$R_J \qquad 41 \quad 17 \quad 14 \quad 16 \quad 39 \quad 13 \quad 39 \quad 37$$

$$\Sigma R_J = 216$$

Equations and computations

$$\frac{\Sigma R_J}{N} = \frac{216}{8}$$

$$= 27$$

$$S = \Sigma \left(R_J - \frac{\Sigma R_J}{N} \right)^2$$

$$= (41 - 27)^2 + (17 - 27)^2 + (14 - 27)^2 + (16 - 27)^2 + (39 - 27)^2 + (13 - 27)^2 + (39 - 27)^2 + (37 - 27)^2$$

$$= 1,170$$

$$W = \frac{12S}{m^2(N^3 - N)}$$

$$= \frac{12(1,170)}{(6)^2(8^3 - 8)}$$

$$= \frac{12(1,170)}{36(504)}$$

$$= \frac{14,040}{18,144}$$

$$= 0.77$$

R_J. The Coefficient of Concordance W is defined by the equation [1]

$$W = \frac{12S}{m^2(N^3 - N)} \qquad (13\text{-}2)$$

where $S = \Sigma \; R_J - \dfrac{\Sigma R_J{}^2}{N}$, m = the number of raters, and N = the number of things rated.

For N of 7 or less, significance levels of the Coefficient of Concordance W are presented in Appendix B-8. For N greater than 7, a chi-square test is appropriate. The following relationship holds between the Coefficient of Concordance and chi square with $(N - 1)$ df

$$\chi^2 = m(N - 1)W \qquad (13\text{-}5)$$

In the example presented in Table 13-4, $m = 6$, $N = 8$, and W was calculated to be 0.77. Thus, chi square becomes

$$\chi^2 = 6(8 - 1)0.77$$
$$= 32.34$$

Utilizing Appendix B-8 for a chi square with 7 df, we find that this Coefficient of Concordance is significant beyond the 0.001 level.

It should be pointed out that the Coefficient of Concordance is on a different scale than that for rho or other PM correlations. The PM coefficient ranges from -1.00 to 1.00, but the Coefficient of Concordance ranges from 0.00 to 1.00. A W of 1.00 means perfect agreement among all sets of ranks, and a W of 0.00 means no agreement at all among the sets of ranks.

Except for being scaled differently, the Coefficient of Concordance is a type

---

[1] When data are inherently in the form of ranks, there are no tied ranks (in this case, therapists ranking patients in terms of improvement); however, when data from interval scales or ratio scales are degenerated into ranks, there are usually many tied ranks resulting. When there are tied ranks, a *correction factor* must be employed in calculating W. This correction factor is

$$T = \frac{\Sigma(t^3 - t)}{12} \qquad (13\text{-}3)$$

where t represents the tied ranks. For example, if the ranks on a measure are 1, 2, 3.5, 3.5, 5, 6, 8, 8, 8, there are two groups of ties, one of two ranks and one of three ranks. In this instance, the correction factor would be

$$T = \frac{(2^3 - 2) + (3^3 - 3)}{12}$$
$$= 2.5$$

When this correction factor is tabulated for each of the N sets of ranks, we apply the correction factor in the equation for W as follows

$$W = \frac{12S}{m^2(N^3 - N) - m\Sigma T} \qquad (13\text{-}4)$$

of average correlation coefficient among the several sets of ranks. An alternative statistic could be obtained by actually correlating all possible pairs of rankings and then averaging these. Thus, if three teachers each rank 12 students with respect to earning a scholarship, then there would be three possible rho correlation coefficients. These could be computed separately and averaged. The resulting statistic would provide essentially the same information as provided by W except for the difference in scale. An equation which relates W to average rho is presented and discussed in Guilford and Fruchter (1973), pp. 265-266.

Both rho and W are excellent descriptive statistics for describing the degree of relationship between sets of ranks. Other statistical methods applied to ranks concern inferential rather than descriptive statistics, and these relate to comparisons of two or more experimental treatments. A discussion of such methods will follow.

Significance Tests for Independent Samples

A primary example of independent samples occurs when 40 students are randomly divided into two groups with respect to two types of instruction in spelling. The samples are independent in the sense that each student appears in only one of the two groups. The usual significance test in this situation would be the t test discussed in Chapter 10. An alternative nonparametric statistic is called the *Mann-Whitney U Test*. This is discussed and illustrated in Guilford and Fruchter (1973), Senter (1969), and Siegel (1956).

What is required in employing the U test is to pool the scores from two groups on a dependent measure and rank them from highest (1) to lowest (total N), or from lowest to highest—the same result is obtained either way. A significance test can then be applied to the average ranks in the two groups. If the number of subjects in either of the two groups being compared is no larger than eight, then the significance level of difference in average ranks can be obtained by special tables presented in Siegel (1956), pp. 271-273. When the N of both groups is 9 or more, a direct computational approach which is illustrated in Table 13-5 can be used. After the combined scores from the two groups are ranked (in Table 13-5 from lowest to highest), the U statistic is obtained by the computational steps indicated. This then can be converted to a normal deviate z, and the resulting z can be referred to probability levels relating to the normal distribution shown in Appendix B-3.

In this example, a teacher wishes to learn whether students perform better on a test of reading achievement near the end of the school year or after coming back to school from summer vacation. Near the end of the year, school topics are fresh in students' minds; consequently, they might perform better at that time. On the other hand, students are somewhat older after three months of summer vacation, and they might have opportunities to improve their reading ability in relation to summer activities. The teacher has a class with 19 students who are

Table 13-5. Use of the Mann-Whitney U Test to Compare the Reading Ability of One Group of Children Tested Before Summer Vacation with That of Another Group of Children Tested After Summer Vacation

	Test before vacation	Rank		Test after vacation	Rank
	87	12		70	6.5
	60	3		93	14
	57	2		72	8.5
	90	13		68	5
$N_1 = 10$	97	15	$N_2 = 9$	77	10
	70	6.5		81	11
	72	8.5		52	1
	98	16		63	4
	99	17.5		99	17.5
	100	19			
		$R_1 = 112.5$			$R_2 = 77.5$

Equations and calculations

Calculation of U_1

$$U_1 = N_1 N_2 + \frac{N_1(N_1 + 1)}{2} - R_1$$

$$= 10(9) + \frac{10(11)}{2} - 112.5$$

$$= 90 + 55 - 112.5$$

$$= 32.5$$

$$U_E = \frac{N_1 N_2}{2}$$

$$= 45$$

$$z_{U_1} = \frac{U_1 - U_E}{\sigma_U}$$

$$= \frac{32.5 - 45}{12.247}$$

$$= -1.02$$

Calculation of U_2

$$U_2 = N_1 N_2 + \frac{N_2(N_2 + 1)}{2} - R_2$$

$$= 10(9) + \frac{9(9 + 1)}{2} - 77.5$$

$$= 90 + 45 - 77.5$$

$$= 57.5$$

$$\sigma_U = \sqrt{\frac{N_1 N_2 (N_1 + N_2 + 1)}{12}}$$

$$= \sqrt{\frac{(10)(9)(20)}{12}}$$

$$= \sqrt{\frac{1{,}800}{12}}$$

$$= \sqrt{150}$$

$$= 12.25$$

$$z_{U_2} = \frac{U_2 - U_E}{\sigma_U}$$

$$= \frac{57.5 - 45}{12.247}$$

$$= 1.02$$

randomly assigned to the two testing groups. The computational procedures are given in Table 13-5.

It should be noted that it is possible to calculate the value of U employing either the scores from the first sample (U_1) or the scores from the second sample (U_2). This is indicated in Table 13-5. The same level of significance is obtained by either approach. The only difference is that z for the lower group will be the same size but negative in sign. In this case, z is far below the level of 1.96, which would be significant at the 0.05 level with a two-tailed test.

The logic underlying the U test can be extended to the comparison of more than two groups. [See discussion in Siegel (1956).] Because of the analogy between such tests and those concerning analysis of variance, a test of significance for more than two groups is frequently spoken of as an *analysis of variance of ranks.* Of course, this is something of a misnomer, in the sense that ranks are being analyzed rather than variances of mean differences between treatment groups. What is involved in these tests is the pooling of dependent measures for all groups combined, ranking all scores from highest to lowest, and performing significance tests on differences among mean ranks. Unless there are extreme violations of the assumptions underlying analysis of variance, it is recommended that ANOVA be employed rather than the companion nonparametric statistics.

Matched Groups

Experimental groups may be matched either on the basis of some variable (such as subjects matched on the basis of intelligence), or the same subjects may appear in two or more treatment groups. In Chapter 10, the use of the t test with matched groups was discussed, and in Chapter 12 the use of the analysis of variance for within-subjects or repeated-measurements designs was discussed. It was mentioned there that when it is feasible to employ the same subjects or matched subjects in a research design, the amount of error for assessing experimental results is frequently reduced. Analogous nonparametric significance tests are available for comparing two or more matched groups.

A simple example would be that of comparing the numbers of familiar pairs and unfamiliar pairs of words that subjects remember in a study of verbal learning. Subjects are given five minutes to rehearse a list of 40 words. Half of the words are highly associated with one another in daily life (for example, chair and table), and the other half are seldom associated with one another (for example, tiger and napkin). Subsequently, subjects are asked to write down all the words that they can remember. This is a classic example of a within-subjects or repeated-measurements design. Ordinarily, one would employ the t test with data of this kind. An alternative nonparametric test would be the *Wilcoxon's matched-pairs signed-rank test.* What is required in this test is the pooling of data for the two groups, the ranking of scores on the dependent measure for the pooled data, and an application of a significance test between the difference in average ranks given to the two groups. The use of this test is illustrated in Table 13-6.

In the example shown in Table 13-6, there are 10 subjects. The first two columns of the table present the number of familiar pairs recalled and the number of novel pairs recalled by each subject. In this case, there are two individuals who have the same score in both treatment conditions. One individual correctly remembers 10 word-pairs under both conditions, and another individual remembers 14 word-pairs under both conditions. Then D is 0 for both individuals and the scores of both individuals are not considered in subsequent computations. The third column contains differences between the two types of word-pairs, with the appropriate algebraic sign indicated. In the fourth column, the differences presented in column 3 are ranked regardless of sign. Thus, in the example given in Table 13-6, 2 and -2 are both given the rank of 3. In the final column of the same table, the ranks presented in the fourth column are given the corresponding signs indicated in the third column. At the bottom of Table 13-6, the sum of the positively signed ranks and of the negatively signed ranks are shown. One then sums the positive and negative ranks separately as indicated in Table 13-6. It should also be noted that scores which are tied for any subject (as for subjects 5 and 7) are disregarded. The number of subjects who do not have tied scores is then defined as N. Next, T is defined as the smallest value of the two sums (in an absolute sense). For example, if $\Sigma+$ had been equal to 2 and $\Sigma-$ had been equal to -4, then T would have been equal to 2. In Table 13-6, there are eight nontied scores; consequently $N = 8$. The smallest of the two sums of ranks is 4 (disregarding the minus sign). Then $N = 4$ is sought in the first column of Appendix B-10. Moving to the right on the row

Table 13-6. **Use of the Wilcoxon Matched-Pairs Signed-Rank Test in Comparing Memory for Familiar Versus Nonfamiliar Pairs of Words in the Same Subjects**

		Familiar pairs	*Novel pairs*	*D*	*Ranked D*	*Signed rank*
	1	18	16	2	3	3
	2	16	14	2	3	3
	3	12	13	-1	1	-1
	4	19	12	7	8	8
Subject	5	10	10	—		
	6	12	7	5	7	7
	7	14	14	—		
	8	8	10	-2	3	-3
	9	12	8	4	5.5	5.5
	10	14	8	4	5.5	5.5

Numbers and ranks of familiar and novel word-pairs remembered

$N = 8$ $\Sigma+ = 32.0$

(Tied scores excluded) $\Sigma- = -4$

$T = 4$

Significant at less than 0.05 level

corresponding to $N = 8$, it is found that $T = 4$ corresponds to the 0.05 level of significance for a two-tailed test. This would provide some encouragement to the experimenter for investigating the difference between types of word-pairs with larger numbers of subjects.

For N's larger than 25, T can be converted to a normal deviate z, and a significance test can be made in the usual way. The first step is to derive a theoretical value for T which would be expected in the case where there really was no difference at all between the two groups in the population. This is referred to as T_E and is derived as follows

$$T_E = \frac{N(N + 1)}{4} \tag{13-6}$$

where T_E = the average value of T expected purely by chance. Similar in principle to the t distribution and the chi-square distribution, T_E is a sampling distribution in relation to the signed-rank test. In this case, the descriptive statistic is T, and T_E represents the average of the different T's that would be expected from many samples in the situation where there really was no difference at all between the two populations underlying the two samples. Then the T obtained in any experiment can be compared with T_E to indicate the extent to which T is different from the expected chance value. Second, it is necessary to obtain a standard error for the difference between T and T_E, which is as follows

$$\sigma_T = \sqrt{\frac{N(N + 1)(2N + 1)}{24}} \tag{13-7}$$

where σ_T = the standard deviation (or standard error) of T obtained from random samples of N pairs in which there was no real difference in the population. The next step, as usual, is to divide the difference between the obtained descriptive statistic and the theoretical descriptive statistic by the standard error

$$z = \frac{T - T_E}{\sigma_T} \tag{13-8}$$

where z = the normal deviate corresponding to the difference between T and T_E. The value of z obtained from Equation (13-8) can be inspected for significance in relation to values of the normal distribution presented in Appendix B-3. This is done in the same way as for all other uses of z. For example, a z of approximately 1.96 is required for significance at the 0.05 level for a two-tailed test, and a z of approximately 2.58 is required for significance at the 0.01 level for a two-tailed test.

Perhaps the most useful of all nonparametric statistics is called the *sign test*. Rather than rank differences between scores in a within-subjects design, all that is required in this test is to count the number of subjects who make higher scores under one treatment condition than under another. This can be illustrated with the data shown in Table 13-6. If there were no difference in effect of the two treatments, then it would be expected that the number (or percentage) of subjects who perform better under one circumstance than another would be no better than chance. Statistics regarding differences of this kind relate to the flipping of coins, where it is expected that a barrel full of pennies tossed on the floor would come up approximately half heads and half tails. Departures from this expected amount follow some simple equations regarding probabilities. [See discussions in Senter (1969) and Siegel (1956).] All that is necessary to employ the sign test is to look up the number of events coming out one way versus the other in the table presented in Appendix B-11. If there is a definite hypothesis regarding the results, then a one-tailed test can be employed. If there is no definite hypothesis regarding the study, then a two-tailed test would be used. In the example shown in Table 13-6, it should be noted that six difference scores came out in the positive direction, two in the negative direction, and there were two ties. As in the Wilcoxon matched-pairs signed-rank test, we disregard ties in determining the N. With an N of eight, and only two difference scores going against the hypothesis, in Appendix B-11 the probability is found to be 0.145. It should be observed in this instance that a one-tailed test is used, the reason being that a rather definite hypothesis favored the performance on the familiar word-pairs. The probabilities in Appendix B-11 all concern one-tailed tests. As usual, these probabilities should be doubled when, as is more commonly the case, a two-tailed test is being made. Thus, the sign test also indicates no significant difference between the groups at even the 0.05 level. In the present example, this was highly predictable because the U test is much more powerful than the sign test. Whereas it was helpful to illustrate the sign test with an N of only 8, the sign test seldom indicates highly significant differences between two groups unless the N is 20 or more.

For two reasons, the sign test is particularly useful when examining the results of any experiment where there are at least 20 matched pairs of scores. First, people who are otherwise unfamiliar with statistics are used to thinking in terms of coin tosses and related events; consequently, statistics relating to this principle are easily understood. Second, in contrast to some other nonparametric statistics, the sign test really is very rapidly computed. All that is necessary is to know the number of events that come out in one direction rather than the other, and this quantity can be rapidly assessed in Appendix B-11. The sign test is highly recommended as an understandable and extremely easily computed test of significance; however, unless the data grossly violate the assumptions required for the t test, it is strongly recommended that the t test be computed instead of, or at least subsequent to, the use of the sign test.

SUMMARY

There are three circumstances in which it is not permissible to employ the types of parametric inferential statistics discussed in Part Three of this book. These occur when the data (1) are inherently in the form of categories, (2) are inherently in the form of ranks, or (3) have a frequency distribution in the sample which is very different from the normal distribution even though the data relate to interval scales or ratio scales.

When data are in the form of categories, the most useful descriptive statistic in most cases is the percentage. Thus, percentages could be used to describe the relative frequency of persons who say that they would vote for one political candidate rather than another or the relative frequencies of high school students who state that they plan to enter various occupations. A very flexible and useful inferential statistic for analyzing categorical data is chi square, which is most conveniently applied to the frequencies themselves rather than to percentages. Chi square is a function of differences between observed frequencies and expected frequencies in a set of categories. Usually, the expected frequency represents what would most probably be obtained from a purely chance distribution of subjects over categories. In this case, chi square is said to provide a test of independence, or a test of the null hypothesis of obtained frequencies in comparison to an alternative of pure randomness.

When data are inherently in the form of ranks, various correlational methods can be employed as descriptive statistics. For comparing two sets of ranks, the special version of the PM coefficient called rho can be employed. The Coefficient of Concordance is quite useful in describing the tendency of three or more sets of ranks to correlate.

Inferential statistics relating to ranks can be applied to differences among the effects of two or more experimental treatments. In some cases, such data arise because the results are inherently in the form of ranks, for example, teachers ranking eight students with respect to receipt of a scholarship. In other cases, the data are originally in the form of interval scales or ratio scales, but the experimenter decides to convert this information to ranks. The major inferential statistics applied in these instances are based on comparisons of average ranks in the different experimental treatments. Such statistics are available both for the case of comparing independent samples and for the one-sample case of comparing the responses of the same individuals to a number of experimental treatments.

It has sometimes been the case that data which met the requirements of parametric descriptive and inferential statistics (such as approximately normally distributed scores from interval or ratio scales) were "degenerated" into ranks or categories; consequently, nonparametric statistics were applied. This is almost always a mistake. Three situations in which it is quite necessary to employ the nonparametric counterparts of parametric statistics were mentioned in the first lines of this summary; however, the parametric statistics should be employed in nearly all cases where their use is justified by the nature of the data. Generally, the parametric statistics are more easily used in mathematical analyses and they provide more information about the results of experiments. To purposefully swap parametric statistics for nonparametric statistics would be as bad a strategy as swapping dimes for nickels.

EXERCISES

Study Questions

1 In what situations is there a choice as to whether to employ parametric or nonparametric statistics, and in what situation is the experimenter absolutely limited to nonparametric statistics?

2 When there is a choice whether to employ parametric or nonparametric statistics, what are the arguments against employing the nonparametric statistics?

3 What are the most frequently employed inferential statistics for analyzing categorical data? Give hypothetical examples of their use. Why would one *not* employ parametric statistics such as the *t* test or *F* test on categorical data?

4 In what sense is chi square spoken of as a test of independence? Illustrate what is meant.

5 When is it necessary to degenerate data from interval scales and ratio scales into categories? If that necessity is not present, is it wise to degenerate such data?

6 Compose an example of the use of the Coefficient of Concordance. In what way is the Coefficient of Concordance similar to the average correlation among a set of ranks?

7 Give a hypothetical example of a situation in which the Mann-Whitney *U* test would be employed. What is the analogous parametric test to the *U* test?

8 When would one employ Wilcoxon's matched-pairs signed-rank test? Give a hypothetical example of its use in research.

9 In what situations would one employ the sign test? Give an example of its use. How does the usefulness of the test relate to the number of subjects involved in the study?

Problems

1 A researcher wishes to determine if the sex of the observer is related to whether or not the observer will judge a given film as pornographic. He randomly selects 20 males and 20 females from a sample of college students and has them view the film in question. Three of the males rate the film as pornographic, and 17 males rate the film as not pornographic. Fifteen of the females rate the film as pornographic, while five of the females rate the film as not pornographic. Is judgment of pornographic content of the film independent of sex? Employ the chi-square test in this case.

2 A gambler in Las Vegas believes that one of the die being used in a game of chance is biased. He rolls this die 50 times and obtains the following distribution of scores

		Frequency of occurrence
	1	8
	2	12
Die score	*3*	9
	4	7
	5	6
	6	8

On the basis of this data, is he justified in calling the die biased? Employ the chi-square test, showing all computational steps and the eventual probability value.

3 Six therapists rank each of eight patients from least to most improved as a function of participation in group psychotherapy. The resulting ranks are given as follows

					Patient			
	1	*2*	*3*	*4*	*5*	*6*	*7*	*8*
1	1	6	3	8	4	5	7	2
2	2	7	3	6	5	4	8	1
Therapist *3*	5	8	4	7	1	3	6	2
4	1	8	4	7	3	5	6	2
5	2	6	5	8	4	3	7	1
6	3	7	4	6	2	1	8	5

Do the six therapists rank the eight patients significantly similar in terms of amount of improvement? Apply the Coefficient of Concordance.

4 A researcher wishes to test the effects of a mnemonic device (aid to memory) on students' memory of a talk. Two sections of a class hear the same talk at the same time. Prior to the talk the first section (with 14 members) is given instructions regarding mnemonic devices, and the second section (with 10 members) is given a discussion concerning memory but with no specific discussion concerning mnemonic devices. Later, both sections are given a test concerning the content of the talk. A high score on this test represents greater retention of the content of the talk. The results are presented as follows

Subject	Mnemonic group (N = 14)	Control group (N = 10)
1	15	8
2	16	17
3	20	20
4	32	19
5	14	13
6	19	12
7	6	15
8	12	10
9	15	2
10	8	5
11	33	
12	37	
13	40	
14	19	

Perform the Mann-Whitney U test on these data, showing all computational steps and the significance level. What conclusion would be reached about the results?

5 A researcher investigates the power of suggestion on students' perceptions of their own levels of anxiety. A low score indicates a high level of anxiety and vice versa for a high score. The 20 subjects are divided into two matched groups of 10 subjects each; that is, each subject in the experimental group is paired with a subject in the control group who has an almost identical score on the test of anxiety. In the experiment, both groups are given a pill that contains no medicinal element at all. The control group is given no information about the pill, but rather they are told that information in that regard will be given after the experiment is completed. The experimental group is told emphatically that the pill is useful in reducing feelings of anxiety, and this theme is elaborated upon in considerable detail. The pill is given daily for ten days. On the following day, the original test is readministered. The results are presented as follows

Subject pairs	Experimental group	Control group
1	15	10
2	15	15
3	23	31
4	14	6
5	19	13
6	28	15
7	17	17
8	32	28
9	24	16
10	25	22

To determine the significance of difference between the two groups, employ the the sign test. What conclusion would be justified on the basis of the result?

6 On the data presented in Problem 5, determine the level of significance utilizing the Wilcoxon matched-pairs signed-rank test. Show all computational steps. What conclusion would be reached?

SUGGESTED ADDITIONAL READINGS

Ferguson, G. A. *Statistical analysis in psychology and education*, 3d ed. New York: McGraw-Hill, 1973, Chaps. 13 and 14.

Guilford, J. P. and B. Fruchter. *Fundamental statistics in psychology and education*, 5th ed. New York: McGraw-Hill, 1973, Chaps. 11 and 12.

Hays, W. L. *Statistics for the social sciences*, 2d ed. New York: Holt, Rinehart & Winston, 1973, Chaps. 17 and 18.

Senter, R. J. *Analysis of data*. Glenview, Illinois: Scott Foresman, 1969, Chaps. 10 and 13.

Siegel, S. *Nonparametric statistics*. New York: McGraw-Hill, 1956.

Appendix A

List of Frequently Used Statistical Terms, Indexed by the Chapter(s) in Which Each Is Discussed in Detail

Analysis of variance (ANOVA): tests of statistical significance for experiments involving one or more factors and two or more levels on each factor (11,12).

Average deviation: a measure of dispersion consisting of the sum of absolute deviations (signs being ignored) about the mean divided by the number of subjects. It is now largely of historical value (5).

Bias, of research results by the experimenter: a misleading influence of the experimenter on the outcome of an experiment, for example, the instructions for an experiment suggest to the subject the ways in which he should perform (4).

Biserial correlation: an estimate based on one dichotomized variable and one relatively continuous variable of the product-moment correlation that would be obtained if both variables were relatively continuous (8).

Categories: the use of numbers to represent groups of objects or persons as in the use of the numbers 1,2, or 3, and so on to stand for various occupations (2).

Central tendency: average performance in a group of scores. The score point about which all obtained scores tend to balance at higher and lower levels (5).

Chi square: a statistical distribution that is employed very widely in significance tests for the analysis of categorical data (13).

Coefficient of Concordance (W): a measure of agreement among any number of sets of ranks, a descriptive statistic that is closely related to the average rho correlation among sets of ranked data (13).

Confidence intervals: probabilities relating a statistic (or relationship among statistics) computed on a sample to values of a statistic to be expected in a population as a whole, for example, the 99 percent confidence interval expected about a sample correlation of 0.50 with an N of 100 (9,10).

Confounding variables: variables that influence the results of an experiment but which are not controlled by the experimenter, for instance, independent variables in addition to the designated independent variable (3).

Contrasted-groups design: a research design in which the independent variable consists of group membership rather than some type of experimental treatment, such as in comparing males and females, mentally ill persons with normal persons, and deaf persons with those who are able to hear (3).

Correlation coefficient: a measure of the degree of relationship between two variables expressed as standard scores. The degree to which subjects are ordered alike on two variables, as in the correlation between scores of a group of students on a test of mathematical achievement and a test of reading comprehension (7).

Cumulative frequency distribution: a graph in which the frequencies in a distribution are successively added to show the total number of subjects who make scores up to any point on the score continuum (4).

Data: facts resulting from an experiment, as evidenced in a dependent variable, such as amount learned, number of words correctly detected in perception, and amount of hostility shown in a study of group interaction (4).

Deductive inference: the drawing of conclusions about the truth or falseness of relations in a system of symbols, most prominently evidenced in deductions in algebra and other mathematical systems (3,9).

Degrees of freedom (df): the effective sample size used in computing probability values associated with inferential statistics, in contrast to the actual number N of subjects in the sample (9).

Dependent variable: a measure of the effects of an experimental treatment on subjects, such as measures of (1) amount retained in a study of memory, (2) cooperation in an experiment in social psychology, and (3) improvement in reading speed after different types of instruction (3).

Descriptive statistics: measures which summarize aspects of data obtained in research (1).

Deviation scores: scores expressed in terms of how far they are either above or below the mean, for example, $X - M_X$ (5).

Experimental design: a plan or blueprint for conducting an experiment in such a way as to provide answers to research issues (1).

F ratio: a family of statistical distributions determined by degrees of freedom and the ratio of two variances. The F ratio is particularly useful in testing for significance of difference among treatment conditions in an ANOVA experimental design (10).

Factorial designs: experimental designs in which more than one treatment variable is present and all possible combinations of treatment levels are usually investigated, for example, an experiment on learning which concerns three amounts of practice and three levels of problem difficulty, resulting in nine treatment conditions (3,12).

Frequency distribution: a graph in which the X axis shows the different possible scores that subjects can make, and the Y axis shows the number of subjects that actually make each score, for example, the number of subjects who correctly spell each number of words on a 40-item test of spelling (4).

Heteroscedasticity: the tendency of points in a correlation scatter diagram to be more diverse at some levels on the X axis than at other levels. The opposite of homoscedasticity (8).

Homoscedasticity: the tendency in a correlation scatter diagram for points at each level of the X axis to scatter up and down approximately the same with respect to the Y axis. The opposite of heteroscedasticity (8).

Independence, in an experiment: the circumstance in an experiment when the responses of one subject are entirely uninfluenced by the responses of any other subject (9).

Independent variable: the variable which the experimenter manipulates, with the intent of having some effect on the outcome of the experiment, for instance, manipulating drug dosage levels, amounts of practice in a learning task, or the amount of time given to recognize geometrical forms (3).

Inductive inference: the drawing of conclusions about unknown events in the world from some known events, for example, inferring how a spacecraft will behave from the inductive laws of gravity (3, 9).

Inferential statistics: characteristics of data obtained from a sample which result in probability statements regarding characteristics to be expected from a population as a whole (1, 3, 9).

Interaction in ANOVA designs: nonadditivity of effects in the results of an experiment, as evidenced in differences among means on one factor being larger at some corresponding levels of another factor than at other levels of the other factor (12).

Interval scales: measurement in which the rank ordering of subjects is known with respect to an attribute, for example, when it is known how far apart subjects are, but no information is available about the absolute magnitude of the attribute for any subject (2).

Inverse-square law: the principle which holds with many inferential statistics that the sampling error tends to be inversely proportional to the square root of the sample size (9).

Labels: the use of numbers to keep track of things, without any suggestion that the numbers can be subjected to mathematical analyses (2).

Law of large numbers: the tendency for the sampling error of a statistic to become smaller and smaller as the number of subjects sampled grows larger and larger. The expectation that any statistic will come closer and closer to the actual population value as the size of the sample grows larger and larger (9).

Linearity, in correlational analysis: the tendency for points in a scatter diagram to fall symmetrically about a best-fitting straight line, rather than about any other type of line (8).

Main effects: effects in an ANOVA design due to the separate factors rather than to any interaction of the factors (12).

Mann-Whitney U test: a nonparametric significance test for difference in central tendency between two independent groups of subjects whose combined scores are ranked (13).

Mean: a measure of central tendency. The sum of the raw scores divided by the number of subjects (1,5).

Mean-square, in ANOVA designs: the sums of squares for any component in an ANOVA design divided by the appropriate degrees of freedom (11, 12).

Measurement, in psychology and education: rules for assigning numbers to objects in such a way as to represent quantities of attributes (2).

Measurement scales: the different interpretations of the quantities obtained from measurement methods, these relating to labels, categories, ordinal scales, interval scales, and ratio scales (2).

Median: a measure of central tendency. The score point in a frequency distribution which divides the upper 50 percent of the people from the lower 50 percent (1, 5).

Mode: a measure of central tendency. The most frequently occurring score (1, 5).

Multiple comparisons, in ANOVA designs: comparison of treatment means with one another by special statistical techniques after obtaining significance in a customary ANOVA (11, 12).

Multivariate correlational analysis: correlational analysis where more than two variables are involved, the most prominent example of which is in finding the combination of scores from several tests that will correlate most highly with some criterion of performance in school or elsewhere (8).

Nonlinearity, in correlational analysis: the tendency for points in a scatter diagram to fall about some type of curved line rather than about a straight line (8).

Nonparametric statistics: descriptive and inferential statistics based on categories and ranks rather than on higher-order scales, as opposed to parametric statistics applied to such higher order scales (13).

Normal distribution: a mathematically ideal bell-shaped frequency distribution, for which the percentages of subjects at different levels of performance can be calculated. The distribution is highly useful because the actual frequency distributions obtained from samples of subjects frequently approximate the normal distribution (5).

Null hypothesis: a hypothesis that differences in central tendency or other statistics obtained from a sample really do not reflect differences in a population as a whole. If a significance test shows a very low probability for the null hypothesis being correct, then it is reasonable to accept the alternative, at least temporarily, that the observed findings from samples are real rather than due only to chance (9).

One-tailed and two-tailed tests of significance: a one-tailed test is that in which the direction of difference among statistics is stated in advance, for instance, there is a clear hypothesis that one method of learning would be superior to another. A two-tailed test is one in which there is no clear prediction in advance, or using the same example, there really is no reason in advance to expect that one method of learning will be superior to another (9).

Ordinal scales: measurement in which the rank order of subjects is known with respect to an attribute, but there is no information regarding the absolute level for any subject nor any information regarding how far apart subjects are with respect to the attribute (2).

Paired observations: in the comparison of two treatment conditions, either placing people in pairs with respect to some variable that is thought to be important for experimental outcome, or applying all treatments to the same subjects. Often referred to as concerning repeated-measurements or within-subjects designs (10, 11, 12, 13).

Percentiles: a method of scoring based essentially on ranks, for example, the percentage of persons who fall below any score point on a score continuum, such as the percentage of people who make IQs less than 130, less than 125, and so on (6).

Phi coefficient: a computational approach to obtaining the product-moment correlation when both of the variables are dichotomous rather than continuous (8).

Point-biserial correlation: a computational approach to obtaining the product-moment correlation coefficient when one of the two variables is dichotomous and the other is relatively continuous (8).

Population: A group of people (usually large) to which research results are to be generalized, this generalization being based on actual results obtained from a subset or sample of the population as a whole (3).

Prediction equations, in correlational analysis: the use of a best-fitting straight line based on the product-moment correlation coefficient to estimate scores on one variable from scores on another variable. Frequently called regression equations (7).

Probability: a number between 0 and 1.0 which is used to estimate the relative frequency with which one rather than other possible events will occur out of a specified collection of events. An example is the relative frequency with which people from a sample say that they will vote for one of three candidates for the mayor's office in a city (2).

Product-moment correlation: by far the most widely used measure of correlation between two variables, consisting of the average product of standard scores on two measures (7)

$$r = \frac{\Sigma z_x z_y}{N}$$

Randomized-groups designs: experimental designs in which members of the available group of subjects are randomly assigned to the various treatment conditions, for example, 60 subjects being randomly sorted into three groups of 20 each for an experiment concerning three treatment conditions (3).

Range: a measure of dispersion consisting of the lowest score obtained in an investigation subtracted from the highest score (5).

Ratio scales: measurement in which the rank ordering among people is known with respect to an attribute, the intervals between people are known, and in addition, the distance from a rational zero is known for each person (2).

Raw score: the score obtained on a dependent variable before it is modified in any way, for example, number of arithmetic problems correctly solved, number of words correctly remembered, and number of friendly responses in an observational study of children's interaction (5).

Regression equations, in correlational analysis: the use of a best-fitting straight line based on the product-moment correlation coefficient to estimate scores on one variable from scores on another variable (7).

Reliability, of measurements: consistency with which measurement results are obtained under differing circumstances of time, place, tester, and slight variations in measurement techniques (2, 4).

Repeated-measures designs: research designs in which all treatments are administered to the same subjects, such as in comparing reaction time to a light signal under three different types of preparatory cues given to the same subjects on different trials (3, 11).

Rho correlation: a computational approach to obtaining the product-moment correlation when scores on both variables are expressed as ranks (8, 13).

s: a relatively unbiased estimate of a population standard deviation from research on a sample of subjects, obtained as follows (5)

$$s = \sqrt{\frac{\Sigma x^2}{N-1}}$$

Sample of subjects: a subset of persons from a larger set (or population) of persons. Ideally the subset is drawn randomly, or approximately so, from the population (1).

Sampling error: the amount of imprecision or lack of sureness in estimating characteristics of a population from known characteristics of a sample of subjects from that population (3).

Sampling error, of correlations: the distribution of correlation coefficients that would be expected for any size N if the correlations were computed on randomly drawn samples of subjects from a population in which the actual correlation is zero (7, 10).

Scatter diagram: a graph used in correlational analysis which shows two scores for each individual expressed as a point. This results in a swarm of points in the graph. The larger the amount of scatter, the lower the correlation between the two variables involved (7).

Scoring method: a predetermined plan for objectively converting behavior of subjects in a research project into an independent variable, usually quantitative in nature (4).

Semi-experimental designs: experimental designs that only partially fulfill the requirements of true experimental designs, and thus leave open the possibility of alternative interpretations of the results. For example, in an experiment concerning three types of psychotherapy, it is not possible to randomly assign people to the different types of psychotherapy; consequently there is an inherent ambiguity about the meaning of the results (3).

Sign test: A nonparametric statistical test of significance of difference between two matched groups, either different groups of subjects that are paired in terms of some characteristic, or the same subjects that appear in both treatment conditions (13).

Significance tests: probabilities associated with descriptive statistics obtained from samples actually being different in the parent population from which the samples were drawn. Inversely, the confidence that can be placed in findings obtained from samples of subjects existing in a population as a whole (9).

Skewed distributions: frequency distributions that are not symmetrical in the sense that either the upper or lower tail of the distribution is stretched out more than the other tail (4, 8).

Smoothed frequency distribution: a graph in which lines are drawn between the midpoints of the "steps" in a nonsmoothed frequency distribution (4).

Standard deviation: a much used measure of dispersion of scores in a distribution, obtained by squaring deviation scores, summing these, dividing by the number of subjects, and taking the square root of this result (5).

$$\sigma = \sqrt{\frac{\Sigma x^2}{N}}$$

Standard error of the mean (σ_M): the standard deviation that would be expected of the means obtained from many samples of any size N that were drawn at random from a large population (9, 10).

Standard error of mean difference (s_{MD}): the standard deviation of expected differences between means of two treatment groups over many samples from a population in which the actual difference between means of the treatment groups is zero (10).

Standard scores (z): scores that are expressed in terms of deviations about the mean and how far from the mean they are with respect to the standard deviation (6)

$$z = \frac{x}{\sigma} \quad \text{or} \quad z = \frac{x - \mu}{\sigma}$$

Standardization, of measurement methods: ensuring the comparability of measurement of all subjects in terms of employing the same test items or other measurement techniques, administering items under the same conditions and instructions, and otherwise ensuring uniformity of application in measurement (2).

Statistical distributions: frequency distributions that would be expected of any statistic if many random samples of subjects were drawn from a population and the statistic was computed on each sample (9).

Statistical inference: a special case of inductive inference in which unknown events in the real world are predicted on the basis of probabilities rather than on the basis of near certainties (3, 9).

Sum of squares, in ANOVA: Sums of squared deviations about various means as components of the total sum of squared deviates in an ANOVA design (11, 12).

t distribution: the distribution of values expected with a particular df when differences between sample means from a population in which the actual mean difference is zero are divided by the standard error of the difference between means (10).

Tetrachoric correlation: an estimate based on two dichotomized variables of the product-moment correlation that would be obtained if both variables were approximately continuous (8).

Unbiased statistic: a statistic computed on a sample for which there is an equal probability ($p = 0.50$) that the population value is either higher or lower than the obtained sample result, for example, the mean (5, 9).

Validity, of measurement methods: the extent to which a measurement method (such as a test of personality) measures what it is purported to measure (2).

Variance: a measure of the dispersion in a distribution of scores, the square of the standard deviation, obtained as follows (5)

$$\sigma^2 = \frac{\Sigma x^2}{N}$$

Wilcoxon's matched-pairs signed-rank test: a nonparametric test for difference in central tendency of paired observations in two experimental treatments, either groups that are matched on some basis or the same subjects appearing in both treatment conditions. This is the analogue in parametric tests of the *t* test for matched-groups (13).

Appendix B

Appendix B-1.   Table of Random Numbers*

12	11	16	11	7		4	13	7	16	16		14	15	7	13	13		10	6	1	8	10		15	16	1	2	1		3	12	1	4	3		2	9	5	13	8		15	10	15	13	3
5	9	9	3	1		2	5	6	3	5		11	7	13	16	7		7	5	13	2	14		4	13	3	4	6		6	10	16	1	8		8	14	4	8	14		6	6	10	5	16
13	15	2	5	6		8	2	11	6	10		13	2	9	15	6		2	8	4	5	8		7	2	9	15	15		14	11	8	6	5		7	2	12	6	2		13	2	13	15	10
16	4	5	16	9		9	16	4	8	15		8	5	12	3	9		13	4	3	10	4		1	15	4	12	9		9	8	12	15	2		12	10	13	10	1		12	14	8	7	5
2	2	13	1	11		11	12	13	5	3		5	8	14	7	3		15	13	11	4	7		9	11	7	1	13		4	16	9	13	12		4	11	3	11	10		8	8	9	12	4
10	12	10	7	14		15	14	10	12	4		3	12	5	14	12		16	2	2	9	15		16	3	14	7	6		10	1	13	7	16		9	15	14	7	11		14	9	4	8	15
8	14	15	14	12		7	1	1	7	13		7	10	6	9	11		9	7	6	16	11		3	12	13	16	16		1	14	15	2	11		15	4	11	16	6		4	11	7	14	6
3	16	3	6	16		6	8	3	9	11		4	16	2	6	5		1	12	10	6	9		5	4	10	13	7		7	9	7	3	10		6	1	16	15	9		16	5	1	4	11
1	1	8	9	2		16	10	14	14	2		10	1	15	5	14		12	14	12	3	2		13	9	5	14	4		5	15	10	12	15		10	16	2	3	13		10	7	2	1	12
15	3	12	8	3		10	11	8	2	14		15	4	11	8	16		8	9	14	14	1		8	5	15	3	8		2	7	5	8	7		13	7	15	14	4		1	4	14	10	7
6	6	1	10	13		13	9	5	15	1		6	13	16	12	15		4	11	8	12	6		12	6	2	8	11		13	2	2	10	14		1	6	7	4	7		9	1	12	16	1
4	10	4	4	15		3	15	2	1	12		1	9	8	1	8		14	16	5	13	5		6	1	8	6	2		16	5	11	16	6		3	13	9	12	5		5	3	16	6	8
7	8	7	15	10		5	3	9	11	7		9	3	10	4	4		3	10	9	1	3		10	7	16	5	10		15	6	14	9	13		16	8	6	1	15		11	15	15	11	14
14	13	6	12	5		12	4	16	4	9		12	14	3	10	1		6	15	16	15	12		11	8	6	11	14		12	13	3	5	9		14	3	1	9	3		2	12	3	3	2
11	5	14	2	4		14	6	15	10	8		16	11	1	2	10		5	1	15	7	13		14	14	11	10	12		11	4	4	14	1		11	12	8	2	16		7	13	5	9	13
9	7	11	13	8		1	7	12	13	6		2	6	4	11	2		11	3	7	11	16		2	10	12	9	3		8	3	6	11	4		5	5	10	5	12		3	16	6	2	9

1	10	1	15	16		10	11	4	6	4		14	12	9	8	7		5	13	3	13	3		12	12	10	2	14		15	3	10	9	2		8	9	12	13	10		3	16	8	9	8
3	3	5	3	6		7	7	8	5	12		10	14	15	1	2		11	4	5	15	9		7	15	8	15	10		4	16	12	13	14		14	8	11	14	2		10	6	11	6	6
10	8	11	11	7		16	12	15	9	9		12	6	16	15	16		9	10	12	16	15		9	9	11	6	2		9	8	1	15	4		6	3	16	12	14		1	12	16	11	2
9	2	4	7	1		3	15	10	14	11		3	3	12	14	15		13	6	4	1	16		4	2	16	4	8		8	15	13	10	8		11	13	4	1	6		7	15	12	14	11
6	16	9	4	8		12	8	2	8	6		2	9	8	16	4		6	5	15	7	8		3	4	3	14	12		2	5	6	14	10		9	12	10	7	13		8	2	1	8	9
2	12	10	9	12		14	9	5	13	5		4	13	7	7	9		12	14	8	8	11		16	10	15	8	3		10	14	2	7	3		15	6	6	3	9		2	3	9	1	13
12	1	15	5	15		6	4	12	4	14		9	5	14	11	10		1	3	13	3	5		8	5	2	7	7		16	11	14	16	13		16	10	3	8	7		9	1	13	7	12
13	6	8	6	13		11	3	1	10	7		11	15	6	12	5		7	11	1	14	4		2	6	4	16	9		5	2	11	2	12		7	5	2	10	16		15	14	5	5	3
14	5	3	16	4		13	10	13	15	3		7	8	3	13	11		8	7	7	12	7		15	14	13	11	6		3	12	3	4	7		2	11	15	16	8		4	10	2	10	4
8	15	2	14	9		1	1	7	3	13		8	1	13	6	3		3	15	9	9	12		11	6	15	11	5		3	14	5	11	15		6	9	6	3	15
11	13	16	12	10		15	2	9	2	16		5	11	10	10	12		15	16	14	5	2		11	8	1	13	5		1	1	5	12	9		5	16	7	4	4		5	13	15	12	16
16	9	6	10	14		5	6	6	7	15		16	4	5	5	13		4	9	16	2	6		10	3	12	12	15		7	13	8	3	16		12	15	14	9	12		11	8	7	15	5
7	14	12	8	3		4	5	16	12	8		15	10	1	4	6		16	2	6	11	1		1	7	14	10	4		13	4	16	1	15		10	4	8	15	5		13	4	10	13	7
4	4	13	2	5		8	14	3	1	1		6	7	11	9	14		10	8	11	4	13		14	1	6	5	13		14	10	4	5	1		4	7	13	5	11		12	5	4	2	1
5	7	14	1	2		2	16	11	16	2		13	2	4	2	1		2	12	2	10	14		5	16	5	1	16		6	9	7	6	6		1	2	1	2	3		14	7	14	16	14
15	11	7	13	11		9	13	14	11	10		1	16	2	3	8		14	1	10	6	10		13	11	7	3	11		12	7	9	8	3		13	1	9	6	1		16	11	3	4	10

*Reproduced from Winer, B.J. *Statistical principles in experimental design,* 2nd ed., New York:McGraw-Hill, 1971, p. 881. In each column is a random ordering of the numbers from 1 through 16. Random numbers for any experiment can be obtained if the experimenter closes his eyes and puts a pencil anywhere on the page. The nearest number is then first in the series. Going to the right, additional random numbers are obtained. If the number of persons being randomly ordered is greater than 16, this can be arranged by considering the numbers in pairs or even in triplicates.

Appendix B-2. Table of Squares and Square Roots

Number	Square	Square root	Number	Square	Square root	Number	Square	Square root
1	1	1.0000	51	26 01	7.1414	101	1 02 01	10.0499
2	4	1.4142	52	27 04	7.2111	102	1 04 04	10.0995
3	9	1.7321	53	28 09	7.2801	103	1 06 09	10.1489
4	16	2.0000	54	29 16	7.3485	104	1 08 16	10.1980
5	25	2.2361	55	30 25	7.4162	105	1 10 25	10.2470
6	36	2.4495	56	31 36	7.4833	106	1 12 36	10.2956
7	49	2.6458	57	32 49	7.5498	107	1 14 49	10.3441
8	64	2.8284	58	33 64	7.6158	108	1 16 64	10.3923
9	81	3.0000	59	34 81	7.6811	109	1 18 81	10.4403
10	1 00	3.1623	60	36 00	7.7460	110	1 21 00	10.4881
11	1 21	3.3166	61	37 21	7.8102	111	1 23 21	10.5357
12	1 44	3.4641	62	38 44	7.8740	112	1 25 44	10.5830
13	1 69	3.6056	63	39 69	7.9373	113	1 27 69	10.6301
14	1 96	3.7417	64	40 96	8.0000	114	1 29 96	10.6771
15	2 25	3.8730	65	42 25	8.0623	115	1 32 25	10.7238
16	2 56	4.0000	66	43 56	8.1240	116	1 34 56	10.7703
17	2 89	4.1231	67	44 89	8.1854	117	1 36 89	10.8167
18	3 24	4.2426	68	46 24	8.2462	118	1 39 24	10.8628
19	3 61	4.3589	69	47 61	8.3066	119	1 41 61	10.9087
20	4 00	4.4721	70	49 00	8.3666	120	1 44 00	10.9545
21	4 41	4.5826	71	50 41	8.4261	121	1 46 41	11.0000
22	4 84	4.6904	72	51 84	8.4853	122	1 48 84	11.0454
23	5 29	4.7958	73	53 29	8.5440	123	1 51 29	11.0905
24	5 76	4.8990	74	54 76	8.6023	124	1 53 76	11.1355
25	6 25	5.0000	75	56 25	8.6603	125	1 56 25	11.1803
26	6 76	5.0990	76	57 76	8.7178	126	1 58 76	11.2250
27	7 29	5.1962	77	59 29	8.7750	127	1 61 29	11.2694
28	7 84	5.2915	78	60 84	8.8318	128	1 63 84	11.3137
29	8 41	5.3852	79	62 41	8.8882	129	1 66 41	11.3578
30	9 00	5.4772	80	64 00	8.9443	130	1 69 00	11.4018
31	9 61	5.5678	81	65 61	9.0000	131	1 71 61	11.4455
32	10 24	5.6569	82	67 24	9.0554	132	1 74 24	11.4891
33	10 89	5.7446	83	68 89	9.1104	133	1 76 89	11.5326
34	11 56	5.8310	84	70 56	9.1652	134	1 79 56	11.5758
35	12 25	5.9161	85	72 25	9.2195	135	1 82 25	11.6190
36	12 96	6.0000	86	73 96	9.2736	136	1 84 69	11.6619
37	13 69	6.0828	87	75 69	9.3274	137	1 87 69	11.7047
38	14 44	6.1644	88	77 44	9.3808	138	1 90 44	11.7473
39	15 21	6.2450	89	79 21	9.4340	139	1 93 21	11.7898
40	16 00	6.3246	90	81 00	9.4868	140	1 96 00	11.8322
41	16 81	6.4031	91	82 81	9.5394	141	1 98 81	11.8743
42	17 64	6.4807	92	84 64	9.5917	142	2 01 64	11.9164
43	18 49	6.5574	93	86 49	9.6437	143	2 04 49	11.9583
44	19 36	6.6332	94	88 36	9.6954	144	2 07 36	12.0000
45	20 25	6.7082	95	90 25	9.7468	145	2 10 25	12.0416
46	21 16	6.7823	96	92 16	9.7980	146	2 13 16	12.0830
47	22 09	6.8557	97	94 09	9.8489	147	2 16 09	12.1244
48	23 04	6.9282	98	96 04	9.8995	148	2 19 04	12.1655
49	24 01	7.0000	99	98 01	9.9499	149	2 22 01	12.2066
50	25 00	7.0711	100	1 00 00	10.0000	150	2 25 00	12.2474

Number	Square	Square root	Number	Square	Square root	Number	Square	Square root
151	2 28 01	12.2882	201	4 04 01	14.1774	251	6 30 01	15.8430
152	2 31 04	12.3288	202	4 08 04	14.2127	252	6 35 04	15.8745
153	2 34 09	12.3693	203	4 12 09	14.2478	253	6 40 09	15.9060
154	2 37 16	12.4097	204	4 16 16	14.2829	254	6 45 16	15.9374
155	2 40 25	12.4499	205	4 20 25	14.3178	255	6 50 25	15.9687
156	2 43 36	12.4900	206	4 24 36	14.3527	256	6 55 36	16.0000
157	2 46 49	12.5300	207	4 28 49	14.3875	257	6 60 49	16.0312
158	2 49 64	12.5698	208	4 32 64	14.4222	258	6 65 64	16.0624
159	2 52 81	12.6095	209	4 36 81	14.4568	259	6 70 81	16.0935
160	2 56 00	12.6491	210	4 41 00	14.4914	260	6 76 00	16.1245
161	2 59 21	12.6886	211	4 45 21	14.5258	261	6 81 21	16.1555
162	2 62 44	12.7279	212	4 49 44	14.5602	262	6 86 44	16.1864
163	2 65 69	12.7671	213	4 53 69	14.5945	263	6 91 69	16.2173
164	2 68 96	12.8062	214	4 57 96	14.6287	264	6 96 96	16.2481
165	2 72 25	12.8452	215	4 62 25	14.6629	265	7 02 25	16.2788
166	2 75 56	12.8841	216	4 66 56	14.6969	266	7 07 56	16.3095
167	2 78 89	12.9228	217	4 70 89	14.7309	267	7 12 89	16.3401
168	2 82 24	12.9615	218	4 75 24	14.7648	268	7 18 24	16.3707
169	2 85 61	13.0000	219	4 79 61	14.7986	269	7 23 61	16.4012
170	2 89 00	13.0384	220	4 84 00	14.8324	270	7 29 00	16.4317
171	2 92 41	13.0767	221	4 88 41	14.8661	271	7 34 41	16.4621
172	2 95 84	13.1149	222	4 92 84	14.8997	272	7 39 84	16.4924
173	2 99 29	13.1529	223	4 97 29	14.9332	273	7 45 29	16.5227
174	3 02 76	13.1909	224	5 01 76	14.9666	274	7 50 76	16.5529
175	3 06 25	13.2288	225	5 06 25	15.0000	275	7 56 25	16.5831
176	3 09 76	13.2665	226	5 10 76	15.0333	276	7 61 76	16.6132
177	3 13 29	13.3041	227	5 15 29	15.0665	277	7 67 29	16.6433
178	3 16 84	13.3417	228	5 19 84	15.0997	278	7 72 84	16.6733
179	3 20 41	13.3791	229	5 24 41	15.1327	279	7 78 41	16.7033
180	3 24 00	13.4164	230	5 29 00	15.1658	280	7 84 00	16.7332
181	3 27 61	13.4536	231	5 33 61	15.1987	281	7 89 61	16.7631
182	3 31 24	13.4907	232	5 38 24	15.2315	282	7 95 24	16.7929
183	3 34 89	13.5277	233	5 42 89	15.2643	283	8 00 89	16.8226
184	3 38 56	13.5647	234	5 47 56	15.2971	284	8 06 56	16.8523
185	3 42 25	13.6015	235	5 52 25	15.3297	285	8 12 25	16.8819
186	3 45 96	13.6382	236	5 56 96	15.3623	286	8 17 96	16.9115
187	3 49 69	13.6748	237	5 61 69	15.3948	287	8 23 69	16.9411
188	3 53 44	13.7113	238	5 66 44	15.4272	288	8 29 44	16.9706
189	3 57 21	13.7477	239	5 71 21	15.4596	289	8 35 21	17.0000
190	3 61 00	13.7840	240	5 76 00	15.4919	290	8 41 00	17.0294
191	3 64 81	13.8203	241	5 80 81	15.5242	291	8 46 81	17.0587
192	3 68 64	13.8564	242	5 85 64	15.5563	292	8 52 64	17.0880
193	3 72 49	13.8924	243	5 90 49	15.5885	293	8 58 49	17.1172
194	3 76 36	13.9284	244	5 95 36	15.6205	294	8 64 36	17.1464
195	3 80 25	13.9642	245	6 00 25	15.6525	295	8 70 25	17.1756
196	3 84 16	14.0000	246	6 05 16	15.6844	296	8 76 16	17.2047
197	3 88 09	14.0357	247	6 10 09	15.7162	297	8 82 09	17.2337
198	3 92 04	14.0712	248	6 15 04	15.7480	298	8 88 04	17.2627
199	3 96 01	14.1067	249	6 20 01	15.7797	299	8 94 01	17.2916
200	4 00 00	14.1421	250	6 25 00	15.8114	300	9 00 00	17.3205

Number	Square	Square root	Number	Square	Square root	Number	Square	Square root
301	9 06 01	17.3494	351	12 32 01	18.7350	401	16 08 01	20.0250
302	9 12 04	17.3781	352	12 39 04	18.7617	402	16 16 04	20.0499
303	9 18 09	17.4069	353	12 46 09	18.7883	403	16 24 09	20.0749
304	9 24 16	17.4356	354	12 53 16	18.8149	404	16 32 16	20.0998
305	9 30 25	17.4642	355	12 60 25	18.8414	405	16 40 25	20.1246
306	9 36 36	17.4929	356	12 67 36	18.8680	406	16 48 36	20.1494
307	9 42 49	17.5214	357	12 74 49	18.8944	407	16 56 49	20.1742
308	9 48 64	17.5499	358	12 81 64	18.9209	408	16 64 64	20.1990
309	9 54 81	17.5784	359	12 88 81	18.9473	409	16 72 81	20.2237
310	9 61 00	17.6068	360	12 96 00	18.9737	410	16 81 00	20.2485
311	9 67 21	17.6352	361	13 03 21	19.0000	411	16 89 21	20.2731
312	9 73 44	17.6635	362	13 10 44	19.0263	412	16 97 44	20.2978
313	9 79 69	17.6918	363	13 17 69	19.0526	413	17 05 69	20.3224
314	9 85 96	17.7200	364	13 24 96	19.0788	414	17 13 96	20.3470
315	9 92 25	17.7482	365	13 32 25	19.1050	415	17 22 25	20.3715
316	9 98 56	17.7764	366	13 39 56	19.1311	416	17 30 56	20.3961
317	10 04 89	17.8045	367	13 46 89	19.1572	417	17 38 89	20.4206
318	10 11 24	17.8326	368	13 54 24	19.1833	418	17 47 24	20.4450
319	10 17 61	17.8606	369	13 61 61	19.2094	419	17 55 61	20.4695
320	10 24 00	17.8885	370	13 69 00	19.2354	420	17 64 00	20.4939
321	10 30 41	17.9165	371	13 76 41	19.2614	421	17 72 41	20.5183
322	10 36 84	17.9444	372	13 83 84	19.2873	422	17 80 84	20.5426
323	10 43 29	17.9722	373	13 91 29	19.3132	423	17 89 29	20.5670
324	10 49 76	18.0000	374	13 98 76	19.3391	424	17 97 76	20.5913
325	10 56 25	18.0278	375	14 06 25	19.3649	425	18 06 25	20.6155
326	10 62 76	18.0555	376	14 13 76	19.3907	426	18 14 76	20.6398
327	10 69 29	18.0831	377	14 21 29	19.4165	427	18 23 29	20.6640
328	10 75 84	18.1108	378	14 28 84	19.4422	428	18 31 84	20.6882
329	10 82 41	18.1384	379	14 36 41	19.4679	429	18 40 41	20.7123
330	10 89 00	18.1659	380	14 44 00	19.4936	430	18 49 00	20.7364
331	10 95 61	18.1934	381	14 51 61	19.5192	431	18 57 61	20.7605
332	11 02 24	18.2209	382	14 59 24	19.5448	432	18 66 24	20.7846
333	11 08 89	18.2483	383	14 66 89	19.5704	433	18 74 89	20.8087
334	11 15 56	18.2757	384	14 74 56	19.5959	434	18 83 56	20.8327
335	11 22 25	18.3030	385	14 82 25	19.6214	435	18 92 25	20.8567
336	11 28 96	18.3303	386	14 89 96	19.6469	436	19 00 06	20.8806
337	11 35 69	18.3576	387	14 97 69	19.6723	437	19 09 69	20.9045
338	11 42 44	18.3848	388	15 05 44	19.6977	438	19 18 44	20.9284
339	11 49 21	18.4120	389	15 13 21	19.7231	439	19 27 21	20.9523
340	11 56 00	18.4391	390	15 21 00	19.7484	440	19 36 00	20.9762
341	11 62 81	18.4662	391	15 28 81	19.7737	441	19 44 81	21.0000
342	11 69 64	18.4932	392	15 36 64	19.7990	442	19 53 64	21.0238
343	11 76 49	18.5203	393	15 44 49	19.8242	443	19 62 49	21.0476
344	11 83 36	18.5472	394	15 52 36	19.8494	444	19 71 36	21.0713
345	11 90 25	18.5742	395	15 60 25	19.8746	445	19 80 25	21.0950
346	11 97 16	18.6011	396	15 68 16	19.8997	446	19 89 16	21.1187
347	12 04 09	18.6279	397	15 76 09	19.9249	447	19 98 09	21.1424
348	12 11 04	18.6548	398	15 84 04	19.9499	448	20 07 04	21.1660
349	12 18 01	18.6815	399	15 92 01	19.9750	449	20 16 01	21.1896
350	12 25 00	18.7083	400	16 00 00	20.0000	450	20 25 00	21.2132

Number	Square	Square root	Number	Square	Square root	Number	Square	Square root
451	20 34 01	21.2368	501	25 10 01	22.3830	551	30 36 01	23.4734
452	20 43 04	21.2603	502	25 20 04	22.4054	552	30 47 04	23.4947
453	20 52 09	21.2838	503	25 30 09	22.4277	553	30 58 09	23.5160
454	20 61 16	21.3073	504	25 40 16	22.4499	554	30 69 16	23.5372
455	20 70 25	21.3307	505	25 50 25	22.4722	555	30 80 25	23.5584
456	20 79 36	21.3542	506	25 60 36	22.4944	556	30 91 36	23.5797
457	20 88 49	21.3776	507	25 70 49	22.5167	557	31 02 49	23.6008
458	20 97 64	21.4009	508	25 80 64	22.5389	558	31 13 64	23.6220
459	21 06 81	21.4243	509	25 90 81	22.5610	559	31 24 81	23.6432
460	21 16 00	21.4476	510	26 01 00	22.5832	560	31 36 00	23.6643
461	21 25 21	21.4709	511	26 11 21	22.6053	561	31 47 21	23.6854
462	21 34 44	21.4942	512	26 21 44	22.6274	562	31 58 44	23.7065
463	21 43 69	21.5174	513	26 31 69	22.6495	563	31 69 69	23.7276
464	21 52 96	21.5407	514	26 41 96	22.6716	564	31 80 96	23.7487
465	21 62 25	21.5639	515	26 52 25	22.6936	565	31 92 25	23.7697
466	21 71 56	21.5870	516	26 62 56	22.7156	566	32 03 56	23.7908
467	21 80 89	21.6102	517	26 72 89	22.7376	567	32 14 89	23.8118
468	21 90 24	21.6333	518	26 83 24	22.7596	568	32 26 24	23.8328
469	21 99 61	21.6564	519	26 93 61	22.7816	569	32 37 61	23.8537
470	22 09 00	21.6795	520	27 04 00	22.8035	570	32 49 00	23.8747
471	22 18 41	21.7025	521	27 14 41	22.8254	571	32 60 41	23.8956
472	22 27 84	21.7256	522	27 24 84	22.8473	572	32 71 84	23.9165
473	22 37 29	21.7486	523	27 35 29	22.8692	573	32 83 29	23.9374
474	22 46 76	21.7715	524	27 45 76	22.8910	574	32 94 76	23.9583
475	22 56 25	21.7945	525	27 56 25	22.9129	575	33 06 25	23.9792
476	22 65 76	21.8174	526	27 66 76	22.9347	576	33 17 76	24.0000
477	22 75 29	21.8403	527	27 77 29	22.9565	577	33 29 29	24.0208
478	22 84 84	21.8632	528	27 87 84	22.9783	578	33 40 84	24.0416
479	22 94 41	21.8861	529	27 98 41	23.0000	579	33 52 41	24.0624
480	23 04 00	21.9089	530	28 09 00	23.0217	580	33 64 00	24.0832
481	23 13 61	21.9317	531	28 19 61	23.0434	581	33 75 61	24.1039
482	23 23 24	21.9545	532	28 30 24	23.0651	582	33 87 24	24.1247
483	23 32 89	21.9773	533	28 40 89	23.0868	583	33 98 89	24.1454
484	23 42 56	22.0000	534	28 51 56	23.1084	584	34 10 56	24.1661
485	23 52 25	22.0227	535	28 62 25	23.1301	585	34 22 25	24.1868
486	23 61 96	22.0454	536	28 72 96	23.1517	586	34 33 96	24.2074
487	23 71 69	22.0681	537	28 83 69	23.1733	587	34 45 69	24.2281
488	23 81 44	22.0907	538	28 94 44	23.1948	588	34 57 44	24.2487
489	23 91 21	22.1133	539	29 05 21	23.2164	589	34 69 21	24.2693
490	24 01 00	22.1359	540	29 16 00	23.2379	590	34 81 00	24.2899
491	24 10 81	22.1585	541	29 26 81	23.2594	591	34 92 81	24.3105
492	24 20 64	22.1811	542	29 37 64	23.2809	592	35 04 64	24.3311
493	24 30 49	22.2036	543	29 48 49	23.3024	593	35 16 49	24.3516
494	24 40 36	22.2261	544	29 59 36	23.3238	594	35 28 36	24.3721
495	24 50 25	22.2486	545	29 70 25	23.3452	595	35 40 25	24.3926
496	24 60 16	22.2711	546	29 81 16	23.3666	596	35 52 16	24.4131
497	24 70 09	22.2935	547	29 92 09	23.3880	597	35 64 09	24.4336
498	24 80 04	22.3159	548	30 03 04	23.4094	598	35 76 04	24.4540
499	24 90 01	22.3383	549	30 14 01	23.4307	599	35 88 01	24.4745
500	25 00 00	22.3607	550	30 25 00	23.4521	600	36 00 00	24.4949

Appendix B-2. Table of Squares and Sqaure Roots (Continued)

Number	Square	Square root	Number	Square	Square root	Number	Square	Square root
601	36 12 01	24.5153	651	42 38 01	25.5147	701	49 14 01	26.4764
602	36 24 04	24.5357	652	42 51 04	25.5343	702	49 28 04	26.4953
603	36 36 09	24.5561	653	42 64 09	25.5539	703	49 42 09	26.5141
604	36 48 16	24.5764	654	42 77 16	25.5734	704	49 56 16	26.5330
605	36 60 25	24.5967	655	42 90 25	25.5930	705	49 70 25	26.5518
606	36 72 36	24.6171	656	43 03 36	25.6125	706	49 84 36	26.5707
607	36 84 49	24.6374	657	43 16 49	25.6320	707	49 98 49	26.5895
608	36 96 64	24.6577	658	43 29 64	25.6515	708	50 12 64	26.6083
609	37 08 81	24.6779	659	43 42 81	25.6710	709	50 26 81	26.6271
610	37 21 00	24.6982	660	43 56 00	25.6905	710	50 41 00	26.6458
611	37 33 21	24.7184	661	43 69 21	25.7099	711	50 55 21	26.6646
612	37 45 44	24.7386	662	43 82 44	25.7294	712	50 69 44	26.6833
613	37 57 69	24.7588	663	43 95 69	25.7488	713	50 83 69	26.7021
614	37 69 96	24.7790	664	44 08 96	25.7682	714	50 97 96	26.7208
615	37 82 25	24.7992	665	44 22 25	25.7876	715	51 12 25	26.7395
616	37 94 56	24.8193	666	44 35 56	25.8070	716	51 26 56	26.7582
617	38 06 89	24.8395	667	44 48 89	25.8263	717	51 40 89	26.7769
618	38 19 24	24.8596	668	44 62 24	25.8457	718	51 55 24	26.7955
619	38 31 61	24.8797	669	44 75 61	25.8650	719	51 69 61	26.8142
620	38 44 00	24.8998	670	44 89 00	25.8844	720	51 84 00	26.8328
621	38 56 41	24.9199	671	45 02 41	25.9037	721	51 98 41	26.8514
622	38 68 84	24.9399	672	45 15 84	25.9230	722	52 12 84	26.8701
623	38 81 29	24.9600	673	45 29 29	25.9422	723	52 27 29	26.8887
624	38 93 76	24.9800	674	45 42 76	25.9615	724	52 41 76	26.9072
625	39 06 25	25.0000	675	45 56 25	25.9808	725	52 56 25	26.9258
626	39 18 76	25.0200	676	45 69 76	26.0000	726	52 70 76	26.9444
627	39 31 29	25.0400	677	45 83 29	26.0192	727	52 85 29	26.9629
628	39 43 84	25.0599	678	45 96 84	26.0384	728	52 99 84	26.9815
629	39 56 41	25.0799	679	46 10 41	26.0576	729	53 14 41	27.0000
630	39 69 00	25.0998	680	46 24 00	26.0768	730	53 29 00	27.0185
631	39 81 61	25.1197	681	46 37 61	26.0960	731	53 43 61	27.0370
632	39 94 24	25.1396	682	46 51 24	26.1151	732	53 58 24	27.0555
633	40 06 89	25.1595	683	46 64 89	26.1343	733	53 72 89	27.0740
634	40 19 56	25.1794	684	46 78 56	26.1534	734	53 87 56	27.0924
635	40 32 25	25.1992	685	46 92 25	26.1725	735	54 02 25	27.1109
636	40 44 96	25.2190	686	47 05 96	26.1916	736	54 16 96	27.1293
637	40 57 69	25.2389	687	47 19 69	26.2107	737	54 31 69	27.1477
638	40 70 44	25.2587	688	47 33 44	26.2298	738	54 46 44	27.1662
639	40 83 21	25.2784	689	47 47 21	26.2488	739	54 61 21	27.1846
640	40 96 00	25.2982	690	47 61 00	26.2679	740	54 76 00	27.2029
641	41 08 81	25.3180	691	47 74 81	26.2869	741	54 90 81	27.2213
642	41 21 64	25.3377	692	47 88 64	26.3059	742	55 05 64	27.2397
643	41 34 49	25.3574	693	48 02 49	26.3249	743	55 20 49	27.2580
644	41 47 36	25.3772	694	48 16 36	26.3439	744	55 35 36	27.2764
645	41 60 25	25.3969	695	48 30 25	26.3629	745	55 50 25	27.2947
646	41 73 16	25.4165	696	48 44 16	26.3818	746	55 65 16	27.3130
647	41 86 09	25.4362	697	48 58 09	26.4008	747	55 80 09	27.3313
648	41 99 04	25.4558	698	48 72 04	26.4197	748	55 95 04	27.3496
649	42 12 01	25.4775	699	48 86 01	26.4386	749	56 10 01	27.3679
650	42 25 00	25.4951	700	49 00 00	26.4575	750	56 25 00	27.3861

Number	Square	Square root	Number	Square	Square root	Number	Square	Square root
751	56 40 01	27.4044	801	64 16 01	28.3019	851	72 42 01	29.1719
752	56 55 04	27.4226	802	64 32 04	28.3196	852	72 59 04	29.1890
753	56 70 09	27.4408	803	64 48 09	28.3373	853	72 76 09	29.2062
754	56 85 16	27.4591	804	64 64 16	28.3549	854	72 93 16	29.2233
755	57 00 25	27.4773	805	64 80 25	28.3725	855	73 10 25	29.2404
756	57 15 36	27.4955	806	64 96 36	28.3901	856	73 27 36	29.2575
757	57 30 49	27.5136	807	65 12 49	28.4077	857	73 44 49	29.2746
758	57 45 64	27.5318	808	65 28 64	28.4253	858	73 61 64	29.2916
759	57 60 81	27.5500	809	65 44 81	28.4429	859	73 78 81	29.3087
760	57 76 00	27.5681	810	65 61 00	28.4605	860	73 96 00	29.3258
761	57 91 21	27.5862	811	65 77 21	28.4781	861	74 13 21	29.3428
762	58 06 44	27.6043	812	65 93 44	28.4956	862	74 30 44	29.3598
763	58 21 69	27.6225	813	66 09 69	28.5132	863	74 47 69	29.3769
764	58 36 96	27.6405	814	66 25 96	28.5307	864	74 64 96	29.3939
765	58 52 25	27.6586	815	66 42 25	28.5482	865	74 82 25	29.4109
766	58 67 56	27.6767	816	66 58 56	28.5657	866	74 99 56	29.4279
767	58 82 89	27.6948	817	66 74 89	28.5832	867	75 16 89	29.4449
768	58 98 24	27.7128	818	66 91 24	28.6007	868	75 34 24	29.4618
769	59 13 61	27.7308	819	67 07 61	28.6182	869	75 51 61	29.4788
770	59 29 00	27.7489	820	67 24 00	28.6356	870	75 69 00	29.4958
771	59 44 41	27.7669	821	67 40 41	28.6531	871	75 86 41	29.5127
772	59 59 84	27.7849	822	67 56 84	28.6705	872	76 03 84	29.5296
773	59 75 29	27.8029	823	67 73 29	28.6880	873	76 21 29	29.5466
774	59 90 76	27.8209	824	67 89 76	28.7054	874	76 38 76	29.5635
775	60 06 25	27.8388	825	68 06 25	28.7228	875	76 56 25	29.5804
776	60 21 76	27.8568	826	68 22 76	28.7402	876	76 73 76	29.5973
777	60 37 29	27.8747	827	68 39 29	28.7576	877	76 91 29	29.6142
778	60 52 84	27.8927	828	68 55 84	28.7750	878	77 08 84	29.6311
779	60 68 41	27.9106	829	68 72 41	28.7924	879	77 26 41	29.6479
780	60 84 00	27.9285	830	68 89 00	28.8097	880	77 44 00	29.6648
781	.60 99 61	27.9464	831	69 05 61	28.8271	881	77 61 61	29.6816
782	61 15 24	27.9643	832	69 22 24	28.8444	882	77 79 24	29.6985
783	61 30 89	27.9821	833	69 38 89	28.8617	883	77 96 89	29.7153
784	61 46 56	28.0000	834	69 55 56	28.8791	884	78 14 56	29.7321
785	61 62 25	28.0179	835	69 72 25	28.8964	885	78 32 25	29.7489
786	61 77 96	28.0357	836	69 88 96	28.9137	886	78 49 96	29.7658
787	61 93 69	28.0535	837	70 05 69	28.9310	887	78 67 69	29.7825
788	62 09 44	28.0713	838	70 22 44	28.9482	888	78 85 44	29.7993
789	62 25 21	28.0891	839	70 39 21	28.9655	889	79 03 21	29.8161
790	62 41 00	28.1069	840	70 56 00	28.9828	890	79 21 00	29.8329
791	62 56 81	28.1247	841	70 72 81	29.0000	891	79 38 81	29.8496
792	62 72 64	28.1425	842	70 89 64	29.0172	892	79 56 64	29.8664
793	62 88 49	28.1603	843	71 06 49	29.0345	893	79 74 49	29.8831
794	63 04 36	28.1780	844	71 23 36	29.0517	894	79 92 36	29.8998
795	63 20 25	28.1957	845	71 40 25	29.0689	895	80 10 25	29.9166
796	63 36 16	28.2135	846	71 57 16	29.0861	896	80 28 16	29.9333
797	63 52 09	28.2312	847	71 74 09	29.1033	897	80 46 09	29.9500
798	63 68 04	28.2489	848	71 91 04	29.1204	898	80 64 04	29.9666
799	63 84 01	28.2666	849	72 08 01	29.1376	899	80 82 01	29.9833
800	64 00 00	28.2843	850	72 25 00	29.1548	900	81 00 00	30.0000

Number	Square	Square root	Number	Square	Square root
901	81 18 01	30.0167	951	90 44 01	30.8383
902	81 36 04	30.0333	952	90 63 04	30.8545
903	81 54 09	30.0500	953	90 82 09	30.8707
904	81 72 16	30.0666	954	91 01 16	30.8869
905	81 90 25	30.0832	955	91 20 25	30.9031
906	82 08 36	30.0998	956	91 39 36	30.9192
907	82 26 49	30.1164	957	91 58 49	30.9354
908	82 44 64	30.1330	958	91 77 64	30.9516
909	82 62 81	30.1496	959	91 96 81	30.9677
910	82 81 00	30.1662	960	92 16 00	30.9839
911	82 99 21	30.1828	961	92 35 21	31.0000
912	83 17 44	30.1993	962	92 54 44	31.0161
913	83 35 69	30.2159	963	92 73 69	31.0322
914	83 53 96	30.2324	964	92 92 96	31.0483
915	83 72 25	30.2490	965	93 12 25	31.0644
916	83 90 56	30.2655	966	93 31 56	31.0805
917	84 08 89	30.2820	967	93 50 89	31.0966
918	84 27 24	30.2985	968	93 70 24	31.1127
919	84 45 61	30.3150	969	93 89 61	31.1288
920	84 64 00	30.3315	970	94 09 00	31.1448
921	84 82 41	30.3480	971	94 28 41	31.1609
922	85 00 84	30.3645	972	94 47 84	31.1769
923	85 19 29	30.3809	973	94 67 29	31.1929
924	85 37 76	30.3974	974	94 86 76	31.2090
925	85 56 25	30.4138	975	95 06 25	31.2250
926	85 74 76	30.4302	976	95 25 76	31.2410
927	85 93 29	30.4467	977	95 45 29	31.2570
928	86 11 84	30.4631	978	95 64 84	31.2730
929	86 30 41	30.4795	979	95 84 41	31.2890
930	86 49 00	30.4959	980	96 04 00	31.3050
931	86 67 61	30.5123	981	96 23 61	31.3209
932	86 86 24	30.5287	982	96 43 24	31.3369
933	87 04 89	30.5450	983	96 62 89	31.3528
934	87 23 56	30.5614	984	96 82 56	31.3688
935	87 42 25	30.5778	985	97 02 25	31.3847
936	87 60 96	30.5941	986	97 21 96	31.4006
937	87 79 69	30.6105	987	97 41 69	31.4166
938	87 98 44	30.6268	988	97 61 44	31.4325
939	88 17 21	30.6431	989	97 81 21	31.4484
940	88 36 00	30.6594	990	98 01 00	31.4643
941	88 54 81	30.6757	991	98 20 81	31.4802
942	88 73 64	30.6920	992	98 40 64	31.4960
943	88 92 49	30.7083	993	98 60 49	31.5119
944	89 11 36	30.7246	994	98 80 36	31.5278
945	89 30 25	30.7409	995	99 00 25	31.5436
946	89 49 16	30.7571	996	99 20 16	31.5595
947	89 68 09	30.7734	997	99 40 09	31.5753
948	89 87 04	30.7896	998	99 60 04	31.5911
949	90 06 01	30.8058	999	99 80 01	31.6070
950	90 25 00	30.8221	1,000	1 00 00 00	31.6228

Appendix B-3. Proportions of the Area in Various Sections of the Normal Distribution*

+ and −	Standard score $(\frac{x}{\sigma})$ (1)	Area between (2)	Area beyond (3)
+ and −	0.00	0.0000	1.0000
	0.05	.0392	.9602
	0.10	.0796	.9204
	0.15	.1192	.8808
	0.20	.1586	.8414
+ and −	0.25	.1974	.8026
	0.30	.2358	.7642
	0.35	.2736	.7264
	0.40	.3108	.6892
	0.45	.3472	.6528
+ and −	0.50	.3830	.6170
	0.55	.4176	.5824
	0.60	.4514	.5486
	0.65	.4844	.5156
	0.70	.5160	.4840
+ and −	0.75	.5468	.4532
	0.80	.5762	.4238
	0.85	.6046	.3954
	0.90	.6318	.3682
	0.95	.6578	.3422
+ and −	1.00	.6826	.3174
	1.05	.7062	.2938
	1.10	.7286	.2714
	1.15	.7498	.2502
	1.20	.7698	.2302
+ and −	1.25	.7888	.2112
	1.30	.8064	.1936
	1.35	.8230	.1770
	1.40	.8384	.1616
	1.45	.8530	.1470

*If, for example, in a normal distribution of test scores you want to estimate the number of persons who make scores between plus one standard deviation of the mean and minus one standard deviation of the mean, you would look opposite 1.00 in the first column at the proportion in the second column. There it is seen that the proportion is 0.6826, or, in other words, approximately 68 percent. This means that approximately 32 percent of the individuals make scores either greater than one standard deviation above the mean or less than one standard deviation below the mean. If you want to determine the proportions of people who lie within or beyond certain standard score units above the mean only or below the mean only, the proportions in columns 2 and 3 should be halved.

Appendix B-3. Proportions of the Area in Various Sections of the Normal Distribution (Continued)

	Z Standard score $(\frac{X}{\sigma})$ (1)	Area between (2)	Area beyond (3)
+ and −	1.50	.8664	.1336
	1.55	.8788	.1212
	1.60	.8904	.1096
	1.65	.9019	.0990
	1.70	.9108	.0892
+ and −	1.75	.9198	.0802
	1.80	.9282	.0718
	1.85	.9356	.0644
	1.90	.9426	.0574
	1.95	.9488	.0512
+ and −	2.00	.9544	.0456
	2.05	.9596	.0404
	2.10	.9642	.0358
	2.15	.9684	.0316
	2.20	.9722	.0278
+ and −	2.25	.9756	.0244
	2.30	.9786	.0214
	2.35	.9812	.0188
	2.40	.9836	.0164
	2.45	.9858	.0142
+ and −	2.50	.9876	.0124
	2.55	.9892	.0108
	2.60	.9906	.0094
	2.65	.9920	.0080
	2.70	.9930	.0070
+ and −	2.80	.9948	.0052
	2.90	.9962	.0038
	3.00	.9973	.0027
	3.10	.99806	.00194
	3.20	.99862	.00138
+ and −	3.40	.99932	.00068
	3.60	.99968	.00032
	3.80	.999856	.000144
	4.00	.9999366	.0000634
	4.50	.9999932	.0000068
	5.00	.9999942	.00000058
	6.00	.999999998	.000000002

Appendix B-4.   Cumulative Normal Probabilities*

z	p	z	p	z	p	z	p
0.00	0.5000000	0.41	0.6590970	0.82	0.7938919	1.23	0.8906514
0.01	0.5039894	0.42	0.6627573	0.83	0.7967306	1.24	0.8925123
0.02	0.5079783	0.43	0.6664022	0.84	0.7995458	1.25	0.8943502
0.03	0.5119665	0.44	0.6700314	0.85	0.8023375	1.26	0.8961653
0.04	0.5159534	0.45	0.6736448	0.86	0.8051055	1.27	0.8979577
0.05	0.5199388	0.46	0.6772419	0.87	0.8078498	1.28	0.8997274
0.06	0.5239222	0.47	0.6808225	0.88	0.8105703	1.29	0.9014747
0.07	0.5279032	0.48	0.6843863	0.89	0.8132671	1.30	0.9031995
0.08	0.5318814	0.49	0.6879331	0.90	0.8159399	1.31	0.9049021
0.09	0.5358564	0:50	0.6914625	0.91	0.8185887	1.32	0.9065825
0.10	0.5398278	0.51	0.6949743	0.92	0.8212136	1.33	0.9082409
0.11	0.5437953	0.52	0.6984682	0.93	0.8238145	1.34	0.9098773
0.12	0.5477584	0.53	0.7019440	0.94	0.8263912	1.35	0.9114920
0.13	0.5517168	0.54	0.7054015	0.95	0.8289439	1.36	0.9130850
0.14	0.5556700	0.55	0.7088403	0.96	0.8314724	1.37	0.9146565
0.15	0.5596177	0.56	0.7122603	0.97	0.8339768	1.38	0.9162067
0.16	0.5635595	0.57	0.7156612	0.98	0.8364569	1.39	0.9177356
0.17	0.5674949	0.58	0.7190427	0.99	0.8389129	1.40	0.9192433
0.18	0.5714237	0.59	0.7224047	1.00	0.8413447	1.41	0.9207302
0.19	0.5753454	0.60	0.7257469	1.01	0.8437524	1.42	0.9221962
0.20	0.5792597	0.61	0.7290691	1.02	0.8461358	1.43	0.9236415
0.21	0.5831662	0.62	0.7323711	1.03	0.8484950	1.44	0.9250663
0.22	0.5870604	0.63	0.7356527	1.04	0.8508300	1.45	0.9264707
0.23	0.5909541	0.64	0.7389137	1.05	0.8531409	1.46	0.9278550
0.24	0.5948349	0.65	0.7421539	1.06	0.8554277	1.47	0.9292191
0.25	0.5987063	0.66	0.7453731	1.07	0.8576903	1.48	0.9305634
0.26	0.6025681	0.67	0.7485711	1.08	0.8599289	1.49	0.9318879
0.27	0.6064199	0.68	0.7517478	1.09	0.8621434	1.50	0.9331928
0.28	0.6102612	0.69	0.7549029	1.10	0.8643339	1.51	0.9344783
0.29	0.6140919	0.70	0.7580363	1.11	0.8665005	1.52	0.9357445
0.30	0.6179114	0.71	0.7611479	1.12	0.8686431	1.53	0.9369916
0.31	0.6217195	0.72	0.7642375	1.13	0.8707619	1.54	0.9382198
0.32	0.6255158	0.73	0.7673049	1.14	0.8728568	1.55	0.9394292
0.33	0.6293000	0.74	0.7703500	1.15	0.8749281	1.56	0.9406201
0.34	0.6330717	0.75	0.7733726	1.16	0.8769756	1.57	0.9417924
0.35	0.6368307	0.76	0.7763727	1.17	0.8789995	1.58	0.9429466
0.36	0.6405764	0.77	0.7793501	1.18	0.8809999	1.59	0.9440826
0.37	0.6443088	0.78	0.7823046	1.19	0.8829768	1.60	0.9452007
0.38	0.6480273	0.79	0.7852361	1.20	0.8849303	1.61	0.9463011
0.39	0.6517317	0.80	0.7881446	1.21	0.8868606	1.62	0.9473839
0.40	0.6554217	0.81	0.7910299	1.22	0.8887676	1.63	0.9484493

*This table is condensed from Table 1 of Pearson, E. S., and H. O. Hartley, (Eds.). *Biometrika tables for statisticians,* Vol. 1, 3d ed., 1965. Reproduced here with the permission of E. S. Pearson and the trustees of Biometrika.

An example of using the table would be in the case where the probability is being sought of randomly selecting an individual for an experiment who is 1.80 standard deviations above the mean in intelligence. Looking at a z of 1.80, it is found that the corresponding p value is 0.964 or 0.96. In other words, only approximately 4 percent of the population have higher IQs and approximately 96 percent have lower IQs. This table gives one-tailed probabilities. Probability statements concerning two-tailed tests would need to be doubled.

z	p	z	p	z	p	z	p
1.64	0.9494974	1.91	0.9719334	2.18	0.9853713	2.45	0.9928572
1.65	0.9505285	1.92	0.9725711	2.19	0.9857379	2.46	0.9930531
1.66	0.9515428	1.93	0.9731966	2.20	0.9860966	2.47	0.9932443
1.67	0.9525403	1.94	0.9738102	2.21	0.9864474	2.48	0.9934309
1.68	0.9535213	1.95	0.9744119	2.22	0.9867906	2.49	0.9936128
1.69	0.9544860	1.96	0.9750021	2.23	0.9871263	2.50	0.9937903
1.70	0.9554345	1.97	0.9755808	2.24	0.9874545	2.51	0.9939634
1.71	0.9563671	1.98	0.9761482	2.25	0.9877755	2.52	0.9941323
1.72	0.9572838	1.99	0.9767045	2.26	0.9880894	2.53	0.9942969
1.73	0.9581849	2.00	0.9772499	2.27	0.9883962	2.54	0.9944574
1.74	0.9590705	2.01	0.9777844	2.28	0.9886962	2.55	0.9946139
1.75	0.9599408	2.02	0.9783083	2.29	0.9889893	2.56	0.9947664
1.76	0.9607961	2.03	0.9788217	2.30	0.9892759	2.57	0.9949151
1.77	0.9616364	2.04	0.9793248	2.31	0.9895559	2.58	0.9950600
1.78	0.9624620	2.05	0.9798178	2.32	0.9898296	2.59	0.9952012
1.79	0.9632730	2.06	0.9803007	2.33	0.9900969	2.60	0.9953388
1.80	0.9640697	2.07	0.9807738	2.34	0.9903581	2.70	0.9965330
1.81	0.9648521	2.08	0.9812372	2.35	0.9906133	2.80	0.9974449
1.82	0.9656205	2.09	0.9816911	2.36	0.9908625	2.90	0.9981342
1.83	0.9663750	2.10	0.9821356	2.37	0.9911060	3.00	0.9986501
1.84	0.9671159	2.11	0.9825708	2.38	0.9913437	3.20	0.9993129
1.85	0.9678432	2.12	0.9829970	2.39	0.9915758	3.40	0.9996631
1.86	0.9685572	2.13	0.9834142	2.40	0.9918025	3.60	0.9998409
1.87	0.9692581	2.14	0.9838226	2.41	0.9920237	3.80	0.9999277
1.88	0.9699460	2.15	0.9842224	2.42	0.9922397	4.00	0.9999683
1.89	0.9706210	2.16	0.9846137	2.43	0.9924506	4.50	0.9999966
1.90	0.9712834	2.17	0.9849966	2.44	0.9926564	5.00	0.9999997
						5.50	0.9999999

Appendix B-5. Significance Levels of the Correlation Coefficient*

Level of significance for one-tailed test

0.05	0.025	0.01	0.005

Level of significance for two-tailed test

df	0.10	0.05	0.02	0.01
1	.988	.997	.9995	.9999
2	.900	.950	.980	.990
3	.805	.878	.934	.959
4	.729	.811	.882	.917
5	.669	.754	.833	.874
6	.622	.707	.789	.834
7	.582	.666	.750	.798
8	.549	.632	.716	.765
9	.521	.602	.685	.735
10	.497	.576	.658	.708
11	.476	.553	.634	.684
12	.458	.532	.612	.661
13	.441	.514	.592	.641
14	.426	.497	.574	.623
15	.412	.482	.558	.606
16	.400	.468	.542	.590
17	.389	.456	.528	.575
18	.378	.444	.516	.561
19	.369	.433	.503	.549
20	.360	.423	.492	.537
21	.352	.413	.482	.526
22	.344	.404	.472	.515
23	.337	.396	.462	.505
24	.330	.388	.453	.496
25	.323	.381	.445	.487
26	.317	.374	.437	.479
27	.311	.367	.430	.471
28	.306	.361	.423	.463
29	.301	.355	.416	.456
30	.296	.349	.409	.449
35	.275	.325	.381	.418
40	.257	.304	.358	.393
45	.243	.288	.338	.372
50	.231	.273	.322	.354
60	.211	.250	.295	.325
70	.195	.232	.274	.303
80	.183	.217	.256	.283
90	.173	.205	.242	.267
100	.164	.195	.230	.254

*Abridged from Fisher, R. A. and F. Yates. *Statistical tables for biological agricultural, and medical research.* Published by Longman Group Ltd., London, (previously published by Oliver & Boyd, Edinburgh), and by permission of the authors and publishers.

Appendix B-6. Significance Levels of t*

Level of significance for one-tailed test

0.05	0.025	0.01	0.005	0.0005

Level of significance for two-tailed test

df	0.10	0.05	0.02	0.01	0.001
1	6.314	12.706	31.821	63.657	636.619
2	2.920	4.303	6.965	9.925	31.598
3	2.353	3.182	4.541	5.841	12.941
4	2.132	2.776	3.747	4.604	8.610
5	2.015	2.571	3.365	4.032	6.859
6	1.943	2.447	3.143	3.707	5.959
7	1.895	2.365	2.998	3.499	5.405
8	1.860	2.306	2.896	3.355	5.041
9	1.833	2.262	2.821	3.250	4.781
10	1.812	2.228	2.764	3.169	4.587
11	1.796	2.201	2.718	3.106	4.437
12	1.782	2.179	2.681	3.055	4.318
13	1.771	2.160	2.650	3.012	4.221
14	1.761	2.145	2.624	2.977	4.140
15	1.753	2.131	2.602	2.947	4.073
16	1.746	2.120	2.583	2.921	4.015
17	1.740	2.110	2.567	2.898	3.965
18	1.734	2.101	2.552	2.878	3.922
19	1.729	2.093	2.539	2.861	3.883
20	1.725	2.086	2.528	2.845	3.850
21	1.721	2.080	2.518	2.831	3.819
22	1.717	2.074	2.508	2.819	3.792
23	1.714	2.069	2.500	2.807	3.767
24	1.711	2.064	2.492	2.797	3.745
25	1.708	2.060	2.485	2.787	3.725
26	1.706	2.056	2.479	2.779	3.707
27	1.703	2.052	2.473	2.771	3.690
28	1.701	2.048	2.467	2.763	3.674
29	1.699	2.045	2.462	2.756	3.659
30	1.697	2.042	2.457	2.750	3.646
40	1.684	2.021	2.423	2.704	3.551
60	1.671	2.000	2.390	2.660	3.460
120	1.658	1.980	2.358	2.617	3.373
∞	1.645	1.960	2.326	2.576	3.291

*Abridged from Fisher, R. A. and F. Yates. *Statistical tables for biological agricultural, and medical research.* Published by Longman Group Ltd., London, (previously published by Oliver & Boyd, Edinburgh), and by permission of the authors and publishers.

Appendix B-7. Significance Levels of F: 0.05 (roman), 0.01 (italic), and 0.001 (bold face)*

n_2 \ n_1	1	2	3	4	5	6	8	12	24	∞
1	161	200	216	225	230	234	239	244	249	254
	4052	*4999*	*5403*	*5625*	*5724*	*5859*	*5981*	*6106*	*6234*	*6366*
	405284	**500000**	**540379**	**562500**	**576405**	**585937**	**598144**	**610667**	**623497**	**636619**
2	18.51	19.00	19.16	19.25	19.30	19.33	19.37	19.41	19.45	19.50
	98.49	*99.01*	*99.17*	*99.25*	*99.30*	*99.33*	*99.36*	*99.42*	*99.46*	*99.50*
	998.5	**999.0**	**999.2**	**999.2**	**999.3**	**999.3**	**999.4**	**999.4**	**999.5**	**999.5**
3	10.13	9.55	9.28	9.12	9.01	8.94	8.84	8.74	8.64	8.53
	34.12	*30.81*	*29.46*	*28.71*	*28.24*	*27.91*	*27.49*	*27.05*	*26.60*	*26.12*
	167.5	**148.5**	**141.1**	**137.1**	**134.6**	**132.8**	**130.6**	**128.3**	**125.9**	**123.5**
4	7.71	6.94	6.59	6.39	6.26	6.16	6.04	5.91	5.77	5.63
	21.20	*18.00*	*16.69*	*15.98*	*15.52*	*15.21*	*14.80*	*14.37*	*13.93*	*13.46*
	74.14	**61.25**	**56.18**	**53.44**	**51.71**	**50.53**	**49.00**	**47.41**	**45.77**	**44.05**
5	6.61	5.79	5.41	5.19	5.05	4.95	4.82	4.68	4.53	4.36
	16.26	*13.27*	*12.06*	*11.39*	*10.97*	*10.67*	*10.27*	*9.89*	*9.47*	*9.02*
	47.04	**36.61**	**33.20**	**31.09**	**29.75**	**28.84**	**27.64**	**26.42**	**25.14**	**23.78**
6	5.99	5.14	4.76	4.53	4.39	4.28	4.15	4.00	3.84	3.67
	13.74	*10.92*	*9.78*	*9.15*	*8.75*	*8.47*	*8.10*	*7.72*	*7.31*	*6.88*
	35.51	**27.00**	**23.70**	**21.90**	**20.81**	**20.03**	**19.03**	**17.99**	**16.89**	**15.75**
7	5.59	4.74	4.35	4.12	3.97	3.87	3.73	3.57	3.41	3.23
	12.25	*9.55*	*8.45*	*7.85*	*7.46*	*7.19*	*6.84*	*6.47*	*6.07*	*5.65*
	29.22	**21.69**	**18.77**	**17.19**	**16.21**	**15.52**	**14.63**	**13.71**	**12.73**	**11.69**
8	5.32	4.46	4.07	3.84	3.69	3.58	3.44	3.28	3.12	2.93
	11.26	*8.65*	*7.59*	*7.01*	*6.63*	*6.37*	*6.03*	*5.67*	*5.28*	*4.86*
	25.42	**18.49**	**15.83**	**14.39**	**13.49**	**12.86**	**12.04**	**11.19**	**10.30**	**9.34**
9	5.12	4.26	3.86	3.63	3.48	3.37	3.23	3.07	2.90	2.71
	10.56	*8.02*	*6.99*	*6.42*	*6.06*	*5.80*	*5.47*	*5.11*	*4.73*	*4.31*
	22.86	**16.39**	**13.90**	**12.56**	**11.71**	**11.13**	**10.37**	**9.57**	**8.72**	**7.81**
10	4.96	4.10	3.71	3.48	3.33	3.22	3.07	2.91	2.74	2.54
	10.04	*7.56*	*6.55*	*5.99*	*5.64*	*5.39*	*5.06*	*4.71*	*4.33*	*3.91*
	21.04	**14.91**	**12.55**	**11.28**	**10.48**	**9.92**	**9.20**	**8.45**	**7.64**	**6.76**
11	4.84	3.98	3.59	3.36	3.20	3.09	2.95	2.79	2.61	2.40
	9.65	*7.20*	*6.22*	*5.67*	*5.32*	*5.07*	*4.74*	*4.40*	*4.02*	*3.60*
	19.69	**13.81**	**11.56**	**10.35**	**9.58**	**9.05**	**8.35**	**7.63**	**6.85**	**6.00**
12	4.75	3.88	3.49	3.26	3.11	3.00	2.85	2.69	2.50	2.30
	9.33	*6.93*	*5.95*	*5.41*	*5.06*	*4.82*	*4.50*	*4.16*	*3.78*	*3.36*
	18.64	**12.97**	**10.80**	**9.63**	**8.89**	**8.38**	**7.71**	**7.00**	**6.25**	**5.42**
13	4.67	3.80	3.41	3.18	3.02	2.92	2.77	2.60	2.42	2.21
	9.07	*6.70*	*5.74*	*5.20*	*4.86*	*4.62*	*4.30*	*3.96*	*3.59*	*3.16*
	17.81	**12.31**	**10.21**	**9.07**	**8.35**	**7.86**	**7.21**	**6.52**	**5.78**	**4.97**

*Reprinted in rearranged form, from Table V of Fisher, R. A. and F. Yates. *Statistical tables for biological, agricultural, and medical research.* Published by Longman Group Ltd., London, (previously published by Oliver & Boyd, Edinburgh), and by permission of the authors and publishers.

n_2 \ n_1	1	2	3	4	5	6	8	12	24	∞
14	4.60	3.74	3.34	3.11	2.96	2.85	2.70	2.53	2.35	2.13
	8.86	*6.51*	*5.56*	*5.03*	*4.69*	*4.46*	*4.14*	*3.80*	*3.43*	*3.00*
	17.14	**11.78**	**9.73**	**8.62**	**7.92**	**7.43**	**6.80**	**6.13**	**5.41**	**4.60**
15	4.54	3.68	3.29	3.06	2.90	2.79	2.64	2.48	2.29	2.07
	8.68	*6.36*	*5.42*	*4.89*	*4.56*	*4.32*	*4.00*	*3.67*	*3.29*	*2.87*
	16.59	**11.34**	**9.34**	**8.25**	**7.57**	**7.09**	**6.47**	**5.81**	**5.10**	**4.31**
16	4.49	3.63	3.24	3.01	2.85	2.74	2.59	2.42	2.24	2.01
	8.53	*6.23*	*5.29*	*4.77*	*4.44*	*4.20*	*3.89*	*3.55*	*3.18*	*2.75*
	16.12	**10.97**	**9.00**	**7.94**	**7.27**	**6.81**	**6.19**	**5.55**	**4.85**	**4.06**
17	4.45	3.59	3.20	2.96	2.81	2.70	2.55	2.38	2.19	1.96
	8.40	*6.11*	*5.18*	*4.67*	*4.34*	*4.10*	*3.79*	*3.45*	*3.08*	*2.65*
	15.72	**10.66**	**8.73**	**7.68**	**7.02**	**6.56**	**5.96**	**5.32**	**4.63**	**3.85**
18	4.41	3.55	3.16	2.93	2.77	2.66	2.51	2.34	2.15	1.92
	8.28	*6.01*	*5.09*	*4.58*	*4.25*	*4.01*	*3.71*	*3.37*	*3.00*	*2.57*
	15.38	**10.39**	**8.49**	**7.46**	**6.81**	**6.35**	**5.76**	**5.13**	**4.45**	**3.67**
19	4.38	3.52	3.13	2.90	2.74	2.63	2.48	2.31	2.11	1.88
	8.18	*5.93*	*5.01*	*4.50*	*4.17*	*3.94*	*3.63*	*3.30*	*2.92*	*2.49*
	15.08	**10.16**	**8.28**	**7.26**	**6.61**	**6.18**	**5.59**	**4.97**	**4.29**	**3.52**
20	4.35	3.49	3.10	2.87	2.71	2.60	2.45	2.28	2.08	1.84
	8.10	*5.85*	*4.94*	*4.43*	*4.10*	*3.87*	*3.56*	*3.23*	*2.86*	*2.42*
	14.82	**9.95**	**8.10**	**7.10**	**6.46**	**6.02**	**5.44**	**4.82**	**4.15**	**3.38**
21	4.32	3.47	3.07	2.84	2.68	2.57	2.42	2.25	2.05	1.81
	8.02	*5.78*	*4.87*	*4.37*	*4.04*	*3.81*	*3.51*	*3.17*	*2.80*	*2.36*
	14.59	**9.77**	**7.94**	**6.95**	**6.32**	**5.88**	**5.31**	**4.70**	**4.03**	**3.26**
22	4.30	3.44	3.05	2.82	2.66	2.55	2.40	2.23	2.03	1.78
	7.94	*5.72*	*4.82*	*4.31*	*3.99*	*3.76*	*3.45*	*3.12*	*2.75*	*2.31*
	14.38	**9.61**	**7.80**	**6.81**	**6.19**	**5.76**	**5.19**	**4.58**	**3.92**	**3.15**
23	4.28	3.42	3.03	2.80	2.64	2.53	2.38	2.20	2.00	1.76
	7.88	*5.66*	*4.76*	*4.26*	*3.94*	*3.71*	*3.41*	*3.07*	*2.70*	*2.26*
	14.19	**9.47**	**7.67**	**6.69**	**6.08**	**5.65**	**5.09**	**4.48**	**3.82**	**3.05**
24	4.26	3.40	3.01	2.78	2.62	2.51	2.36	2.18	1.98	1.73
	7.82	*5.61*	*4.72*	*4.22*	*3.90*	*3.67*	*3.36*	*3.03*	*2.66*	*2.21*
	14.03	**9.34**	**7.55**	**6.59**	**5.98**	**5.55**	**4.99**	**4.39**	**3.74**	**2.97**
25	4.24	3.38	2.99	2.76	2.60	2.49	2.34	2.16	1.96	1.71
	7.77	*5.57*	*4.68*	*4.18*	*3.86*	*3.63*	*3.32*	*2.99*	*2.62*	*2.17*
	13.88	**9.22**	**7.45**	**6.49**	**5.88**	**5.46**	**4.91**	**4.31**	**3.66**	**2.89**
26	4.22	3.37	2.98	2.74	2.59	2.47	2.32	2.15	1.95	1.69
	7.22	*5.53*	*4.64*	*4.14*	*3.82*	*3.59*	*3.29*	*2.96*	*2.58*	*2.13*
	13.74	**9.12**	**7.36**	**6.41**	**5.80**	**5.38**	**4.83**	**4.24**	**3.59**	**2.82**
27	4.21	3.35	2.96	2.73	2.57	2.46	2.30	2.13	1.93	1.67
	7.68	*5.49*	*4.60*	*4.11*	*3.78*	*3.56*	*3.26*	*2.93*	*2.55*	*2.10*
	13.61	**9.02**	**7.27**	**6.33**	**5.73**	**5.31**	**4.76**	**4.17**	**3.52**	**2.75**
28	4.20	3.34	2.95	2.71	2.56	2.44	2.29	2.12	1.91	1.65
	7.64	*5.45*	*4.57*	*4.07*	*3.75*	*3.53*	*3.23*	*2.90*	*2.52*	*2.06*
	13.50	**8.93**	**7.19**	**6.25**	**5.66**	**5.24**	**4.69**	**4.11**	**3.46**	**2.70**

n_2 \ n_1	1	2	3	4	5	6	8	12	24	∞
29	4.18	3.33	2.93	2.70	2.54	2.43	2.28	2.10	1.90	1.64
	7.60	*5.42*	*4.54*	*4.04*	*3.73*	*3.50*	*3.20*	*2.87*	*2.49*	*2.03*
	13.39	**8.85**	**7.12**	**6.19**	**5.59**	**5.18**	**4.64**	**4.05**	**3.41**	**2.64**
30	4.17	3.32	2.92	2.69	2.53	2.42	2.27	2.09	1.89	1.62
	7.56	*5.39*	*4.51*	*4.02*	*3.70*	*3.47*	*3.17*	*2.84*	*2.47*	*2.01*
	13.29	**8.77**	**7.05**	**6.12**	**5.53**	**5.12**	**4.58**	**4.00**	**3.36**	**2.59**
40	4.08	3.23	2.84	2.61	2.45	2.34	2.18	2.00	1.79	1.51
	7.31	*5.18*	*4.31*	*3.83*	*3.51*	*3.29*	*2.99*	*2.66*	*2.29*	*1.80*
	12.61	**8.25**	**6.60**	**5.70**	**5.13**	**4.73**	**4.21**	**3.64**	**3.01**	**2.23**
60	4.00	3.15	2.76	2.52	2.37	2.25	2.10	1.92	1.70	1.39
	7.08	*4.98*	*4.13*	*3.65*	*3.34*	*3.12*	*2.82*	*2.50*	*2.12*	*1.60*
	11.97	**7.76**	**6.17**	**5.31**	**4.76**	**4.37**	**3.87**	**3.31**	**2.69**	**1.90**
120	3.92	3.07	2.68	2.45	2.29	2.17	2.02	1.83	1.61	1.25
	6.85	*4.79*	*3.95*	*3.48*	*3.17*	*2.96*	*2.66*	*2.34*	*1.95*	*1.38*
	11.38	**7.31**	**5.79**	**4.95**	**4.42**	**4.04**	**3.55**	**3.02**	**2.40**	**1.56**
∞	3.84	2.99	2.60	2.37	2.21	2.09	1.94	1.75	1.52	1.00
	6.64	*4.60*	*3.78*	*3.32*	*3.02*	*2.80*	*2.51*	*2.18*	*1.79*	*1.00*
	10.83	**6.91**	**5.42**	**4.62**	**4.10**	**3.74**	**3.27**	**2.74**	**2.13**	**1.00**

Appendix B-8. Significance Levels of Chi Square*

df	0.05	Probability† 0.02	0.01	0.001
1	3.84	5.41	6.64	10.83
2	5.99	7.82	9.21	13.82
3	7.82	9.84	11.34	16.27
4	9.49	11.67	13.28	18.46
5	11.07	13.39	15.09	20.52
6	12.59	15.03	16.81	22.46
7	14.07	16.62	18.48	24.32
8	15.51	18.17	20.09	26.12
9	16.92	19.68	21.67	27.88
10	18.31	21.16	23.21	29.59
11	19.68	22.62	24.72	31.26
12	21.03	24.05	26.22	32.91
13	22.36	25.47	27.69	34.53
14	23.68	26.87	29.14	36.12
15	25.00	28.26	30.58	37.70
16	26.30	29.63	32.00	39.29
17	27.59	31.00	33.41	40.75
18	28.87	32.35	34.80	42.31
19	30.14	33.69	36.19	43.82
20	31.41	35.02	37.57	45.32
21	32.67	36.34	38.93	46.80
22	33.92	37.66	40.29	48.27
23	35.17	38.97	41.64	49.73
24	36.42	40.27	42.98	51.18
25	37.65	41.57	44.31	52.62
26	38.88	42.86	45.64	54.05
27	40.11	44.14	46.96	55.48
28	41.34	45.42	48.28	56.89
29	42.56	46.69	49.59	58.30
30	43.77	47.96	50.89	59.70

*Abridged from Table IV of Fisher R. A. and F. Yates. *Statistical tables for biological, agricultural, and medical research.* Published by Longman Group Ltd., London, (previously published by Oliver & Boyd, Edinburgh), and by permission of the authors and publishers.
†An example of using the table would be in the case where a chi square of 9.8 is obtained with 2 df. It can be seen that with 2 df, a chi square of 9.21 is significant at the 0.01 level.

Appendix B-9. Significance Levels of *s* in the Kendall Coefficient of Concordance*

k	*N*					Additional values † for *N* = 3	
	3†	4	5	6	7	*k*	*s*

Values at the 0.05 level of significance

k	3†	4	5	6	7	*k*	*s*
3			64.4	103.9	157.3	9	54.0
4		49.5	88.4	143.3	217.0	12	71.9
5		62.6	112.3	182.4	276.2	14	83.8
6		75.7	136.1	221.4	335.2	16	95.8
8	48.1	101.7	183.7	299.0	453.1	18	107.7
10	60.0	127.8	231.2	376.7	571.0		
15	89.8	192.9	349.8	570.5	864.9		
20	119.7	258.0	468.5	764.4	1,158.7		

Values at the 0.01 level of significance

k	3†	4	5	6	7	*k*	*s*
3			75.6	122.8	185.6	9	75.9
4		61.4	109.3	176.2	265.0	12	103.5
5		80.5	142.8	229.4	343.8	14	121.9
6		99.5	176.1	282.4	422.6	16	140.2
8	66.8	137.4	242.7	388.3	579.9	18	158.6
10	85.1	175.3	309.1	494.0	737.0		
15	131.0	269.8	475.2	758.2	1,129.5		
20	177.0	364.2	641.2	1,022.2	1,521.9		

*Adapted from Friedman, M. "A comparison of alternative tests of significance for the problem of rankings." *Annals of mathematical statistics,* 1940, Vol. 11, pp. 86-92, with the permission of the publisher.
† Notice that additional critical values of *s* for *N* = 3 are given in the right-hand column of this table.

Appendix B-10. Significance Levels of T in the Wilcoxon's Matched-Pairs Signed-Rank Test*

N	Level of significance for one-tailed test		
	0.025	0.01	0.005
	Level of significance for two-tailed test		
	0.05	0.02	0.01
6	0	—	—
7	2	0	—
8	4	2	0
9	6	3	2
10	8	5	3
11	11	7	5
12	14	10	7
13	17	13	10
14	21	16	13
15	25	20	16
16	30	24	20
17	35	28	23
18	40	33	28
19	46	38	32
20	52	43	38
21	59	49	43
22	66	56	49
23	73	62	55
24	81	69	61
25	89	77	68

*Adapted from Table II of Wilcoxon, F. and R. A. Wilcox. *Some rapid approximate statistical procedures.* Pearl River, New York: Lederle Laboratories, 1964, p. 28, with the permission of the publisher.

Appendix B-11. Significance Levels of the Sign Test: p Values with Decimal Points Omitted*

N＼m	0	1	2	3	4	5	6	7	8	9	10	11	12	13	14	15
5	031	188	500	812	969	*										
6	016	109	344	656	891	984	*									
7	008	062	227	500	773	938	992	*								
8	004	035	145	363	637	855	965	996	*							
9	002	020	090	254	500	746	910	980	998	*						
10	001	011	055	172	377	623	828	945	989	999	*					
11		006	033	113	274	500	726	887	967	994	*	*				
12		003	019	073	194	387	613	806	927	981	997	*	*			
13		002	011	046	133	291	500	709	867	954	989	998	*	*		
14		001	006	029	090	212	395	605	788	910	971	994	999	*	*	
15			004	018	059	151	304	500	696	849	941	982	996	*	*	*
16			002	011	038	105	227	402	598	773	895	962	989	998	*	*
17			001	006	025	072	166	315	500	685	834	928	975	994	999	*
18			001	004	015	048	119	240	407	593	760	881	952	985	996	999
19				002	010	032	084	180	324	500	676	820	916	968	990	998
20				001	006	021	058	132	252	412	588	748	868	942	979	994
21				001	004	013	039	095	192	332	500	668	808	905	961	987
22					002	008	026	067	143	262	416	584	738	857	933	974
23					001	005	017	047	105	202	339	500	661	798	895	953
24					001	003	011	032	076	154	271	419	581	729	846	924
25						002	007	022	054	115	212	345	500	655	788	885

*Adapted from Table IV, B, of Walker, Helen, and J. Lev. *Statistical inference.* New York: Holt, 1953, p. 458, with the permission of the authors and publisher.

Presented in the table are one-tailed probabilities associated with the smaller number of signs. One example would be in the case where a one-tailed prediction is made in an experiment concerning 12 matched observations. It is predicted that one set of scores will be larger than the other. It is found that five scores are smaller (have negative signs). In this case the probability is found to be 0.387 or 0.39 (not significant at the 0.05 level). Another example of using the table would be in the case of 20 matched pairs of scores, where a one-tailed test is being made. It is found that 17 of the differences in scores are in the predicted direction. This corresponds to a one-tailed probability of 0.001 or a two-tailed probability of 0.002.

References

Albig, W. *Modern public opinion*. New York: McGraw-Hill, 1956.

Anastasi, A. *Psychological testing*, 3d ed. New York: MacMillan, 1968.

Blough, D. S. and P. M. Blough, *Experiments in psychology. Laboratory studies of animal behavior*. New York: Holt, Rinehart & Winston, 1964.

Campbell, D. T. "Reforms as experiments." *American Psychologist*, 1969, Vol. 24, pp. 409-429.

Campbell, D. T. and J. C. Stanley, *Experimental and quasi-experimental designs for research*. Chicago: Rand-McNally, 1966.

Chase, C. I. *Elementary statistical procedures*. New York: McGraw-Hill, 1967.

Cronbach, L. J. *Essentials of psychological testing*, 3d ed. New York: Harper & Row, 1970.

Eves, H. *An introduction to the history of mathematics*. New York: Holt, Rinehart & Winston, 1964.

Ferguson, G. A. *Statistical analysis in psychology and education*, 3d ed. New York: McGraw-Hill, 1971.

Guilford, J. P., and B. Fruchter, *Fundamental statistics in psychology and education*, 5th ed. New York: McGraw-Hill, 1973.

Hays, W. L. *Statistics for the social sciences*, 2d ed. New York: Holt, Rinehart & Winston, 1973.

Kirk, R. E. *Experimental design procedures for the behavioral sciences*. Belmont, California: Brooks/Cole, 1968.

Kish, L. *Survey sampling*. New York: John Wiley, 1956.

McNemar, Q. *Psychological statistics*. New York: John Wiley, 1962.

Nunnally, J. C. *Psychometric theory*. New York: McGraw-Hill, 1967.

Nunnally, J. C. *Introduction to psychological measurement*. New York: McGraw-Hill, 1970.

Nunnally, J. C. *Educational measurement and evaluation*, 2d ed. New York: McGraw-Hill, 1972.

Scott, W. A., and M. Wertheimer, *Introduction to psychological research*. New York: John Wiley, 1967.

Senter, R. J. *Analysis of data*. Glenview, Illinois: Scott Foresman, 1969.

Siegel, S. *Nonparametric statistics*. New York: McGraw-Hill, 1956.

Underwood, B. J. *Experimental psychology*, 2d ed. New York: Appleton-Century-Crofts, 1966.

Webster's New World Dictionary, 1970, p. 1391.

Winer, B. J. *Statistical principles in experimental design*, 2d ed. New York: McGraw-Hill, 1971.

Yates, F. *Sampling methods for censuses and surveys*. New York: Hafner, 1949.

Index